THE

COLLECTED WORKS

OF

THEODORE PARKER,

MINISTER OF THE TWENTY-EIGHTH CONGREGATIONAL
SOCIETY AT BOSTON. U.S.

CONTAINING HIS

THEOLOGICAL, POLEMICAL, AND CRITICAL WRITINGS,
SERMONS, SPEECHES, AND ADDRESSES,
AND LITERARY MISCELLANIES.

EDITED BY

FRANCES POWER COBBE.

VOL. VI.

DISCOURSES OF SLAVERY.—VOL. II.

LONDON:
TRÜBNER & CO., 60, PATERNOSTER ROW.
1864.

LONDON:
W. STEVENS, PRINTER, 37, BELL YARD,
TEMPLE BAR.

DISCOURSES

OF

SLAVERY.

BY

THEODORE PARKER.

VOL. II.

LONDON:

TRÜBNER & CO., 60, PATERNOSTER ROW.

1864.

CONTENTS TO VOL. II.

SOME THOUGHTS ON THE PROGRESS OF AMERICA, AND THE INFLUENCE OF HER DIVERSE INSTITUTIONS.

AN ADDRESS

PREPARED FOR THE ANTI-SLAVERY CONVENTION IN BOSTON, MAY 31, 1854.

AT this day there are two great tribes of men in Christendom, which seem to have a promising future before them—the Sclavonic and the Anglo-Saxon. Both are comparatively new. For the last three hundred years each has been continually advancing in numbers, riches, and territory; in industrial and military power. To judge from present appearances, it seems probable that a hundred years hence there will be only two great national forces in the Christian world—the Sclavonic and the Anglo-Saxon.

The Anglo-Saxon tribe is composite, and the mingling so recent, that we can still easily distinguish the main ingredients of the mixture. There are, first, the Saxons and Angles from North Germany; next, the Scandinavians from Denmark and Sweden; and, finally, the Normans, or Romanized Scandinavians, from France.

This tribe is now divided into two great political branches, namely, the Anglo-Saxon Briton, and the Anglo-Saxon American; but both are substantially the same people, though with different antecedents and surroundings. The same fundamental characteristics belong to the Briton and the American.

Three hundred years ago, the Anglo-Saxons were scarce three millions in number; they did not own the whole of Great Britain. Now there are thirty or forty millions of men with Anglo-Saxon blood in their veins. They possess

the British Islands; Heligoland, Gibraltar, Malta, and the
Ionian Isles; St. Helena, South Africa, much of East and
West Africa; enormous territories in India, continually
increasing; the whole of Australia; almost all of North
America, and I know not how many islands scattered
about the Atlantic and Pacific seas. Their geographical
spread covers at least one-sixth part of the habitable globe;
their power controls about one-fifth of the inhabitants of
the earth. It is the richest of all the families of mankind.
The Anglo-Saxon leads the commerce and the most important manufactures of the world. He owns seven-
eighths of the shipping of Christendom, and half that of
the human race. He avails himself of the latest dis-
coveries in practical science, and applies them to the
creation of "comforts" and luxuries. Iron is his favourite
metal; and about two-thirds of the annual iron crop of the
earth is harvested on Anglo-Saxon soil. Cotton, wheat,
and the potato, are his favourite plants.

The political institutions of the Anglo-Saxon secure
National Unity of Action for the State, and Individual
Variety of Action for each citizen, to a greater degree
than other nations have thought possible. In all Christendom, there is scarce any freedom of the Press except on
Anglo-Saxon soil. Ours is the only tongue in which
Liberty can speak. Anglo-Saxon Britain is the asylum of
exiled patriots, or exiled despots. The royal and patrician
wrecks of the revolutionary storms of continental Europe,
in the last century and in this, were driven to her hospit-
able shore. Kossuth, Mazzini, Victor Hugo, and Comte,
relics of the last revolution, are washed to the same coast.
America is the asylum of exiled nations, who flee to her
arms, four hundred thousand in a year, and find shelter.

The Sclavonians fight with diplomacy and the sword,
the Anglo-Saxon with diplomacy and the dollar. He is
the Roman of productive industry, of commerce, as the
Romans were Anglo-Saxons of destructive conquest, of
war. The Sclavonian nations, from the accident of their
geographical position, or from their ethnological peculiarity of nature, invade and conquer lands more civilized
than their own. They have the diplomatic skill to control
nations of superior intellectual and moral development.
The Anglo-Saxon is too clumsy for foreign politics; when

he meddles with the affairs of other civilized people, he is often deceived. Russia outwits England continually in the political game now playing for the control of Europe. The Anglo-Saxon, more invasive than the Sclavonian, prefers new and wild lands to old and well-cultivated territories; so he conquers America, and tills its virgin soil: seizes on Africa,—the dry nurse of lions and of savage men,—and founds a new empire in Australia. If he invades Asia, it is in the parts not Christian. His rule is a curse to countries full of old civilization; I take it that England has been a blight to India, and will be to China, if she sets there her conquering foot. The Anglo-Saxon is less pliable than the Romans, a less indulgent master to conquered men; with more plastic power to organize and mould, he has a less comprehensive imagination, limits himself to a smaller number of forms, and so hews off and casts away what suits him not. Austria conquers Lombardy, France Algiers, Russia Poland, to the benefit of the conquered party, it seems. Can any one show that the British rule has been a benefit to India? The Russians make nothing of their American territory. But what civilization blooms out of the savage ground wherever the Saxon plants his foot!

I must say a word of the leading peculiarities of this tribe.

1. There is a strong love of individual freedom. This belongs to the Anglo-Saxons in common with all the Teutonic family. But with them it seems eminently powerful. Circumstances have favoured its development. They care much for freedom, little for equality.

2. Connected with this, is a love of law and order, which continually shows itself on both sides of the ocean. Fast as we gain freedom, we secure it by law and constitution, trusting little to the caprice of magistrates.

3. Then there is a great federative power—a tendency to form combinations of persons, or of communities and states—special partnerships on a small scale for mercantile business; on a large scale, like the American Union, or the Hanse towns, for the political business of a nation.

4. The Anglo-Saxons have eminent practical power to organize things into a mill, or men into a state, and then

to administer the organization. This power is one which contributes greatly to both their commercial and political success. But this tribe is also most eminently material in its aims and means; it loves riches, works for riches, fights for riches. It is not warlike, as some other nations, who love war for its own sake, though a hard fighter when put to it.

5. We are the most aggressive, invasive, and exclusive people on the earth. The history of the Anglo-Saxon, for the last three hundred years, has been one of continual aggression, invasion, and extermination.

I cannot now stop to dwell on these traits of our tribal anthropology, but must yet say a word touching this national exclusiveness and tendency to exterminate.

Austria and Russia never treated a conquered nation so cruelly as England has treated Ireland. Not many years ago, four-fifths of the population of the island were Catholics, a tenth Anglican churchmen. All offices were in the hands of the little minority. Two-thirds of the Irish House of Commons were nominees of the Protestant gentry; the Catholic members must take the declaration against Transubstantiation. Papists were forbidden to vote in elections of members to the Irish Parliament. They suffered "under a universal, unmitigated, indispensable, exceptionless disqualification." "In the courts of law, they could not gain a place on the bench, nor act as a barrister, attorney, or solicitor, nor be employed even as a hired clerk, nor sit on a grand jury, nor serve as a sheriff, nor hold even the lowest civil office of trust and profit; nor have any privilege in a town corporation; nor be a freeman of such corporation; nor vote at a vestry."* A Catholic could not marry a Protestant: the priest who should celebrate such a marriage was to be hanged. He could not be "a guardian to any child, nor educate his own child, if its mother were a Protestant," or the child declared in favour of Protestantism. "No Protestant might instruct a Papist. Papists could not supply their want by academies and schools of their own; for a Catholic to teach, even in a private family, or as usher to a Protestant, was a felony, punishable by imprisonment, exile, or death." "To be educated in any foreign Catholic school

* Bancroft, *History of United States,* vol. v. p. 66, et seq.

was an unalterable and perpetual outlawry." "The child sent abroad for education, no matter of how tender an age, or himself how innocent, could never after sue in law or equity, or be guardian, executor, or administrator, or receive any legacy or deed of gift; he forfeited all his goods and chattels, and forfeited for his life all his lands;" whoever sent him incurred the same penalties.

The Catholic clergy could not be taught at home or abroad: they "were registered and kept, like prisoners at large, within prescribed limits." "All Papists exercising ecclesiastical jurisdiction; all monks, friars, and regular priests, and all priests not actually in parishes, and to be registered, were banished from Ireland under pain of transportation; and, on a return, of being hanged and quartered." "The Catholic priest abjuring his religion, received a pension of thirty, and afterwards of forty pounds." "No non-conforming Catholic could buy land, or receive it by descent, devise, or settlement; or lend money on it as security; or hold an interest in it through a Protestant trustee; or take a lease of ground for more than thirty-one years. If under such a lease he brought his farm to produce more than one-third beyond the rent, the first Protestant discoverer might sue for the lease before known Protestants, making the defendant answer all interrogations on oath; so that the Catholic farmer dared not drain his fields, nor inclose them, nor build solid houses on them." "Even if a Catholic owned a horse worth more than five pounds, any Protestant might take it away," on payment of that sum. "To the native Irish, the English oligarchy appeared as men of a different race and creed, who had acquired the island by force of arms, rapine, and chicane, and derived revenues from it by the employment of extortionate underlings or overseers." *

The same disposition to invade and exterminate showed itself on this side of the ocean.

In America, the Frenchman and the Spaniard came in contact with the red man; they converted him to what they called Christianity, and then associated with him on equal terms. The pale-face and the red-skin hunted in company; they fished from the same canoe in the Bay of

* Bancroft, *ubi sup.* p. 67, *et seq.*

Fundy and Lake Superior; they lodged in the same tent, slept on the same bear-skin; nay, they knelt together before the same God, who was "no respecter of persons," and had made of one blood all nations of men! The white man married the Indian's daughter; the red man wooed and won the pale child of the Caucasian. This took place in Canada, and in Mexico, in Peru, and Equador. In Brazil, the negro graduates at the college; he becomes a general in the army. But the Anglo-Saxon disdains to mingle his proud blood in wedlock with the "inferior races of men." He puts away the savage—black, yellow, red. In New England, the Puritan converted the Indians to Christianity, as far as they could accept the theology of John Calvin; but made a careful separation between white and red, "my people and thy people." They must dwell in separate villages, worship in separate houses; they must not intermarry. The general court of Massachusetts once forbade all extra-matrimonial connection of white and red, on pain of death! The Anglo-Saxon has carefully sought to exterminate the savages from his territory. The Briton does so in Africa, in Van Diemen's Land, in New Zealand, in New Holland—wherever he meets them. The American does the same in the western world. In New England the Puritan found the wild woods, the wild beasts, and the wild men; he undertook to eradicate them all, and has succeeded best with the wild men. There are more bears than Indians in New England. The United States pursues the same destructive policy. In two hundred years more there will be few Indians left between the Lake of the Woods and the Gulf of Mexico, between the Atlantic and Pacific Oceans.

Yet the Anglo-Saxons are not cruel; they are simply destructive. The Dutch, in New York, perpetrated the most wanton cruelties: the savages themselves shuddered at the white man's atrocity: "Our gods would be offended at such things," said they; "the white man's God must be different!" The cruelties of the French, and, still more, of the Spaniards in Mexico, in the West Indies, and South America, are too terrible to repeat, but too well known to need relating. The Spaniard put men to death with refinements of cruelty, luxuriating in destructiveness. The Anglo-Saxon simply shot down his foe, offered a reward for homicide, so much for a scalp, but tolerated no needless cruelty. If the problem is to destroy a race of men with the least expenditure of destructive force on one side, and the least suffering on the other, the Anglo-Saxon, Briton, or American, is the fittest instrument to be found on the whole globe.

So much for the Anglo-Saxon character in general, as introductory to an examination of America in special. It is well to know the anthropology of the stock before attempting to appreciate the character of the special people. America has the general characteristics of this powerful tribe, but modified by her peculiar geographical and historical position. Our fathers emigrated from their home in a time of great ferment, and brought with them ideas which could not then be organized into institutions at home. This was obviously the case with the theological ideas of the Puritans, who, with their descendants, have given to America most of what is new and peculiar in her institutions. Still more, the early settlers of the North brought with them sentiments not ripened yet, which, in due time, developed themselves into ideas, and then into institutions.

At first necessity, or love of change, drove the wanderers to the wilderness; they had no thought of separating from England. The fugitive pilgrims in the Mayflower, who subscribed the compact, which so many Americans erroneously regard as the "seed-corn of the republican tree, under which millions of her men now stand," called themselves "loyal subjects of our dread sovereign, King James," undertaking to plant a colony "for the glory of God, and advancement of the Christian faith, and honour of our king and country." In due time, as the colonists developed themselves in one, and the English at home in a different direction, there came to be a great diversity of ideas, and an opposition of interests. When mutuality of ideas and of interests, as the indispensable condition of national unity of action, failed, the colony fell off from its parent: the separation was unavoidable. Before many years, we doubt not, Australia will thus separate from the mother country, to the advantage of both parties.

In America, two generations of men have passed away

since the last battle of the Revolution. The hostility of that contest is only a matter of history to the mass of Britons or Americans, not of daily consciousness ; and as this disturbing force is withdrawn, the two nations see and feel more distinctly their points of agreement, and become conscious that they are both but one people.

The transfer of the colonists of England to the western world was an event of great importance to mankind ; they found a virgin continent, on which to set up and organize their ideas, and develop their faculties. They had no enemies but the wilderness and its savage occupants. I doubt not that, if the emigrant had remained at home, it would have taken a thousand years to attain the same general development now reached by the free States of North America. The settlers carried with them the best ideas and the best institutions of their native land—the arts and sciences of England, the forms of a representative government, the trial by jury, the common law, the ideas of Christianity, and the traditions of the human race. In the woods, far from help, they were forced to become self-reliant and thrifty men. It is instructive to see what has come of the experiment. It is but two hundred and forty-six years since the settlement of Jamestown—not two hundred and thirty-four years since the Pilgrims landed at Plymouth ; what a development since that time—of numbers, of riches, of material and spiritual power !

In the ninth century, Korb Flokki, a half-mythical person, " let loose his three crows," it is said, seeking land to the west and north of the Orkneys, and went to Iceland. In the tenth century, Gunnbjiorn, and Eirek the Red, discovered Greenland, an " ugly and right hateful country," as Paul Egede calls it. In the eleventh century, Leife, son of Eirek, with Tyrker the Southerner, discovered Vinland, some part of North America, but whether Newfoundland, Nova Scotia, or New England, I shall leave others to determine. It is not yet four hundred years since Columbus first dropped his anchor at San Salvador, and Cabot discovered the continent of America, and cruised along its shores from Hudson's Bay to Florida, seeking for a passage to the East Indies. In 1608 the first permanent British settlement was made in

America, at Jamestown; in 1620 the Pilgrims began their far-famed experiment at Plymouth. What a change from 1608 to 1854! It is not in my power to determine the number of immigrants before the Revolution. There was a great variety of nationalities—Dutch in New York, Germans in Pennsylvania and Georgia, Swedes and Finns in Delaware, Scotch in New England and North Carolina, Swiss in Georgia; Acadians from Nova Scotia; and Huguenots from France.

America has now a stable form of government. Her pyramid is not yet high. It is only humble powers that she develops, no great creative spirit here as yet enchants men with the wonders of literature and art;—but her foundation is wide and deeply laid. It is now easy to see the conditions and the causes of her success. The conditions are, the new continent, a virgin soil to receive the seed of liberty; the causes were, first, the character of the tribe, and next, the liberal institutions founded thereby.

The rapid increase of America in most of the elements of national power, is a remarkable fact in the history of mankind.

Look at the increase of numbers. In 1689, the entire population of the English colonies, exclusive of the Indians, amounted to about 200,000. Twenty-five years later there were 434,000, now 24,000,000.*

* *Table of Population in 1715.*

Colonies.	Whites.	Negroes.	Total.
New Hampshire	9,500	150	9,650
Massachusetts	94,000	2,000	96,000
Rhode Island	8,500	500	9,000
Connecticut	46,000	1,500	47,500
New York	27,000	4,000	31,000
New Jersey	21,000	1,500	22,500
Pennsylvania and Delaware . . .	43,300	2,500	45,800
Maryland	40,700	9,500	50,200
Virginia	72,000	23,000	95,000
North Carolina	7,500	3,700	11,200
South Carolina	6,250	10,500	16,750
	375,750	58,850	134,600

The present population of the United States consists of

In 1754, another return was made to the Board of Trade, in the following

Table of Population in 1754.

Whites.	Blacks.	Total.
1,192,896	292,738	1,485,634

We will now give the population at seven successive periods, as indicated by the returns of the official census of the United States.

Table of Population from 1790 to 1850.

Years.	Whites.	Free Coloured.	Slaves.	Total.
1790	3,172,464	59,466	697,897	3,929,827
1800	4,304,489	108,395	893,041	5,305,925
1810	5,862,004	186,446	1,191,364	7,239,814
1820	7,872,711	238,197	1,543,688	9,654,596
1830	10,537,378	319,599	2,009,043	12,866,020
1840	14,189,555	386,348	2,487,355	17,069,453
1850	19,630,738	428,661	3,198,324	23,257,723

The following is the official report of Immigration from 1790 to 1850. Much of it is conjectural and approximate.

Table of Immigration from 1790 to 1850.

From 1790 to 1800	120,000
,, 1810 to 1820	114,000
,, 1820 to 1830	203,979
,, 1830 to 1840	778,500
,, 1840 to 1850	1,542,840
	2,759,329

The immigrants are thus conjecturally distributed among the nations of the earth. The estimate is a rough one.

Table of Nationality.

Celtic—Irish (one-half)	1,350,000
Teutonic—Germans, Danes, Swedes, etc. (one-fourth)	675,000
Miscellaneous—All other nations	734,329

The following statement exhibits the nationality of the immigration to the United States for the calendar year, 1851 (Dec. 31, 1850, to Dec. 31, 1851) :—

Nationality of Immigrants in 1851.

From Great Britain and Ireland	264,222
,, Germany	72,283
,, France	20,107
Of these there were Males	245,017
,, ,, Females	163,745
,, ,, Unknown	66

Table of Immigration for the first four months of 1853.

From the British Islands	15,023
,, French Ports	8,768
,, German Ports	3,511
,, Belgian and Dutch	2,747
,, Spanish, Portuguese, and Italian	135

the following ingredients.   The numbers are conjectural
and approximate :—

Table of Nationality.

White Immigrants since 1790, and their white descendants	4,350,934
Africans, and their descendants . . .	3,626,585
White Immigrants previous to 1790, and their white descendants	15,279,804

This does not include the Indians living within the
territories and States of the Union.   These facts show that
a remarkable mingling of families of the Caucasian stock
is taking place.   The exact statistics would disclose a yet
more remarkable mingling of the Caucasian and the
Æthiopian races going on.   The Africans are rapidly
" bleaching " under the influence of democratic chemistry.
If only one-tenth of the "coloured population" has
Caucasian blood in its veins, then there are 362,698
descendants of this " amalgamation;" but if you estimate
these *hybrids* as one in five, which is not at all excessive,
we have then 725,397.

The thirty-one States now organized have a surface of
1,485,870 square miles, while the total area of the United
States, so far as I have information, on the 17th of May,
1853, was 3,220,000 square miles.   In the States, on an
average, there are not sixteen persons to the square mile ;
in the whole territory, not eight to a mile.   Massachusetts,
the most densely peopled State, has more than one hundred
and twenty-six to the mile, while Texas has but eighty-
nine men for a hundred miles of land, more than eight
hundred acres to each human soul.

In 1840, there were ten States, whose united populations
exceeded 4,000,000, which yet had no town with 10,000
inhabitants.*

* The following table shows the occupation of 4,798,870 persons in
1840, ascertained by the census :—

Table of Occupation.

Engaged in Mining	15,211
„	Agriculture	3,719,951
„	Commerce	117,607
„	Manufactures . . .	791,749
„	Navigation (Ocean) . . .	56,021
„	„ (Inland Waters) . .	33,076
„	Learned Professions . . .	65,255

Look next at the products of industry in the United
States.*

* I take these results of the census of 1840, as deduced by Professor
Tucker, in his admirable book, *Progress of the United States in Population
and Wealth in Fifty Years.*   New York, 1843.   1 vol. 8vo.

Value of Annual Products of Industry, 1840.

Agriculture	$654,387,597
Manufactures	236,836,224
Commerce	79,721,086
Mining	42,358,761
The Forest	16,835,060
The Ocean	11,996,108
Total . . .	$1,063,134,736

In 1850, the iron-crop in the United States amounted to 564,755 tons.
The ship-crop was 1360 vessels, with a measurement of 272,218 tons.
The increase of American shipping is worth notice, and is shown in the
following

Table of American Tonnage from 1815 to 1850.

Years.	Tons.
1815	1,368,127
1820	1,280,165
1825	1,423,110
1830	1,181,986
1835	1,824,939
1840	2,180,763
1845	2,417,001
1850	3,535,454

The tonnage is still on the increase.   In 1851 it amounted to 3,772,439,
and at this moment must be considerably more than 4,000,000.   The
first ship built in New England was the "Blessing of the Bay," a "bark
of thirty tons," launched in 1634.   Nor far from the spot where her keel
was laid, a ship has recently been built, three hundred and ten feet long,
and more than six thousand tons burden.

On the 30th September, 1851, there were, if the accounts are reliable,
12,805 miles of railroad in the United States.   At present, there are
probably about 15,000 miles.

To show the increase of American commerce, consider the following

Table of Imports and Exports from 1800 to 1852.

Years.	IMPORTS.	EXPORTS.
1800	$91,252,768	$70,971,780
1805	120,000,000	95,566,021
1810	85,400,000	66,757,974
1815	113,041,274	52,557,753
1820	74,450,000	69,691,669
1825	96,340,075	99,535,388
1830	70,876,920	73,849,508
1835	149,895,742	121,693,577
1840	107,141,519	132,085,946
1845	117,254,564	114,646,606
1850	178,138,318	161,898,720
1852	212,613,282	209,641,625

The contrast between the Spanish and the Anglo-Saxon settlements in America is amazing. A hundred years ago, Spain, the discoverer of America, had undisputed sway over all South America, except Brazil and the Guianas. All Mexico was hers—all Central America, California unbounded on the north, extending indefinitely, Louisiana, Florida, Cuba, Porto Rico, and part of Hayti. She ruled a population of twenty million men. Now Cuba trembles in her faltering hand; all the rest has dropped from the arms of that feeble mother of feeble sons. In 1750 her American colonies extended from Patagonia to Oregon. The La Plata was too far north for her southern limit, the Columbia too far south for her northern bound. The Mississippi and the Amazon were Spanish rivers, and emptied the waters of a continent into the lap of America, the Mexique Gulf, which was also a Spanish sea. But Spain allowed only eight-and-thirty vessels to ply between the mother country and the family of American daughters on both sides of the continent. The empire of Spain, mother country and colonies, extending from Barcelona to Manilla, with more sea-coast than the whole continent of Africa, employed but sixteen thousand sailors in her commercial marine. Portugal forbade Brazil to cultivate any of the products of the Indies.

Look at this day at Anglo-Saxon, and then at Spanish America. In 1606 there was not an English settlement

The most important articles of export for five-and twenty years appear in the following

Table of the chief articles of Export from 1825 to 1850.

Years.	Cotton.	Breadstuffs and Provisions.	Tobacco.
1825	$36,846,649	$11,634,449	$6,115,623
1830	29,674,883	12,075,430	5,586,365
1835	64,961,302	12,009,399	8,250,577
1840	63,870,307	19,067,535	9,883,957
1845	51,739,643	16,743,421	7,469,819
1850	71,484,616	26,051,373	9,951,023
1852	87,965,732	25,857,177	10,031,283

The greatest amount of cotton was exported in 1852,—1,093,230,639 pounds; but the greatest value of cotton was in 1851, amounting to $112,351,317. In 1847, the value of breadstuffs and provisions exported was $68,701,921.

The government revenues for the fiscal year 1852 were $49,728,386.89; there was a balance in the treasury of $10,911,645.68; making the total means for that year $60,640,032.57. On the 1st January, 1853, the national debt amounted to $65,131,692.

in America. In 1627 only two, Jamestown and Plymouth. But the Spanish colonies date back to 1493. Compare the history of the basin of the Amazon with the valley of the Mississippi. The Amazon, with its affluents, commands seventy thousand miles of internal navigation, draining more arable land than all Europe contains, the largest, the most fertile valley in the world. It includes 1,796,000 square miles. Everything which finds a home on earth will flourish in the basin of the Amazon, between the level of the Atlantic and the top of the Andes. But the tonnage on the Amazon does not probably equal the tonnage on Lake Champlain. Only an Anglo-Saxon steamer ruffles the waters of the Amazon. Parà, at its mouth, more than three hundred years old, contains less than 20,000 inhabitants.

The Mississippi with its tributaries drains 982,000 square miles, and affords 16,694 miles of steam navigation. In 1851 there were 1190 steamboats on its bosom, measuring 249,054 tons, running at an annual cost of $39,774,194; the value of the merchandise carried on the river in 1852 was estimated at $432,651,240, more than double the whole foreign trade of the United States for that year. New Orleans, at the mouth of the Mississippi, was founded in 1719, and in 1850 contained 119,461 inhabitants: in 1810 it had not 18,000!

The Anglo-Saxon colonists brought with them the vigorous bodies and sturdy intellect of their race; the forms of representative and constitutional government; publicity of political transactions; trial by jury; a fondness for local self-government; an aversion to centralization; the Protestant form of religion; the Bible; the right of private judgment; their national administrative power; and that stalwart self-reliance and thrift which mark the Englishman and American wherever they go. New Spain had priests and soldiers; New England ministers and schoolmasters. In two centuries, behold what consequences come of such causes! No Chilian vessel ever went to Spain!

But America itself is not unitary; there is a Spanish America in the United States. Unity of idea and interest by no means prevails here.

America was settled by two very different classes of men, one animated by moral or religious motives, coming to realize an idea; the other animated by only commercial ideas, pushing forth to make a fortune or to escape from gaol. Some men brought religion, others only ambition; the consequence is, two antagonistic ideas, with institutions which correspond, antagonistic institutions.

First there is the Democratic idea: that all men are endowed by their Creator with certain natural rights; that these rights are alienable only by the possessor thereof; that they are equal in all men; that government is to organize these natural, unalienable, and equal rights into institutions designed for the good of the governed; and therefore government is to be of all the people, by all the people, and for all the people. Here government is development, not exploitation.

Next there is the Oligarchic idea, just the opposite of this; that there is no such thing as natural, unalienable, and equal rights, but accidental, alienable, and unequal powers; that government is to organize the might of all, for the good of the governing party; is to be a government of all, by a part, and for the sake of a part. The governing power may be one man, King Monarch; a few men, King Noble; or the majority, King Many. In all these cases, the motive, the purpose, and the means, are still the same, and government is exploitation of the governed, not the development thereof. So far as the people are developed by the government, it is that they may be thereby exploitered.

Neither the Democratic nor the Oligarchic idea is perfectly developed as yet: but the first preponderates most at the north, the latter at the south—one in the free, the other in the slave States.

The settlers did not bring to America the Democratic idea fully grown. It is the child of time. In all great movements there are three periods—first, that of Sentiment —there is only a feeling of the new thing; next of Idea —the feeling has become a thought; finally of Action— the thought becomes a thing. It is pleasant to trace the growth of the Democratic sentiment and idea in the human race, to watch the efforts to make the thought a thing, and found domestic, social, ecclesiastical, and political institutions, corresponding thereto. Perhaps it is easier to trace this here than elsewhere. It has sometimes been claimed that the Puritans came to America to found such institutions. But they had no fondness for a Democracy; the thought did not enter their heads that the substance of man is superior to the accidents of men, his nature more than his history. New England men on the 4th of July claim the compact on board the Mayflower, as the foundation of Democracy in America, and of the Declaration of Independence. But the signers of that famous document had no design to found a Democracy. Much of the liberality of the settlers at Plymouth seems to have been acquired by their residence in Holland, where they saw the noblest example of religious toleration then in the world.

The Democratic idea has had but a slow and gradual growth, even in New England. The first form of government was a theocracy, an intense tyranny in the name of God. The next world was for the "Elect" said Puritan theology; "let us also have this," said the Elect. The distinction between clerical and laical was nowhere more prominent than in Puritan New England. The road to the ballot-box lay under the pulpit; only church-members could vote, and if a man's politics were not marked with the proper stripe it was not easy for him to become a church-member. The "Lords Brethren" were as tyrannical in the new world as the "Lords Bishops" in the old.

There was a distinction between "gentlemen," with the title of *Mr.*, and men, with only the name, *John, Peter,* and *Bartholomew,* or the title "*Goodman.*"

Slavery was established in the new world; there were two forms of it:—absolute bondage of the Africans and the Indians; the conditional bondage of white men, called "servants," slaves for a limited period. Before the Revolution the latter were numerous, even in the north.

The Puritan had little religious objection to the establishment of Slavery. But the red man would fight, and would not work. It was not possible to make useful slaves of Indians: the experiment was tried; it failed, and the savage was simply destroyed.

In theocratic and colonial times at the north, the Democratic idea contended against the church; and gradually weakened and overcame the power of the clergy and of all ecclesiastical corporations. At length all churches stand on the same level. The persecuted Quaker has vindicated his right to free inspiration by the Holy Ghost;

the Baptist enjoys the natural right to be baptized after the apostolic fashion; the Unitarian to deny the Holy Trinity; the Universalist to affirm the eternal blessedness of all men; and the philosophical critic to examine the claims of Christianity as of all religions, to sweep the whole ocean of religious consciousness, draw his net to land, gather the good into vessels, and cast the bad away.

The spirit of freedom contended against the claims of ancestral gentility. In the woods of New England it was soon found that a pair of arms was worth more than a "coat of arms," never so old and horrid with griffins. A man who could outwit the Indians, "whip his weight in wild cats," hew down tress, build ships, make wise laws, and organize a river into a mill, or men into towns and states, was a valuable person; and if born at all was well born. "Men of no family" grew up in the new soil, and often overtopped the twigs cut from some famous tree. In the humblest callings of life, I have found men of the most eminent European stocks. But it was rare that men of celebrated families settled in America: monarchy, nobility, prelacy did not emigrate, it was the people who came over. And in 1780, the Convention of Massachusetts put this in the first Article of the Constitution of the State: "All men are born free and equal, and have certain natural, essential, and unalienable rights." All distinction of gentle and simple, bond and free, perished out of Massachusetts. The same thought is repeated in the constitutions of many Northern States.

This spirit of freedom contended against the claims of England. "Local self-government" was the aim of the colonies. Opposition to centralization of authority is very old in America. I hope it will be always young. England was a hard master to her western children; she left them to fight their own battles against the Indians, against the French; and this circumstance made all men soldiers. In King Philip's war every man capable of bearing arms took the field, first or last. The frontier was a school for soldiers. The day after the battle of Lexington, a hundred and fifty men, in a large farming town of New Hampshire, shouldered their muskets and marched for Boston, to look after their brethren.

It was long before there was a clear and distinct expres-

sion of the Democratic idea in America. The Old Testament helped it to forms of denunciatory speech. The
works of Milton, Sidney, Locke, and the writers on the
law of nature and of nations, were of great service. Rousseau came at the right time, and aided the good cause.
Calvin and Rousseau, strange to say, fought side by side in
the battle for freedom. It was a great thing for America
and the world, that this idea was so clearly set forth in the
Declaration of Independence, announced as a self-evident
truth. A young man's hand came out of the wall, and
wrote words which still make many tremble as they read.

The battle for human freedom yet goes on; its victory
is never complete. But now in the free States of the
North the fight is against all traditional forms of evil.
The domestic question relates to the equal rights of men
and women in the family and out of it; there is a great
social question,—" Shall money prevail over man, and the
rich and crafty exploiter the poor and the simple?" In
the church, men ask—"Shall authority—a book or an
institution, each an accident of human history—prevail
over reason, conscience, the affections, and the soul—the
human substance?" In the State, the minority looks for
the eternal principles of Right; and will not heed the
bidding of famous men, of conventions, and majorities;
appeals to the still, small voice within, which proclaims
the Higher Law of God. Even in the North a great
contest goes on.

The Democratic idea seems likely to triumph in the
North, and build up its appropriate institutions—a family
without a slave, a family of equals; a community without
a lord, a community of co-operators; a church without a
bishop, a church of brethren; a State without a king, a
State of citizens.

The institutions of the free States are admirably suited
to produce a rapid development of the understanding.
The State guarantees the opportunity of education to all
children. The free schools of the north are her most
original institution, quite imperfect as yet. The attempts
to promote the public education of the people have already
produced most gratifying results.

More than half of the newspaper editors in the United
States have received all their academical education in the

common school. Many a Methodist and Universalist minister, many a member of Congress, has been graduated at that beneficent institution. The intelligence and riches of the North are due to the common schools. In the free States books are abundant; newspapers in all hands; skilled labour abounds. Body runs to brain, and work to thought. The head saves the hands. Under the benignant influence of public education, the children of the Irish emigrant, poor and despised, grow up to equality with the descendants of the rich; two generations will efface the difference between them. I have seen, of a Sunday afternoon, a thousand young Irish women, coming out of a Catholic church, all well dressed, with ribbons and cheap ornaments, to help elevate their self-respect; and when remembering the condition of these same women in their native land, barefoot, dirty, mendicant, perhaps thievish, glad of a place to serve at two pounds a year, I have begun to see the importance of America to the world; and have felt as John Adams, when he wrote in his diary, "I always consider the settlement of America with reverence and wonder, as the opening of a grand scene and design of Providence, for the illumination of the ignorant, and the emancipation of the slavish part of mankind, all over the earth."

The educational value of American institutions, in the free States is seldom appreciated. The schools open to all, where all classes of the people freely mingle, and the son of a rude man is brought into contact with the good manners and self-respectful deportment of children from more fortunate homes; * the churches, where everybody is welcome (if not black); the business which demands intelligence, and educates the great mass of the people; the public lectures, delivered in all the considerable towns of New England, the winter through; the newspapers abundant, cheap, discussing everything with as little reserve as the summer wind; the various social meetings of incorporated companies to discuss their affairs; the constitution of the towns, with their meetings, two or three times a year, when officers are chosen, and taxes voted, and all municipal affairs abundantly discussed; the public pro-

* In the large towns of the north—even of Massachusetts—the *coloured children* are not allowed in the common schools.

ceedings of the courts of law, so instructive to jurors and spectators; the local legislatures of the States—each consisting of from two to four hundred members, and in session four or five months of the year; the politics of the nation brought home to every voter in the land,—all these things form an educational power of immense value, for such a development of the lower intellectual faculties, as men esteem most in these days.

But, the Oligarchic idea is also at work. You meet this in all parts of the land, diligently seeking to organize itself. It takes no new forms, however, which are peculiar to America. It re-enacts the old statutes which have oppressed mankind in the eastern world: it attempts to revive the institutions that have cursed other lands in darker days. Now the few tyrannize over the many, and devise machinery to oppress their fellow-mortals; then the majority thus tyrannize over the few, over the minority. There are two forms of Democracy—the Satanic and the Celestial: one is Selfishness, which knows no higher law; the other Philanthropy, that bows to the justice of the infinite God, with a " Thy will be done." In America we find both—the democratic Devil and the democratic Angel.

The idea of the North is preponderatingly democratic in the better sense of the word; new justice is organized in the laws; government becomes more and more of all, by all, and for all. You trace the progress of humanity, of liberty, equality, and fraternity in the constitution of the free States from Massachusetts to Wisconsin.

But in the Southern States the Oligarchic idea prevails to a much greater extent, and becomes more and more apparent and powerful. The South has adopted the institution of slavery, elsewhere discarded, and clings to it with strange tenacity. In South Carolina, the possession of slaves is made the condition, *sine quâ non,* of eligibility to certain offices. The constitution provides that a citizen shall not " be eligible to a seat in the House of Representatives, *unless legally seized and possessed in his own right,* of a settled freehold estate of five hundred acres of land, and *ten negroes.**

* Art. I. § 6.

The Puritans of New England made no very strong objection to Slavery. It was established in all the colonies of the North and South. White servitude continued till the Revolution. As late as 1757, white men were kidnapped, "spirited away," as it was called in Scotland, and sold in the colonies.

Negro slavery began early. Even the gentler Puritans at Plymouth had the Anglo-Saxon antipathy to the coloured race. The black man must sit aloof from the whites in the meeting-house, in a "negro pew;" he must "not be joined unto them in burial;" a place was set apart, in the graveyard at Plymouth, for coloured people, and still remains as "from time immemorial." In 1851, an Abolitionist, before his death, insisted on being buried with the objects of his tender solicitude. The request was complied with.

After the Revolution, the Northern States gradually abolished slavery, though not without violent opposition in some places. In 1788 three coloured persons were kidnapped at Boston and carried to the West Indies; the crime produced a great excitement, and led to executive and legislative action. The same year, the General Presbyterian Assembly of America issued a pastoral letter, recommending "the abolition of Slavery, and the instruction of the negroes in letters and religion." In 1790, Dr. Franklin, president of the "Pennsylvanian Society for the Abolition of Slavery," signed a memorial to Congress, asking that body "to countenance the restoration of liberty to the unhappy men who alone in this land of freedom are degraded into perpetual bondage, and who, amid the general joy of surrounding provinces, are groaning in servile subjection; that you will devise means for removing this inconsistency from the character of the American people; that you will permit mercy and justice towards this distressed race; and that you will step to the very verge of the power vested in you for discouraging every species of traffic in the persons of our fellow-men."

The memorial excited a storm of debate. Slavery was defended as a measure of political economy, and a principle of humanity, South Carolina leading in the defence of her favourite institution. Yet many eminent Southern men were profoundly convinced of the injustice of slavery; others saw it was a bad tool to work with.

Since that time the Southern idea of Slavery appears to have changed. Formerly, it was granted by the defenders of slavery that it was wrong; but they maintained:—
1. That Americans were not responsible for the wrong, as England had imposed it upon the colonies. 2. That it was profitable to the owners of slaves. 3. That it was impossible to get rid of it. Now the ground is taken that slavery is not a wrong to the slave, but that the negro is fit for a slave, and a slave only.

I pass by the arguments of the Southern clergy and the Northern clergy—whose conduct is yet more contemptible —to cite the language of the prominent secular organs of the South. The *Richmond Examiner*, one of the most able journals of the South, declares:—

"When we deprive the negro of that exercise of his will which the white calls liberty, we deprive him of nothing; on the contrary, when we give him the guidance and protection of a master, we confer on him a great blessing." *

".To treat two creatures so utterly different as the white man and the negro man on the same system, is an effort to violate elementary laws." "The aphorisms of the Declaration of Independence" are illogical when applied to the negro. "They involve the assumption that the negro is the white man, only a little different in external appearance and education. But this assumption cannot be supported." "A law rendering perpetual the relation between the negro and his master is no wrong, but a right." "Negroes are not men, in the meaning of the Declaration of Independence."

"'Haven't negroes got souls?' asks some sepulchral voice. 'Have they no souls?' That question we never answer; we know nothing about it. *Non mi ricordo;* they may have souls, for aught we know to the contrary; so may horses and hogs."

"We expect the institution of Slavery to exist for ever." "The production of cotton, rice, sugar, coffee, and tobacco, demand that which Slavery only can supply. And in all

* See above, vol. i. p. 394, *et seq.*

portions of this Union where these staples are produced, it will be retained. And when we get Hayti, Mexico, and Jamaica, common sense will doubtless extend it, or rather, re-establish it there too." *

I will now quote a little from the Mr. De Bow's large work :—†

"No amount of education or training can ever render the negro equal in intellect with the white." " 'You cannot make a silk purse out of a sow's lug,' is an old and homely adage, but not the less true ; so you cannot make anything from a negro but negroism, which means barbarism and inferiority." "As God made them so they have been, and so they will be; the white man, the negro, and the jackass ; each to his kind, and each to his nature ; true to the finger of destiny (which is the finger of God), and undeviatingly pursuing the track which that finger as undeviatingly points out." ‡

" Is the negro made for slavery ? God in heaven! what are we, that because we cannot understand the mystery of this Thy will, we should dare rise in rebellion, and call it wrong, unjust, and evil ? The kindness of nature fits each creature to fulfil its destiny. The very virtues of the negro fit him for slavery, and his vices cry aloud for the shackles of bondage ! " " It is the destiny of the negro, if by himself, to be a savage ; if by the white, to be a serf." "They may be styled human beings, though of an inherently degraded species. To attempt to relieve them from their natural inferiority is idle in itself, and may be mischievous in its results." §

"Equality is no thought nor creation of God. Slavery, under one name or another, will exist as long as man exists ; and abolition is a dream whose execution is an impossibility. Intellect is the only divine right. The negro cannot be schooled, nor argued, nor driven into a love of freedom."‖

"Alas for their folly! (the abolitionists.) But woe!

* Richmond (Va.) *Semi-weekly Examiner*, January 4, 1853.

† "The Industrial Resources, etc., of the Southern and Western States : embracing a View of their Commerce, Agriculture, Manufactures, Internal Improvements ; Slave and Free Labour, Slavery Institutions, Products, etc., of the South, etc., with an Appendix." By J. D. B. de Bow, etc. In 3 vols. 8vo. New Orleans, 1852.

‡ De Bow, vol. ii. p. 199.   § *Id.* p. 203.   ‖ *Id.* p. 204.

woe! a woe of darkness and of death, a woe of hell and perdition to those who, better knowing, goad folly on to such an extreme. This is, indeed, the sin not to be forgiven; the sin against the Holy Ghost, and against the Spirit of God! The beautiful order of creation breathed down from Almighty intelligence, is to be moulded and wrought by fanatic intelligence, until dragged down, at last, to negro intelligence!" *

Chancellor Harper, of South Carolina, in an address delivered before "the Society for the Advancement of Learning," at Charleston, makes some statements a little remarkable:—

"The institution of Slavery is a principle cause of civilization." "It is as much the order of nature that men should enslave each other, as that other animals should prey upon each other." "The savage can only be tamed by being enslaved or by having slaves." "The African slave-trade has given and will give the boon of existence to millions and millions in our country who would otherwise never have enjoyed it." †

He quotes the Bible to justify Slavery:—

" 'They shall be your bondmen for ever.' " "Servitude is the condition of civilization. It was decreed when the command was given, 'Be fruitful and multiply, and replenish the earth and subdue it;' and when it was added 'In the sweat of thy face shalt thou eat bread.' Slavery was "forced on us by necessity, and further forced upon us by the superior authority of the mother country. I, for one, neither deprecate nor resent the gift." "I am by no means sure that the cause of humanity has been served by the change in jurisprudence which has placed their murder on the same footing with that of a freeman." "The relation of master and slave is naturally one of kindness." "It is true that the slave is driven to his labour by stripes; such punishment would be degrading to a freeman, who had the thoughts and aspirations of a freeman. In general, it is not degrading to a slave, nor is it felt to be so." ‡

It is alleged that "the slave is cut off from the means of intellectual, moral, and religious improvement, and in consequence his moral character becomes depraved, and he

* De Bow, vol. ii. p. 197.   † Id. pp. 206—210.   ‡ Id. pp. 214—217.

addicted to degrading vices." To this the democratic Chancellor of South Carolina replies :—

" The Creator did not intend that every individual human being should be highly cultivated, morally and intellectually." " It is better that a part should be highly cultivated, and the rest utterly ignorant." " Odium has been cast upon our legislation on account of its forbidding the elements of education to be communicated to slaves. But, in truth, what injury is done them by this ? He who works during the day with his hands does not read in intervals of leisure for his amusement, or the improvement of his mind." " Of the many slaves whom I have known capable of reading, I have never known one to read anything but the Bible, and this task they imposed on themselves as matter of duty." " Their minds generally show a strong religious tendency, . . . and perhaps their religious notions are not much more extravagant than those of a large portion of the free population of our country." " It is certainly the master's interest that they should have proper religious sentiments."

" A knowledge of reading, writing, and the elements of arithmetic, is convenient and important to the free labourer . . . but of what use would they be to the slave ?" " Would you do a benefit to the horse or the ox by giving him a cultivated understanding or fine feelings ?" *

" The law has not provided for making those marriages [of slaves] indissoluble ; nor could it do so." " It may perhaps be said, ' that the chastity of wives is not protected by law from the outrages of violence.' " " Who ever heard of such outrages being offered ? . . . One reason, doubtless, may be, that often there is no disposition to resist, . . . there is little temptation to this violence as there is so large a population of this class of females [slave wives] who set little value on chastity." " It is true that in this respect the morals of this class are very loose, . . . and that the passions of the men of the superior caste tempt and find gratification in the easy chastity of the females. This is evil, . . . but evil is incident to every condition of society."

" The female slave [who yields to these temptations] is not a less useful member of society than before. . . . She

* De Bow, vol. ii. p. 217, et seq.

has done no great injury to herself or any other human
being; her offspring is not a burden but an acquisition to
her owner; his support is provided for, and he is brought
up to usefulness; if the fruit of intercourse with a free
man, his condition is perhaps raised somewhat above that
of his mother."

"I do not hesitate to say, that the intercourse which
takes place with enslaved females is less debasing in its
effects [on man] than when it is carried on with females
of their own caste, . . . the attraction is less, . . . the
intercourse is generally casual, . . . he is less liable to
those extraordinary fascinations."

"He [the slave husband] is also liable to be separated
from wife or child, . . . but from native character and
temperament, the separation is much less severely felt." *

"The love of liberty is a noble passion. But, alas! it is
one in which we know that a large portion of the human
race can never be gratified." "If some superior power
should impose on the laborious poor of this, or any other
country, this ['a condition which is a very near approach
to that of our slaves'] as their undeniable condition, . . .
how inappreciable would the boon be thought." "The
evils of their situation they [the slaves] but slightly feel,
and would hardly feel at all if they were not sedulously
instructed into sensibility." "Is it not desirable that the
inferior labouring class should be made up of such who will
conform to their condition without painful aspirations and
vain struggles?" †

"I am aware that, however often assumed, it is likely
to be repeated again and again:—How can that institution
be tolerable, by which a large class of society is cut off
from the hope of improvement and knowledge; to whom
blows are not degrading, theft no more than a fault, false-
hood and the want of chastity almost venial; and in which
a husband or parent looks with comparative indifference on
that which to a free man would be the dishonour of a wife
or child? But why not, if it produce the greatest aggregate of good? Sin and ignorance are only evils because
they lead to misery." ‡

"The African negro is an inferior variety of the human

* De Bow, vol. ii. p. 219, et seq.   † Id. p. 222.   ‡ Id.

race, . . . and his distinguishing characteristics are such as peculiarly mark him out for the situation which he occupies among us; . . . the most remarkable is their indifference to personal liberty." "Let me ask if this people do not present the very material out of which slaves ought to be made?" "I do not mean to say that there may not be found among them some of superior capacity to many white persons. . . . And why should it not be so? We have many domestic animals—infinite varieties, distinguished by various degrees of sagacity, courage, strength, swiftness, and other qualities."

"Slavery has done more to elevate a degraded race in the scale of humanity; to tame the savage, to civilize the barbarous, to soften the ferocious, to enlighten the ignorant, and to spread the blessing of Christianity among the heathen, than all the missionaries that philanthropy and religion have ever put forth." "The tendency of Slavery is to elevate the character of the master," "to elevate the female character." "There does not now exist a people in a tropical climate, or even approaching to it, where Slavery does not exist that is in a state of high civilization. Mexico and the South American republics, having gone through the farce of abolishing slavery, are rapidly degenerating." "Cuba is daily and rapidly advancing in industry and civilization; and it is owing exclusively to her slaves. St. Domingo is struck out of the map of civilized existence, and the British West Indies shortly will be so." "Greece is still barbarous, and scantily peopled." "Such is the picture of Italy—nothing has dealt upon it more heavily than the loss of domestic Slavery. Is not this evident?" *

A writer in the same work, speaking of the future of the South, refers to the British and French West Indies as follows :—

"The mind of the devout person who contemplates the condition of the *ci-devant* slave-colonies of these two powers, must become impressed with the fact, that Providence must have raised up those two examples of human folly for the express purpose of a lesson to these States, to save which from human errors it has, on more than one

* De Bow, vol. ii. pp. 222—229.

occasion, manifestly and directly interposed." "England itself . . . is in some sort the slave of Southern blacks."

"The few articles which are most necessary to modern civilization—sugar, coffee, cotton, and tobacco—are products of compulsory black labour." *

Another writer, whom I take to be a clergyman and a Jesuit,† goes so far as to forbid all sympathy for the sufferings of slaves :—

"Sympathy for them could do them no good, because a relief from slavery could not elevate them—could do them no good, but an injury. Hence such sympathy is forbidden;" meaning it is forbidden by God, in such passages as this: "Thine eye shall not pity him" (Deut. xix. 13). He maintains that African slavery is a punishment divinely inflicted on the descendants of Ham for his offence. Ham, he thinks, married a descendant of Cain, and his children inherited the "mark" set upon the first murderer!

Let us now look at some facts connected with Slavery in America.

No nation has, on the whole, treated its African slaves so gently as the Americans. This is proved by the rapid increase of the slave population. Compare America in this respect with some of the British West Indies.‡

In seventy-three years, from 1702 to 1775, the increase of the coloured population of Jamaica was 158,614; but in that period there were imported and retained in the island, 360,622; so the slave-owners in seventy-three years must have used up and destroyed about 300,000 human beings. This dreadful exploitation continued a long time. From 1775 to 1794, about 113,000 more were imported;

* De Bow, vol. iii. pp. 39, 40.

† "John Fletcher of Louisiana," in his *Studies on Slavery in* (119) *Easy Lessons.* Natchez, 1852. 8vo. pp. xiv. and 637. The author luxuriates in the idea of Slavery, and gives the public a paradigm of the Hebrew verb עָבַד, *to slave*, in *kal, niphal, pihel, puhol, hiphil hophal, hithpael*; and a declension of the "*factitious euphonic segholate*" noun, עֶבֶד, *a slave.*

‡ In 1658 there were in Jamaica   1,400 slaves.
   1670   "   "   8,000   "
   1673   "   "   9,504   "
   1702   "   "   36,000   "
   1734   "   "   86,546   "   [persons.
   1775   "   "   194,614   "   and free coloured

but in 1791 there were only 260,000 coloured persons in Jamaica. In sixteen years, the loss was more than 47,000 greater than the entire importation. To say it all in a word : in 1702, Jamaica started with 36,000 slaves ; up to 1791, she had imported and retained in bondage 473,000 more ; making a total of 509,000 souls, and in 1791, she had only 260,000 to show as the result of her traffic in human souls. There was a waste of 249,000 lives ! *

About 750,000 slaves were imported into Jamaica between 1650 and 1808. If that number seems excessive, diminish it to 700,000, which is certainly below the fact ; then add all the children born in the one hundred and eighty-four years which elapsed before the day of emancipation came. Remember that only 311,000 were there to be emancipated in 1834, and it is plain what a dreadful massacre of human life had been going on in that garden of the western world.†

About 1,700,000 slaves have been imported into the

* From 1791 to 1808, about 150,000 more were imported, and the slave population in 1808 was only 323,827, showing a waste of more than 86,000 lives in eighteen years ! Importation was illegal, but still carried on after the latter date ; at least 80,000 must have been smuggled in, in the next nine years.

In 1817 the number of slaves was 346,150
In 1826 it had fallen to . . . 331,119
In 1833 ,, ,, . . . 311,692

After the importation ceased, more pains were taken to preserve the Africans ; but the table shows how mortality went on with increased velocity.

Years.	Registered Births.	Registered Deaths.
From 1817 to 1820	24,348	25,104
,, 1823 to 1826	23,026	25,171
,, 1826 to 1829	21,728	25,137

† The same thing took place in all the British West Indies. Look at the following

Table of Slave Population of British Guiana.

Number in 1820		77,376
,,	1826	71,382
,,	1832	65,517
Loss in twelve years		11,859

Table of Births and Deaths.

Years.	Registered Births.	Registered Deaths.
1817 to 1820	4868	7140
1820 to 1823	4512	7188
1823 to 1826	4494	7634
1826 to 1829	4684	5731
1829 to 1832	4086	7016

British West Indies. Of all this number, and the'vast families of children born thereof, in 1834 there were only 780,993 to be emancipated.

Look at the course of things in the United States. In 1714, the number of coloured persons was 58,850; in 1850, 3,626,985.*

The United States can show ten Africans now living for every one brought into the country, while the British West Indies, in 1834, could not show one living man for each two brought thither as slaves.†

* Here is a conjectural and approximate

Table of Importation of African Slaves to the United States.

Before	1714	. .	30,000
From 1715 to 1750	.	90,000
„ 1750 to 1760	. .	35,000
„ 1760 to 1770	.	74,000
„ 1770 to 1790	. .	34,000
After 1790	. . .	70,000

Total   .   .   . 333,500

† The above facts, and the authorities for them, are taken from a valuable and readable book, by H. C. Carey, *The Slave Trade, Domestic and Foreign; why it exists, and how it may be extinguished.* Philadelphia, 1853. 1 vol. 12mo., pp. 426. Another work, by M. Charles Comte, contains much information relative to slavery, and its effects in ancient and modern times:—*Traité de Législation ou Exposition des Lois Générales suivant lesquelles les Peuples prospèrent, deperissent, ou restent stationaires,* etc. (3me Edition. Bruxelles, 1837.) Livre v.

In De Bow, vol. ii. p. 340, *et seq.,* is a statement of the importation of Slaves to Charleston, from 1804 to 1807, whence I construct the following

Table of South Carolina Slave-Trade 1804–1807.

70	vessels owned in	England	. .	brought	19,649	slaves.
3	„ „	France .	. .	„	1,078	„ .
61	„ „	Charleston	.	„	7,723	„
59	„ „	Rhode Island	.	„	8,238	„
4	„ „	Baltimore .	.	„	750	„
3	„ „	other Southern Ports	„	787	„
3	„ „	„ Northern Ports	„	650	„

39,075   „

Of these, 3433 were imported on account of citizens of the slave-holding States, and 35,642 on account of capitalists in countries where Slavery was prohibited! Newport, in Rhode Island, was famous for the slave-trade, and its prosperity fell with that business. The cost of paving the only street in the town paved with stone was defrayed by a tax of ten dollars on each slave brought into the harbour. So late as 1850, Boston vessels were engaged in the African slave-trade. The domestic slave-trade still employs many northern vessels,—1033 slaves were shipped at Baltimore, for various southern ports, in 1851.

A Texan newspaper, the *Columbian Planter*, of April 5, 1853, deprecates all discussion of Slavery, and thus speaks of the slave code of that State:—" We consider it the duty of the County Court to have these local laws compiled and printed in a cheap form, and a copy placed on each plantation in the county. But we cannot, with what we consider the true policy and interest of the South, open the columns of the *Planter* for their publication."

" We regard the institution of domestic slavery as purely a local subject, which should lie at the feet of the Southern press with deathlike silence; for its great importance will not admit of its discussion."

I will mention three cases of cruelty which have lately come to my knowledge. A black free man, in a city of Kentucky, had a wife who was a slave. One evening her master, who had a grudge against the husband, found him in the kitchen with her, and ordered him out of the house. He went, but left the gate of the back yard open as he passed out. The white man ordered him to return and shut it; the black man grumbled and refused; whereupon the white man shot him dead! The murderer was a " class leader" in the church, and attended a meeting shortly after this transaction. He was asked to " comfort the souls of the meeting, and improve his gift" by some words of exhortation. He declined on the ground that he felt dissatisfied with himself, that he himself " needed to be strengthened, and wished for the prayers of the brethren." They appointed a committee to look into the matter, who reported that he had done nothing wrong. The affair was also brought before a magistrate, who dismissed the case!

Here is another, yet more atrocious. A slave-holder in South Carolina had inflicted a brutal and odious mutilation, which cannot be named, on two male slaves for some offence. Last year the master attempted to inflict the same barbarity upon a third slave. He ordered another black man to help bind the victim. The slave, struggling against them both, seized a knife, killed the master, and then took his own life. The neighbours came together, ascertained the facts, and hung up the slave's dead body at the next four corners, as a terror to the coloured people of the place! No account of it was published in the newspapers. Slavery "should lie at the feet of the Southern press with deathlike silence!"

While writing this address I receive intelligence of a slave woman recently whipped to death in Missouri. An incautious German, who had not been long enough in the country to become converted to "American Christianity," and so callous to such things, published an account of the transaction in a German newspaper. The murderers were not punished.

The following advertisement is taken from a newspaper published in Wilmington (North Carolina), in March, 1853. Nothing in Mrs. Stowe's work is so atrocious; for American fiction halts this side of the American fact :—

225 DOLLARS REWARD.—State of North Carolina, New Hanover County. —Whereas, complaint upon oath has this day been made to us, two of the Justices of the Peace for the State and county aforesaid, by Benjamin Hallett, of the said county, that two certain male slaves belonging to him, named Lott, aged about twenty-two years, five feet four or five inches high, and black, formerly belonging to Lott Williams, of Onslow Co.; and Bob, aged about sixteen years, five feet high, and black, have absented themselves from their said master's service, and supposed to be lurking about this county, committing acts of felony and other misdeeds. These are, therefore, in the name of the State aforesaid, to command the said slaves forthwith to return home to their masters; and we do hereby, by virtue of the Act of the General Assembly in such cases made and provided, intimate and declare, that if the said Lott and Bob do not return home and surrender themselves, any person may kill and destroy the said slaves, by such means as he or they may think of, without accusation or impeachment of any crime or offence for so doing, and without incurring any penalty or forfeiture thereby.
Given under our hands and seals, this 28th day of February, 1853.
         W. N. PEDEN, J. P.   [seal.]
         W. C. BETTENCOURT, J. P. [seal.]

225 DOLLARS REWARD.—Two hundred dollars will be given for negro Lott, either dead or alive; and twenty-five dollars for Bob's head, delivered to the subscriber in the town of Wilmington.
                    BENJAMIN HALLETT.
March 2, 1853.

I will next proceed to show some of the effects of democracy at the North, and despotism at the South.

First notice the effect on the increase of population. In 1790, the entire population of the territory now occupied by the slave States was 1,961,372 exclusive of Indians; that of the free States was 1,968,455.

In 1850, with an addition of immense territories— Florida, Louisiana, Texas, New Mexico—the population of the slave States amounted to 9,719,779; the free States and territories, not including Oregon and California, had 13,348,371 souls. The population of the free States has increased about six hundred per cent., that of the slave only about four hundred per cent.

Let us compare a free and a slave State which lie side by side. In soil and climate, Kentucky is superior to Ohio—only the stream separates them. Slavery is on one side, freedom on the other; and what a difference!

Kentucky contains 37,680 square miles. It is well watered with navigable rivers—the Ohio, Cumberland, Kentucky, Green, and Salt. The soil is admirable, producing abundantly; the climate mild and salubrious. It abounds in minerals—coal, iron, lead. The salt springs were famous even with the French and Indians. Rice, cotton, and the sugar-cane grow in Kentucky.

Ohio contains 39,964 square miles of land, no better watered, with a soil not superior, less favoured with mineral riches, yet also abounding in iron and coal; the climate is sterner, the water power less copious.

In 1790, Kentucky had 73,077 inhabitants; Ohio not a white man. In 1800, Kentucky had 220,959; Ohio only 45,365. But in 1850, Kentucky had only 982,405; while Ohio had grown to 1,980,427 souls. To-day, Kentucky has not 775,000 freemen, while Ohio has more than 2,000,000.

In 1810, Louisville, the capital of Kentucky, numbered 4,012 persons; Cincinnati, the chief town of Ohio, contained 9,644. Now Louisville has less than 50,000, and Cincinnati more than 150,000; while Cleveland and Columbus, in the same State, have risen from nothing to cities each containing 20,000 inhabitants.

Look next at the effect of these different institutions on the productive industry of the different sections of the land. In the North, labour is respected. In 1845, there were in Boston 19,037 private families; there were 15,744 who kept no servant, and only 1,069 who had more than one. Is Boston poor? In 1854, the property of her citizens, taxable on the spot, is more than $225,000,000.

In 1847, the real property in Boston was valued at $97,764,500,—$45,271,120 more than the value of all the real estate of South Carolina, with her 24,500 square miles of land. South Carolina "owns" 384,984 slaves; at $400 a head, they would come to $153,993,600. The actual property of the inhabitants of Boston, in 1854, is sufficient to buy all those slaves, and then leave a balance sufficient to pay the market value of all the houses and land in that proud State.

In 1839, the census value of the annual agricultural products of the entire South was $312,380,151; that of the free States, $342,007,446. Yet the South had an advantage by nature, and 249,780 more persons engaged in agriculture.

The manufactures of the South for that year were worth $42,178,184; of the North, $197,658,040.

The aggregate earnings of all the South were $403,429,718, of the North, $658,705,108. The entire earnings of the two Carolinas, Georgia, Alabama, Mississippi, and Louisiana, amounted to $189,321,719; those of New York to $193,806,433.

Omitting the territories and California from the estimate, in 1850, the fifteen slave States contained 190,297,188 acres of land in farms; the fifteen Northern States only 97,087,778 acres. But the Northern farms were worth $283,023,483, while the Southern were valued at only $253,583,234. The South has 93,000,000 acres the most land, and it is worth $30,000,000 the least.

The South has invested $95,918,842 in manufacturing establishments which give an annual return of $167,906,350: while the North has $431,290,351 in manufactures, with a yearly earning of $845,430,428.

In 1853, the South had 438,297 tons of shipping; at $40 a ton it was worth $17,331,880. The North had 3,831,047 tons, worth $153,241,880.

On the 1st of September, 1852, the South had 2,144 miles of railroad; the North 9,661 miles. The cost of 1,140 miles of railroad in Massachusetts with its equipment was $56,559,982.

In 1850, the aggregate value of all the property real and personal of the fifteen slave States was $2,755,411,554; that of fifteen free States — omitting California — was $3,186,683,924. But in the Southern estimate the value of the working men is included; appraising the 3,200,412 at $400 apiece, they come to $1,280,164,800; deduct this from the gross sum, and there remains $1,475,246,754 as the worth of all the material property of all the persons in the fifteen slave States; while the inhabitants of the free States have material property amounting to $3,186,683,924.

The different effects of democracy and despotism appear in the higher forms of industry—the inventions which perform the work of human hands. From 1790 to 1849, there were 16,514 patents granted for inventions made in the free States, and only 2,202 in the slave States. I omit patents granted to citizens of the district of Columbia, and to foreigners. In 1851, 64 patents were granted to citizens of the slave States; 656 to those of the free States. Besides; many of the Southern patents are granted to men born and bred at the North.

It is not too much to say, that the machinery of Pennsylvania, New York, and Massachusetts, driven by water and steam, earns every year more than all the 3,000,000 slaves of the entire South. Even Chancellor Harper confesses that "free labour is cheaper than the labour of slaves." The South kidnaps men, breeds them as cattle, brands them as cattle, beats them as cattle, sells them as cattle—does not know "whether they have a soul or not;" declares them cursed by God, not fit for human sympathy, incapable of development, indifferent to liberty, to chastity, without natural affection; breaks up their marriages, forbids them to be taught reading and writing—behold the practical results!

Look at the effect of these two institutions, the democratic and the despotic, on the intellectual education of the people, in the North and South.

In 1839, there were in the slave States, at schools and colleges, 301,172 pupils; in the free States, 2,212,444 pupils at school and college. New York sends, to school and college, more than twice as many young persons as all the slave States.

At that time there were in Connecticut 163,843 free persons over twenty years of age; of these only 526 were unable to read and write. In South Carolina, there were 111,663 free persons over twenty, and of these 20,615 were reported as unable to write or read. The ignorant men of

Connecticut were almost all foreigners, those of South
Carolina natives of that soil.   A sixth part of the voters
of South Carolina are unable to read the ballot they cast.

According to the census of 1850, in the year 1849, the
South paid $2,717,771 for public schools; the North
$6,834,388.   The South had 976,966 children at school;
the North, 3,106,961.

The South had 2,867,567 native whites over twenty
years of age; of these 532,605 were unable even to read—
more than eighteen per cent.   In the North there were
6,649,001 native whites over twenty, and only 278,575
thus illiterate—not four and one-fourth per cent.

In 1850, there were in the United States 2,800 newspapers and other periodicals, from the daily to the quar-
terly, issuing annually about 422,700,000 copies, to about
5,000,000 subscribers.   Of these journals, 716 were in the
slave States—including those printed in the capital of
America—and 2,084 in the free States.   The circulation of
Southern periodicals, however, is limited: their average
is not more than one-half or two-thirds that of the northern
journals.

Almost all who are eminent in science, literature, or art
—naturalists, historians, poets, preachers—are Northern
men.   The Southern pulpit produces nothing remarkable
but evidences of the Divinity of Slavery.

The respective military power of the democratic and
despotic institutions was abundantly tested in the revolutionary war.   From 1775 to 1783, the free population of
the slave States was 1,307,549; there were also 657,527
slaves.   New England contained 673,215 free persons,
and 3,886 slaves.   During the nine years of that war, the
slave States furnished the continental army with 58,421
regular soldiers; New England alone furnished 118,380
regulars.   The slave States had also 12,719 militia-men,
and New England 46,048 militia-men.

After the battle of Bunker Hill, when the States in
Congress were called on to furnish soldiers, South Carolina,
in consequence of her "peculiar institutions," asked that
hers might remain at home.   In 1779 (March 29th) a
committee of Congress reported that "the State of South
Carolina is unable to make any effectual effort, with militia,

by reason of the great proportion of the citizens necessary
to remain at home, to prevent insurrection among the
negroes, and prevent the desertion of them to the enemy."
From 1775 to 1783, South Carolina contained 166,018
free persons, Connecticut only 158,760. During the
nine years of the war, South Carolina sent 5,508 soldiers
to the army, and Connecticut 39,831. While the six
slave States could raise only 58,421 soldiers, and 12,779
militia-men, Massachusetts alone contributed 67,937 soldiers to the continental army, and 15,155 militia-men—in
all 83,092 !

The demoralizing influence of American despotism is
fearfully obvious in the conduct of the general Government. It debases the legislative and the executive power;
the Supreme Court is its venal prostitute. You remember
the Inaugural of Mr. Pierce :—
"I believe that involuntary servitude is recognised by
the Constitution. I believe that it stands like any other
admitted right. I hold that the laws of 1850 [the Fugitive Slave Act] commonly called the 'compromise measures,' are strictly constitutional, and to be unhesitatingly
carried out." "The laws to enforce these [rights to property in the body and soul of men] should be respected
and obeyed, not with a reluctance encouraged by abstract
opinions as to their propriety in a different state of society,
but cheerfully, and according to the decisions of the
tribunal to which their exposition belongs."
The effect of Slavery on the morality of the North is
painful to reflect upon. Northern merchants engage in
the internal slave trade; in the foreign slave trade; they
own plantations at the South; they lend money to the
South, and take slaves as security. The Northern church
is red with the guilt of bondage; most of its eminent
preachers are deadly enemies to the freedom of the African.
How many clerical defenders has the Fugitive Slave Act
found in the North? The court-house furnished kidnappers at Philadelphia, New York, and Boston; the
church justified them in the name of God. I know of no
church which has ever showed itself more cowardly than
the American. Since 1849, the Bible Society dares not
distribute the Scriptures to slaves. The American Tract

Society adapts its publications to the Southern market, by expunging every word hostile to the patriarchal institution. Mr. Gurney says, "If this love had always prevailed among professing Christians, where would have been the sword of the crusader? *Where the African slave-trade? Where the odious system which permits to man a property in his fellow-man, and converts rational beings into marketable chattels?*" The American Tract Society alters the text, and instead of what I have italicized, it prints: "Where the tortures of the Inquisition? Where every system of oppression and wrong by which he who has the power revels in luxury and ease at the expense of his fellow-men!"

In 1850 and 1851, the most prominent preachers in the North came out in public and justified the kidnapping of men in Philadelphia, New York, and Boston. It is true some noble ministers lifted up their voices against it; but the theological leaders went for man-stealing, and knew no higher law.

Commercial and political journals denounced every minister who applied the golden rule of the Gospel to the poor fugitives from Slavery. Several clergymen were driven from their parishes in Massachusetts, because they preached against kidnapping. Metropolitan newspapers invited merchants to refuse to trade with towns where the Fugitive Slave Bill was unpopular; lawyers and doctors opposed to Slavery must not be employed.

Anti-Slavery sentiments are carefully excluded from school-books: the writers want a Southern market. The principal men in the Northern colleges appear to be on the side of oppression. The political and commercial press of the North is mainly on the side of the slave-holder. While preparing this paper I find in a Northern newspaper (the *Boston Courier*, of April 26, 1853) an advertisement as follows:—

"A RARE CHANCE FOR CAPITALISTS!

"FOR SALE.

"The Pulaski House, at Savannah, and Furniture, and a number of PRIME NEGROES, accustomed to hotel business," etc.

The advertisement is dated "Savannah, 19*th April*."
On that day, 1851, Boston landed at Savannah a man

whom she had kidnapped in her own streets; on that day, in 1775, a few miles from Boston, a handful of farmers and mechanics first drew the sword of America against the oppressions of her parent, "in the sacred cause of God and their country." Nemesis is never asleep! If men are to be advertised for sale in a Boston newspaper, it is well that the advertisement should date from the Battle of Lexington, or the Declaration of Independence.

Last year the State of Illinois passed "An Act to prevent the immigration of free negroes" into that State. A man who brings a free negro or mulatto into the State is to be fined not less than $100, nor more than $500, and to be imprisoned not more than a year. Every negro thus coming, shall be fined fifty dollars, and, if unable to pay, shall be sold to any person "who will pay said fine and costs, for the shortest time." "Every person who shall have one-fourth negro blood shall be deemed a mulatto." Delaware has just passed a similar law, though with penalties less severe.

In the commercial journals of the free and the slave States, the most scandalous abuse has been poured out upon Mrs. Stowe for her *Uncle Tom's Cabin*, and its Key. "Priestess of Darkness" is one of the pleasant epithets applied to her. The Duchess of Sutherland receives, also, a large share of abuse from the same quarter. When the kidnapper is honoured; when "prime negroes" are advertised for sale; when clergymen recommend man-stealing in the name of Christ and of God, it is very proper that ladies of genius and philanthropy should be held up as objects of scorn and contempt! Men who know no law higher than the Fugitive Slave Bill, must work after their kind.

It is a strange spectacle which America just now offers. Exiles flee hither, four hundred thousand in a year, and are welcome; while Americans born take their lives in their hand, and fly to Canada, to Nova Scotia, for an asylum. Unsuccessful "rebels," who have committed "treason" at home, find a shelter in America, a welcome, and the protection of the democratic government; while 3,300,000 men, guilty of no crime, are kept in a bondage worse than Siberian. The "chief judicial officer" of

South Carolina thinks of all "distinguishing character-istics" of the negroes "the most remarkable is their indifference to personal liberty." But democratic Calhoun, with Clay, Webster, and all the leaders of the South, must unite to make the Fugitive Slave Bill, and hinder those men who are indifferent to personal liberty from running away! After all the tumult, fifteen hundred fugitives got safely out of the slave soil of the United States in the year 1853. Alas, they must escape to the territories of a monarch! Of all the ground covered by the Declaration of Independence, not an inch is free soil, except the five thousand miles which Britain regained by the Ashburton treaty. Every foot of monarchic British soil can change a slave to a free man; while in all the three million square miles of democratic America, there is not an inch of land where he can claim the natural and unalienable right to life, liberty, and the pursuit of happiness. English is the only tongue for liberty; it is also the only speech in which kidnapping is justified by the clergy in the name of God. The despots of the European continent point with delight to the American democrats enslaving one another, and declaring there is no higher law.

There can be no lasting peace between the two conflicting ideas I have named above. One wants a Democracy, the other a Despotism; each is incursive, aggressive, exter-minating. Which shall yield? The answer is plain: Slavery is to perish out of America; Democracy is to triumph. Every census makes the result of the two ideas more apparent. The North increases in numbers, in riches, in the intellectual development of the great mass of its people—out of all proportion to the South. Slavery is a bad tool to work with. In the South, there is little skilled labour, little variety of industry; rude farm labour, rearing corn, coffee, tobacco, sugar, cotton, that is all. At Boston, at New York, on the Kennebec, and the Penobscot, Northern men build ships of oak from Virginia, and hard pine from Georgia; they get the pitch and tar from Carolina, the hemp from Kentucky—that State which has no shipping. Labour is cheap on the fair land of the Carolinas, the best in the world for red wheat; labour is dear in Pennsylvania, but she undersells the Carolinas in

the wheat market. Tennessee has rich mines of iron ore
—the fine bloomer iron; slave labour is cheap, coal
abundant. Work is dear in Pennsylvania; but there free
labour makes better iron at cheaper rates. The South is
full of water power; within six miles of the President's
house there is force enough to turn all the mills of British
Manchester; it runs by as idle as a cloud. The Southerner
draws water in a Northern bucket, drinks from a Northern
cup; with a Northern fork and spoon he eats from a
Northern dish, set on a Northern table. He wears
Northern shoes made from Southern hides; Northern
coats, hats, shirts; he keeps time with a Northern watch;
his wife wears Northern jewels, plays on a Northern
pianoforte; he sleeps in a Northern bed; reads (if read he
can) a Northern book; and writes (if writing be not a
figure of speech) on Northern paper, with a pen from the
North. The laws of Mississippi must be printed in a
Northern town! The Southerner has no market near at
hand, no variety of labour, little that is educational in toil;
industry is dishonourable. It is the curse of Slavery which
makes it so!

Three forces now work against this institution: Political
Economy, showing that it does not pay; the Public
Opinion of England, France, Germany, of all Christendom,
heaping shame on the "model republic"—"the first and
most enlightened nation in the world;" the still small
voice of Conscience in all men. The Political Economist
scoffs at the absolute Right; the Partisan Politician mocks
at the Higher Law; the Pharisee in the pulpit makes
mouths at the invisible Spirit, which silently touches the
hearts of women and of men. But he who knows the
world because he knows man, and man's God, understands
very well, that though Justice has feet of wool, her hands
are of iron. These three forces—it is plain what they will
do with American Slavery.

This institution of Slavery has brought us into most
deadly peril. A story is told of some Italian youths, of
famous family, in the Middle Ages. Borgia and his com-
rades sat riotously feasting, long past midnight, hot with
young blood, giddy with passion, crazed with fiery wine.

In their intemperate laughter they hear the hoarse voice of monks in the street, coming round the corner, chanting the *Miserere* as service for the dying, "Have mercy upon me, O God, according to thy loving-kindness!" "What is that?" cries one. "Oh," answers another, "it is only some poor soul going to hell, and the priests are trying to cheat the devil of his due! Push round the wine." Again comes the chant, "For I acknowledge my transgression, and my sin is ever before me!" "How near it is; under the windows," says a reveller, turning pale. "What if it should be meant for one of us; let me look." He opens the window, the torches flash in from the dark street, and the chant pours on them, "Purge me with hyssop, and I shall be clean: wash me, and I shall be whiter than snow!" They all spring to their feet. "Whom is it for?" they cry out. "Deliver me from blood-guiltiness, O God, thou God of my salvation; and my tongue shall sing aloud of thy righteousness," is the answer. They throw open the door—the mother of Borgia rushes in: "You are all dead men," she cries; "I poisoned the wine myself. Confess, and make your peace with God; here are His ministers." The white-robed priests fill up the room, chanting, "The sacrifices of God are a broken spirit: a broken and a contrite heart, O God, thou wilt not despise!" "But here is an antidote for my son," cries the mother of Borgia. "Take it!" He dashes the cup on the ground—and the gay company lies there, pale-blue, poisoned, and dead! Shall that be the fate of America? Yes; if she cast the cup of healing to the ground! Other admonitions must come, yet more terrible, before we learn for whom the *Miserere* is now wailing forth.

If America were to keep this shameful pest in the land, then ruin is sure to follow,—ruin of all the dear-bought institutions of our fathers. The slaves double in about twenty-five years; so in A.D. 1930, there would be 27,000,000 of slaves! What a thought! The question is not merely, shall we have Slavery and Freedom, but Slavery OR Freedom. The two cannot long continue side by side.

When this hinderance is taken away, there is a noble career open before this young giant. There is a new continent, now for the first time married to the civilized world. Various races of men mingle their blood—Indians, Africans, Caucasians; various tribes—Celtic Irish, Welsh, Scotch, Anglo-Saxon, Norwegian, Swedish, Danish, Dutch, German, Polish, Swiss, French, Spanish; all these are here. Each will contribute its best to the general stock. Democratic institutions and Democratic education will give an intellectual development to the mass of men such as the world never saw. There is no fear of war; the army and the navy do not number thirty thousand men. The energies of the nation will be directed to their natural work—subduing material Nature, and developing human Nature into its higher forms. Now we are excessively material in our tastes—one day, if this great obstacle be overcome, America will be eminent also for science, letters, art, and for the noblest virtues which adorn mankind. No nation had ever so fair an opportunity—shall we be false to our origin, and the heart's high hope? Humanity says, "No!"

THE NEW CRIME AGAINST HUMANITY.

A SERMON

PREACHED AT

The Music Hall, in Boston, on Sunday, June 4, 1854.

WITH

THE LESSON FOR THE DAY OF THE PREVIOUS SUNDAY.

INTRODUCTORY.

On Sunday, May 28, after the usual introductory services, Mr. Parker pronounced the following

LESSON FOR THE DAY.

I SEE by your faces, as well as by your number, what is expected of me to-day. A person has just sent me a request, asking me, "Cannot you extemporize a sermon for this day?" It is easier to do it than not. But I shall not extemporize a sermon for to-day—I shall extemporize the Scripture. I therefore pass over the Bible words, which I designed to read from the Old Testament and the New, and will take the Morning Lesson from the circumstances of the past week. The time has not come for me to preach a sermon on the great wrong now enacting in this city. The deed is not yet fully done: any counsel that I have to offer is better given elsewhere than here, at another time than now. Neither you nor I are quite calm enough to-day to look the matter fairly in the face and see entirely what it means. Before the events of the past week took place, I had proposed to preach this morning on the subject of war, taking my theme from the present commotions in Europe, which also will reach us, and have already.

That will presently be the theme of my morning's sermon. Next Sunday, I shall preach on THE PERILS INTO WHICH AMERICA IS BROUGHT AT THIS DAY BY THE NEW CRIME AGAINST HUMANITY. That is the theme for next Sunday: the other is for to-day. But before I proceed to that, I have some words to say in place of the Scripture lesson, and instead of a selection from the Old Testament prophets.

Since last we came together, there has been a man stolen in this city of our fathers. It is not the first; it may not be the last. He is now in the great slave pen in the city of Boston. He is there against the law of the Commonwealth, which, if I am rightly informed, in such cases prohibits the use of State edifices as United States gaols. I may be mistaken. Any forcible attempt to take him from that barracoon of Boston, would be wholly without use. For besides the holiday soldiers who belong to the city of Boston, and are ready to shoot down their brothers in a just or an unjust cause, any day when the city government gives them its command and its liquor, I understand that there are one hundred and eighty-four United States marines lodged in the Court House, every man of them furnished with a musket and a bayonet, with his side arms, and twenty-four ball cartridges. They are stationed also in a very strong building, and where five men, in a passage-way, about the width of this pulpit, can defend it against five-and-twenty, or a hundred. To "keep the peace," the Mayor, who, the other day "regretted the arrest" of our brother, Anthony Burns, and declared that his sympathies were wholly with the alleged fugitive—and of course wholly against the claimant and the Marshal—in order to keep the peace of the city, the Mayor must become corporal of the guard for kidnappers from Virginia. He must keep the peace of our city, and defend these guests of Boston over the graves, the unmonumented graves, of John Hancock and Samuel Adams.

A man has been killed by violence. Some say he was killed by his own coadjutors: I can easily believe it; there is evidence enough that they were greatly frightened. They were not United States soldiers, but volunteers from the streets of Boston, who, for their pay, went into the

Court House to assist in kidnapping a brother man. They were so cowardly that they could not use the simple cut-lasses they had in their hands, but smote right and left, like ignorant and frightened ruffians as they are. They may have slain their brother or not—I cannot tell. It is said by some that they killed him. Another story is, that he was killed by a hostile hand from without. Some say by a bullet, some by an axe, and others still by a knife. As yet nobody knows the facts. But a man has been killed. He was a volunteer in this service. IIe liked the business of enslaving a man, and has gone to render an account to God for his gratuitous wickedness. Twelve men have been arrested, and are now in gaol to await their examination for wilful murder!

Here, then, is one man butchered, and twelve men brought in peril of their lives. Why is this? Whose fault is it?

Some eight years ago, a Boston merchant, by his mer-cenaries, kidnapped a man " between Faneuil Hall and old Quincy," and carried him off to eternal slavery. Boston mechanics, the next day, held up the half-eagles which they received as pay for stealing a man. The matter was brought before the grand jury for the county of Suffolk, and abundant evidence was presented, as I understand, but they found " no bill." A wealthy merchant, in the name of trade, had stolen a black man, who, on board a ship, had come to this city, had been seized by the mer-cenaries of this merchant, kept by them for, awhile, and then, when he escaped, kidnapped a second time in the city of Boston. Boston did not punish the deed!

The Fugitive Slave Bill was presented to us, and Boston rose up to welcome it! The greatest man in all the North came here, and in this city told Massachusetts she must obey the Fugitive Slave Bill with alacrity—that we must all conquer our prejudices in favour of justice and the unalienable rights of man. Boston did conquer her pre-judices in favour of justice and the unalienable rights of man.

Do you not remember the " Union Meeting " which was held in Faneuil Hall, when a " political soldier of fortune," sometimes called the " Democratic Prince of the Devils," howled at the idea that there was a law of God higher than the Fugitive Slave Bill? He sneered, and asked, "Will you have the 'Higher Law of God' to rule over you?" and the multitude which occupied the floor, and the multitude that crowded the galleries, howled down the Higher Law of God! They treated the Higher Law to a laugh and a howl! That was Tuesday night. It was the Tuesday before Thanksgiving-day. On that Thanksgiving-day, I told the congregation that the men who howled down the Higher Law of Almighty God, had got Almighty God to settle with; that they had sown the wind, and would reap the whirlwind. At that meeting Mr. Choate told the people—"REMEMBER! REMEMBER! *Remember!*" Then nobody knew what to "remember." Now you know. That is the state of that case.

Then you "remember" the kidnappers came here to seize Thomas Sims. Thomas Sims was seized. Nine days he was on trial for more than his life; and never saw a judge—never saw a jury. He was sent back into bondage from the city of Boston. You remember the chains that were put around the Court House; you remember the judges of Massachusetts stooping, crouching, creeping, crawling under the chain of Slavery, in order to get to their own courts. All these things you "remember." Boston was non-resistant. She gave her "back to the smiters"—from the South; she "withheld not her cheek"—from the scorn of South Carolina, and welcomed the "spitting" of kidnappers from Georgia and Virginia. To-day we have our pay for such conduct. You have not forgotten the "fifteen hundred gentlemen of property and standing," who volunteered to conduct Mr. Sims to slavery—Marshal Tukey's "gentlemen." They "remember" it. They are sorry enough now. Let us forgive—we need not forget. "REMEMBER! REMEMBER! *Remember!*"

The Nebraska Bill has just now been passed. Who passed it? The fifteen hundred "gentlemen of property and standing" in Boston, who, in 1851, volunteered to carry Thomas Sims into slavery by force of arms. They passed the Nebraska Bill. If Boston had punished the kidnapping of 1845, there would have been no Fugitive Slave Bill in 1850. If Massachusetts, in 1850, had declared the Bill should not be executed, the kidnapper would

never have shown his face in the streets of Boston. If,
failing in this, Boston had said, in 1851, " Thomas Sims
shall not be carried off," and forcibly or peacefully, by the
majesty of the great mass of men, had resisted it, no
kidnapper would have come here again. There would
have been no Nebraska Bill. But to every demand of
the slave power, Massachusetts has said, " Yes, yes !—we
grant it all ! " " Agitation must cease ! " " Save the
Union ! "

Southern Slavery is an institution which is in earnest.
Northern Freedom is an institution that is not in earnest.
It was in earnest in '76 and '83. It has not been much
in earnest since. The compromises are but provisional!
Slavery is the only finality! Now, since the Nebraska
Bill is passed, an attempt is made to add insult to insult,
injury to injury. Last week, at New York, a brother of
the Rev. Dr. Pennington, an established clergyman, of
large reputation, great character, acknowledged learning,
who has his diploma from the University of Heidelberg,
in Germany—a more honourable source than that from
which any clergyman in Massachusetts has received one—
his brother and two nephews were kidnapped in New
York, and without any trial, without any defence, were
hurried off into bondage. Then, at Boston, you know
what was done in the last four days. Behold the consequences of the doctrine that there is no higher law.
Look at Boston to-day. There are no chains round your
Court House—there are only ropes round it this time. A
hundred and eighty-four United States soldiers are there.
They are, I am told, mostly foreigners—the scum of the
earth—none but such enter into armies as common soldiers,
in a country like ours. I say it with pity—they are not
to blame for having been born where they were and what
they are. I pity the scum as well as I pity the mass of
men. The soldiers are there, I say, and their trade is to
kill. Why is this so ?

You remember the meeting at Faneuil Hall, last Friday,
when even the words of my friend, Wendell Phillips, the
most eloquent words that get spoken in America in this
century, hardly restrained the multitude from going, and
by violence storming the Court House. What stirred
them up ? It was the spirit of our fathers—the spirit of

justice and liberty in your heart, and in my heart, and in the heart of us all. Sometimes it gets the better of a man's prudence, especially on occasions like this; and so excited was that assembly of four or five thousand men, that even the words of eloquent Wendell Phillips could hardly restrain them from going at once rashly to the Court House, and tearing it to the ground.

Boston is the most peaceful of cities. Why? Because we have commonly had a peace which was worth keeping. No city respects laws so much. Because the laws have been made by the people, for the people, and are laws which respect justice. Here is a law which the people will not keep. It is a law of our Southern masters; a law not fit to keep.

Why is Boston in this confusion to-day? The Fugitive Slave Bill Commissioner has just now been sowing the wind, that we may reap the whirlwind. The old Fugitive Slave Bill Commissioner stands back; he has gone to look after his "personal popularity." But, when Commissioner Curtis does not dare appear in this matter, another man comes forward, and for the first time seeks to kidnap his man also in the city of Boston. Judge Loring is a man whom I have respected and honoured. His private life is mainly blameless, so far as I know. He has been, I think, uniformly beloved. His character has entitled him to the esteem of his fellow-citizens. I have known him somewhat. I never heard a mean word from him—many good words. He was once the law-partner of Horace Mann, and learned humanity of a great teacher. I have respected him a good deal. He is a respectable man—in the Boston sense of that word, and in a much higher sense; at least, I have thought so. He is a kind-hearted, charitable man; a good neighbour; a fast friend—when politics do not interfere; charitable with his purse; an excellent husband; a kind father; a good relative. And I should as soon have expected that venerable man who sits before me, born before your Revolution [SAMUEL MAY],—I should as soon have expected him to go and kidnap Robert Morris, or any of the other coloured men I see around me, as I should have expected Judge Loring to do this thing. But he has sown the wind, and we are reaping the whirlwind. I need

not say what I now think of him. He is to act to-
morrow, and may yet act like a man. Let us wait and see.
Perhaps there is manhood in him yet. But, my friends,
all this confusion is his work. He knew he was stealing
a man born with the same unalienable right to "life,
liberty, and the pursuit of happiness" as himself. He
knew the slave-holders had no more right to Anthony
Burns than to his own daughter. He knew the consequences of stealing a man. He knew that there are men
in Boston who have not yet conquered their prejudices—
men who respect the higher law of God. He knew
there would be a meeting at Faneuil Hall—gatherings in
the streets. He knew there would be violence.

EDWARD GREELEY LORING, Judge of Probate for the
county of Suffolk, in the State of Massachusetts, Fugitive Slave Bill Commissioner of the United States, before
these citizens of Boston, on Ascension Sunday, assembled
to worship God, I charge you with the death of that
man who was killed on last Friday night. He was your
fellow-servant in kidnapping. He dies at your hand.
You fired the shot which makes his wife a widow, his
child an orphan. I charge you with the peril of twelve
men, arrested for murder, and on trial for their lives. I
charge you with filling the Court House with one hundred
and eighty-four hired ruffians of the United States, and
alarming not only this city for her liberties that are in
peril, but stirring up the whole Commonwealth of Massachusetts with indignation, which no man knows how to
stop—which no man can stop. You have done it all!

This is my Lesson for the Day.

SERMON.[*]

––––––

"Then one of the twelve, called Judas Iscariot, went unto the chief priests, and said unto them, What will ye give me, and I will deliver him unto you? And they covenanted with him for thirty pieces of silver. And from that time he sought opportunity to betray him."—MATT. xxvi. 14–16.

"Then Judas, which had betrayed him, when he saw that he was condemned, repented himself, and brought again the thirty pieces of silver to the chief priests and elders, saying, I have sinned in that I have betrayed the innocent blood. And they said, What is that to us? see thou to that."—MATT. xxvii. 3, 4.

WITHIN the last few days, we have seen some of the results of despotism in America, which might indeed easily astonish a stranger; but a citizen of Boston has no right to be surprised. The condition of this town from May 24th to June 2nd is the natural and unavoidable result of well-known causes, publicly and deliberately put in action. It is only the first-fruit of causes which in time will litter the ground with similar harvests, and with others even worse. Let us pretend no amazement that the seed sown has borne fruit after its kind. Let us see what warning or what guidance we can gather from these events, their cause and consequence. So this morning I ask your attention to a SERMON OF THE NEW CRIME AGAINST

[*] The Sermon which follows was printed in the *Boston Commonwealth*, on Monday, from the Phonographic Report of Messrs. Slack and Yerrinton. They copied out the notes at my house, and I revised them. We did not complete our labours till half-past three o'clock Monday morning. It may easily be imagined that some errors appeared in the print—for the perishable body weigheth down the mind, and, though the spirit be willing, the flesh is too weak to work four-and-twenty hours continuously. Yet the errors were surprisingly few. In this edition of the Sermon some passages have been added which were omitted in the Report, and some also which, though written, were not delivered on Sunday.

BOSTON, *June* 10, 1854.

HUMANITY COMMITTED IN THE MIDST OF US, of the LAST KIDNAPPING which has taken place in Boston.

I know well the responsibility of the place I occupy this morning. To-morrow's sun shall carry my words to all America. They will be read on both sides of the continent. They will cross the ocean. It may astonish the minds of men in Europe to hear of the iniquity committed in the midst of us. Let us be calm and cool, and look the thing fairly in the face.

Of course, you will understand, from my connection with what has taken place in part, that I must speak of some things with a good deal of reserve, and others pass by entirely. However, I have only too much to say. I have have had but short time for preparation, the deed is so recent. Perhaps I shall trespass a little on your patience this morning, that hand overrunning my customary hour some twenty or thirty minutes. If any of you find your patience exhausted, and standing too wearisome, you can retire; and, if without noise, none will be disturbed, and none offended.

On Wednesday night, the 24th of May, a young man, without property, without friends—I will continue to call his name Anthony Burns—was returning home from his usual lawful and peaceful work in the clothing shop of Deacon Pitts, in Brattle Street. He was assaulted by six ruffians, who charged him with having broken into a jeweller's shop. They seized him, forced him to the Court House, thrust him into an upper chamber therein, where he was surrounded by men, armed, it is said, with bludgeons and revolvers. There he was charged with being a fugitive slave. A man from Virginia, claiming to be his owner, and another man, likewise from Virginia, confronted the poor victim, and extorted from him a confession, as they allege, that he was the claimant's fugitive slave—if, indeed, the confession was not purely an invention of his foes, who had made the false charge of burglary; for they who begin with a lie are not to be trusted after that lie has been told. He was kept all night, guarded by ruffians hired for the purpose of kidnapping a man. No friend was permitted to see him; but his deadliest foes, who clutched at what every one of us holds tenfold dearer than life itself, were allowed access. They came and went freely, making their inquisition, extorting or inventing admissions to be used for Mr. Burns's ruin.

At nine o'clock the next morning, Thursday (May 25th), the earliest hour at which the courts of Massachusetts ever open, he was brought tot he court-room and arraigned before Edward Greeley Loring, Judge of Probate, one of the Fugitive Slave Bill Commissioners of the city of Boston, and immediately put on trial. "Intimidated" by the mob about him, and stupefied with terror and fear, he makes no defence. "As a lamb before his shearers is dumb, so he opened not his mouth." How could he dare make a defence, treated as he had been the night before?—confronted as he was by men clutching at his liberty?—in a court-room packed with ruffians, where the slaveholders' counsel brought pistols in their breasts? He had been in duress all night, with inquisitors about him. His claimant was there, with documents manufactured in Alexandria; with a witness brought from Richmond; with two lawyers of Boston to aid them.

What a scene it was for a Massachusetts court! A merchant from Richmond, so Mr. Brent called himself; another from Alexandria, who was a sheriff and member of the Virginia Legislature—for such Colonel Suttle has been —they were there to steal a man! They had him already in gaol; they went out and came in as they liked, and shut from his presence everybody who was not one of the minions hired to aid them in their crime.

Further, they had two lawyers of Boston giving them the benefit of their education and their knowledge of the law; and, in addition to that, the senior lawyer, Seth J. Thomas, brought considerable experience, acquired on similar occasions—for he has been the kidnappers' counsel from the beginning. The other lawyer was a young man of good culture and amiable deportment, I think with no previous stain on his reputation. This is his first offence. I trust it will be also his last—that he will not bring shame on his own and his mother's head. I know not how the kidnappers enticed the young man to do so base a deed; nor what motive turned him to a course so foul as this. He is a young man, sorely penitent for this early treason against humanity. Generous emotions are com-

monly powerful in the bosoms of the young. A young
man with only cruel calculation in his heart is a rare and
loathsome spectacle. Let us hope better things of this
lawyer; that a generous nature only sleeps in him. It is
his first offence. I hope he will bring forth "fruits
meet for repentance." Judge of him as charitably as you
can. Of Mr. Thomas I have only this to add:—that he is
chiefly known in the courts as the associate of Mr. Curtis
in attempts like this; the regular attorney of the stealers
of men, and apparently delighted with his work. He
began this career by endeavouring to seize William and
Ellen Craft. He is a member of the Democratic party
who has not yet received his reward.

On the side of the kidnapper there were also the district
marshal, the district attorney, the Fugitive Slave Bill
Commissioner, and sixty-five men whom I counted as the
marshal's "guard." When the company was ordered to
disperse, and the guard to remain, I tarried late, and
counted them. I reckoned sixty-five in the court-room,
and five more outside. I may have been mistaken in the
count.

On the other side there was a poor, friendless negro,
sitting between two' bullies, his wrists chained together
by stout handcuffs of steel—a prisoner without a crime,
chained; on trial for more than life, and yet there was no
charge against him, save that his mother had been a slave!

Mr. Burns had no counsel. The kidnapper's lawyers
presented their documents from Alexandria, claiming
him as a slave of Colonel Suttle, who had escaped from
"service." They brought a Virginia merchant to identify
the prisoner. He was swiftly sworn, and testified with
speed. The claimant's lawyers declared that Mr. Burns
had acknowledged already that he was Colonel Suttle's
slave, and willing to go back. So they demanded a
"certificate;" and at first it seemed likely to be granted
at once. Why should a Fugitive Slave Bill Commissioner
delay? Why does he want evidence? Injustice is swift
of foot. You know what was done in New York, the very
same week:—three men were seized, carried before a commissioner, and, without even a mock trial, without any
defence, hurried to bondage, pitiless and for ever! Only
an accident, it seems, saved Boston from that outrage.

.. But there came forward in the court-room two young
lawyers, Richard H. Dana and Charles M. Ellis, noble and
honourable men, the pride of the mothers that bore them,
and the joy of the fathers who have trained them up to
piety and reverence for the law of God. Voluntarily,
gratuitously, they offered their services as counsel for Mr.
Burns. But it was said by the kidnappers that he did
"not want counsel;" that he "would make no defence;"
that he was "willing to go back." Messrs. Dana and
Ellis did not wish to speak with him, or seemed to plead
that he might be their client. I spoke with him. His
fear gave him a sad presentiment of his fate. He feared
that he should be forced into slavery. How could he
think otherwise? Arrested on a lying charge; kept in
secret under severe and strict duress; guarded by armed
men; confronted by his claimant; seeing no friends about
him; how could he do otherwise than despair? If he went
back at all, it was natural that he should "wish to go back
easily," fearing that, if he resisted his claimant in Boston,
he "must suffer for it in Alexandria." His "conqueror,"
he thought, would take "vengeance" on him when he got
him home, if he resisted his claim. That is the best
evidence which I have seen that the man had ever been a
slave : he knew the taste and the strength of the slave-
driver's whip. That was not brought forward in
"evidence." If I had been the kidnapper's counsel I
should have said, "The man is doubtless a slave; he is
afraid to go back!" When I was in the court-room, as
I was about to ask poor Burns if he would have counsel,
one of the "guard" said to me, "You will never get him
to say he wants a defence." Another more humanely said,
"I hope he will; at any rate, it will do no harm to try."
I asked him, and he said, "Do as you think best."
But still the counsel felt a delicacy in engaging under
such circumstances. For they thought that, if, after all,
he was to be sent to bondage, and when in the hands of the
slave-master should be tortured the more for the defence
they had made for him in Boston Court House, it would
surely be better to let the marshal take his victim as soon as
he liked, and allow the Fugitive Slave Bill Commissioner
to earn his "thirty pieces of silver" without delay. They
begged for time, however, that the intimidated man might

make up his mind, and determine whether he would have a defence or not.

There is no end to human atrocity. The kidnapper's lawyers objected to the delay, and wished the "trial" to proceed at once "forthwith." They said that the claimant, Colonel Suttle, was here, having come all the way from Alexandria to Boston, at great cost; that the case was clear; that Burns made no defence: and they asked for an instant decision. The Democratic lawyer [THOMAS] thought it was not worth while to delay; there was only the liberty of a man at stake—a poor man, with no reputation, no friends, nothing but the "natural, essential, and unalienable rights" wherewith he was "endowed by his Creator"—nothing but that:—let the Virginia colonel have his slave! That is Administration Democracy in Massachusetts. There are two Democracies—the Celestial and the Satanic. One—it is the Democracy of the Beatitudes of the New Testament and of Jesus Christ; that says, "My brother, you are as good as I: come up higher, and let me take you by the hand, and we will help each other." Such Democracy is the worship of the great God. The other—it says, "I am as good as you, and, if you don't let me triumph over you, I will smite you to the ground." That is the Democracy of Caleb Cushing, the Democracy of the Administration, and of a great many political men, Democrat and Whig, and neither Whig nor Democrat.

Commissioner Loring asked Mr. Burns if he wanted time to think of the matter, and counsel to aid in his defence. I shall never forget how he looked round that court-room, at the marshal, at the kidnapper's lawyers, at the commissioner, the claimant and his witness! Save the counsel, whom he had never seen before, there was scarce a friendly face that his eye rested on. At length he said timidly, and catching for breath, "Yes." Mr. Loring put off the case until Saturday. The Fugitive Slave Bill Commissioner was to lecture at Cambridge on Friday. He is a Professor at Harvard College, and he could not conveniently hold court on that day. He is a Judge of Probate, and looks after widows and orphans; he must be in the Probate Office on Monday. Saturday was the most convenient day for the commissioner. So, in a

matter which was to determine whether the prisoner should
be a free man or only a thing which might be sold and
beaten as a beast, the "court" allowed him forty-eight
hours' delay! It really gave him time to breathe a little.
Let us be grateful to the commissioner! He gave more
favour than any Fugitive Slave Bill Commissioners have
done before, I believe.

You know the rest. He was on trial ten days. He was
never in a court; all this time he has not seen a jury; he
has not even seen a judge; the process is "summary,"
not "summary in time," as Mr. Loring declares; but it
is "without due form of law." The Democratic *chargé
d'affaires* at Turin says "the negro is the connecting link
between the human and brute creation." * Why do you
want a court to make a negro a slave in Boston? Surely,
a commissioner is enough in such a case. Let him proceed as swiftly as he will:—the kidnapper's lawyers said
—"forthwith;" not in a hurry, but "immediately."

You remember what followed. You have seen the
streets crowded with armed men. You have read the
newspapers, the handbills, and the posters. You remember the Faneuil Hall meeting, when all the influence of
the platform scarce kept the multitude from tearing the
Court House that night to the ground. You remember
the attack on the Court House—a man killed and twelve
citizens in gaol, charged with crimes of an atrocious
character. You recollect the conventions—Free Soil and
Anti-Slavery. You call to mind the aspect of Court Square
last Monday. Boston never saw such an Anniversary
week. There were meetings of theological societies, philanthropic societies, reformatory societies, literary societies:
and Boston was in a state of siege—the Court House full
of United States soldiers—marines from the navy yard,
troops from the forts, from New York, from Portsmouth,
from Rhode Island. The courts sat with muskets at their
backs, or swords at their bosoms; drunken soldiers charged
bayonet on the witnesses, on counsel, and on strangers, who
had rights where the soldier had none. The scene last Friday
you will never forget—business suspended, the shops shut,
the streets blocked up, all the "citizen-soldiery" under
arms. Ball cartridges were made for the city government on

* See above, vol. i. p. 394.

Thursday afternoon in Dock Square, to be fired into your
bosoms and mine; United States soldiers loaded their
pieces in Court Square, to be discharged into the crowd of
Boston citizens whenever a drunken officer should give
command; a six-pound cannon, furnished with forty
rounds of canister shot, was planted in Court Square,
manned by United States soldiers, foreigners before they
enlisted. The town looked Austrian. And, at high
change, over the spot where, on the 5th of March, 1770,
fell the first victim in the Boston Massacre,—where the
negro blood of Christopher Attucks stained the ground,—
over that spot Boston authorities carried a citizen of Massachusetts to Alexandria as a slave; "and order reigns in
Boston"—or Warsaw, call it which you will.

So much for a brief statement of facts.

Pause with me a moment, and look at the general causes
of the fact. Here are two great forces in the nation. One
is Slavery, Freedom is the other. The two are hostile,
deadly foes—irreconcilable. They will go on fighting till
one kills the other outright. From 1775 to 1788, Freedom
generally prevailed over Slavery. It was the period of
revolution, when the nation fell back on its religious
feelings, and thence developed the great political ideas of
America. But even then Slavery was in the midst of us.
It came into the constitution, and, from the adoption of the
Federal constitution to the present time, it has advanced,
and freedom declined. It has gone over the Alleghanies,
over the Rio del Norte, over the Cordilleras; it extends
from the forty-ninth parallel to the thirty-second, from the
Atlantic to the Pacific; it has gone into ten new States,
into all the territories except Oregon.

Since the annexation of Texas, in 1845, Slavery has been
the obvious master, Freedom the obvious servant. Fidelity
to Slavery is the *sine quâ non* for office-holders. Slavery
is the "peculiar institution" of the industrial democracy
of America. Slavery is terribly in earnest, as Freedom has
never been since the Revolution. It controls all the politics of the country. It strangles all our "great men."
There is not a great democrat, nor a great Whig, who dares
openly op ose Slavery. All the commercial towns are on
its side. There is not an anti-Slavery governor of any

State in the Union. The supreme courts of the States are all pro-Slavery, save in Vermont. The leading newspapers are nearly all on the side of wrong—almost all the commercial, almost all the political newspapers. I know but few exceptions—of course I do not speak of those devoted to philanthropy—the democratic *Evening Post,* truly democratic, of New York; and the *New York Tribune,* which is truly democratic, though it hoists another banner. Many of the theological journals—Protestant as well as Catholic—are cruelly devoted to Slavery. But proudly above all the religious journals of the land rises the *Independent,* and bears a noble witness to the humane spirit of Christianity. These are eminent exceptions, which would do honour to any nation.

The friends of Freedom appeal religiously to the souls and consciences of men : piety and justice demand that all be free ; the appeal immediately touches a few. They address also the reason and the understanding of men : Freedom is the great idea of politics ; it is self-evident that " all men are created equal." That argument touches a few more. But the religious, who reverence God's higher law, and the intellectual, who see the great ideas of politics, they are few. Slavery addresses the vulgar interests of vulgar men. To the slave-holder it gives political power, pecuniary power ; and here is an argument which the dullest can understand, and the meanest appreciate. Able and cunning men feel this, and avail themselves of Slavery to secure money and political power. These are the objects of most intense desire in America. They are our highest things—marks of our " great men." Office is transient nobility ; money is permanent, heritable nobility. Accordingly, Slavery is the leading idea of America—the " great American institution." I think history furnishes no instance of one section of a country submitting so meanly to another as we have done in America. The South is weak in numbers and in money—the North strong in both. The South has few schools, no commerce, few newspapers, no large mass of intelligent men, wherein the North abounds. But the most eminent Southern men are devoted to politics, while the Northern turn to trade : and so the South commands the North. I am only translating facts into ideas, and bringing the condition of America to the consciousness of America. Some men knew these things before, but the mass of men know them not.

So much for the general causes.

Now look at some of the special causes. I shall limit myself chiefly to those which Massachusetts has had a share in putting into activity.

In 1826, on the 9th of March, Mr. Edward Everett made a speech in Congress. He was the representative of Middlesex County. Once he was a minister of the church where John Hancock used to worship, and as clergyman officially resided in the house which John Hancock gave to that church. Next, he was a Professor in Harvard College, where the Adamses—the three Adamses, Samuel, John, and John Quincy—were educated, and where John Hancock had graduated. He represented Lexington, and Concord, and Bunker Hill, and in his speech he said :—

"Neither am I one of those citizens of the North who would think it immoral and irreligious to join in putting down a servile insurrection at the South. I am no soldier, sir. My habits and education are very unmilitary; but there is no cause in which I would sooner buckle a knapsack to my back, and put a musket to my shoulder, than that." "Domestic slavery . . . is not, in my judgment, to be set down as an immoral or irreligious institution." "Its duties are presupposed by religion." "The New Testament says, 'Slaves, obey your masters.'"

The *Daily Advertiser* defended Mr. Everett, declaring that it was perfectly right in him to justify the continuance of the relation between the master and his slaves, and added (I am now quoting from the *Daily Advertiser* of March 28th, 1826) :—"We hold that it is not time, and never will be, that we should be aroused to any efforts for their redemption." That was the answer which the "respectability of Boston" gave to Mr. Everett's speech. True, some journals protested against the iniquitous statement; even the *Christian Register* was indignant. But Middlesex County sent him again. Lexington, and Concord, and Bunker Hill, returned their apostate representative a second, a third, a fourth, and a fifth time. And, when he was weary of that honour, the State of Massachusetts made him her Governor, and he carried to the State

House the same proclivities to despotism which he had evinced in his maiden speech.

In 1835, the anti-Slavery men and women were mobbed in Boston by an assembly of "respectable gentlemen;" the Mayor did not stop the tumult, the destruction of property, and the peril to life! There were no soldiers in the streets then; nobody, I think, was punished.

The next winter, the General Assemblies of several Southern States sent resolutions to the Massachusetts General Court, whereof this is one from South Carolina:— "The formation of abolition societies, and the acts and doings of certain fanatics, calling themselves abolitionists, in the non-slaveholding States of this confederacy, are in direct violation of the obligations of the compact of the Union."

South Carolina requested the Government "promptly and effectually to suppress all those associations," and would consider "the abolition of Slavery in the district of Columbia as a violation of the rights of citizens, and a usurpation to be at once resisted." Georgia asked Massachusetts "to crush the traitorous designs of the abolitionists." Virginia required the non-slaveholding States "to adopt penal enactments, or such other measures as will effectually suppress all associations within their respective limits, purporting to be, or having the character of, abolition societies;" and that they "will make it highly penal to print, publish, or distribute newspapers, pamphlets, or other publications, calculated or having a tendency to incite the slaves of the Southern States to insurrection and revolt." How do you think Massachusetts answered? In solemn resolutions the committee of the Massachusetts Legislature declared that "the agitation of the question of domestic slavery had already interrupted the friendly relations between the several States of the Union;" expressed its "entire disapprobation of the doctrines and speeches of such as agitate the question," and advised them "to abstain from all such discussion as might tend to disturb and agitate the public mind." That was the voice of a committee appointed by the Massachusetts Legislature. True, it was not accepted by the House of Representatives, but the report was only too significant. What followed?

In 1844, one of the most eminent lawyers of this State
was sent by Massachusetts to the city of Charleston, to
proceed legally and secure the release of Massachusetts
coloured citizens from the gaols of Charleston, where they
were held without charge of crime, and contrary to the
Constitution of the United States. Mr. Hoar was mobbed
out of Charleston by a body of respectable citizens, the
high sheriff aiding in driving him out.

Mr. Hoar made his report to the Governor of Massachusetts, and said :—

"Has the Constitution of the United States the least
practical validity or binding force in South Carolina,
excepting when she thinks its operation favourable to her?
She prohibits the trial of an action in the tribunals established under the Constitution for determining such cases,
in which a citizen of Massachusetts complains that a citizen
of South Carolina has done him an injury; saying that she
has herself already tried that cause, and decided against
the plaintiff."

The evil complained of continues unabated to this day.
South Carolina imprisons all the free coloured citizens of the
North who visit her ports in our ships.

In 1845, Texas was admitted, and annexed as a slave
State, with the promise that she might bring in four other
slave States.

In 1847 and '48 came the Mexican War, with the
annexation of an immense territory as slave soil. Many
of the leading men of Massachusetts favoured the annexation of Texas. New England might have stopped it;
Massachusetts might have stopped it; Boston might have
stopped it. But Mr. Webster said "she could not be
aroused." The politicians of Massachusetts favoured the
Mexican war. It was a war for Slavery. Boston favoured
it. The newspapers came out in its defence. The Governor
called out the soldiers, and they came. From the New
England pulpit we heard but a thin and feeble voice
against the war.

But there were men who doubted that wrong was right,
and said, "Beware of this wickedness!" The sober people
of the country disliked the war: they said, "No! let us
have no such wicked work as this!" Governor Briggs,
though before so deservedly popular, could never again get

elected by the people. He had violated their conscience by issuing his proclamation calling for volunteers.

In 1850 came the Fugitive Slave Bill. You all remember Mr. Webster's speech on the 7th of March. Before that time he had opposed all the great steps of the slave power—the Missouri Compromise, the annexation of Texas, the Mexican War, the increase of slave territory. He had voted, I think, against the admission of every slave State. He was opposed to the extension of American Slavery, "at all times, now and for ever." He claimed the Wilmot proviso as his "thunder." He "could stand on the Buffalo platform" in 1848. But, in 1850, he proffered his support to the Fugitive Slave Bill, "with all its provisions, to the fullest extent." He volunteered the promise that Massachusetts would "obey," and that "with alacrity." You remember his speech at the Revere House —discussion "must be suppressed, in Congress and out;" Massachusetts must "conquer her prejudices" in favour of the unalienable rights of man, which she had fought the Revolution to secure. You have not forgotten his speeches at Albany, at Syracuse, at Buffalo; nor his denial of the Higher Law of God at Capron Springs in Virginia—"The North Mountain is very high; the Blue Ridge higher still; the Alleghanies higher than either; yet this 'Higher Law' ranges an eagle's flight above the highest peak of the Alleghanies." What was the answer from the crowd? "Laughter." The multitude laughed at the Higher Law. There is no law above the North Mountain, above the Blue Ridge, above the peaks of the Alleghany— is there? The Fugitive Slave Bill reaches up where there is no God!

Men of property and standing all over New England supported the apostacy of Mr. Webster. You remember the letters from Maine, from New Hampshire, and the one from Newburyport. I am sure you have not forgotten the letter of the nine hundred and eighty-seven prominent men in and about Boston, telling him that he had "convinced the understanding and touched the conscience of a nation." Good men, whom I have long known, and tenderly loved, put their names to that letter. Did they think the "Union in danger?" Not one of them. A man of great understanding beguiled them.

You remember the tone of the newspapers, Whig and Democratic. With alacrity they went for kidnapping to the fullest extent. They clasped hands in order to seize the black man. When the time came, Mr. Eliot gave the vote of Boston for the Fugitive Slave Bill. When he returned to his home, some of the most prominent men of the city went and thanked him for his vote. They liked it. I believe no "eminent man" of Boston spoke against it. They "strained their consciences," as Mr. Walley has just said, "to aid in the passage of the Fugitive Slave Act." Boston fired a hundred guns on the Common, at noon-day, in honour of that event.

I know there was opposition—earnest and fierce opposition; but it did not come from the citizens of "eminent gravity," whom Boston and Massachusetts are accustomed stupidly to follow. You know what hatred was felt in Boston against all men who taught that the natural law of God was superior to the Fugitive Slave Bill, and Conscience above the Constitution.

You have not forgotten the "Union meeting" in Faneuil Hall. I never saw so much meanness and so little manhood on that platform. The Democratic Herods and the Whig Pilates were made friends that day that they might kidnap the black man. You recollect the howl of derision against the Higher Law of God, which came from that ignoble stage, and was echoed by that ignoble crowd above it and below—speakers fit for fitting theme.

When the Fugitive Slave Bill was proposed, prominent men said, "It cannot pass: the North will reject it at once; and, even if it were passed, it would be repealed the next day. We will petition for its repeal." After it was passed, they said: "It cannot be executed, and never will be." But, when asked to petition for its repeal, the same men refused—"No, it would irritate the South." I received the petitions which our fellow-citizens sent from more than three hundred towns in Massachusetts. I took the smallest of them all, and sent it to the representative of Boston, Mr. Eliot, with a letter, asking him to present it to the House. He presented it—to me! It was not "laid on the table;" he put it in the post-office. I sent it back to Washington, to some Southern or Western member, and he presented it in Congress.

The next Congress re-affirmed the Fugitive Slave Bill.

> "Twice they routed all their foes,
> And twice they slew the slain."

The new Representative from Boston, Mr. Appleton, gave the vote of Boston for it. He was never censured for that act. He was approved, and re-elected.

You remember the conduct of the Boston newspapers. Almost all of them went for the Fugitive Slave Bill. They made Atheism the first principle in American politics— "There is no Higher Law." The instinct of commerce is adverse to the natural rights of labour: so the chief leaders in commerce wish to have the working man but poorly paid ; the larger gain falls into their hands ; their labourer is a mill, they must run him as cheap as they can. So the great cities of the North were hostile to the slave—hostile to freedom. The wealthy capitalists did not know that in denying the Higher Law of God they were destroying the rock on which alone their money could rest secure. The mass of men in cities, servants of the few, knew not that in chaining the black man they were also putting fetters on their own feet. Justice is the common interest of all men ! Alas, that so few know what God writes in letters of fire on the world's high walls !

You have not forgotten the general tone of the pulpit,— "Conscience and the Constitution," at Andover. Mr. Stuart says, " Keep the laws of men, come what may come of the Higher Law of God." One minister of Boston said, "I would drive the fugitive from my own door." The most eminent Doctor of Divinity in the Unitarian ranks declared he would send his own mother into slavery. He says he said brother ! Give him the benefit of the ethical distinction : he would send back his own brother ! What had Andover and New Haven to say, in their collegiate churches ? What the churches of commerce in New York. Boston, Philadelphia, Albany, Buffalo ? They all went for kidnapping. " Down with God and up with iniquity." That was the short of the lower law religion which littered the land. The ecclesiastical teachers did more to strengthen infidelity then, than all the " infidels" that ever taught. What else could you expect from lower law divines ? All at once this blessed Bible seemed to have become a treatise in favour of man-stealing. Kidnapping arguments were strewn all the way through from Genesis to Revelation. These were the reverend gentleman who call me "infidel," or "atheist!" Nothing has so weakened the Church in America as this conduct of these "leading ministers" at that time. I mean ministers of churches that are rich in money, which lead the fashion and the opinion of the day. What defences of kidnapping have I heard from clerical lips! "No matter what the law is—it must be executed. The men who made the Fugitive Slave Bill, and those who seek to execute it, are ' Christian men,' ' very conscientious!'" Turn back and read the newspapers of 1850 and 1851. Nay, read them not—they are too bad to read!

When the Fugitive Slave Bill was before Congress, some of the northern politicians said to the people, "Let it pass; it will ' save the Union,' and we will repeal it at the next session of Congress." After it had passed they said, "Do not try to repeal it; that would irritate the South, and ' dissolve the Union;' it will never be executed; it is too bad to be." But when the kidnapper came to Boston, and demanded William and Ellen Craft, the same advisers said, "Of course the *niggers* must be sent back; the law must be enforced because it is law!"

At length the time came to execute the Act. Morton was busy in New York, Kane in Philadelphia, Curtis, the Boston Commissioner, was also on his feet. William and Ellen Craft fled off from the stripes of America to the lion of England. Shadrach—he will be remembered as long as Daniel—sang his psalm of deliverance in Canada. Taking him out of the Kidnappers' Court was high treason. It was "levying war." Thomas Sims will not soon be forgotten in Boston. Mayor Bigelow, Commissioner Curtis, and Marshal Tukey, they will also be remembered; they will all three be borne down to posterity, riding on the scourged and bleeding shoulders of Thomas Sims. The government of Boston could do nothing for the fugitive but kidnap him. The officers of the county nothing; they were only cockade and vanity. The Supreme Court could do nothing; the Judges crouched, and crawled, and went under the chain. The Free Soil Governor could do nothing; the Free Soil Legislature nothing. The Court House was in chains. Faneuil Hall was shut. The victim was on trial. A thousand able-bodied men sat in Tremont Temple all day in a Free Soil Convention, and—went home at night ! Most of the newspapers in the city were for kidnapping. The greater part of the clergy were for returning the fugitive :—"Send back our brother." Some of the towns held meetings, and passed resolutions against the rendition of the fugitive—Lynn, New Bedford, Worcester. And, in consequence, the leading commercial papers of Boston threatened to cut off all trade with New Bedford; they would not buy its oil : would have no dealings with Lynn, they would not tread her shoes under their feet: they would starve out Worcester. In Boston, wealthy traders entertained the kidnappers from the South. Merchants and railroad directors withdrew their advertising from newspapers which opposed the stealing of men. More than one minister in New England was driven from his pulpit for declaring the Golden Rule superior to the Fugitive Slave Bill !

When Judge Woodbury decided not to grant the writ of *habeas corpus*, and thus at one spurt of his pen cut off Mr. Sims's last chance for liberty and life, the Court House rang with plaudits, and the clapping of hands of " gentlemen" who had assembled there ! Fifteen hundred " gentlemen, of property and standing," volunteered to escort the poor fugitive out of the State, and convey him to bondage for ever. It was not necessary. When he stepped from Long Wharf on board John H. Pearson's brig,—the owner is sorry for it now, and has repented, and promises to bring forth fruits meet for repentance ; let that be remembered to his honour,—when Thomas Sims stepped on board the " Acorn," these were his words : " And this is Massachusetts liberty !" There was that great stone finger pointing from Bunker Hill towards heaven ; and this was " Massachusetts liberty !" " Order reigned in Warsaw." But it was some comfort that he could not be sent away till soldiers were billeted in Faneuil Hall ; then, only in the darkest hour of the night !

Boston sent back the first man she ever stole since the Declaration of Independence. Thomas Sims reached Savannah on the 19th of April, seventy-six years after the first battle of the Revolution, fought on the soil of Lexington. He was sent back on Saturday, and the next

Sunday the "leading ministers" of this city—I call them leading, though they lead nobody—gave God thanks. They forgot Jesus. They took Iscariot for their exemplar. "The Fugitive Slave Bill must be kept," they said, "come what will come to justice, liberty, and love; come what may come of God."

I know there were noble ministers, noble men in pulpits, whose hearts bled in them, and who spoke brave warning words of liberty; some were in the country, some in town. I know one minister, an "orthodox man," who in five months helped ninety-and-five fugitives flee from American stripes to the freedom of Canada! I dare not yet tell his name! Humble churches in the country towns—Methodist, Baptist, Unitarian—of all denominations save that of commerce—dropped their two mites of money into the alms-box for the slave, and gave him their prayers and their preaching too. But the "famous churches" went for "law" and stealing men.

Slavery had long been master at Washington: the "Union meeting" proved that it was master at Boston; proved it by words. The capture and sending back of Thomas Sims proved it by deeds. No prominent Whig openly opposed the Fugitive Slave Bill or its execution. No prominent democrat opposed it. Not a prominent clergyman in Boston spoke against it. I mean a clergyman of a "rich and fashionable church"—for in these days the wealth and social standing of the church make the minister "prominent." Intellectual power, eloquence, piety,—they do not make a "prominent minister" in these days.* Not ten of the rich men of Massachusetts gave the weight of their influence against it. Slavery is master; Massachusetts is one of the inferior counties of Virginia; Boston is only a suburb of Alexandria. Many of our lawyers, ministers, merchants, politicians, were negro-drivers for the South. They proved it by idea before; then by deed. Yet there were men in Boston who hated slavery—alas! they had little influence.

Let me not pass by the Baltimore conventions, and the two platforms. The Fugitive-Slave Bill was the central

* Dr. Charles Lowell, with the humane piety which has beautified his long and faithful ministry, at that time opposed the Fugitive Slave Bill with manly earnestness.

and topmost plank in them both.   Each confessed Slavery
to be master; it seemed that there was no North; slave
soil all the way from the south of Florida to the north of
Maine.   All over the land Slavery ruled.

You cannot forget Mr. Pierce's inaugural address, nor
the comments of the Boston press thereon.   He says the
Fugitive Slave Bill is to be "unhesitatingly carried into
effect;" "not with reluctance," but "cheerfully and willingly."   The newspapers of Boston welcomed the sentiment; and now Mr. Pierce's organ, the *Washington Union*,
says it is very proper this Bill should be enforced at
Boston, for "Boston was among the first to approve of
this emphatic declaration."   So let the promise be executed
here till we have enough of it!

You know the contempt which has been shown towards
everybody who opposed Slavery here in Massachusetts.
Horace Mann—there is not a man in the State more hated
than he by the "prominent politicians,"—or more loved
by the people—because he opposed Slavery with all his
might; and it is a great might.   Robert Rantoul, though
a politician and a party man, fought against Slavery; and
when he died, though he was an eminent lawyer, the
members of the Suffolk bar, his brother lawyers, took no
notice of him.   They wore no crape for Robert Rantoul!
He had opposed Slavery; let him die unnoticed, un-
honoured, unknown.   Massachusetts sent to the Senate a
man whose chief constitutional impulse is the instinct of
decorum—Mr. Everett, who had been ready to buckle on
his knapsack, and shoulder his musket, to put down an insurrection of slaves; a Cambridge professor of Greek, he
studied the original tongue of the Bible to learn that the
Scripture says "slaves," where the English Bible says
only "servants."   Fit Senator!

Then came the Nebraska Bill.   It was at once a measure
and a principle.   As a measure, it extends the old curse of
Slavery over half a million square miles of virgin soil, and
thus hinders the growth of the territory in population,
riches, education, in moral and religious character.   It
makes a South Carolina of what might else be a Connecticut, and establishes Paganism in the place of Christ's
piety.   As a principle, it is worse still—it makes Slavery
national and inseparable from the national soil; for the

principle which is covertly endorsed by the Nebraska Bill might establish Slavery in Massachusetts—and ere long the attempt will be made.

In the House of Representatives, forty-four Northern men voted for the enslavement of Nebraska. They are all Democrats—it is an administration measure. Mr. Everett, the senator from Boston, "did not know exactly what to do." The thing was discussed in committee, of which he was a member; but when it came up in public, it "took him by surprise." He wrote, I am told, to eleven prominent Whig gentlemen of Massachusetts, and asked their advice as to what he should do. With singular unanimity, every man of them said, "Oppose it with all your might!" But he did not. Nay, his vote has not been recorded against it yet. I am told his vote was in favour of prohibiting aliens from voting in that territory; his name against the main question has never been recorded yet. Nay, he did not dare to present the remonstrance which three thousand and fifty of his fellow-clergymen manfully sent to their clerical brother, and asked him to lay before the senate. Did any one suppose that he would dare do it? None who knew his antecedents.

There was an Anti-Nebraska meeting in Boston at Faneuil Hall. It was Siberian in its coldness—it was a meeting of icebergs. The platform was Arctic. There seemed to be no heart in the speeches. It must have been an encouragement to the men at Washington who advocated the bill. I suppose they understood it so. I am sure I should. The mass of the people in Massachusetts who think at all, are indignant; but so far as I can learn, the men who control the politics of Boston, or who have controlled them until the last week, feel no considerable interest in the matter. In New York, men of great property and high standing came together and protested against this iniquity. New York has been, for once, and in one particular, morally in advance of Boston. The platform there was not Arctic, not even Siberian. Such a meeting could not have been held here.

Now, put all these things together, and you see the causes which bore the fruits of last week;—in general, the triumph of Slavery over Freedom, and in special, the indifference of Massachusetts, and particularly of Boston, to the efforts which are made for Freedom; her zeal to promote Slavery and honour its defenders. Men talk of dividing the Union. I never proposed that. Before last week I should not have known where to .begin. I should have had to draw the line somewhere north of Boston.

Last week Massachusetts got part of her pay for obeying the Fugitive Slave Bill with alacrity; for suppressing discussion; for conquering her prejudices; pay for putting cowardly, mean men, in the place of brave, honourable men; pay for allowing the laws of Massachusetts to be trodden underfoot, and her court-house of Northern granite to be surrounded by Southern chains. Thomas Sims was scourged on the 19th of April, when he was carried back to Savannah. Boston did not feel it then. She felt it last week—felt it sorely. In September, 1850, we heard the hundred guns fired on Boston Common, in honour of the Fugitive Slave Bill—fired by men of "eminent gravity." Last Friday you saw the cannon! One day you will see it again grown into many cannons. That one was only a devil's grace before a devil's meat! No higher law, is there? Wait a little longer, and you shall find there is a "lower law," a good deal lower than we have yet come to! Sow the wind, shall we? When the whirlwind comes up therefrom, it has a course of its own, and God only can control the law of such storms as those. We have not yet seen the full consequences of sowing atheism with a broad hand among the people of this continent. We have not yet seen the end. These are only the small early apples that first fall to the earth. There is a whole tree full of them. When some autumnal storm shakes the boughs, they will cover the ground—sour and bitter in our mouths, and then poison.

Yet this triumph of Slavery does not truly represent the wishes of the Northern people. Not a single Pro-Slavery measure has ever been popular with the mass of men in New England or Massachusetts. The people disliked the annexation of Texas in that unjust manner: they thought the Mexican War was wicked. They were opposed to the extension of Slavery; they hated the Fugitive Slave Bill, and rejoiced at the rescue of Shadrach. The kidnapping

of Thomas Sims roused a fierce indignation. Only one
town in all New England has ever returned a fugitive—
all the rest hide the outcasts, while Boston bewrays him
that wandereth. The Nebraska Act is detested by the
people.

A few editors have done a manly duty in opposing all
these manifold iniquities. A few ministers have been
faithful to the spirit of this Bible, and to their own conscience, heedless of law and constitution. Manly preachers
of all denominations—save the commercial—protested
against kidnapping, against enacting wickedness by statute.
From humble pulpits their voices rang out in Boston and
elsewhere. But what were they among so many? There
were Theological Journals which stoutly resisted the
wickedness of the prominent men, and rebuked the mam-
mon-worship of the churches of commerce. The *Independent* at New York, the *Congregationalist* at Boston, not to
mention humbler papers, did most manly service—now
with eloquence, now with art, then with satiric scorn,—
always with manly religion. Even in the cities, there were
editors of secular prints who opposed the wicked law and
its execution.

No man in New England, within the last few years, has
supported Slavery without at the same time losing the confidence of the best portion of the people—sober, serious,
religious men, who believe there is a law of God writ in the
nature of things. Even Mr. Webster quailed before the
conscience of the North: the Supreme Court of Massachusetts no longer enjoys the confidence of the people; the
most "prominent clergymen" of New England—pastors,
I mean, of the richest churches—are not looked up to with
the same respect as before.

The popularity of *Uncle Tom's Cabin* showed how
deeply the feelings of the world were touched by this
great outrage. No one of the encroachments of Slavery
could have been sustained by a direct popular vote. I
think seven out of every ten of all the New England men
would have voted against the Fugitive Slave Bill; nine
out of ten against kidnapping. But alas! we did not
say so—we allowed wicked men to rule over us. Now
behold the consequences! Men who will not love God
must fear the devil.

Boston is the test and touchstone of political principles and measures. Faneuil Hall is "the cradle of liberty," and therein have been rocked the great ideas of America—rocked by noble hands.

Well, if Boston had said, "No Texan annexation in that wicked way!" we might have had Texas on fair conditions. If Boston had opposed the Mexican War, all New England would have done the same—almost all the North. We might have had all the soil we have got, without fighting a battle, or taking or losing a life, at far less cost; and have demoralized nobody. If, when the Fugitive Slave Bill was before Congress, Boston had spoken against that iniquity, all the people would have risen, and there would have been no Fugitive Slave Act. If, after that Bill was passed, she had said, "No kidnapping," there would have been none. Then there would have been no Nebraska Bill, no repeal of the Missouri Compromise, no attempt to seize Cuba and Saint Domingo. If the fifteen hundred gentlemen of "property and standing" in Boston, who volunteered to return Mr. Sims to bondage, or the nine hundred and eighty-seven who thanked Mr. Webster for the Fugitive Slave Bill, had come forward on the side of justice, they might have made every Commissioner swear solemnly that he would not execute that Act. Thus the "true sons of liberty," on the 17th of December, 1765, induced Commissioner Oliver to swear solemnly, at noon-day, in "presence of a great crowd," and in front of the Liberty Tree, that he would not issue a single stamp! Had that been done, there would have been no man arrested. There are only eight Commissioners, and public opinion would have kept them all down. We should have had no kidnappers here.

Boston did not do so; Massachusetts did no such thing. She did just the opposite. In 1828, the Legislature of Georgia passed resolutions relative to the Tariff, declaring that the General Government had no right to protect domestic manufactures, and had been guilty of a "flagrant usurpation;" she will insist on her construction of the Constitution, and "will submit to no other." Georgia carried her point. The Tariff of 1828 went to the ground! South Carolina imprisons our coloured citizens: we bear it with a patient shrug,—and pay the cost: Massachusetts is non-resistant; New England is a Quaker,—when a blustering little State undertakes to ride over us. Georgia offers a reward of five thousand dollars for the head of a non-resistant in Boston,—and Boston takes special pains to return Ellen Craft to a citizen of Georgia, who wished to sell her as a harlot for the brothels of New Orleans! Northern clergymen defended the character of her " owner"—a man of " unquestionable piety." You know what denunciations were uttered in this city against the men and women who sheltered her! Boston could not allow the poor woman to remain. Did the churches of commerce " put up a prayer" for her? " Send back my own mother!" Not a Northern minister lost his pulpit or his professional respectability by that form of practical atheism. Not one! At the South not a minister dares preach against Slavery ; at the North—think of the preaching of so many " eminent divines!" *

* My friend, the Rev. Dr. Edward Beecher, thinks I have been unjust to the ministers,—judging from the Sermon as reported in the *Commonwealth*. So he published the following article in that paper on Friday, June 9. I gladly insert it below. It comes from a powerful and noble man. I wish he had made out a stronger case against me.

"THEODORE PARKER AND THE MINISTRY.

"*Mr. Editor*,—In his Sermon, last Sabbath, Mr. Parker seems to charge the clergy of the country with a general, if not universal, delinquency in the cause of freedom with respect to the Fugitive Slave Law. He says, ' You all remember the tone of *the pulpit*.' As if on that subject *the pulpit* had been a unit. He adds, ' What had Andover and New Haven to say in their collegiate churches? What the churches (of commerce) of New York, of Boston, of Philadelphia, of Albany, of Buffalo? They all went for kidnapping. "Down with God and up with kidnapping." That was the short of the lower law religion that littered the land. The ecclesiastical teachers did more to strengthen infidelity than all the infidels that ever taught.' He does not say that these charges are true of a part only of the ministry. His language would convey to any reader, ignorant of the fact, the opposite impression. He says that when Thomas Sims was sent back, ' the clergy were for returning the Fugitive. "Send back our brother."' ' The next Sunday the leading ministers of the city —I call them *leading*, though they lead nobody—gave God thanks.'

"Speaking of the Slave Bill and its execution, he says, ' Not a prominent clergyman spoke against it.'

"And when he speaks of the Nebraska Bill, he scarcely mentions the petition of the three thousand and fifty ministers. And then, not as if he desired to give them due praise, he merely mentions it incidentally in dealing with Mr. Everett—'He did not dare to present the remonstrance which three thousand and fifty of his fellow-clergyman sent to their clerical brother, and asked him to lay before the Senate.' And

My friends, we deserve all we have suffered. We are
the scorn and contempt of the South. They are our

---

again : 'The cowardice of Mr. Everett has excited the clergy of New
England—of all the North; they are stung with the reproach of the
people, and ashamed of their past neglect.' Just as if they had not been
self-moved by their own honourable impulses. The bearing of all these
passages, considered in the general drift of the Sermon, is undeniably to
implicate the clergy as a whole in the delinquencies charged.

"Now, if Mr. Parker were to be represented, on both continents, as an
advocate of kidnapping, and of the Fugitive Slave Law, he would probably regard it as unjust. But he does not seem to be sufficiently alive
to the idea, that it is unjust to convey the idea that this is true of
clergymen who have from the first opposed these measures as earnestly
and decidedly as he himself. He seems to be fully convinced that to rob
even one slave of his liberty is a crime. He does not seem as deeply to
feel that it is a crime to rob even our ministers of that reputation which
in his own case he prizes so highly. Even if the cases of fidelity were
few, for that very reason they should receive from a lover of the cause
the more careful and particular notice and praise. In cases like these, if
ever, discriminations and truthful statements of facts are a sacred duty.
Let those be censured who deserve censure, and let those be commended
who deserve praise.

"Allow me, then, to state some of the facts of the case chiefly concerning the Orthodox Congregational pastors and churches, leaving to
other denominations, if they see fit, to state similar facts, more at large,
in their own case. From my own knowledge, I am assured that it would
not be difficult to multiply them, especially if a full account were to be
given of all the unpublished sermons of the times.

"It is not true, as Mr. P.'s statements imply, that Mr. Parker was the
only one who preached and wrote and prayed against the Fugitive Slave
Law.

"The *Congregationalist*, then edited by the Rev. H. M. Dexter, Rev.
Mr. Storrs, and myself, devoted all its energies to a conflict with the
Fugitive Slave Bill, and a vindication of the claim of the higher law.
Some of its articles were considered of such importance as to be honoured
with special attention and censure by Mr. Choate, at the Boston Union
Saving meeting. Our articles, if collected, would make a large volume.

"The law was also most earnestly opposed from the pulpit by many
ministers, Mr. Stone, Mr. Dexter, and myself among the number. The
same thing was true of a large number of the clergymen of New England
and the Middle States. I have before me published Sermons or other
Addresses to this effect from Storrs and Spear, of Brooklyn, N. Y.;
Beecher, of Newark, N. J.; Thompson and Cheever, of New York;
Bacon, of New Haven, Conn.; Colver, of Boston; Wallcott, now of
Providence; Leavit, then of Newton, Mass.; Withington, of Newbury,
Mass.; Whitcomb, of Stoneham, Mass.; Thayer, of Ashland, Mass.;
Arvine, of West Boylston, Mass., and others. Nothing can be more able
and eloquent than their defence of God's law, as opposed to the infamous
Slave Bill. Others also were published which I have not on file, and I
know of several very able discourses against the law which were not
published. If a true report could be made of all the Sermons then
preached, and of the influence then exerted in other ways by the ministry

masters, and treat us as slaves. It is ourselves who made
the yoke. We offer our back to the slave-driver's whip.

---

of the North, there is reason to believe that a very large majority would
be found to have set themselves decidedly against the law, and to have
advocated its entire disobedience.

"The fact is, that undue importance has been given to those of the
ministry who favoured obedience to that law, and they have been made
to overshadow its more numerous opponents.

"In relation to Andover, the facts are these :—Professor Stuart, who
for some years had ceased to act as Professor in the Seminary, published
his views, greatly to the regret of a large portion of his brethren. That
the body of the Professors of the Institution did not sympathize in these
views, is evident from the fact that when a paper approving the compromise was circulated there, Professors Park, Phelps, and Edwards
refused to sign. Only one acting Professor did sign, much to his own
subsequent regret. This does not justify the sweeping affirmation.

"'Andover went for kidnapping.' Mr. Parker ought to be more careful, and less free in the use of such wholesale charges. Moreover, the
positions of Professor Stuart were thoroughly exposed by members of his
own denomination.

"The Rev. Rufus Clark, now of East Boston, published in the columns
of the *Atlas* a thorough refutation of his pamphlet in a series of very
able articles, which were subsequently republished in a pamphlet form.

"Rev. George Perkins, of Connecticut, performed a similar service in
that State. Rev. Mr. Dexter, of Boston, exposed himself to an excited
retort from Professor Stuart, for his keen and able exposure of his course
on the Compromises.

"That there was a sad failure on the part of too many of the clergy of
Boston and other commercial cities, cannot be denied; nor do I desire
to avert from them merited censure. But ought the labours of such men
as the clerical editors and contributors of the *Independent* to be passed
by in silence in speaking of the prominent clergy of the city of New
York?

"As to the other cities named, if there were but one exception in each,
it ought to have been prominently named and honoured. I do not doubt
that there were more.

"As to the country churches and pastors of New England, I have
already stated my opinion that the vast majority were opposed to the
Fugitive Slave Law. It is not just to regard the Nebraska protest as a
virtual confession and reparation of past neglect, but rather as a development of the real feeling of the clergy of New England. Charity thinketh
no evil, and there is no gain at this time in depreciating the merits of
any earnest opponents of the aggressions of Slavery.

"As Mr. Parker expects to be read in all parts of this nation and on
both sides of the Atlantic, I will not doubt that his strongly avowed
appreciation of what is just and honourable in action will induce him to
revise and correct his statement of facts, and instead of such sweeping
and indiscriminate censure, to give honour where honour is due.

                                                "EDWARD BEECHER."

I have repeatedly and in the most public manner done honour to the
ministers who have opposed this great iniquity, and did not suppose that
any one would misunderstand the expressions which Dr. Beecher con-

A Western man travels all through Kentucky—he was in Boston three days ago—and hears only this rumour : " the

---

siders as " sweeping." When he reads in the Bible that " *Jerusalem and all Judea went out,*" I suppose he thinks that some persons stayed at home. But I am sorry he could not make out a stronger case for his side. I know nothing of what was said *privately,* or of sermons which never get spoken of out of the little parish where they are written. He mentions *sixteen Orthodox ministers* who published matter in opposition to the Fugitive Slave Bill. It is not a very large number for all the churches in New Jersey, New York, Connecticut, Rhode Island, and Massachusetts to furnish. I can mention more.

These are the facts in respect to Andover : Professor Stuart, the most distinguished clergyman in all New England, wrote an elaborate defence of the Fugitive Slave Bill, and of Mr. Webster's conduct in defending it. He was induced to do this by Mr. Webster himself. The work is well known—*Conscience and the Constitution*—and it is weak and doting as it is wicked. Professor Stuart and two other Andover Professors—Rev. Ralph Emerson, D.D., and Rev. Leonard Woods, D.D.—signed the letter to Mr. Webster expressing their " deep obligations for what this speech has done and is doing ;" thanking him " for recalling us to our duties under the Constitution, and for the broad, national, and patriotic views" it inculcates, and desiring to " express to you our entire concurrence in the sentiments of your speech." It seems three other Professors— Messrs. Park, Phelps, and Edwards—did not sign it, and one of the signers—Dr. Woods or Dr. Emerson—did it much to his own subsequent regret. But did he make his regret public? Did Andover in public say anything against the conduct of the signers ?

At the Annual Conference of Unitarian Ministers, in May, 1851, long and public defences of kidnapping were made by " the most eminent men in the denomination." One Doctor of Divinity vindicated the attempt of his parishioners to kidnap mine, whom I took to my house for shelter. Dr. Dewey's promise to send back his own mother or brother got the heartiest commendation from more than one " prominent minister." Dr. Dewey was compared with " faithful Abraham ;" his declaration was " imputed to him for righteousness." Many of the country ministers were of a different opinion. Some of them declared his conduct " atrocious." Of course there were noble men in the Unitarian denomination, who were faithful to the great principles of Christianity. I have often spoken in their praise, and need not now mention their names ; too well known to require honour from me.

But I am sorry to say that I can retract nothing from what I have said in general respecting the conduct of the clergy of all denominations at that time. At a large public meeting in Boston a Vigilance Committee was appointed to look after the fugitives and furnish them aid. The Committee sent a circular to every church in Massachusetts, asking for the fugitives donations of money and clothes ; and received replies from *eighty-seven churches,* which gave us $148,456!

Here is my letter in reply to Dr. Beecher, from the *Commonwealth* of June 10, 1854 :—

DR. EDWARD BEECHER AND THEODORE PARKER.

Rev. Edward Beecher, D.D.,—My dear Sir, I have just read your letter

Yankees are cowards; they dare not resist us. We will drive them just where we like. We will force the Nebraska Bill down their throats, and then force Saint Domingo and Cuba after it." That is public opinion in Kentucky. My brothers, it is very well deserved.

The North hated the Missouri Compromise. Daniel Webster fought against it with all his manly might; and then it was very manly and very mighty. When he collects his speeches, in 1850, for electioneering purposes—a political pamphlet in six octavos—he leaves out all his speeches and writings against the Missouri Compromise! His friend, Mr. Everett, writes his memoir, and there is nothing about Mr. Webster's opposition to the extension of Slavery; about the Missouri Compromise not one single word.

---

in the *Commonwealth* of this morning, in which you maintain that the statements in my last sermon respecting the delinquency of the Northern clergy were too sweeping, and that I did injustice to the ministers who stoutly resisted the Fugitive Slave Bill and its execution. Perhaps the language of the sermon would seem to warrant your opinion. But I have so many times, and in so public a manner, expressed my respect and veneration for those noble men who have been found faithful in times of peril, that I cannot think I am in general obnoxious to the charge you make against me.

In respect to the special sermon of last Sunday, I beg leave to inform you that the *whole* was neither printed nor preached; the entire sermon is now in press, and when you see it, I think you will find that I do no injustice to the men you speak of. As I spoke on Sunday, I did not suppose any one would misunderstand my words, or think I wished to be regarded as the only one found faithful. Certainly I have many times done honour to the gentlemen you mention, and to the journals you refer to—with others you do not name. And allow me to say, the conduct of yourself and all your family has not only been a strong personal encouragement to me, but a theme of public congratulation which I have often brought forward in lectures, and sermons, and speeches. I am a little surprised that you should suppose that by the *churches of commerce* in New York, Boston, &c., I mean *all the churches* of those towns. I still think that from 1850 to 1852 the general voice of the New England churches, so far as it was heard through the press, was in favour of the Fugitive Slave Bill and its execution. This was especially true of the rich and fashionable churches in the great commercial towns. Surely you cannot forget the numerous clerical eulogies on the late Mr. Webster, which sought to justify all his political conduct. I do not think you have made out a very strong case for Andover.

I am sorry to have given pain to a man whose life is so noble and his character so high; but believe me,

Respectfully and truly yours,

THEODORE PARKER.

My friends, the South treat us as we deserve. They make compromises, and then break them. They say we are cowards. Are they mistaken? They put our seamen in gaol for no crime, but their complexion. We allow it. Then they come to New England, and in Boston steal our fellow-citizens—no! our fellow-subjects, our fellow-slaves. We call out the soldiers to help them! Go into a bear's den, and steal a young cub; and if you take only one, all the full-grown bears in the den will come after you and follow till you die, or they die, or their strength fails, and they must give up the pursuit.

> " O Justice! thou art fled to brutish beasts,
> And men have lost their reason!"

The Nebraska Bill has hardly got back to the Senate again when a Virginian comes here to see how much Boston will bear. He brings letters to " eminent citizens of Boston," lodges at the Revere House, and bravely shows himself to the public in the streets. He walks upon the Common, and looks at the eclipse—the eclipse of the sun I mean, not the eclipse of Boston: that he needs no glass to look at, as there is none smoked dark enough to hinder it from dazzling his eyes. He gets two Boston lawyers to help him kidnap a man. He finds a Commissioner, a Probate Officer of Massachusetts, ready to violate the tenure of his own trust, prepared for the work; a Marshal anxious to prove his democracy by stealing a man; he finds newspapers ready to sustain him; the Governor lets him go unmolested; the Mayor lends him all the police of the city; and then, illegally and without any authority, against the protestations of the Aldermen, calls out all the soldiers among a hundred and sixty thousand people, in order to send one innocent negro into bondage, and gives them orders, it is said, to shoot down any citizen who shall attempt to pass their lines! The soldiers, half drunk, present their horse-pistols at the heads of women—their thumb on the hammer! They stab horses, and with their sabres slash the heads of men!

When Mr. Burns was first seized by the kidnappers, nearly all the daily newspapers took sides against the fugitive. The city was full of ministers all the week; two Anti-Slavery conventions were held, one of them two thousand men strong; the Worcester "Freedom Club" came down here to visit us: they all went home, and "order reigns in Warsaw." In South Carolina there is a public opinion stronger than the law. Let Massachusetts send an honoured citizen to Charleston, to remonstrate against an iniquitous statute, and most respectable citizens drive him away. Coloured citizens of Massachusetts rot in the gaols of Charleston. Northern merchants pay the costs. Boston merchants remonstrated years ago, and the Boston senator did not dare to offer their paper in Congress! Yes, a Boston senator did not dare present the remonstrances of Boston merchants! The South despises us. Do you wonder at the treatment we receive? I wonder not at all.

Now, let me say another word—it must be a brief one—of this particular case. When Mr. Burns was kidnapped, a public meeting was called in Faneuil Hall. Who went there? Not one of the men who are accustomed to control public opinion in Boston. If ten of them had appeared on that platform, Mr. Phillips and myself would not have troubled the audience with our speech. We would have yielded the place—to citizens of "eminent gravity" giving their counsel, and there would have been no man carried out of Boston. I could mention ten men, known to every man here, who, if they had been there, would have so made such public opinion, that the Fugitive Slave Bill Commissioner never would have found "evidence" or "law" enough to send Anthony Burns back to Alexandria. There was not one of them there. They did not wish to be there. They cared nothing for freedom!

In general, the blame of this wickedness rests on the city of Boston, much of it on Massachusetts, on New England, and on all the North. But here I must single out some of the individuals who are personally responsible for this outrage.

I begin with the Commissioner. He was the primo mover.

Now, as a general thing, the Commissioners who kidnap men in America have had a proclivity to wickedness. It has been structural, constitutional. Man-stealing was in their bones. It was an osteological necessity. A phrenologist, examining their heads, would have said : " Beware of this man. He is ' fit for treason, stratagems, and spoils.' "

It seems natural that Mr. Kane should steal men in Philadelphia. His name is warrant to bear out the deed. In Boston, the former kidnapper lost no "personal popularity" by the act. His conduct seems alike befitting the disposition he was born with, and the culture he has attained to ; and so appears equally natural and characteristic. But I thought Mr. Loring of a different disposition. His is a pleasant face to look at, dignified, kindly—a little weak, yet not without sweetness and a certain elevation. I have seen him sometimes in the Probate Office, and it seemed to me a face fit to watch over the widow and the fatherless. When a bad man does a wicked thing, it astonishes nobody. When one otherwise noble and generous is overtaken in a fault, we " weep to record, and blush to give it in," and in the spirit of meekness seek to restore such a one. But when a good man deliberately, voluntarily, does such a deed as this, words cannot express the fiery indignation which it ought to stir up in every man's bosom. It destroys confidence in humanity.

The wickedness began with the Commissioner. He issued the writ. It was to end with him,—he is sheriff, judge, jury. He is paid twice as much for condemning as for acquitting the innocent.

He was not obliged to be a Commissioner. He was not forced into that bad eminence. He went there voluntarily fifteen years ago, as United States Commissioner, to take affidavits and acknowledgments. Slave-catching. was no part of his duty. The soldiers of Nicholas execute their master's tyranny, because they are forced into it. The only option with them is to shoot with a musket, or be scourged to death with the knout. If Mr. Loring did not like kidnapping, he need not have kept his office. But he liked it. He wrote three articles, " cold and cruel," in the *Daily Advertiser*, defending the Fugitive Slave Bill.

But if he kept the office he is not officially obliged to do the work. The District Attorney is not suspected of being so heavily fraught with conscience that he cannot trim his craft to sail with any political wind which offers to carry him to port ; but even Mr. Hallett refused to

kidnap Ellen Craft. He did not like the business. It was
not a part of Mr. Loring's official obligation. A man lets
himself to a sea-captain as a mariner to go a general
voyage. He is not obliged to go privateering or pirating
whenever the captain hoists the black flag. He can leave
at the next port. A labourer lets himself to a farmer to
do general farm work. By and by his employer says, " I
intend to steal sheep." The man is not obliged by his
contract to go and steal sheep because his employer will.
That would be an illegal act, no doubt. But suppose the
general government had made a law, authorizing every
farmer to steal all the black sheep he can lay his hands
on; nay, commanding the felony. Is this servant, who
is hired to do general farm work, obliged in his official
capacity to go and steal black sheep? I do not look at it
so. I do not think any man does. A lawyer turns off
many a client. A constable refuses many a civil job. He
does not like the business. The Commissioner took this
business because he liked to take it. I do not say he was
not " conscientious." I know nothing of that. I only
speak of the act. Herod was " conscientious," for aught
I know, and Iscariot and Benedict Arnold, and Aaron
Burr. I do not touch that question. To their own
master they stand or fall. The tortures of the Spanish
Inquisition may have been " conscientious."

It was entirely voluntary for Mr. Loring to take this
case. There was no official obligation, no professional
honour, that required him to do it. He had a " great
precedent," even, in Mr. Hallett, to decline it.

In 1843, Massachusetts enacted a law prohibiting any
State officer from acting as slave-catcher, for fear of abuse
of our own law. Since that, Mr. Loring has become
Judge of Probate. There was a chance for a good man
to show his respect for the law of the State which gives
him office.

Now see how the case was conducted. I am no lawyer,
and shall not undertake to judge the technical subtleties of
the case. But look at the chief things which require no
technical skill to judge.

The Commissioner spoke very kindly, and even pater-
nally, when he consulted Burns. I confess the tear started
to my eye when he looked so fatherly towards the man,

like a Judge of Probate, and asked him, " Would you like a little time to prepare to make a defence ?" And when Mr. Burns replied, " Yes," he honourably gave him some time, forty-eight hours, to decide whether he would make a defence on Saturday, May 27. He also honourably gave Mr. Burns and his counsel a little time to make ready for trial. He gave them from Saturday until Monday! True it was only twenty-four hours ; Sunday intervened, and lawyers, like other laymen, and ministers, are supposed to be at meeting on Sunday. That twenty-four hours—it was not very much time to allow for the defence of a man whose liberty was in peril ! If Mr. Burns had been arraigned for murder, he would have had several months to prepare for his trial, the purse and the arm of Massachusetts to summon witnesses for his defence. But as he was charged with no crime, only with being the involuntary slave of one of our Southern masters—as the Fugitive Slave Act was not designed to " establish justice," but its opposite, or to " insure the blessings of liberty," but the curse of bondage—he may have only twenty-four hours to make ready for his defence : his counsel and a minister may visit him—others are excluded !

If Mr. Burns had been arraigned for stealing a horse, for slander, or anything else, not twenty-fours, or days, but twenty-four weeks would have been granted him to make ready for trial. A common lawsuit, for a thousand dollars, in the Supreme Court of Suffolk, is not ordinarily tried within a year ; and, if any questions of law are to be settled, not disposed of within two years. Here, however, a man was on trial for more than life, and but twenty-four hours were granted him ! I accept that thankfully, and tender Mr. Loring my gratitude for that ! It is more than I looked for from any Fugitive Slave Bill Commissioner, except him. I never thought him capable of executing this wickedness. Honour him for this with due honour— no more; no less.

When the hearing began, the kidnapper's counsel urged that the testimony taken at first, when Mr. Burns was brought up, was in the case. The Commissioner held to this monstrous position ; and it was only after the urgent opposition of the prisoner's counsel that he consented it should be put in *de novo*.

G 2

But after the kidnapping lawyers put in their evidence, the counsel for Mr. Burns asked time for conference and consultation, as the most important questions of law and fact came up; they were weary with long service and exhausting labour—and they begged the Commissioner to adjourn for an hour or two. It was already almost three o'clock. When hard pressed, he granted them thirty minutes to get up their law and their evidence, take refreshment, and come back to court. At length he extended it to forty minutes! Much of that time was lost to one of the counsel by the troops, who detained him at the door. But the next day, after Mr. Burns's counsel had brought in evidence to show that he was in Boston on the 1st of March,—which nobody expected, for Brent alleges that he saw him in Virginia on the 19th of March, and that he escaped thence on the 24th,—then, after a conference with the Marshal, he grants the kidnapper's lawyers an hour and a quarter to meet this new and unexpected evidence. Of course he knew that in granting them this, he really gave them all night to get up their evidence, prepare their defence, and come into court the next morning, and rebut what had been said. Is that fair? Consider what a matter there was at stake—a man's liberty for ever and ever on earth! Consider that Mr. Loring was judge and jury;—that it was a "court" without appeal; that no other court could pass upon his verdict, and reverse it, if afterwards it was shown to be suspicious or proved to be wrong. He grants Mr. Burns thirty minutes, and the other side, at once, an hour and a quarter, virtually all night! That is not all. His decision was limited to one point, namely, the identity of the prisoner. If Mr. Burns answered the description of the fugitive given in the record, the Commissioner took it for granted, first, that he was a slave,—there was no proof; second, that he had escaped into another State,—that was not charged in the record, nor proved by testimony; third, that he owed service and labour to Colonel Suttle, not to the lessee, who had a limited fee in his services, nor to the mortgagee, who had the conditional fee of his person; but to Colonel Suttle, the reversioner, the original claimant of his body.

Now the statute leaves the party claimant his choice

between two processes; one under its sixth section, the other under the tenth.

The sixth section obliges the claimant to prove three points—1, That the persons claimed *owes* service; 2, That he has *escaped;* and, 3, That the party before the court is the *identical one* alleged to be a slave.

The tenth section makes the claimant's certificate conclusive as to the first two points, and only leaves the identity to be proved.

In this case, the claimant, by offering proof of service and escape, made his election to proceed under the sixth section.

Here he failed: failed to prove service; failed to prove escape. Then the Commissioner allowed him to swing round and take refuge in the tenth section, leaving identity only to be proved; and this he proved by the prisoner's confession, made under duress and in terror, if at all; wholly denied by him; and proved only by the testimony of a witness of whom we know nothing, but that he was contradicted by several witnesses as to the only point to which he affirmed capable of being tested.

So, then, the Commissioner reduced the question precisely to this: Is the prisoner at the bar the same Anthony Burns whom Brent saw in Virginia on the 19th day of March last, and who the claimant swears in his complaint escaped from Virginia on the 24th of March?

One man, calling himself "William Brent, a merchant of Richmond," testified as to the question of identity —"This is Burns." He was asked, "When did you see him in Virginia?" and he answered, "On the 19th of March last." But nobody in court new Mr. Brent, and Mr. Loring himself confessed that he stood "under circumstances that would bias the fairest mind." He had come all the way from Richmond to Boston to make out the case. Doubtless he expected his reward—perhaps in money, perhaps in honour; for it is an honour in Virginia to support the institutions of that State. But on the other side, many witnesses testified that Burns was here in Boston on the 1st of March, and worked several days at the Mattapan Iron Works, at South Boston. Several men, well known in Boston—persons of unimpeached integrity—testified to the fact. No evidence rebutted their

testimony.   Nothing was urged to impugn their veracity.
The Commissioner says their "integrity is admitted," and
"no imputation of bias could be attached" to them.   So,
to decide between these two, Mr. Loring takes the admissions of the fugitive, alleged to have been made under
duress, in the presence of his "master," made in gaol; when
he was surrounded by armed ruffians; when he was "intimidated" by fear,—admissions which Mr. Burns denied to
the last, even after the decision.   This was the proof of
identity !

The record called Burns a man with "dark complexion."
The prisoner is a "full-blooded negro."   His complexion
is black almost as my coat.   The record spoke of Burns as
having a scar on his right hand.   The right hand of this
man had been broken; it was so badly injured that when
it was opened he could only shut it by grasping it with
his left.   The bone stuck out prominent.   The kidnapper's
witness testified that Burns was in Virginia on the 19th
of March.   Several witnesses—I know not how many—
testified that he was in Boston nineteen days before !

Mr. Brent stated nothing to show that he had ever had
any particular knowledge of Mr. Burns, or particularly
observed his person.   Some of the witnesses for the prisoner
did not testify merely from general observation of his form
or features, but they stated that they had noted especially
the scar on his cheek, and his broken hand, and they knew
him to be the man.   Besides, this testimony is of multiplied force, not being that of so many to one fact; that of
each stands by itself.   There was a cloud of witnesses to
prove that Mr. Burns was in Boston from the 1st of
March.   If their evidence could be invalidated, it was not
attacked in court.   Their fairness was admitted.

Not many years ago, a woman was on trial in Boston
for the murder of her own child.   At first she pleaded
guilty, and, weeping, stated the motives which led to the
unnatural crime.   But the court interfered, induced her
to retract the plea, and to make a defence.   And in spite
of her voluntary admissions made in court, she was ac-
quitted—for there was not evidence to warrant a legal
conviction.

Mr. Loring seemed to regard Slavery as a *crimen ex-
ceptum;* and when a man is charged with it he is presup-

posed to be guilty, and must be denied the usual means of defence. So out of the victim's own mouth he extorts the proof that this is the man named in the record.

A man not known to anybody in court brings a paper from Alexandria claiming Anthony Burns as his slave; the paper was drawn up five hundred miles off; in the absence of Mr. Burns; by his enemies, who sought for his liberty and more than his life. He brought one witness to testify to the identity of the man, who says that, in his fear, Burns said, "I am the man." But seven witnesses, whose veracity was not impeached in the court, testify that the prisoner *was in Boston* in the early part of March; and therefore it appears that he is not the Burns who *was in Virginia* on the 19th of March, and thence escaped on the 24th. To decide between the two testimonies— that of one Virginian under circumstances that would bias the fairest mind, and seven Bostonians free from all bias— the Commissioner takes the words put into the mouth of Mr. Burns.

Now, the Fugitive Slave Bill provides that the testimony of the fugitive shall not be received as evidence in the case. Mr. Loring avoids that difficulty. He does not call it "testimony" or "evidence." He calls it "admissions;" accepts it to prove the "identity," and decides the case against him. But who proves that Mr. Burns made the admissions? There are two witnesses: 1. A man hired to kidnap him, one of the Marshal's "guard," a spy, a hired informer, set to watch the prisoner and make inquisition. Of what value was his testimony? 2. Mr. Brent, who had come five hundred miles to assist in catching a runaway slave, and claimed Mr. Burns as the slave. This was the only valuable witness to prove the admission. So the admission is proved by the admission of Mr. Brent, and the testimony of Mr. Brent is proved by the admission! Excellent Fugitive Slave Bill "evidence!" Brent confirms Brent! There is, I think, a well-known axiom of the common law, that "admissions shall go in entire" —all that the prisoner said. Now, Mr. Loring rules in just what serves the interest of the claimant, and rules out everything that serves Mr. Burns's interest. And is that Massachusetts justice?

Remember, too, that Commissioner Loring is the whole

court—a "judge," not known to the Constitution; a "jury" only known in the inquisition! There is no appeal from his decision. The witness came from Virginia to swear away the freedom of a citizen of Massachusetts, charged with no crime. When the Marshal, and the men hired to kidnap, are about the poor black man, it is said he makes an admission that he is the fugitive; and on that "evidence" Mr. Loring decides that he is to go into bondage for ever. It was conduct worthy of the Inquisition of Spain!* Let doubts weigh for the prisoner, is a rule as old as legal attempts at justice. Here, they weigh against him. The case is full of doubts—doubts on every side. He rides over them all. He takes the special words he wants, and therewith strikes down the prisoner's claim to liberty.

Suppose, in the present instance, the fugitive had been described as a man of light complexion, blue eyes, and golden hair: then, suppose some white man, you or I, answered the description, and some ruffian swore to the identity. By that form of law, any man, any woman, in the city of Boston, might have been taken and carried off into bondage straightway, irredeemable bondage, bondage for ever.

Commissioner Loring had no better ground for taking away the liberty of Anthony Burns than in the case I have just supposed.

Suppose Colonel Suttle had claimed the Mayor and Aldermen of Boston as his slaves; had brought a "record" from Alexandria reciting their names, and setting forth the fact of their owing service, and their escape from it; had them kidnapped and brought before Mr. Loring. According to his own ruling, the only question he has to determine is this: "the identity of the persons." A witness testifies that the Mayor and Aldermen of Boston are the parties named in the record as owing service and having escaped therefrom. The Commissioner says, "The facts to be proved by the claimant are three.

"1. That the parties charged owed him service in Virginia.

---

* Tacitus thinks it a piece of good fortune that Agricola died before such "admissions" were made evidence to ruin a man, as in Domitian's time *quum Suspiria nostra subscriberentur!*—Agricola, c. xlv.

"2. That they escaped from that service.

"These facts he has proved by the record which the statute (sec. 10) declares 'shall be held, and taken to be full and conclusive evidence of the fact of escape, and that the service or labour of the person escaping is due to the party in such record mentioned.'

"Thus these two facts are removed entirely and absolutely from my jurisdiction, and I am entirely and absolutely precluded from applying evidence to them; if, therefore, there is in the case evidence capable of such application, I cannot make it.

"3. The third fact is the identity of the parties before me with the parties mentioned in the record.

"This identity is the only question I have a right to consider. To this, and to this alone, I am to apply the evidence.

"And then, on the whole testimony, my mind is satisfied beyond a reasonable doubt of the identity of the respondents with the parties named in the record.

"On the law and facts of the case, I consider the claimant entitled to the certificate from me which he claims."

The Mayor and Aldermen go into bondage for ever. The liberty of all this audience might be thus sworn away by a Commissioner and another kidnapper.

But the "ruling" is not the worst thing in the case. The Commissioner had prejudged it all. He had prejudged it entirely before he had even begun this mock trial; before he heard the defence; before the prisoner had any counsel to make a defence. Here is my proof. On Friday (May 26), Wendell Phillips went to Cambridge to see Mr. Loring. He is a professor of law in Harvard College, teaching law and justice to the young men who go up thither to learn law and justice! Mr. Phillips went there to get permission to visit Mr. Burns, and see if he would make a defence and have counsel. Mr. Loring advised Mr. Phillips to make no defence. He said: "Mr. Phillips, I think the case is so clear that you would not be justified in placing any obstructions in the way of the man's going back, as he probably will."

So, as the matter was decided beforehand, it was to be only a mock trial, and might just as well have been dispensed with. It keeps up some hollow semblance to the form of the Fugitive Slave Bill; but it was all prejudged before Mr. Burns had selected his counsel or determined to have any. Place no "obstructions in the way of the man's going back, *as he probably will!*"

Nor is that all. Before any defence had been made, on Saturday night, Mr. Loring drew up a bill of sale of Anthony Burns. Here it is, in his own handwriting:—

"Know all men in these Presents — That I, Charles F. Suttle, of Alexandria, in Virginia, in consideration of twelve hundred dollars, to me paid, do hereby release and discharge, quitclaim and convey to Antony Byrnes, his liberty; and I hereby manumit and release him from all claims and services to me for ever, hereby giving him his liberty to all intents and effects for ever.

" In testimony whereof, I have hereto set my hand and seal, this twenty-seventh day of May, in the year of our Lord eighteen hundred and fifty-four."

What should you say of a Judge of the Supreme Court of Massachusetts who should undertake to negotiate a note of hand which was a matter of litigation before him in court? What if the Chief-Justice, before he had heard a word of the case of the last man tried for murder—before the prisoner had any counsel—had told some humane man taking an interest in the matter, "You would not be justified in placing any obstructions in the way of the man's being hanged, as he probably will?" Add this, also: here Commissioner Loring is Justice to draw the writ, Judge, Jury, all in one! Do the annals of judicial tyranny show a clearer case of judgment without a hearing?

This is not yet the end of the wickedness. Last Wednesday night the Kidnapper's Court adjourned till Friday morning at nine o'clock. Then the "decision" was to be made. But the kidnapper and his assistants, the Marshal, etc., knew it on Thursday night. How long before, I know not. The men who hired Mr. Loring to steal a man, with the Fugitive Slave Bill for his instrument, they knew the decision at least fourteen hours before it was announced in court—I think twenty hours before.

First, he judged the case before he heard it; second, he judged it against evidence when he heard it; third, he clandestinely communicated the decision to one of the

parties half a day before he declared it openly in court.
Could Kane or Curtis do worse? I do not find that they
have ever done so bad. Does Boston teem with Epsoms
and Dudleys, the vermin of the law? Does New England
spawn Jeffreyses and Scroggses, whom we supposed impossible—fictitious characters too bad to be?

Look at the Marshal's conduct. Of his previous character
I say nothing. But his agents arrested Mr. Burns on a
false charge; threatened violence if he should cry out; they
kept him in secret. Nobody came nigh unto him.

The trial was unfairly conducted on the Marshal's part.
The public was excluded from the Court House. His servants lined the stairways, insulting the people. Southerners
were freely admitted, but Northern gentlemen kept out.
Rude, coarse, and insolent fellows found no check. Clergymen and lawyers were turned back, and Southern students
of law let in. Two gentlemen were refused admission; but
when one declared he was from Virginia, the other from
South Carolina, they were both admitted on the instant.
The whole Court House seemed to be the property of the
slave power.

He crowded the Court House with soldiers. Some of
them were drunk, and charged bayonet upon the counsel
and witnesses for Burns, and thrust them away. He employed base men for his guard. I never saw such a motley
crew as this kidnapper's gang collected together, save in
the darkest places of London and Paris, whither I went to
see how low humanity might go down, and yet bear the
semblance of man. He raked the kennels of Boston. He
dispossessed the stews, bawding the courts with unwonted
infamy. He gathered the spoils of brothels; prodigals not
penitent, who upon harlots had wasted their substance in
riotous living; pimps, gamblers, the *succubus* of Slavery;
men which the gorged gaols had cast out into the streets
scarred with infamy; fighters, drunkards, public brawlers;
convicts that had served out their time, waiting for a second
conviction; men whom the subtlety of counsel, or the
charity of the gallows, had left unhanged. "No eye hath
seen such scarecrows." The youngest of the Police Judges
found ten of his constituents there. Gaoler Andrews, it is
said, recognised forty of his customers among them. It is

said that Albert J. Tirrell was invited to move in that leprous gang, and declined!* "The wicked walk on every side when the vilest men are exalted!" The publican who fed those locusts of Southern tyranny, said that out of the sixty-five, there was but one respectable man, and he kept aloof from all the rest. I have seen courts of justice in England, Holland, Belgium, Germany, France, Italy, and Switzerland, and I have seen just such men. But they were always in the dock, not the servants of the Court. The Marshal was right; "the statute is so cruel and wicked that it should not be executed by good men." He chose fit tools for fitting work. I do not think Herod sent the guardian of orphans to massacre the innocents of Bethlehem. I doubt that Pontius Pilate employed a Judge of Probate to crucify Jesus between two thieves!

There was an unfairness about the offer to sell Mr. Burns. I do not know whose fault that was. His claimant pretended that he would sell; but when the money was tendered, his agents delayed, equivocated, wore out the time, till it was Sunday; and the deed could not legally be done. It was the man, and not the money they wanted. He offered to sell the man for twelve hundred dollars. The price was exorbitant, he would not bring eight hundred at Alexandria.†

* While these sheets are passing through the press I learn that three of the Marshal's guard have been arrested for crimes of violence committed *within twenty-four hours after the rendition.* Set a thief to serve a thief.

† "MR. ATTORNEY HALLETT'S INTERFERENCE WITH THE PURCHASE OF THE FUGITIVE.

"Boston, Saturday, June 3, 1854.

"*To the Editors of the Atlas:*—You have called my attention to an article in your paper this morning signed 'L.,' and to a contradiction of its statement in the *Journal* of this evening, by authority of the United States District Attorney. I know nothing of the origin of either of these articles, but will, at your request, give you a narrative of my own connection with the recent negotiation for the freedom of 'Byrnes,' believing that such a narrative will be altogether pertinent to the fact which you seek to establish, namely, the interference of the United States District Attorney in the negotiation above referred to.

"On Saturday afternoon last, the Rev. Mr. Grimes called upon me and said that the owner of Byrnes had offered to sell him for twelve hundred dollars, and that he (Grimes) was anxious to raise the money at once. He desired my advice and assistance in the matter, and requested me to draw up a suitable subscription paper for that purpose, which I did in these words:—

There was another trick. At one time it was thought the evidence would compel the reluctant Commissioner to

---

. " ' Boston, May 27, 1854.

" ' We, the undersigned, agree to pay to Anthony Byrnes, or order, the sum set against our respective names, for the purpose of enabling him to obtain his freedom from the United States Government, in the hands of whose officers he is now held as a slave.

" ' This paper will be presented by the Rev. L. A. Grimes, pastor of the 12th Baptist Church.'

" Upon this paper Mr. Grimes obtained signatures for six hundred and sixty-five dollars, and with the aid of Colonel Suttle's counsel, Messrs. Parker and Thomas, who interested themselves in this matter, four hundred dollars more were got in a check, conditionally, and held by Mr. Parker. It was agreed by me that I should be near at hand on Saturday night, to assist and advance the money, which was accordingly done ; and my check for eight hundred dollars, early in the night, was placed in the hands of the United States Marshal for this purpose. About eleven o'clock, all parties being represented, we met at Mr. Commissioner Loring's office. This gentleman, with commendable alacrity, prepared necessary papers.

" At this juncture the actual money was insisted on, which threatened for a time the completion of the negotiation ; but anticipating this contingency, which, under all circumstances, was not an unreasonable demand, we adjourned to the Marshal's office, and I prepared myself with the needful tender. The United States Attorney, Mr. Hallett, was in attendance, and the respective parties immediately discussed the mode of procedure. The hour of twelve was rapidly approaching, after which no action could be taken. Mr. Grimes was prepared to receive Byrnes, and anxious to take him as he might peacefully. The matter lingered, and official action ceased.

" I am not disposed to charge any one with designedly defeating the desired end on that occasion. The business was new, the questions raised novel. But when we had proceeded thus far, and were ready in good faith to make good the sum requisite on Monday, in view also of the friendly understanding had after midnight with all parties in interest, we had a right to expect Byrnes's liberation on Monday. When that day came, the owner refused to treat. Learning from rumour only that four thousand dollars had been named as the sum then asked for, I on Monday addressed Colonel Suttle, then in court, a respectful note, reminding him of the position of things on Saturday night, and urging that Mr. Grimes had the right to expect the original agreement to be carried out, but further asking him if any additional sum was required ; to which he replied, that the ' case is before the Court, and must await its decision.'

" Tuesday morning, I had an interview with Colonel Suttle in the U. S. Marshal's office. He seemed disposed to listen to me, and met the subject in a manly way. He said he wished to take the boy back, after which he would sell him. He wanted to see the result of the trial, at any rate. I stated to him that we considered his claim to Byrnes clear enough, and that he would be delivered over to him, urging particularly upon him that the boy's liberation was not sought for except with his free consent, and his claim being fully satisfied. I urged upon him no consideration of the fear of a rescue, or possible unfavourable result of

free his victim.   Then it was proposed that he should be
seized in the court, and either summarily declared a slave by

---

the trial to him, but offered distinctly, if he chose, to have the trial proceed, and whatever might be the result, still to satisfy his claim.

"I stated to him that the negotiation was not sustained by any society
or association whatsoever, but that it was done by some of our most
respectable citizens, who were desirous not to obstruct the operation of
the law, but in a peaceable and honourable manner sought an adjustment
of this unpleasant case; assuring him that this feeling was general
among the people.   I read to him al etter, addressed to me by a highly-
esteemed citizen, urging me to renew my efforts to accomplish this, and
placing at my disposal any amount of money that I might think proper
for the purpose.

"Colonel Suttle replied that he appreciated our motives, and that he felt
disposed to meet us.   He then stated what he would do.   I accepted his
proposal at once; it was not entirely satisfactory to me, but yet, in view
of his position, as he declared to me, I was content.   At my request, he
was about to commit our agreement to writing, when Mr. B. F. Hallett
entered the office, and they two engaged in conversation apart from me.
Presently Colonel Suttle returned to me, and said : 'I must withdraw
what I have done with you.'   We both immediately approached Mr.
Hallett, who said, pointing to the spot where Mr. Batchelder fell, in sight
of which we stood, 'That blood must be avenged.'   I made some pertinent reply, rebuking so extraordinary a speech, and left the room.

"On Friday, soon after the decision had been rendered, finding Colonel
Suttle had gone on board the Cutter at an early hour, I waited upon his
counsel, Messrs. Thomas and Parker, at the Court-house, and there
renewed my proposition.   Both these gentlemen promptly interested
themselves in my purpose, which was to {tender the claimant full satis-
faction, and receive the surrender of Byrnes from him, either there, in
State Street, or on board the Cutter, at his own option.   It was arranged
between us that Mr. Parker should go at once on board the Cutter, and
make an arrangement, if possible, with the Colonel.

"I provided ample funds, and returned immediately to the Court-
house, when I found that there would be difficulty in getting on board
the Cutter.   Application was made by me to the Marshal; he interposed
no objection, and I offered to place Mr. Parker alongside the vessel.
Presently Mr. Parker took me aside and said these words : 'Colonel
Suttle has pledged himself to Mr. Hallett that he will not sell his boy
until he gets him home.'   Thus the matter ended.

"In considering, Mr. Editor, whose interference was potent in thus
defeating the courteous endeavours of citizens of Boston, peacefully and
with due respect to the laws of the land, to put to rest the painful scenes
of the past week, it must be borne in mind that the United States
Marshal, who, throughout this unfortunate negotiation, has conducted
himself towards us with great consideration, consented individually to
hold the funds, as a party not in interest, thus early acquiescing in the
success of our plan; the owner himself was willing to release his claim;
his counsel, Messrs. Thomas and Parker, volunteered their aid in raising
the money, urged it, and interested themselves in its speedy accomplish-
ment—even in the latest moment when it could be effected, with commendable alacrity, they offered their assistance; the United States

some other Commissioner, or else carried off with no further mock trial. I think it would have been done; but Commissioner Loring was ready to do the work demanded of him, and earn his twofold pay.

The conduct of the Governor requires some explanation. The law of Massachusetts was cloven down by the sword of the Marshal; no officer could be found to serve the writ of personal replevin, designed by the Massachusetts Legislature to meet exactly such cases, and bring Mr. Burns before a Massachusetts court. The Governor could not be induced to attend to it: Monday he was at the meeting of the Bible Society; Thursday at the meeting of the Sunday Schools. If the United States Marshal had invaded the sovereignty of South Carolina, where do you think her Governor would have been?

The conduct of the Mayor of Boston deserves to be remembered. He had the police of the city in Court Square, aiding the kidnapper. It was not their fault. They served against their will. Captain Hayes, of the police, that day magnanimously resigned his charge.* The Mayor called out the soldiers at great cost, to some one.

Commissioner himself consented to be at his post until midnight of Saturday, to give his official service for the object—I repeat, in view of all these considerations, the conclusion must come home irresistibly to every candid mind, that there was one personage who, officially or individually, in this connection either did do, or left undone, something whereby his interference became essential to a less painful termination of this case.

"Respectfully,
"HAMILTON WILLIS."

* Here is the note of Mr. Hayes to the city authorities; one day his children will deem it a noble trophy:—

"Boston, June 2, 1854.

"*To His Honour the Mayor and the Aldermen of the City of Boston:*—

"Through all the excitement attendant upon the arrest and trial of the fugitive by the United States Government, I have not received an order which I have conceived inconsistent with my duties as an officer of the police until this day, at which time I have received an order which, if performed, would implicate me in the execution of that infamous 'Fugitive Slave Bill.'

"I therefore resign the office which I now hold as a Captain of the Watch and Police from this hour, 11 A.M.

"Most respectfully yours,
"JOSEPH K. HAYES."

He did this on his own responsibility. Five Aldermen have publicly protested against the breach of honour and justice. After the wicked deed was over, he attended a meeting of Sunday School children in Faneuil Hall. When he was introduced to the audience, "Out of the mouth of babes and sucklings" came a hiss! At night, the "citizen soldiery" had a festival. The Mayor was at the supper, and toasted the military—eating and drinking and making merry. What did they care, or he, that an innocent citizen of Boston was sent into bondage for ever, and by their hands! The agony of Mr. Burns only flavoured their cup. So the butcher's dog can enjoy himself in the shambles, while the slaughter of the innocent goes on around him, "battening on garbage!"

Thus, on the 2nd of June, Boston sent into bondage the second victim. It ought to have been fifteen days later—the 17th of June. What a spectacle it was! The day was brilliant; there was not a cloud; all about Boston there was a ring of happy summer loveliness; the green beauty of June; the grass, the trees, the heaven, the light; and Boston itself was the theatre of incipient civil war!

What a day for Boston! Citizens applauding that a man was to be carried into bondage! Drunken soldiers, hardly able to stand in the street, sung their ribald song— "Oh, carry me back to old Virginia!" *

Daniel Webster lies buried at Marshfield; but his dead

---

* I copy this from one of the newspapers :—

"*The Pay of the Boston Military for their Aid in the Rendition of Anthony Burns.*

"We write with an ' iron pen' for the benefit of some future historian, that in the year of our Lord eighteen hundred and fifty-four, in the City of Boston, there was received for their aid in consigning to the bondage of American chattel Slavery one Anthony Burns,—by the grace of God and his own efforts a freeman,—by the independent volunteer militia of said city, the following sums :—

"National Lancers, Capt. Wilmarth	$820.00
Boston Light Dragoons, Capt. Wright	1,128.00
Fifth Regiment of Artillery, by Col. Cowdin, for himself, staff, and regiment	3,946.00
Boston Light Infantry, Capt. Rogers . . .	460.00
New England Guards, Capt. Henshaw . . .	432.00
Pulaski Guards, Capt. Wright	328.00
Boston Light Guard, Capt. Follett	500.00

hand put the chain on Anthony Burns. Last winter it was proposed to build him a monument. He needs it not. Hancock has none; Samuel Adams sleeps in a nameless grave; John Adams has not a stone. We are their monuments; the homage of the people is their epitaph. Daniel Webster also had his monument last Friday. It was the Court House crowded with two hundred and twenty United States soldiers and flanked with a cannon. His monument reached all the way from John Hancock's house in Court Street to the T Wharf; nay, it went far out to sea

Boston City Guard, Capt. French	488.00
(of which $190 was paid by order to George Young for 'refreshments.')	
Boston Independent Fusileers, Capt. Cooley . .	320.00
Washington Light Infantry, Capt. Upton . . .	536.00
Mechanic Infantry, Capt. Adams	428.00
National Guard, Lieut. Harlow commanding . . .	416.00
Union Guard, Capt. Brown	476.00
Sarsfield Guard, Capt. Hogan	308.00
Boston Independent Cadets, Capt. Amory . . .	1,136.00
Boston Light Artillery, Capt. Cobb	168.00
Major-General Edmands and staff	715.00
Major Pierce and staff of the First Battalion Light Dragoons	146.00
Colonel Holbrook and staff of the first Regiment of Light Infantry	26.00
Brigadier-General Andrews and staff of the First Brigade	107.50
Major Burbank and staff of the Third Battalion of Light Infantry	76.00
William Read, hardware and sporting apparatus dealer, for ammunition	155.28
Total . . $13,115.78"	

The sum paid to the *civil officers* of Boston for their services has not yet been made public.

Mr. Burns was subsequently sold to David McDaniel, of Nash county, N. C., on condition that he "*should never be sold to go North.*" A most piteous letter was received from him in January, 1855, full of pious gratitude to all who sought to preserve for him the unalienable Right to Life, Liberty, and the Pursuit of Happiness.

Presently, after Commissioner Loring had accomplished his "legal" kidnapping, he tried to purchase a piece of meat of a noble-hearted butcher in Boylston Market. "I will take that pig," said the Commissioner. "You can't have it," replied the butcher. "What, is it sold?" "No, sir! But you can't buy your meat of me. I want none of your blood-money. It would *burn my pocket!*"

Rev. Nehemiah Adams, D.D., subsequently sent to the Commissioner a presentation copy of his *South Side View of Slavery*, with the author's regards!

in the Revenue Cutter, and is borne seaward or shoreward. Conquer your prejudices! No higher law! On the brass cannon you could read, I STILL LIVE.

Mr. Burns was seized on that day which the Christian church has consecrated to two of the martyrs, Saints Donatian and Rogatian. They seem to have been put to death by Rictius Varus, the Commissioner of Belgic and Celtic Gaul. They suffered death at Nantes. They were impeached for professing themselves Christians. Simple death was not torment enough for being a Christian in the year 287. They were put to the rack first. Their bodies, still held in great veneration, now sleep their dusty slumber in the great cathedral of the town. The antiquarian traveller wonders at the statues of those two martyrs still standing at the corner of the Money-Changers' Street, and telling the tale of times when the Christians only suffered persecution. St. Rogatian's day was not an unfitting time for Puritanic Boston to steal a man!

The day on which Mr. Burns was sent from Boston into Alexandrian bondage is still more marked in the Christian church. It is consecrated to a noble army of martyrs who tasted death at Vienna, in Gaul,—now Vienne, in the south of France—in the year 178 after Christ. I shall never forget the little town, once famous and eminent, where the dreadful event took place. A letter written, it is said, by St. Irenæus himself details the saddening history. It begins, "We the Servants of Christ [Mr. Everett might translate it ' Slaves'], dwelling at Vienna and Lyons in Gaul to the brethren in Asia and Phrygia who have the same faith and hope with us. Peace, and Grace, and Glory from God the Father, and from our Lord Jesus Christ." The whole letter is a most touching memorial of the faithful piety of the Christians in days when it cost life to be religious. Anybody may read what remains of it in Eusebius. Here is the story in short:—

A law was passed forbidding Christians to be out of their own houses "in any place whatsoever." The most cruel punishments were denounced against all persons who professed the Christian religion.

The Governor, who was also a commissioner appointed for persecuting and murdering the Christians, had the most prominent members of the Church arrested and

brought before him. In the "examination" they were
treated with such cruelty that Vettius Epagathus, a
Christian of distinguished family, undertook their defence,
a man so exactly virtuous, that, though young, he won the
honour of old Zacharias—"walking in all the command-
ments and ordinances of the Lord blameless." The commissioner asked him, "Art thou also a Christian?" Epagathus made his "admission" in a loud voice, and shared
the fate of the martyrs. The Christians called him the
Comforter of Christians,—"for he had the Comforter, the
Spirit, in him, more than Zacharias himself;" a title as
hateful then as Friend of the Slave now is in the Court or
the Church of Kidnappers in Boston.

Sanctus, the Deacon; Maturus, a new convert; Attalus,
from Asia Minor, one of the pillars of the Church; Blandina, a female Slave; Pothinus, ninety years old, and
Bishop of Lyons, hard by, were put to the most cruel
tortures. Four of them were exposed to the wild beasts
in the amphitheatre to divert the spectators! Blandina
was fastened to a post to be eaten up by the beasts, and
when they left her untouched, the Marshal haled her to
prison again. "But, last of all, St. Blandina, like a well-
born mother who has nursed her children and sent them
victorious to the King, hastened after them, rejoicing and
leaping for joy at her departure; thrown, indeed, to the
wild beasts, she went as if invited to a bridal feast; and
after the scourging, after the exposure to wild beasts, after
the chair of fire, she was wrapped in a net and tossed by a
bull—and at last killed." Others fell with them: Ponticus, a boy of fifteen; Alexander the Phrygian, and many
more. They were tortured with cudgels, with whips, with
wild beasts, and red-hot plates of iron; at last they died,
one by one. The tormentors threw their dead bodies to
the dogs: some raged and gnashed their teeth over the
dead, seeking to take yet more abundant vengeance thereon;
others laughed and made mockery thereof. And others,
more gentle, seeming to sympathize as much as they dared,
made grievous reproaches, and said, "Where is now their
God, and of what profit is their piety, which they loved
better even than their own life! Now we shall see if they
will ever rise from the dead, and if their God can help and
deliver them out of our hands!"

*H 2

So things went at Allobrogian Vienna on the 2nd of
June, sixteen hundred and seventy-six years ago last
Friday.   The murder of those Christians was just as
"legal" as the rendition of Anthony Burns.   It would
be curious to know what the "respectable" men of the
town said thereupon : to see the list of fifteen hundred
citizens volunteering their aid ; to read the letter of nine
hundred and eighty-seven men thanking the commissioner
for touching their conscience.   The preaching of the priests
must have been edifying :—"I would drive a Christian
away from my own door!   I would murder my own
mother!"

Doubtless some men said, "The statute which commands
the torturous murder of men, women, and children, for no
crime but piety, if constitutional, is wicked and cruel."
And doubtless some heathen "Chief-Justice Parker"
choked down the rising conscience of mankind, and answered, "Whether the statute is a harsh one or not, it is
not for us to determine."[*]   No! it is not for the bloodhound to ask whether the victim he rends to quivering
fragments is a sinner or a saint ; the bloodhound is to bite,
and not consider ; he has teeth, not conscience.   The
Fugitive Slave Bill Commissioner is not to do justly, and
love mercy, and walk humbly with his God ; he is to
kidnap men in Boston at ten dollars a head!   The pagan
murder of Christians at Vienna under Aurelian, did not
differ much from the Christian kidnapping of Mr. Burns
in Boston under Pierce.   But, alas for these times—it is
not recorded of the Romans that any heathen Judge of
Probate came forward and volunteered to butcher the
widows and orphans of the early Church!   Then the tor-
mentor worshipped Mars and Bellona ; now he sits in the
Church of Jesus Christ.

Boston chose a fit day to consummate her second kidnapping.   St. Pothinus was a Christian preacher, so was
Anthony Burns—"a minister of the Baptist denomination," "regularly ordained!"   Commissioner Loring could
not have done better than select this time to execute his
"decision."   On St. Pothinus's day, let Anthony Burns
be led to a martyrdom more atrocious!   The African

* Reference is here made to the words used by Commissioner Loring
in his "decision," citing the words of the late Chief-Justice Parker.

churches of Boston may write a letter to-day, which three or four thousand years hence will sound as strange as now the Epistle of St. Irenæus. Sixteen hundred and seventy-six years hence, it may be thought the Marshal's "guard" is a fair match for the bullies who tortured Blandina. In the next world the District Marshal may shake hands with the heathen murderer who put the boy Ponticus to cruel death. I make no doubt there were men at the corners of the streets who clapped hands, as one by one the lions in the public square rent the Christian maidens limb from limb, and strewed the ground with human flesh yet palpitating in its severed agony. Boston can furnish mates for them. But the Judge of Probate, the teacher of a Sunday-school, the member of a church of Christ,—he may wander through all Hades, peopled thick with Roman tormentors, nor never meet with a heathen guardian of orphans who can be his match. Let him pass by. Declamation can add nothing to his deed.

> "To gild refined gold, to paint the lily,
> To throw a perfume on the violet,
> To smooth the ice, or add another hue
> Unto the rainbow, or with taper light
> To seek the beauteous eye of heaven to garnish,
> Is wasteful and ridiculous excess."

No doubt the commissioner for murdering the Christians at Vienna reasoned as "legally" and astutely in the second century as the Fugitive Slave Bill Commissioner at Boston in the nineteenth. Perhaps the "argument" was after this wise :—*

"This statute has been decided to be constitutional by the unanimous opinion of the Judges of the Supreme Court of the Province of Gaul, after the fullest argument and the maturest deliberation, to be the law of this province, as well as and because it is a constitutional law of the Roman Empire; and the wise words of our revered chief-justice † may well be repeated now, and remembered always. The chief-justice says : —

" 'The torture, persecution, and murder of Christians was not created, established, or perpetuated by the consti-

---

* See the Commissioner's " decision."
† Hon. Lemuel Shaw. See his "opinion" on the constitutionality of the Fugitive Slave Bill, in 7 Cushing's Reports, p. 285, *et seq.*

tution; it existed before; it would have existed if the constitution had not been made. The framers of the constitution could not abrogate the custom of persecuting, torturing, and murdering Christians, or the rights claimed under it. They took it as they found it, and regulated it to a limited extent. The constitution, therefore, is not responsible for the origin or continuance of this custom of persecuting, torturing, and murdering Christians—the provision it contains was the best adjustment which could be made of conflicting rights and claims to persecute, torture, and murder, and was absolutely necessary to effect what may now be considered as the general pacification by which harmony and peace should take the place of violence and war. These were the circumstances, and this the spirit in which the constitution was made—the regulation of persecution, torture, and murder of Christians, so far as to prohibit provinces by law from harbouring fugitive Christians, was an essential element in its formation; and the union intended to be established by it was essentially necessary to the peace and happiness and highest prosperity of all the provinces and towns. In this spirit, and with these views steadily in prospect, it seems to be the duty of all judges and magistrates to expound and apply these provisions in the constitution and laws of the Roman Empire, and in this spirit it behoves all persons bound to obey the laws of the Roman Empire to consider and regard them.'

"Therefore *Christianos ad Leones*—Let the Christians be torn to pieces by the wild beasts."

Wednesday, the 24th of May, the city was all calm and still. The poor black man was at work with one of his own nation, earning an honest livelihood. A Judge of Probate, Boston born and Boston bred, a man in easy circumstances, a professor in Havard College, was sitting in his office, and with a single spurt of his pen he dashes off the liberty of a man—a citizen of Massachusetts. He kidnaps a man endowed by his Creator with the unalienable right to life, liberty, and the pursuit of happiness. He leaves the writ with the Marshal, and goes home to his family, caresses his children, and enjoys his cigar. The frivolous smoke curls round his frivolous head, and at length he lays him down to sleep, and, I suppose, such dreams as haunt such heads. But when he wakes next morn, all the winds of indignation, wrath, and honest scorn, are let loose. Before night, they are blowing all over this commonwealth—ay, before another night they have gone to the Mississippi, and wherever the lightning messenger can tell the tale. So have I read in an old mediæval legend, that one summer afternoon there came up a "shape, all hot from Tartarus," from hell below, but garmented and garbed to represent a civil-suited man, masked with humanity. He walked quiet and decorous through Milan's stately streets, and scattered from his hand an invisible dust. It touched the walls; it lay on the streets; it ascended to the cross on the minster's utmost top. It went down to the beggar's den. Peacefully he walked through the streets, vanished and went home. But the next morning, the pestilence was in Milan, and ere a week had sped half her population were in their graves; and half the other half, crying that hell was clutching at their hearts, fled from the reeking City of the Plague!

Why did the Commissioner do all this? He knew the consequences that must follow. He knew what Boston was. We have no monument to Hancock and Adams; but still we keep their graves; and Boston, the dear old mother that bore them, yet in her bosom hides the honoured bones of men whom armies could not terrify, nor England bribe. Their spirit only sleeps. Tread roughly, tread roughly on the spot—their spirit rises from the ground! He knew that here were men who never will be silent when wrong is done. He knew Massachusetts; he knew Boston; he knew that the Fugitive Slave Bill had only raked the ashes over fires which were burning still, and that a breath might scatter those ashes to the winds of heaven, and bid the slumbering embers flame. Had he determined already what should happen to Anthony Burns? He knew what had befallen Thomas Sims. Did he wish another inhabitant of Boston whipped to death?

I have studied the records of crime—it is a part of my ministry. I do not find that any college professor has ever been hanged for murder in all the Anglo-Saxon family of men, till Harvard College had that solitary shame. Is not that enough? Now she is the first to have a professor that kidnaps men. "The Athens of America" furnished both.

I can understand how a man commits a crime of passion, or covetousness, or rage,—nay, of revenge, or of ambition. But for a man in Boston, with no passion, no covetousness, no rage, with no ambition nor revenge, to steal a poor negro, to send him into bondage,—I cannot comprehend the fact. I can understand the consciousness of a lion, not a kidnapper's heart. Once Mr. Loring defined a lawyer to be "a human agent for effecting a human purpose by human means." Here, and now, the Commissioner seems an inhuman agent for effecting an inhuman purpose by inhuman means.

I belong to a school that reverences the infinite perfection of God,—if, indeed, there be such a school. I believe, also, in the nobleness of man; but last week my faith was somewhat sorely tried. As I looked at that miscreant crew, the kidnapper's body-guard, and read in their faces the record and the prophecy of many a crime,

> "Felons by the hand of nature marked,
> Quoted and signed to do a deed of shame,"

I could explain and not despair. They were tools, not agents. But as I looked into the Commissioner's face, mild and amiable, a face I have respected, not without seeming cause; as I remembered his breeding and his culture, his social position, his membership of a Christian church, and then thought of the crime he was committing against humanity, with no temptation, I asked myself, can this be true? Is man thus noble, made in the dear image of the father God? Is my philosophy a dream: or are these facts a lie?

But there is another court. The Empsons and the Dudleys have been summoned there before; Jeffreys and Scroggs, the Kanes, and the Curtises, and the Lorings, must one day travel the same unwelcome road. Imagine the scene after man's mythologic way. "Edward, where is thy brother Anthony?" "I know not; am I my brother's keeper, Lord?" "Edward, where is thy brother Anthony?" "Oh, Lord, he was friendless, and so I smote him; he was poor, and I starved him of more than life. He owned nothing but his African body. I took that away from him, and gave it to another man!"

Then listen to the voice of the Crucified—"Did I not tell thee, when on earth, 'Thou shalt love the Lord thy God with all thy understanding and thy heart?'" "But I thought thy kingdom was not of this world."

"Did I not tell thee that thou shouldst love thy neighbour as thyself? Where is Anthony, thy brother? I was a stranger, and you sought my life; naked, and you rent away my skin; in prison, and you delivered me to the tormentors—fate far worse 'than death. Inasmuch as you did it to Anthony Burns, you did it unto me."

The liberty of America was never in greater peril than now. Hessian bayonets were not half so dangerous as the gold of the National treasury in the hands of this Administration. Which shall conquer, Slavery or Freedom? That is the question. The two cannot long exist side by side. Think of the peril; remember the rapacity of this Administration; its reckless leaders: think of Douglas, Cushing, and the rest. They aimed at the enslavement of Nebraska. The Northern majority in Congress yielded that.

Now they aim at Hayti and Cuba. Shall they carry that point? Surely, unless we do our duty. Shall Slavery be established at the North, at the West, and the East; in all the free States? Mr. Toombs told Mr. Hale—"Before long the master will sit down at the foot of Bunker Hill Monument with his slaves." Will do it. He has done it already, and not an officer in the State of Massachusetts made the least resistance. Our laws were trod down by insolent officials, and Boston ordered out her soldiers to help the disgraceful deed. Strange that we should be asked to make the fetters which are to chain us. Mr. Suttle is only a feeler. Soon there will be other Suttles in Boston. Let them come!

It is not only wicked; it is costly. The kidnapping of Mr. Burns must have cost in all at least one hundred thousand dollars, including the loss of time and travelling expenses of our friends from the country. The publican's bill for feeding the Marshal's crew is already more than six thousand dollars!

Consider the demoralization of the people produced by such a deed. Mr. Dana was knocked down in the street by one of the Marshal's posse—as it is abundantly proved.* The blow might easily have been fatal. It is long since a bully has attacked a respectable citizen in Boston before. Hereafter I fear it will be more common. You cannot employ such a body-guard as the Marshal had about him in such business without greatly endangering the safety of the persons and the property of the town. We shall hear from them again. What a spectacle it was ; the army of the United States, the soldiers of Boston, sending an innocent man into Slavery ! What a lesson to the children in the Sunday Schools — to the vagrant children in the streets, who have no school but the Sights of the City ! What a lesson of civilization to the Irish population of Boston ! Men begin to understand this. There never was so much Anti-Slavery feeling in Boston before—never so much indignation in my day. If a law aims at justice, though it fail of the mark we will respect the law—not openly resist it or with violence : wait a little, and amend it or repeal it. But when the law aims at injustice, open, manifest, palpable wickedness, why, we must be cowards and fools too, if we submit.

Massachusetts has never felt so humiliated before. Soldiers of the Government enforcing a law in peaceful Boston, the most orderly of Christian cities ! We have had no such thing since the Declaration of Independence ! The rendition of Mr. Burns fills New England with sorrow and bitter indignation. The people tolled the bells at Plymouth. The bones of the forefathers gave that response to the kidnappers in Boston. At Manchester and several other towns they did the same. To-day, ministers are preaching as never before. What will it all come to ? Men came to Boston peacefully last week. Will they always come " with only the arms God gave ?" One day in the seventeenth century five thousand country gentlemen rode into London with a " petition to the King"—with only the arms God gave them. Not long after they went

---

* The culprit was held in trifling bail by the Court, one of the Marshal's gang became his surety. But the ruffian absconded, was subsequently arrested at New Orleans, and sent to the House of Correction for a year and a half.

thither with Oliver Cromwell at their head and other "arms" which God also had given. May such times never return in New England! *

We want no rashness, but calm, considerate action, deliberate, prudent far-seeing. The Fugitive Slave Bill is a long wedge, thin at one end, wide at the other; it is entered between the bottom planks of our SHIP OF STATE; a few blows thereon will "enforce" more than the South thinks of. A little more,—and we shall go to pieces. Men talk wildly just now, and I do not credit what cool men say in this heat. But I see what may come—what must come, if a few more blows be struck in that quarter. It was only Mr. Webster's power to manufacture public opinion by his giant will and immense eloquence, which made the North submit at all to the Fugitive Slave Bill. He strained his power to the utmost—and died! Now there is no Webster or Clay; not even a Calhoun; not a first-rate man in the Pro-Slavery party, North or South. Slavery is not well manned—many hands, dirty, cunning, stealthy,—not a single great, able head.

The cowardice of Mr. Everett has excited the clergy of New England; of all the North. They are stung with the reproach of the people, and ashamed of their own past neglect. The Nebraska Bill opens men's eyes. Agitation was never so violent as at this day. The prospect of a war with Spain is not inviting to men who own ships, and want a clear sea and open market. Pirates, privateers,—

---

* While this Sermon is passing through the press, I find the following paragraph in a newspaper :—

"One of the Fourth of July celebrations at Columbus, Ga., was the sale of ninety or a hundred men, women, and boys, by the order of Robert Toombs, United States Senator. Here is the advertisement :—

"'ADMINISTRATOR'S SALE.—Will be sold on the first Tuesday in July next, at the Court House door of Stewart County, within the usual hours of sale, between ninety and one hundred negroes, consisting of men, women, boys, etc. These negroes are all very likely, and between forty and fifty of the number are men and boys. Sold as the property of Henry J. Pope, deceased, in pursuance of an order of the Court of Ordinary of Stewart County, for the benefit of heirs and creditors. Terms of sale, a credit (with interest) until 25th December next.

"'ROBERT TOOMBS,
"'Adm'r of Henry J. Pope, deceased.'

"'Men, women, and boys,' bought on the Fourth of July,—paid for on Christmas !"

Algerine, Greek, Spanish, Portuguese, West Indian,—are not welcome to the thoughts of men. The restoration of the Slave Trade is not quite agreeable to the farmers and mechanics of the North. This attempt to seize a man in Boston; the display of force; the insolence of the officials; the character of the men concerned in this iniquity—all is offensive. Then there was insult, open and intentional. Mr. Burns was carried through State Street at "high change." Boston merchants feel as they never did before. All Massachusetts is incensed. The wrath of Massachusetts is slow, but she has wrath, has courage, "perseverance of the saints."

Let us do nothing rashly. What is done hastily must be done over again—it is not well done. This is what I would recommend.

1. A convention of all Massachusetts, without distinction of party, to take measures to preserve the rights of Massachusetts. For this we want some new and stringent laws for the defence of personal liberty, for punishing all who invade it on our soil. We want powerful men as officers to execute these laws.

2. A general convention of all the States to organize for mutual protection against this new master.

It is not speeches that we want—but action; not rash, crazy action, but calm, deliberate, systematic action—organization for the defence of personal liberty and the State Rights of the North. Now is a good time; let us act with cool energy. By all means let us do something, else the liberties of America go to ruin—then what curses shall mankind heap upon us!

> " And deep, and more deep—as the iron is driven,—
>   Base slaves, will the whet of our agony be,
> When we think—as the damned haply think of the Heaven
>   They had once in their reach—that we might have been free."

But, my friends, out of all this dreadful evil we can bring relief. The remedy is in our hearts and hands. God works no miracles. There is power in human nature to end this wickedness. God appointed the purpose, provided the means—a divine purpose, human means. Only be faithful, and in due time we shall triumph over the destroyer. Every noble quality of man works with us;

each attribute of God. We are His instruments. Let us faithfully do the appointed work! Darkness is about us! Journey forward; light is before us!

> " O God, who in thy dear still heaven
>   Dost sit and wait to see
> The errors, sufferings, and crimes
>   Of our humanity;
> How deep must be thy Causal love,
>   How Whole thy final care,
> Since Thou who rulest all above
>   Canst see, and yet canst bear!" *

* See Appendix.

A SERMON

OF THE

DANGERS WHICH THREATEN THE RIGHTS OF MAN IN AMERICA.

PREACHED AT THE MUSIC HALL, ON SUNDAY, JULY 2, 1854.

" And He gave them their request; but sent leanness into their soul."—
PSALM cvi. 15.

NEXT Tuesday will be the seventy-eighth anniversary of
American Independence. The day suggests a national
subject as theme for meditation this morning. The condition of America makes it a dark and a sad meditation. I
ask your attention, therefore, to a "Sermon of the Dangers
which threaten the Rights of Man in America."

The human race is permanent as the Mississippi, and
like that is fed from springs which never dry; but the
several nations are as fleeting as its waves. In the great
tide of humanity, States come up, one after the other, a
wave or a bubble; each lasts its moment, then dies—passed
off, forgot:

> " Or like the snow-falls in the river,
> A moment white—then melts for ever,"

while the great stream of humanity rolls ever forward,
from time to eternity :—not a wave needless; not a snow
flake, no drop of rain or dew, no ephemeral bubble, but
has its function to perform in that vast, unmeasured, never-
ending stream.

How powerless appears a single man! He is one of a
thousand million men; the infinitesimal of a vulgar fraction; one leaf on a particular tree in the forest. A single
nation, like America, is a considerable part of mankind
now living; but when compared with the human race of all
time, past and to come, it seems as nothing; it is but one

bough in the woods. Nay, the population of the earth, to-day, is but one tree in the wide primeval forest of mankind, which covers the earth and outlasts the ages. The leaf may fall and not be missed from the bough; the branch may be rudely broken off, and its absence not marked; the tree will die and be succeeded by other trees in the forest, green with summer beauty, or foodful and prophetic with autumnal seed. Tree by tree, the woods will pass away, and, unobserved, another forest take its place,—arising, also, tree by tree.

How various the duration of States or men—dying at birth, or lasting long periods of time! For more than three thousand years, Egypt stood the queen of the world's young civilization, invincible as her own pyramids, which yet time and the nations alike respect. From Romulus, the first half-mythologic king of the seven-hilled city, to Augustulus, her last historic emperor, it is more than twelve centuries. At this day the Austrian, the Spanish, the French and German sovereigns sit each on a long-descended throne. Victoria is "daughter of a hundred kings." Pope Pius the Ninth claims two hundred and fifty-six predecessors, canonical and "infallible." His chair is reckoned more than eighteen hundred years old; and it rests on an Etrurian platform yet ten centuries more ancient. The Turkish throne has been firmly fixed at Constantinople for four hundred years. Individual tyrants, like summer flies, are short-lived; but tyranny is old and lasting. The family of ephemera, permanent amid the fleeting, is yet as old as that of elephants, and will last as long.

But free governments have commonly been brief. If the Hebrew people had well-nigh a thousand years of independent national life, their Commonwealth lasted but about three centuries; the flower of their literature and religion was but little longer. The historic period of Greece begins 776 B. C.; her independence was all over in six hundred and thirty years. The Roman deluge had swallowed it up. No Deucalion and Pyrrha could re-people the land with men. Her little States—how brief was their hour of freedom for the people! From the first annual archon of Athens to her conquest by Philip, and the death of her liberty, it was only two hundred and forty-five years!

Her tree of freedom grew in a narrow field of time and briefly bore its age-outlasting fruit of science, literature, and art. Now the tree is dead; its fragments are only curious Athenian stone. The Grecian colonies in the East, Ætolian, Dorian, Ionian—how fair they flourished in the despotic waste of Asia! how soon those liberal blossoms died! Even her colonies in the advancing West had no long independent life. Cyrene, Syracusa, Agrigentum, Crotona, Massilia Saguntum,—how soon they died!—flowers which the savage winter swiftly nipped.

The Roman Commonwealth could not endure five hundred years. Her theocratic Tarquin the Proud must be succeeded by a more despotic dictator, with the style of democrat; and Rome, abhorring still the name of king, see all her liberties laid low. The red sea of despotism opened to let pass one noble troop—the elder Brutus at the head, the younger bringing up the rear—then closed again and swallowed up that worse than Ægyptian host, clamouring only for "bread and games!"

The republics of Italy in the Middle Ages were no more fortunate. The half-Grecian Commonwealths, Naples, Amalphi, Gaëta,—what promise they once held forth; and what a warning fate! They were only born to die. A similar destiny befell the towns of more northern Italy, where freedom later found a home,—Milan, Padua, Genoa, Verona, Venice, Bologna, Florence, Pisa. Nay, in the midnight of the dark ages, seven hundred years ago, in the very city of the Popes and Cæsars, in the centre of that red Roman sea of despotism, there was a momentary spot of dry free land; and Arnaldo da Brescia eloquently spoke of "Roman Liberty." The "Roman Republic" and "Roman Senate" became once more familiar words. Italian liberty, Lombard republics,—how soon they all went down! No city—not even Florence—kept the people's freedom safe three hundred years. Silently the wealthy nobles and despotic priests sapped the walls. Party spirit blinded the else clear eyes: "the State may perish; let the faction thrive." The republicans sought to crush the adjacent feeble States. They forgot justice, the higher law of God: unworthy of liberty, they fell and died! Let the tyrant swallow up the Italian towns; they were unfit for freedom. "A generous disdain of one man's will is to republics what chastity is to woman;" they spurned this austere virtue. Let them serve their despots. "Liberty withdrew from a people who disgraced her name." Let Dante burn his poetic brand of infamy into the forehead of his countrymen. But while freedom lasted, how fair was her blossom, how rich and sweet her fruit! What riches, what beauty, what science, letters, art, came of that noble stock! Italy was the world's wonder—for a day; its sorrow ever since. So the cactus flowers into one gorgeous ecstasy of bloom; then the excessive blossom, with withering collapse, swoons and dies of its voluptuous and tropical delight.

Liberty wanders from the North, through Italy, the fairest of all earthly lands; then sits sadly down on the tallest of the Alps, and once more reviews those famous towns; the jewels that adorn the purple robe of history—all tarnished, shattered, spoiled. Slowly she turns her face northward and longs for hope. But even the Teutonic towns, where freedom ever wore a sober dress, were only spots of sunshine in a day of wintry storm. Swiss, German, Dutch, they were brief as fair. In Novogorod and in Poland, how soon was Slavonian freedom lost!

So in a winter day in the country have I seen a little frame of glass screening from the northern snow and ice a nicely sheltered spot, where careful hands tended little delicate plants, for beauty and for use. How fair the winter garden seemed amid the wildering snow, and else all-conquering frost! The little roses lifted up their face and kissed the glass which sheltered from the storm. But anon, some rude hand broke the frail barrier down, and in an hour the plants were frozen, stiff and dead; and the little garden was all filled with snow and ice;—a garden now no more!

How often do you see in a great city a man perish in his youth, bowed down by lusts of the body. The graves of such stand thick along the highway of our mortal life,—numberless, nameless, or all too conspicuously marked. Other men we see early bowed down by their ambition, and they live a life far worse than merely sensual death—themselves the ghastliest monuments, beacons of ruin! And so, along the highway that mankind treads, there are the open sepulchres of nations, which perished of their sin;

or else transformed to stone, the gloomy sphinxes sit there by the wayside—a hard, dread, awful lesson to the nations that pass by.   Let America,

"The Heir of all the ages! and the youngest born of time!"

gather up every jewel which the prodigal scattered from his hand, look down into his grave, and then confront these gloomy, awful sphinxes, and learn what lessons of guidance they have; or of warning, if it alone is to be found!   Even the sphinx has a riddle which we needs must learn, or else perish.

The greater part of a nation's life is not delight; it is discipline. A famous political philosopher, who has survived two revolutionary storms in France, has just now written, "God has made the condition of all men more severe than they are willing to believe. He causes them at all times to purchase the success of their labours and the progress of their destiny at a dearer price than they had anticipated."

The merchant knows how difficult it is to acquire a great estate; the scholar, youthful and impatient, well understands that the way of science or of letters is steep and hard to climb; the farmer, knowing the stern climate of New England, her niggard soil, rises early and retires late, and is never off his guard. These men all thrive. But, alas! the people of America do not know on what severe conditions alone national welfare is to be won. Human nature is yet only a New England soil and climate for freedom to grow in.

Nations may come to an end through the decay of the family they belong to; and thus they may die out of old age,—for there is an infancy, manhood, and old age to a nation as well as to a man. Then the nation comes to a natural end, and like a shock of corn fully ripe, in its season it is gathered to its people. But I do not find that any State has thus lived out its destiny, and died a natural death.

Again, States may perish by outward violence, military conquest,—for as the lion in the wilderness eateth up the wild ass, so the strong nations devour the weak. But this happened most often in ancient times, when men and States were more rapacious even than now.

Thirdly, States may perish through their own vice, moral or political. Their national institutions may be a defective machine which works badly, and fails of producing national welfare of body or spirit. It may not secure national unity of action—there being no national gravitation of the great masses which fly asunder; or it may fail of individual variety of action—having no personal freedom; excessive national gravitation destroys individual cohesion, and pulls the people flat; the men are slaves; they cannot reach the moral and spiritual welfare necessary for a nation's continuous life. In both these cases the vice is political; the machinery is defective, made after false ideas. Or when the institutions are good and capable of accommodating the nation's increase and growth, the vice may be moral, lying deeper in the character of the people. They may have a false and unimprovable form of religion, which suits not the nature of man or of God, and which consequently produces a false system of morals, and so corrupts the nation's heart. They may become selfish, gross, cowardly, atheistic, and so decay inwardly and perish. If left all alone, such a people will rot down and die of internal corruption. Mexico is in a perishing condition to-day; so is Spain; so are some of the young nations of South America, and some of the old of Asia and Europe. Nothing can ever save Turkey,—not all the arms of all the allied West; and though Protestant and Catholic join hands, Christendom cannot propagate Mahometanism, nor keep it from going down.

Leave these nations to their fate and they will die. But commonly, they are not left to themselves; other people rush in and conquer. The wild individual man is rapacious by instinct. The present nations are rapacious also by calculation; they prey on feeble States. The hooded crow of Europe watches for the sickly sheep. In America the wolves prowl round the herd of buffaloes and seize the sickly, the wounded, and the old. And so there are scavengers of the nations,—fillibusters, the flesh-flies and carrion-vultures of the world, who have also their function to perform. Wealth and power are never left without occupants. Rome was corrupt, her institutions

bad, her religion worn out, her morals desperate; northern
nations came upon her. "Wheresoever the body is, thither
the eagles will be gathered together."

In Europe there are nations in this state of decay, from
moral or political vice. All the Italo-Greek populations,
most of the Celto-Roman, all the Celtic, all the old Asiatic
populations—the Hungarians and Turks. The Teutonic
and Slavic families alone seem to prosper, full of vigorous,
new life, capable of making new improvements, to suit the
altered phases of the world.

In America there is only one family in a condition of
advance, of hardy health. Spanish America is in a state
of decay; she has a bad form of religion, and bad morals;
her republics only "guarantee the right of assassination;"
an empire is her freest state. But in the north of North
America the Anglo-Saxon British colonies rapidly advance
in material and spiritual development, and one day doubtless they will separate from the parent stem and become
an independent tree. The roots of England run under the
ocean; they come up in Africa, India, Australia, America,
in many an island of all the seas. Great fresh, living
trunks grow up therefrom. One day these offshoots will
become self-supporting, with new and independent roots,
and ere long will separate from the parent stem; then there
will be a great Anglo-Saxon trunk in Australia, another
in India, another in Africa, another in the north of our
own continent, and yet others scattered over the manifold
islands of the sea, an Anglo-Saxon forest of civilization.

But in the centre of the North American continent, the
same Anglo-Saxons have passed from their first condition
of scattered and dependent colonies, and become a united
and independent nation, five-and-twenty millions strong.
Our fellow-countrymen here in America compose one-
fortieth part of all the inhabitants of the globe. We are
now making the greatest political experiment which the
sun ever looked down upon.

First, we are seeking to found a State on industry, and
not war. All the prizes of America are rewards of toil,
not fighting. We are ruled by the constable, not by the
soldier. It is only in exceptional cases, when the liberal
institutions of America are to be trodden under foot, that
the constable disappears, and the red arm of the soldier

clutches at the people's throat. That is the first part of our scheme—we are aiming to found an industrial State.

Next, the national theory of the government is a democracy—the government of all, by all, for all. All officers depend on election, none are foreordained. There are to be no special privileges, only natural, universal rights.

It would be a fair spectacle,—a great industrial Commonwealth, spread over half the continent, and folding in its bosom one-fortieth of God's whole family! It is a lovely dream; nor Athenian Plato, nor English Thomas More, nor Bacon, nor Harrington, ever dared to write on paper so fair an ideal as our fathers and we have essayed to put into men. I once thought this dream of America would one day become a blessed fact! We have many elements of national success. Our territory for quantity and quality is all we could ask; our origin is of the Caucasian's best. No nation had ever so fair a beginning as we. The Anglo-Saxon is a good hardy stock for national welfare to grow on. To my American eye, it seems that human nature had never anything so good for popular liberty to be grafted into. We are already strong, and fear nothing from any foreign power. The violent cannot take us by force. No nation is our enemy.

But the question now comes, Is America to live or to die? If we live, what life shall it be? Shall we fall into the sepulchre of departed States—a new debauchee of the nations? Shall we live petrified to stone, a despotism many-headed, sitting—another sphinx—by the wayside of history, to scare young nations in their march and impede their progress? Or shall we pursue the journey—a great, noble-hearted Commonwealth, a nation possessing the continent, full of riches, full of justice, full of wisdom, full of piety, and full of peace? It depends on ourselves. It is for America, for this generation of Americans, to say which of the three shall happen. No fate holds us up. Our character is our destiny.

I am not a timid man; I am no excessive praiser of times passed by; I seldom take counsel of my fears, often of my hopes;—but now I must say that since '76 our success was never so doubtful as at this time. England is in peril; the despots on the continent hate her free Parliament, which makes laws for the people—just laws; they hate her free speech, which tells every grievance at home or abroad; they hate her free soil, which offers a home to every exile, republican or despotic. England is in peril, for every tyrant hates her. Russia is in danger, for the two strongest powers of Christendom have just clasped hands, and sworn an oath to fight against that great marauding empire of the East. . Their armies threaten her cities; her sovereign deserts his capital; her treasure is carried a thousand miles inward; the Western fleets blockade her ports and sweep her navies from the sea. But Russia has no peril like ours; England has no danger so great as that which threatens us this day. In the darkest periods of the American Revolution, when Washington's army, without blankets, without coats, without shoes, fled through the Jerseys, when they marked the ice of the Delaware, and left revolutionary tracks in frozen blood, we were not in such peril as to-day. When General Gage had the throat of Boston in his hand, and perfidiously disarmed the people, we were not in such danger. Yea, when four hundred houses in yonder town went up in one great cloud of smoke towards heaven, the liberties of America were not in such peril as they are to-day. Then we were called to fight with swords—and when that work was to be done, was America ever found wanting? Then our adversary was the other side of the sea, and wicked statutes were enacted against us in Westminster Hall. Now our enemy is at home; and something far costlier than swords is to be called into service.

Look at some of these dangers. I shall pass by all that are trifling. I find four great perils. Here they are:—

I. There comes the danger from our exclusive Devotion to Riches.

II. The danger from the Roman Catholic Church, established in the midst of us.

III. The danger from the idea that there is no Higher Law above the Statutes which men make.

IV. The danger from the Institution of Slavery, which is based on that atheistic idea last named.

I. Of the danger which comes from our exclusive Devotion to Riches.

Power is never left without a possessor : when it fell from the theocratic and military classes, from the priest, the noble, and the king, it passed to the hands of the capitalists. In America, ecclesiastical office is not power ; noble or royal birth is of small value. If Madison or Jefferson had left any sons but mulattoes, their distinguished birth would avail them nothing. The son of Patrick Henry lived a strolling schoolmaster, and a pauper's funeral was asked for his body. Money is power ; the only permanent and transmissible power ; it goes by device. Money "can ennoble sots and slaves and cowards."

It gives rank in the Church. The millionaire is always a saint. The priests of commerce will think twice before damning a man who enhances their salary and gives them dinners. In one thing the American Heaven resembles the New Jerusalem:—its pavement is "of fine gold." The capitalist has the chief seat in our Christian synagogue. It is a rare minister who dares assail a vice which has riches on its side. Is there a clergyman at the South who speaks against the profitable wickedness which chains three million American men ? How few at the North ! European gentility is ancient power ; American is new money hot from the stamping.

In society, money is genteel ; it is always respectable. The high places of society do not belong to ecclesiastical men, as in Rome ; to military men, as in St. Petersburg ; to men of famous family, as in England and Spain ; to men of science and literature, men of genius, as in Berlin ; but to rich men.

Money gives distinction in literature, so far as the literary class can control the public judgment. The colleges revere a rich man's son ; they name professorships after such as endow them with money, not mind. Critics respect a rich man's book ; if he has not brains, he has brass, which is better. The capitalist is admitted a member of the Academies of Arts and Sciences, of collegiate societies ; if he cannot write dissertations, he can give suppers, and there must be a material basis for science. At anniversaries, he receives the honorary degree. " 'Tis easier to weigh purses, sure, than brains." A dull scholar is expelled from college for idleness, and twenty years later returns to New England with half a million of money, and gets his degree. As he puzzles at the Latin diploma, he asks, "If I had come home poor, I wonder how long it would have taken the 'Alma Mater' to find out that I was ever a 'good scholar,' and now 'merited an honorary degree'—facts which I never knew before!"

In politics, money has more influence than in Turkey, Austria, Russia, England, or Spain. For in our politics the interest of property is preferred before all others. National legislation almost invariably favours capital, and not the labouring hand. The Federalists feared that riches would not be safe in America—the many would plunder the wealthy few. It was a groundless fear. In an industrial commonwealth, property is sure of popular protection. Where all own hayricks no one scatters firebrands. Nowhere in the world is property so secure or so much respected; for it rests on a more natural basis than elsewhere. Nowhere is wealth so powerful, in Church, Society, and State. In Kentucky and. elsewhere, it can take the murderer's neck out of the halter. It can make the foolish "wise;" the dull man "eloquent;" the mean man "honourable, one of our most prominent citizens;" the heretic "sound orthodox;" the ugly "fair;" the old man a "desirable young bridegroom." Nay, vice itself becomes virtue, and man-stealing is Christianity!

Here, nothing but the voter's naked ballot holds money in check: there are no great families with their historic tradition, as in all Europe; no bodies of literary or scientific men to oppose their genius to mere material gold. The Church is no barrier, only its servant, for when the minister depends on the wealth of his parish for support, you know the common consequence. Lying rides on obligation's back. The minister respects the hand that feeds him: "the ox knoweth his owner, and the ass his master's crib." Yet now and then a minister looks starvation in the face, and continues his unpopular service of God. No political institutions check the authority of wealth; it can bribe and buy the venal; the brave it sometimes can intimidate and starve. Money can often carry a bill through the legislature—state or national. The majority is hardly strong enough to check this pecuniary sway.

In the "most democratic" States, gold is most powerful. Thus, in fifteen States of America, three hundred thousand proprietors own thirteen hundred millions of money invested in men. In virtue thereof they control the legislation of their own States, making their institutions despotic, and not republican ; they keep the poor white man from political power, from comfort, from the natural means of education and religion ; they destroy his self-respect, and leave him nothing but his body ; from the poorest of the poor, they take away his body itself. Next they control the legislation of America ; they make the President, they appoint the Supreme Court, they control the Senate, the Representatives ; they determine the domestic and foreign policy of the nation. Finally, they affect the laws of all the other sixteen States—the Southern hand colouring the local institutions of New Haven and Boston.

That is only one example—one of many. Russia is governed by a long-descended Czar ; England by a Queen, nobles, and gentry,—men of ancient family, with culture and riches. America is ruled by a troop of men with nothing but new money and what it brings—three hundred thousand slaveholders and their servants, North and South. Boston is under their thumb ; at their command the mayor spits in the face of Massachusetts law, and plants a thousand bayonets at the people's throat. They make ball cartridges under the eaves of Faneuil Hall.

Accordingly, money is the great object of desire and pursuit. There are material reasons why this is so in many lands :—in America there are also social, political, and ecclesiastical reasons for it. "To be rich is to be blessed : poverty is damnation :" that is the popular creed.

The public looks superficially at the immediate effect of this opinion, at this exceeding and exclusive desire for riches ; they see its effect on Israel and John Jacob, on Stephen, Peter, and Robert : it makes them rich, and their children respectable and famous. Few ask, What effect will this have on the nation ? They foresee not the future evil it threatens. Nay, they do not consider how it debauches the institutions of America—ecclesiastical, academic, social, political ; how it corrupts the hearts of the people, making them prize money as the end of life, and manhood as only the means thereto, making money master, and human nature its tool or servant, but no more.

The political effect of this unnatural esteem for riches is

not at all well understood. History but too plainly tells of
the dangerous power of priests or nobles consolidated into
a class, and their united forces directed by a single able
head. The power of allied kings, concentrating whole
realms of men and money on a single point ; the effect of
armies and navies collected together and marshalled by a
single will ; is all too boldly written in the ruin of many a
State. We have often been warned against the peril from
forts, and castles, and standing armies. But the power of
consolidated riches, the peril which accumulated property
may bring upon the liberties of an industrial commonwealth, though formidably near, as yet is all unknown, all
unconsidered too. Already the consolidated property of
one-eightieth part of the population controls all the rest.

Two special causes, both exceptional and fleeting, just
now stimulate the acquisitiveness of America almost to
madness.

One is the rapid development of the art of manufacturing
the raw materials gathered from the bosom or the surface
of the earth. The invention of printing made education
and freedom possible on a large scale; one of the immediate
results thereof is this—the head briefly performs the else
long-protracted labour of the hand. Wind, water, fire,
steam, lightning, have become pliant forces to manufacture
wood, flax, cotton, wool, and all the metals. This result
is nowhere so noticeable as in New England, where education is almost universal. The New England school-house
is the machine-shop of America. What the State invests
in slates and teachers pays dividends in hard coin. This
new power over the material world, the first and unexpected commercial result of the public education of the
people, gives a great and perhaps lasting stimulus to the
pursuit of wealth. It affects the most undisciplined portions of the world,—for the educated man leaves much
rough labour for the ignorant, and enhances the demand
for the results of their toil. The thinking head raises the
wages of all mere hands. Hence arises the increased
value of slaves at the South, and the rapid immigration of
the most ignorant Irishmen to the North. They are to
the thoughtful projector what the Merrimack is to the
cotton-spinner—a rude force pliant before his will. Dr.
Faustus is the unconscious pioneer of many a pilgrimage.

The other cause is the discovery of gold in California and then in Australia. This doubles or trebles the pecuniary momentum of America. Its stimulating influence on our covetousness, accumulation, and luxury, is obvious. What further and ultimate effects it will produce I shall not now pause to inquire. When a whirlwind rises, all men can see that dust is mounting to the sky.

Besides, the form of American industry is changed. Once New England and all the North were chiefly agricultural; manufactures and commerce were conducted on a small scale; and therein each man wrought on his own account. There was a great deal of individual activity, individuality of character. Few men worked for wages. Now New England is mainly manufacturing and commercial, Vermont is the only farming State. Mechanics, men and women, work for wages; many in the employment of a single man; thousands in the pay of one company, organized by superior ability. The workman loses his independence, and is not only paid but governed also by his employer's money. His opinions and character are formed after the prescribed pattern, by the mill he works in. The old military organizations for defence or aggression brought freedom of body distinctly in peril: the new industrial organizations jeopardize spiritual individuality, all freedom of mind and conscience. New England is a monumental proof thereof.

Another change also follows: the military habits of the North are all gone. Once New England had more firelocks than householders; every man was a soldier and a marksman. Now the people have lost their taste for military discipline, and neither keep nor bear arms. Of course a few holiday soldiers, called out by a doctor, and commanded by an apothecary, can overawe the town.

The Northern, and especially the Eastern and Middle States, are the great centre of this industrial development. Here, and especially in New England, the desire for riches has become so powerful that a very large proportion of our men of the greatest practical intellect have almost exclusively turned their attention to purely productive business, to commerce and manufactures. They rarely engage in the work of politics—unprofitable and distasteful to the individual, and, at first sight, merely preservative and defensive to the community. This they shun or neglect, as the mass of men avoid military discipline.

The statutes must be made and administered by politicians. Here they are not able men. Of the forty-one New England delegates in Congress, of the six governors, of the many other professional leaders in politics, how many first-rate men are there? how many middle-sized second-rate men? The control of the national affairs passes out of the fingers of the North—which has .yet three-fifths of the population, and more than four-fifths of the speculative and practical intelligence and material wealth. The nation is controlled by the South, whose ablest men almost exclusively attend to politics. Besides, the State politics of the North fall into the hands of men quite inadequate to such a weighty trust. This mistake is as fatal as it would be in time of war to send all the able-bodied men to the plough, and the women and children to the camp. We are mismanaged at home, and dishonourably routed in the Federal capital. In the present state of the world I think no nation would be justified in turning non-resistant, tearing down its forts, disbanding its armies, melting up its guns and swords; and I am sure the North suffers sadly from devoting so large a part of its masterly, practical men to the productive work of commerce and manufactures. Her politicians are not strong enough for her own defence. In American politics the great battle of ideas and principles, yea, of measures, is to be fought. Shall we keep our Washingtons surveying land?

The national effect of this estimate and accumulation of riches is to produce a great and rapid development of the practical understanding; a great love for vulgar finery which pleases the palate or the eye; great luxury of dress, ornament, furniture. You see this in the hotels and public carriages on land and sea, in the costume of the nation, at public and private tables. Along with this there comes a certain refinement of the public taste.

But there is no proportionate culture of the higher intellectual faculties — of the reason and imagination; still less of yet nobler powers—moral, affectional, and religious. From the common school to the college, the chief things taught are arithmetic and elocution; not the art to reason and create, but the trade to calculate and express. Everything is measured by the money standard. "The protection of property is the great object of government." The politician must suit the pecuniary interest of his constituency, though at the cost of justice; the writer, author, or editor, the pecuniary interest of his readers, though at the sacrifice of truth; the minister, the pecuniary interest of his audience, though piety and morality both come to the ground. Mammon is a profitable god to worship—he gives dinners!

I think it must be confessed in the last eighty years the general moral and religious tone of the people in the free States has improved. This change comes from the natural forward tendency of mankind, the instinct of development quickened by our free institutions. But, at the same time, it is quite plain to me that the moral and religious tone of American politicians, writers, and preachers, has proportionately and absolutely gone down. You see this in the great towns: if Boston were once the "Athens of America," she is now only the "Corinth." Athens has retreated to some inland Salamis.

But, in general, this peril from the excessive pursuit of riches comes unavoidably from our position in time and space, and our consequent political institutions. It belongs to the period of transition from the old form of vicarious rule by theocratic, military, and aristocratic governments, to the personal administration of an industrial commonwealth. I do not much fear this peril, nor apprehend lasting evil from it. One of the great things which mankind now most needs is power over the material world as the basis for the higher development of our spiritual faculties. Wealth is indispensable; it is the material pulp around the spiritual seed. No nation was ever too rich, too well fed, clad, housed, and comforted. The human race still suffers from poverty, the great obstacle to our progress. Doubtless we shall make many errors in our national attempt to organize the productive forces into an industrial State, as our fathers—thousands of years ago—in organizing their destructive powers into a military state. Once, man cut his fingers with iron; he now poisons them with gold. All Christendom shares this peril, though America feels it most. She is now like a thriving man who gets rich fast, and thinks more than he ought of his money, and less of his manhood. Some misfortune, the ruin of a prodigal son perishing in quicksands of gold, will, by-and-by, convince him that riches is not the only thing in life.

II. OF THE DANGER WHICH COMES FROM THE ROMAN CATHOLIC CHURCH.

The Roman Catholic Church claims infallibility for itself, and denies spiritual freedom, liberty of mind or conscience, to its members. It is therefore the foe to all progress; it is deadly hostile to democracy. To mankind this is its first command—Submit to an external authority; subordinate your human nature to an element foreign and abhorrent thereto! It aims at absolute domination over the body and the spirit of man. The Catholic Church can never escape from the consequences of her first principle. She is the natural ally of tyrants, and the irreconcileable enemy of freedom. Individual Catholics in America, as elsewhere, are inconsistent, and favour the progress of mankind. Alas! such are exceptional; the Catholic Church has an iron logic, and consistently hates liberty in all its forms—free thought, free speech.

I quote the words of her own authors in America, recently uttered by the press. "Protestantism . . . has not and never can have any rights where Catholicity is triumphant." "We lose all the breath we expend in declaiming against bigotry and intolerance, and in favour of religious liberty." "Religious liberty [in America] is merely endured until the opposite can be carried into execution without peril to the Catholic world." "Catholicity will one day rule in America, and then religious liberty is at an end." "The very name of Liberty . . . ought to be banished from the very domain of religion." "No man has a right to choose his religion." "Catholicism is the most intolerant of creeds. It is intolerance itself, for it is the truth itself."*

The Catholic population is not great in numbers. In 1853, there were in America 1,712 churches, 1,574 priests,

---

* The above, and many more similar declarations, may be found in a little pamphlet—"Familiar Letters to John B. Fitzpatrick, the Catholic Bishop of Boston, by an Independent Irishman." Boston, 1854.

396 theological students, 32 bishops, 7 archbishops, church-property worth about \$10,000,000, and 1,728,000 Catholics. But most of them are of the Celtic stock, which has never much favoured Protestantism or individual liberty in religion; and in this respect is widely distinguished from the Teutonic population, who have the strongest ethnological instinct for personal freedom.

Besides, the Catholics are governed with absolute rigour by their clergy, who are celibate priests, a social caste by themselves, not sympathizing with mankind, but emasculated of the natural humanities of our race. There are exceptional men amongst them, but such seems to be the rule with the class of Catholic priests in America. They are united into one compact body, with complete corporate unity of action, and ruled despotically by their bishops, archbishops, and Pope. The Catholic worshipper is not to think, but to believe and obey; the priest not to reason and consider, but to proclaim and command; the voter is not to inquire and examine, but to deposit his ballot as the ecclesiastical authority directs. The better religious orders do not visit America; the Jesuits, the most subtle enemies of humanity, come in abundance; some are known, others stealthily prowl about the land, all the more dangerous for their disguise. They all act under the direction of a single head. One shrewd Protestant minister may be equal to one Jesuit, but no ten or forty Protestant ministers is a match for a combination of ten Jesuits, bred to the business of deception, knowing no allegiance to truth or justice, consciously disregarding the higher law of God, with the notorious maxim that "the end justifies the means," bound to their order by the most stringent oath, and devoted to the worst purposes of the Catholic Church.

All these priests owe allegiance to a foreign head. It is not an American Church; it is Roman, not free, individual, but despotic; nay, in its designs not so much human as merely Papal.

The Catholic Church opposes everything which favours democracy and the natural rights of man. It hates our free churches, free press, and, above all, our free schools. No owl more shuns the light. It hates the rule of majorities, the voice of the people; it loves violence, force, and blood.

The Catholic clergy are on the side of Slavery. They

find it is the dominant power, and pay court thereto that they may rise by its help. They love Slavery itself; it is an institution thoroughly congenial to them, consistent with the first principles of their Church. Their Jesuit leaders think it is "an ulcer which will eat up the Republic," and so stimulate and foster it for the ruin of Democracy, the deadliest foe of the Roman hierarchy.

Besides, most of the Catholics are the victims of oppression,—poor, illiterate, oppressed, and often vicious. Their circumstances have ground the humanity out of them. No sect furnishes half so many criminals—victims of society before they become its foes; no sect has so little philanthropy; none is so greedy to oppress. All this is natural. The lower you go down the coarser and more cruel do you find the human being.

I am told there is not in all America a single Catholic newspaper hostile to Slavery; not one opposed to tyranny in general; not one that takes sides with the oppressed in Europe. There is not in America a man born and bred in the Catholic Church, who is eminent for philosophy, science, literature, or art; none distinguished for philanthropy! The water tastes of the fountain.

Catholic votes are in the market; the bishops can dispose of them—politicians will make their bid. Shall it be the sacrifice of the free schools? of other noble institutions? In some States it seems not unlikely.

I do not think our leading men see all this danger. But the baneful influence of the Church of the dark ages begins to show itself in the press, in the schools, and still more in the politics of America. Yet I am glad the Catholics come here. Let America be an asylum for the poor and the down-trodden of all lands; let the Irish ships, reeking with misery, land their human burdens in our harbours. The continent is wide enough for all. I rejoice that in America there is no national form of religion;—let the Jew, the Chinese Buddhist, the savage Indian, the Mormon, the Protestant, and the Catholic have free opportunity to be faithful each to his own conscience. Let the American Catholic have his bishops, his archbishops, and his Pope, his Jesuits, his convents, his nunneries, his celibate priesthood of hard drinkers, if he will. Let him oppose the public education of the people; oppose the press, the meeting-house, and the ballot-box; nay, oppose temperance and religion, if he likes. If, with truth and justice on our side, the few Catholics can overcome the many Protestants, we deserve defeat. We should be false to the first principles of democratic theory, if we did not grant them their unalienable rights. Let there be no tyranny; let us pay the Catholics good for ill; and cast out Satan by the finger of God, not by the Prince of Devils. This peril is easily mastered. The Catholic Church has still many lessons to offer the Protestants.

III. Of the danger from the Idea that there is no Higher Law above the Statutes of Men.

Of late years, it has been industriously taught in America that there is no law of nature superior to the statutes which men enact; that politics are not amenable to conscience or to God. Accordingly, the American Congress knows no check in legislation but the Constitution of the United States and the will of the majority; none in the Constitution of the Universe and the will of God. The atheistic idea of the Jesuits, that the end justifies the means, is made the first principle in American politics. Hence it has been repeatedly declared by "prominent clergymen" that politics should not be treated of in the pulpit; they are not amenable to religion; Christianity has nothing to do with making or administering the laws. When the Pharisees and Sadducees have silenced the prophet and the apostle, it is not difficult to make men believe that Machiavelli is a great saint, and Jesuitism the revealed religion of politics! Let the legislators make what wicked laws they will against the rights of man; the priest of commerce is to say nothing. Nay, the legislators themselves are never to refer to justice and the eternal right, only to the expediency of the hour.

Then when the statute is made, the magistrate is not to ask if it be just, he is only to execute it; the people are to obey and help enforce the wicked enactment, never asking if it be right. The highest virtue in the people is—"unquestioning submission to the Constitution;" or, when the statute violates their conscience, to do "a disagreeable duty!" Thus the political action of the people is exempted from the jurisdiction of God and His natural moral law! "Christianity has nothing to do with politics!"

Within a few years this doctrine has been taught in a great variety of forms. At first it came in with evil laws, simply as the occasional support of a measure; at length it is announced as a principle. It has taken a deep hold on the educated classes of the community; for our "superior education" is almost wholly of the intellect, and of only its humbler powers. It appears among the lawyers, the politicians, the editors, and the ministers. Some deny the natural distinction between right and wrong. "Justice," is a matter of convention; things are not "true," but "agreed upon;" not "right," only "assented to." There is no "moral obligation." Government rests on a compact, having its ultimate foundation on the caprice of men, not in their moral nature. What are called natural rights are only certain conveniences agreed upon amongst men; legal fictions—their recognition is their essence, they are the creatures of a compact. Property has no foundation in the nature of things; it may consist of whatever the legislature determines—land, cattle, food, clothing; or of men, women, and children. Dives may own Lazarus as well as the dogs who serve him at the gate. There is no political morality, only political economy.

This conclusion arises from the philosophy of Hobbes and Filmer; yes, from the first principles of Locke and Rousseau. It is one of the worst results of materialism and practical atheism. It takes different forms in different nations. In a monarchy it has for its axiom, "The King can do no wrong; he is the Norm of Law—*Vox Regis vox Dei.*" In a Democracy, "The majority can do no wrong; they are the Norm of Law—*Vox Populi vox Dei.*" So the Statute becomes an idol; loyalty takes the place of religion, and despotism becomes enthroned on the necks of the people.

It is not surprising that this doctrine should be taught from the pulpit in Catholic countries—it is conformable to the general conduct of the Roman Church. It belongs also with the sensational philosophy which has yet done so much to break to pieces the theology of the Dark Ages;—and does not astonish one in the sects which build thereon. But at first sight it seems amazing that American Christians of the Puritanic stock, with a philosophy that transcends sensationalism, should prove false to the only principle which at once justifies the conduct of Jesus, of Luther, and the Puritans themselves. For certainly if obedience to the established law be the highest virtue, then the Patriots and Pilgrims of New England, the Reformers of the Church, the glorious company of the Apostles, the goodly fellowship of the Prophets, and the noble army of martyrs,—nay, Jesus himself,—were only criminals and traitors. To appreciate this denial of the first principle of all religion, it would be necessary to go deep into the theology of Christendom, and touch the fatal error of all the three parties just referred to. For that there is now no time.

One of the consequences of this atheistic denial of the natural foundation of human laws is, the preponderance of parties. An opinion before it becomes a law, while it is yet a tendency, becomes organized into a faction, or party. Members of the party feel the same loyalty thereto which narrow patriots feel for their nation, or bigots for their sect; they give up their mind and conscience to their party. So fidelity to their party, right or wrong, is deemed a great political virtue; the individual member is bound by the party opinion. Thus is the private conscience still further debauched by the second act in this atheistic popular tragedy.

Thus both national and party politics are taken out of the jurisdiction of morals, declared not amenable to conscience: in other words, are left to the control of political Jesuits. An American may read the natural result of such principles in the downfall of the Grecian and Italian Republics, or wait to behold it in his own land.

IV. OF THE DANGERS FROM THE INSTITUTION OF SLAVERY WHICH RESTS ON THIS FALSE IDEA.

Slavery is the child of Violence and Atheism. Brute material force is its father: the atheistic idea that there is no law of God above the passions of men—that is the mother of it. I have lately spoken so long, so often, and with such publicity, both of speech and print, respecting the extent of Slavery in America, and its constant advance since 1788, that I shall pass over all that theme, and speak

K 2

more directly of the present danger it brings upon our freedom.

There can be no national welfare without national unity of action. That cannot take place unless there is national unity of idea in fundamentals. Without this a nation is a "house divided against itself;" of course it cannot stand. It is what mechanics call a figure without equilibrium; the different parts thereof do not balance.

Now, in the American State there are two distinct ideas —Freedom and Slavery.

The idea of freedom first got a national expression seventy-eight years ago next Tuesday. Here it is. I put it in a philosophic form. There are five points to it.

First. All men are endowed by their Creator with certain natural rights, amongst which is the right to life, liberty, and the pursuit of happiness.

Second. These rights are unalienable; they can be alienated and forfeited only by the possessor thereof; the father cannot alienate them for the son, nor the son for the father; nor the husband for the wife, nor the wife for the husband; nor the strong for the weak, nor the weak for the strong; nor the few for the many, nor the many for the few; and so on.

Third. In respect to these all men are equal; the rich man has not more, and the poor less; the strong man has not more, and the weak man less:—all are exactly equal in these rights, however unequal in their powers.

Fourth. It is the function of government to secure these natural, unalienable, and equal rights to every man.

Fifth. Government derives all its divine right from its conformity with these ideas, all its human sanction from the consent of the governed.

That is the idea of Freedom. I used to call it "the American idea;" it was when I was younger than I am to-day. It is derived from human nature; it rests on the immutable laws of God; it is part of the natural religion of mankind. It demands a government after natural justice, which is the point common between the conscience of God and the conscience of mankind, the point common also between the interests of one man and of all men.

Now this government, just in its substance, in its form must be democratic: that is to say, the government of all, by all, and for all. You see what consequences must follow from such an idea, and the attempt to re-enact the law of God into political institutions. There will follow the freedom of the people, respect for every natural right of all men, the rights of their body, and of their spirit— the rights of mind and conscience, heart and soul. There must be some restraint—as of children by their parents, as of bad men by good men; but it will be restraint for the joint good of all parties concerned; not restraint for the exclusive benefit of the restrainer. The ultimate consequence of this will be the material and spiritual welfare of all — riches, comfort, noble manhood, all desirable things.

That is the idea of Freedom. It appears in the Declaration of Independence; it re-appears in the Preamble to the American Constitution, which aims " to establish justice, insure domestic tranquillity, provide for the common defence, promote the general welfare, and secure the blessings of liberty." That is a religious idea ; and when men pray for the " reign of justice" and the " kingdom of heaven," to come on earth politically, I suppose they mean that there may be a commonwealth where every man has his natural rights of mind, body, and estate.

Next is the idea of Slavery. Here it is. I put it also in a philosophic form. There are three points which I make.

First. There are no natural, unalienable, and equal rights, wherewith men are endowed by their Creator ; no natural, unalienable, and equal right to life, liberty, and the pursuit of happiness.

Second. There is a great diversity of powers, and in virtue thereof the strong man may rule and oppress, enslave and ruin the weak, for his interest and against theirs.

Third. There is no natural law of God to forbid the strong to oppress the weak, and enslave and ruin the weak.

That is the idea of Slavery. It has never got a national expression in America ; it has never been laid down as a principle in any act of the American people, nor in any single State, so far as I know. All profess the opposite;

but it is involved in the measures of both State and nation. This idea is founded in the selfishness of man; it is atheistic.

The idea must lead to a corresponding government; that will be unjust in its substance—for it will depend not on natural right, but on personal force; not on the Constitution of the universe, but on the compact of men. It is the abnegation of God in the universe and of conscience in man. Its form will be despotism—the government of all by a part, for the sake of a part. It may be a single-headed despotism, or a despotism of many heads; but whether a Cyclops or a Hydra, is is alike "the abomination which maketh desolate." Its ultimate consequence is plain to foresee—poverty to a nation, misery, ruin.

At first Slavery came as a measure; nothing was said about it as a principle. But in a country full of school-masters, legislatures, newspapers, talking men—a measure without a principle to bear it up is like a single twig of willow cast out on a wooden floor; there is nothing for it to grow by; it will die. So of late the principle has been boldly avowed. Mr. Calhoun denied the self-evident truths of the Declaration of Independence; denied the natural, unalienable, and equal rights of man. Many since have done the same—political, literary, and mercantile men, and, of course, ecclesiastical men; there are enough of them always in the market. All parts of the idea of Slavery have been affirmed by prominent men at the North and the South. It has been acted on in the formation of the constitution of every slave State, and in the passage of many of its laws. It lies at the basis of a great deal of national legislation.

Hear the opinions of some of our Southern patriots: "Slavery is coeval with society:" "It was commended by God's chosen theocracy, and sanctioned by His Apostles in the Christian Church." All ancient literature "is the literature of slaveholders;" "Rome and Greece owed their literary and national greatness exclusively to the institution of Slavery;" "Slavery is as necessary for the welfare of the Southern States as sunshine is for the flowers of the prairies;" "A noble and necessary institution of God's creation."* "Nature is the mother and protector of

* *Richmond Examiner* for June 30, 1854.

THE RIGHTS OF MAN IN AMERICA.

Slavery;" "Domestic Slavery is not only *natural* and *necessary*, but a great blessing." "Free society is a sad and signal failure;" "it does well enough in a new country." "Free society has become diseased by abolishing Slavery. It can only be restored to pristine health, happiness, and prosperity by re-instituting Slavery." "Slavery may be administered under a new name." "Free society is a monstrosity. Like all monsters it will be short-lived. We dare and do vindicate Slavery in the abstract." The negro "needs a master to protect and govern him ; so do the ignorant poor in old countries."*

"There is no moral wrong in Slavery;" it "is the normal condition of human society." "The benefits and advantages which so far have resulted from this institution we take as lights to guide us to the brighter truths of its future history." "We belong to that society of which Slavery is the distinguishing element, and we are not ashamed of it. We find it marked by every evidence of Divine approval."†

These two ideas are now fairly on foot. They are hostile ; they are both mutually invasive and destructive. They are in exact opposition to each other, and the nation which embodies these two is not a figure of equilibrium. As both are active forces in the minds of men, and as each idea tends to become a fact—a universal and exclusive fact—as men with these ideas organize into parties as a means to make their idea into a fact, it follows that there must not only be strife amongst philosophical men about these antagonistic principles and ideas, but a strife of practical men about corresponding facts and measures. So the quarrel, if not otherwise ended, will pass from words to what seems more serious ; and one will overcome the other.

So long as these two ideas exist in the nation as two political forces there is no national unity of idea, of course, no unity of action. For there is no centre of gravity common to Freedom and Slavery. They will not compose an equilibrious figure. You may cry, "Peace ! peace !"

* *Richmond Examiner*, June 23, 1854.
† *Charleston Standard* (S.C.), June 21, 1854.

but so long as these two antagonistic ideas remain, each
seeking to organize itself and get exclusive power, there
is no peace; there can be none.

The question before the nation to day is, Which shall
prevail—the idea and fact of Freedom, or the idea and the
fact of Slavery; Freedom, exclusive and universal, or Slavery,
exclusive and universal? The question is not merely,
Shall the African be bond or free? but shall America be a
democracy or a despotism? For nothing is so remorseless
as an idea, and no logic is so strong as the historical
development of a national idea by millions of men. A
measure is nothing without its principle. The idea which
allows Slavery in South Carolina will establish it also in
New England. The bondage of a black man in Alexandria
imperils every white woman's daughter in Boston. You
cannot escape the consequences of a first principle more
than you can "take the leap of Niagara and stop when
half-way down." The principle which recognises Slavery
in the constitution of the United States would make all
America a despotism; while the principle which made
John Quincy Adams a free man would extirpate Slavery
from Louisiana and Texas. It is plain America cannot
long hold these two contradictions in the national consciousness. Equilibrium must come.

Now there are three possible ways of settling the quarrel
between these two ideas; only three. The categories are
exhaustive.

This is the first: The discord may rend the nation
asunder and the two elements separate and become distinct
nations—a despotism with the idea of Slavery, a democracy
with the idea of Freedom. Then each will be an equilibrious figure. The Anglo-Saxon despotism may go to
ruin on its own account, while the Anglo-Saxon democracy
marches on to national welfare. That is the first hypothesis.

Or, second: The idea of Freedom may destroy Slavery,
with all its accidents—attendant and consequent. Then
the nation may have unity of idea, and so a unity of
action, and become a harmonious whole, a unit of freedom,
a great industrial democracy, re-enacting the laws of God,
and pursuing its way, continually attaining greater degrees

of freedom and prosperity. That is the second hypothesis.

Here is the third: The idea of Slavery may destroy
Freedom, with all its accidents—attendant and consequent.
Then the nation will become an integer; only it will be a
unit of despotism. This involves, of course, the destructive revolution of all our liberal institutions, State as well
as national. Democracy must go down; the free press
go down; the free church go down; the free school go
down. There must be an industrial despotism, which will
soon become a military despotism. Popular legislation
must end; the Federal Congress will be a club of officials,
like Nero's senate, which voted his horse first consul. The
State legislature will be a knot of commissioners, tide-
waiters, postmasters, district attorneys, deputy-marshals.
The town-meeting will be a gang of government officers,
like the "Marshal's Guard," revolvers in their pockets,
soldiers at their back. The *Habeas Corpus* will be at an
end; trial by jury never heard of, and open courts as
common in America as in Spain or Rome. Commissioners
Curtis, Loring, and Kane will not be exceptional men;
there will be no other "judges;" all courts, courts of the
kidnapper; all process summary; all cases decided by the
will of the Government; arbitrary force the only rule.
The constable will disappear, the soldier come forth. All
newspapers will be like the "Satanic press" of Boston
and New York, like the journal of St. Petersburg, or the
Diario Romano, which tell lies when the ruler commands,
or tell truth when he insists upon it. Then the wicked
will walk on every side, for the vilest of men will be
exalted, and America, become the mock and scorn and
hissing of the nations, will go down to worse shame than
was ever heaped upon Sodom; for with her lust for wealth,
land, and power, she will also have committed the crime
against nature. Then America will be another Italy,
Greece, Asia Minor, yea, like Gomorrah—for the Dead
Sea will have settled down upon us with nothing living
in its breast, and the rulers will proclaim peace where
they have made solitude.

Which of these three hypotheses shall we take?

I. Will there be a separation of the two elements, and

a formation of two distinct States,—Freedom with democracy, and Slavery with a tendency to despotism? That
may save one half the nation, and leave the other to voluntary ruin.   Certainly it is better to enter into life halt or
maimed, rather than having two hands and two feet to be
cast into everlasting fire.

Now, I do not suppose it is possible for the Anglo-Saxons
of America to remain as one nation for a great many years.
Suppose we become harmonious and prosper abundantly :
when there are a hundred millions on the Atlantic slope,
another hundred millions in the Mississippi Valley, a third
hundred millions on the Pacific slope, and a fourth hundred
millions in South America,—it is not likely that all these
will hold together.   We shall be too wide spread.   And,
besides, it is not according to the disposition of the Teutonic
family to aggregate into one great State any very large
body of men ; division, not conglomeration, is after the ethnologic instinct and the historical custom of the Teutonic
family, and especially of its Anglo-Saxon tribe.   We do
not like centralization of power, but have such strong individuality that we prefer local self-government ; we are
social, not gregarious like the Celtic family.   I, therefore,
do not look on the union of the States as a thing that is
likely to last a great length of time, under any circumstances.   I doubt if any part of the nation will desire it a
hundred years hence.

True, there are causes which tend to keep us united :
community of ethnologic origin—fifteen millions are Anglo-
Saxon ; — unity of language, literature, religion ; historic
and legal traditions, and commercial interest.   But all
these may easily be overcome, and doubtless will be.   So a
dissolution of the great Anglo-Saxon State seems likely to
take place, when the territory is spread so wide that there
is a practical inconvenience in balancing the nation on a
single governmental point ; when the numbers are so great
that we require many centres of legislative and administrative action in order to secure individual freedom of the
parts, as well as national unity of the whole ; or when the
Federal Government shall become so corrupt that the
trunk will not sustain the limbs.   Then the branches
which make up this great American banyan-tree will
separate from the rotten primeval trunk, draw their sup-

port from their own local roots, and spread into great and independent trees. All this may take place without fighting. Massachusetts and Maine were once a single State; now friendly sisters.

But I do not think this "dissolution•of the Union" will take place immediately, or very soon. For America is not now ruled—as it is commonly thought—either by the mass of men who follow their national, ethnological, and human instincts; or by a few far-sighted men of genius for politics, who consciously obey the Law of God made clear in their own masterly mind and conscience, and make statutes in advance of the calculation or even the instincts of the people, and so manage the ship of State that every occasional tack is on a great circle of the Universe, a right line of justice, and therefore the shortest way to welfare: but by two very different classes of men; — by mercantile men, who covet money, actual or expectant capitalists; and by political men, who want power, actual or expectant office-holders. These appear diverse; but there is a strong unanimity between the two;—for the mercantile men want money as a means of power, and the political men power as a means of money. There are noble men in both classes, exceptional, not instantial, men with great riches even, and great office. But as a class, these men are not above the average morality of the people, often below it: they have no deep, religious faith, which leads them to trust the Higher Law of God. They do not look for principles that are right, conformable to the constitution of the universe, and so creative of the nation's permanent welfare; but only for expedient measures, productive to themselves of selfish money or selfish power. In general, they have the character of adventurers, the aims of adventurers, the morals of adventurers; they begin poor, and of course obscure, and are then "democratic," and hurrah for the people: "Down with the powerful and the rich" is the private maxim of their heart. If they are successful, and become rich, famous, attaining high office, they commonly despise the people: "Down with the people!" is the axiom of their heart—only they dare not say it; for there are so many others with the same selfishness, who have not yet achieved their end, and raise the opposite cry. The line of the nation's course is a resultant of the compound selfishness of these two classes.

From these two, with their mercantile and political selfishness, we are to expect no comprehensive morality, which
will secure the rights of mankind; no comprehensive
policy, which will secure expedient measures for a long
time. Both will unite in what serves their apparent interest, brings money to the trader, power to the politician,
—whatever be the consequence to the country.

As things now are, the Union favours the schemes of
both of these classes of men; thereby the politician gets
power, the trader makes money.

If the Union were to be dissolved and a great Northern
Commonwealth were to be organized, with the idea of
freedom, three quarters of the politicians, Federal and
State, would pass into contempt and oblivion; all that
class of Northern demagogues who scoff at God's Law,
such as filled the offices of the late Whig administration in
its day of power, or as fill the offices of the Democratic
administration to-day—they would drop down so deep that
no plummet would ever reach them; you would never hear
of them again.

Gratitude is not a very common virtue; but gratitude
to the hand of Slavery, which feeds these creatures, is their
sole and single moral excellence; they have that form of
gratitude. When the hand of Slavery is cut off, that class
of men will perish just as caterpillars die when, some day
in May, the farmer cuts off from the old tree a great branch
to graft in a better fruit. The caterpillars will not vote
for the grafting. That class of men will go for the Union
while it serves them.

Look at the other class. Property is safe in America :
and why ? Because we have aimed to establish a government on natural rights, and property is a natural right;
say oligarchic Blackstone and socialistic Proudhon what
they may, property is not the mere creature of compact, or
the child of robbery; it is founded in the nature of man.
It has a very great and important function to perform.
Nowhere in the world is it so much respected as here.

But there is one kind of property which is not safe just
now :—Property in men. It is the only kind of property
which is purely the creature of violence and law; it has
no root in itself.

Now, the Union protects that " property." There are

three hundred thousand slave-holders, owning thirteen hundred millions of dollars invested in men. Their wealth depends on the Union; destroy that, and their unnatural property will take to itself legs and run off, seeking liberty by flight, or else stay at home and, like an Anglo-Saxon, take to itself firebrands and swords, and burn down the master's house and cut the master's throat. So the slave-holder wants the Union; he makes money by it. Slavery is unprofitable to the nation. No three millions earn so little as the three million slaves. It is costly to every State. But it enriches the owner of the slaves. The South is agricultural; that is all. She raises cotton, sugar, and corn; she has no commerce, no manufactures, no mining. The North has mills, ships, mines, manufactures; buys and sells for the South, and makes money by what impoverishes the South. So all the great commercial centres of the North are in favour of Union, in favour of Slavery. The instinct of American trade just now is hostile to American freedom. The money power and the slave power go hand in hand. Of course such editors and ministers as are only the tools of the money power, or the slave power, will be fond of "Union at all hazards." They will sell their mothers to keep it. Now these are the controlling classes of men; these ministers and editors are the mouthpieces of these controlling classes of men; and as these classes make money and power out of the Union, for the present I think the Union will hold together. Yet I know very well that there are causes now at work which embitter the minds of men, and which, if much enforced, will so exasperate the North that we shall rend the Union asunder at a blow. That I think not likely to take place, for the South sees the peril and its own ruin.

II. The next hypothesis is, Freedom may triumph over Slavery. That was the expectation once, at the time of the Declaration of Independence; nay, at the formation of the Constitution. But only two national steps have been taken against Slavery since then — one the Ordinance of 1787, the other the abolition of the African Slave-Trade; really that was done in 1788, formally twenty years after. In the individual States, the white man's freedom enlarges every year; but the Federal Government becomes more and more addicted to Slavery. This hypothesis does not seem very likely to be adopted.

III. Shall Slavery destroy Freedom? It looks very much like it. Here are nine great steps, openly taken since '87, in favour of Slavery. First, America put Slavery into the Constitution. Second, out of old soil she made four new slave States. Third, America, in 1793, adopted Slavery as a Federal institution, and guaranteed her protection for that kind of property as for no other. Fourth, America bought the Louisiana territory in 1803, and put Slavery into it. Fifth, she thence made Louisiana, Missouri, and then Arkansas slave States. Sixth, she made Slavery perpetual in Florida. Seventh, she annexed Texas. Eighth, she fought the Mexican war, and plundered a feeble sister republic of California, Utah, and New Mexico, to get more slave soil. Ninth, America gave ten millions of money to Texas to support Slavery, passed the Fugitive Slave Bill, and has since kidnapped men in New England, New York, New Jersey, Pennsylvania, Ohio, Michigan, Wisconsin, Illinois, Indiana, in all the East, in all the West, in all the Middle States. All the great cities have kidnapped their own citizens. Professional slave-hunters are members of New England churches; kidnappers sit down at the Lord's table in the city of Cotton, Chauncey, and Mayhew. In this very year, before it is half through, America has taken two more steps for the destruction of Freedom. The repeal of the Missouri compromise and the enslavement of Nebraska: that is the tenth step. Here is the eleventh: The Mexican treaty, giving away ten millions of dollars and buying a little strip of worthless land, solely that it may serve the cause of Slavery.

Here are eleven great steps openly taken towards the ruin of liberty in America. Are these the worst? Very far from it! Yet more dangerous things have been done in secret.

I. Slavery has corrupted the mercantile class. Almost all the leading merchants of the North are pro-Slavery men. They hate freedom, hate your freedom and mine! This is the only Christian country in which commerce is hostile to freedom.

II. See the corruption of the political class. There are forty thousand officers of the Federal Government. Look at them in Boston—their character is as well known as this Hall. Read their journals in this city—do you catch a whisper of freedom in them? Slavery has sought its menial servants—men basely born and basely bred : it has corrupted them still further, and put them in office. America, like Russia, is the country for mean men to thrive in. Give him time and mire enough, a worm can crawl as high as an eagle flies. State rights are sacrificed at the North; centralization goes on with rapid strides; State laws are trodden under foot.* The Northern President is all for Slavery. The Northern members of the Cabinet are for Slavery; in the Senate, fourteen Northern Democrats were for the enslavement of Nebraska; in the House of Representatives, forty-four Northern Democrats voted for the bill,—fourteen in the Senate, forty-four in the House, fifty-eight Northern men voted against the conscience of the North and the law of God. Only eight men out of all the South could be found friendly to justice and false to their own local idea of injustice. The present administration, with its supple tools of tyranny, came into office while the cry of "No Higher Law" was echoing through the land !

III. Slavery has debauched the Press. How many leading journals of commerce and politics in the great cities do you know that are friendly to Freedom and opposed to Slavery? Out of the five large daily commercial papers in Boston, Whig or Democratic, I know of only one that has spoken a word for freedom this great while. The American newspapers are poor defenders of American liberty. Listen to one of them, speaking of the last kidnapping in Boston : "We shall need to employ the same measures of coercion as are necessary in monarchical countries." There is always some one ready to do the basest deeds. Yet there are some noble journals—

* While this volume is passing through the press, another example of this same corruption appears. The Senate passes a bill to protect United States officers engaged in kidnapping citizens of the free States, from the justice of the people. Such kidnappers are to be tried in the kidnappers' court.

political and commercial; such as the *New York Tribune* and *Evening Post*.

IV. Then our colleges and schools are corrupted by Slavery. I do not know of five colleges in all the North which publicly appear on the side of Freedom. What the hearts of the presidents and professors are, God knows, not I. The great crime against humanity, practical atheism, found ready support in Northern colleges, in 1850 and 1851. Once, the common reading books of our schools were full of noble words. Read the school-books now made by Yankee pedlers of literature, and what liberal ideas do you find there? They are meant for the Southern market. Slavery must not be offended!

V. Slavery has corrupted the churches! There are twenty-eight thousand Protestant clergymen in the United States. There are noble hearts, true and just men among them, who have fearlessly borne witness to the truth. I need not mention their names. Alas! they are not very numerous; I should not have to go over my fingers many times to count them all. I honour these exceptional men. Some of them are old, far older than I am; older than my father need have been; some of them are far younger than I; nay, some of them younger than my children might be: and I honour these men for the fearless testimony which they have borne—the old, the middle-aged, and the young. But they are very exceptional men. Is there a minister in the South who preaches against Slavery? How few in all the North!

Look and see the condition of the Sunday schools. In 1853, the Episcopal Methodists had 9,438 Sunday schools; 102,732 Sunday school teachers; 525,008 scholars. There is not an anti-Slavery Sunday school in the compass of the Methodist Episcopal church. Last year, in New York, they issued, on an average, two thousand bound volumes every day in the year, not a line against Slavery in them. They printed also two thousand pamphlets every day; there is not a line in them all against Slavery; they printed more than two hundred and forty million pages of Sunday school books, not a line against Slavery in them all; not a line showing that it is wicked to buy and sell a man, for whom, according to the Methodist Episcopal Church, Christ died !

The Orthodox Sunday School Union spent last year $248,201 ; not a cent against Slavery, our great national sin. They print books by the million. Only one of them contains a word against Slavery; that is Cowper's *Task*, which contains these words—my mother taught them to me when I was a little boy, and sat in her lap :—

> " I would not have a slave to till my ground,
>   To carry me, to fan me when I sleep,
>   And tremble when I wake, for all the wealth
>   That sinews, bought and sold, have ever earned ! "

You all know it : if you do not, you had better learn and teach it to your children. That is the only anti-Slavery work they print. Once they published a book written by Mr. Gallaudet, which related the story, I think, of the selling of Joseph: at any rate, it showed that Egyptian Slavery was wrong. A little girl in a Sunday school in one of the Southern States one day said to her teacher, "If it was wrong to make Joseph a slave, why is it not wrong to make Dinah, and Sambo, and Chloe slaves?" The Sunday school teacher and the church took the alarm, and complained of the Sunday School Union : "You are poisoning the South with your religion, telling the children that Slavery is wicked." It was a serious thing, "dissolution of the Union," "levying war," or at least, "misdemeanor," for aught I know, "obstructing an officer of the United States." What do you think the Sunday School Union did ? It suppressed the book! It printed one Sunday school book which had a line against Egyptian Slavery and then suppressed it ! and it cannot be had to-day. Amid all their million books, there is not a line against Slavery, save what Cowper sung. There are five million Sunday school scholars in the United States, and there is not a Sunday school manual which has got a word against Slavery in it.

You all know the American Tract Society. Last year the American Tract Society in Boston spent $79,983.46 ; it visited more than fourteen thousand families ; it distributed 3,334,920 tracts—not a word against Slavery in them all. The American Tract Society in New York last year visited 568,000 families, containing three million persons; it spent for home purposes $406,707; for foreign purposes $422,294; it distributed tracts in English, French, German, Dutch, Danish, Swedish, Norwegian, Italian, Hungarian, and Welsh—and it did not print one single line, nor whisper a single word against this great national sin of Slavery! Nay, worse:—if it finds English books which suit its general purpose, but containing matter adverse to Slavery, it strikes out all the anti-Slavery matter, then prints and circulates the book. Is the Tract Society also managed by Jesuits from the Roman Church?

At this day, 600,000 slaves are directly and personally owned by men who are called "professing Christians," "members in good fellowship" of the churches of this land; 80,000 owned by Presbyterians, 225,000 by Baptists, 250,000 owned by Methodists:—600,000 slaves in this land owned by men who profess themselves Christians, and in churches sit down to take the Lord's Supper, in the name of Christ and God! There are ministers who own their fellow-men—"bought with a price."

Does not this look as if Slavery were to triumph over Freedom?

VI. Slavery corrupts the judicial class. In America, especially in New England, no class of men has been so much respected as the judges; and for this reason: we have had wise, learned, excellent men for our judges; men who reverenced the higher law of God, and sought by human statutes to execute justice. You all know their venerable names, and how reverentially we have looked up to them. Many of them are dead; some are still living, and their hoary hairs are a crown of glory on a judicial life, without judicial blot. But of late Slavery has put a different class of men on the benches of the Federal Courts —mere tools of the Government; creatures which get their appointment as pay for past political service, and as pay in advance for iniquity not yet accomplished. You see the consequences. Note the zeal of the Federal Judges to execute iniquity by statute and destroy liberty. See how ready they are to support the Fugitive Slave Bill, which tramples on the spirit of the Constitution, and its letter too; which outrages justice and violates the most sacred principles and precepts of Christianity. Not a United States judge, circuit or district, has uttered one

word against that "bill of abominations." Nay, how
greedy they are to get victims under it! No wolf loves
better to rend a lamb into fragments than these judges to
kidnap a Fugitive Slave, and punish any man who dares to
speak against it. You know what has happened in Fugitive Slave Bill Courts. You remember the "miraculous"
rescue of Shadrach; the peaceable snatching of a man from
the hands of a cowardly kidnapper was "high treason;"
it was "levying war." You remember the "trial" of the
rescuers! Judge Sprague's charge to the Grand Jury,
that, if they thought the question was which they ought
to obey, the law of man or the law of God, then they must
"obey both!" serve God and Mammon, Christ and the
devil, in the same act! You remember the "trial," the
"ruling" of the Bench, the swearing on the stand, the
witness coming back to alter and "enlarge his testimony"
and have another gird at the prisoner! You have not
forgotten the trials before Judge Kane at Philadelphia, and
Judge Grier at Christiana and Wilkesbarre.

These are natural results of causes well known. You
cannot escape a principle. Enslave a negro, will you?—
you doom to bondage your own sons and daughters, by
your own act.

Do you forget the Union meeting in Faneuil Hall,
November 26th, 1850, the Tuesday before Thanksgiving
Day? It was called to indorse the Fugitive Slave Bill—a
meeting to promote the stealing of men in Boston, of your
fellow-worshippers and my parishioners. Do you remember
the Democratic Herods and Whig Pilates, who were made
friends that day, melted into one unity of despotism,
in order that they might enslave men? They had unity
of idea and unity of action, that day. Do you remember
the speeches of Mr. Curtis and Mr. Hallett; their yelp
against the unalienable rights of men; their howl at God's
Higher Law? The worser half of that platform is now the
United States Court;—the Fugitive Slave Bill judge, the
United States attorney. They got their offices for their
political services past and for their character—very fitting
reward to very fitting men! A man professes a fondness
for kidnapping, hurrahs for it in Faneuil Hall:—give him
the United States judgeship; make him United States
attorney—fit to fit! When Slavery dispenses offices,

L 2

every service rendered to despotism is well paid. Men
with foreheads of brass, with iron elbows, with consciences
of gum elastic, whose chief commandment of their law,
their prophets, and their gospel, is to

> "—— crook the pregnant hinges of the knee,
>   Where thrift may follow fawning;"

verily they shall have their reward! They shall become
Fugitive Slave Bill judges; yea, attorneys of the United
States!

In 1836, a poor slave girl named Med, who had been
brought from Louisiana to Boston by her master, sued for
her freedom in the courts of Massachusetts. Mr. Benjamin
R. Curtis appeared as the slave-hunter's counsel, long, and
stoutly, and learnedly contending that she should not receive her freedom by the laws, constitution, and usages of
this Commonwealth, but should be sent back to eternal
bondage.* On the 7th of March, 1850, Mr. Webster
made his speech against Freedom, so fatal to himself; but
soon after found such a fire in his rear that he must
return to Massachusetts to rescue his own popularity—
then apparently in great peril. On the 29th of April,
the same Mr. Curtis, faithful to his proclivities towards
Slavery, made a public address to the apostate senator, at
the Revere House, and expressed his "abounding gratitude for the ability and fidelity" which Mr. Webster had
"brought to the defence of the Constitution and the Union;"
praising him as "eminently vigilant, wise, and faithful to
our country, without shadow of turning." At the Union
meeting in Faneuil Hall (Nov. 26th), Mr. Curtis declared
the fugitive slaves "a class of foreigners," "with whose
rights Massachusetts has nothing to do. It is enough for
us that they have no right to be *here*." Other services,

* The girl was set free, and the principle laid down that slaves coming
to a free State with the consent of their masters, secured their freedom.
An account of the case was published in the *Boston Daily Advertiser* of
August 29, 1836, and introduced with the following editorial comment:—
"In some of the States there is, we believe, legislative provision for cases
of this sort [namely, allowing the master to bring and keep slaves in
bondage], and it would seem that some such provision is necessary in
this State, unless we would prohibit citizens of the slave-holding States
from travelling in this State with their families, and unless we would permit such of them as wish to emancipate their slaves, to throw them at
their pleasure upon the people of this State."

similar or analogous, which he has rendered to the cause of inhumanity, I here pass by.

This is a world in which "men do nothing for nothing;" the workman is worthy of his hire; in due time Mr. Curtis received his reward.

He has lately (June 7th) "charged" the Grand Jury of the Circuit Court of the United States, pointing out their duty in respect to recent events in Boston. A federal enactment of 1790 provides that, if any person shall wilfully obstruct, resist, or oppose any officer of the United States in executing any legal writ or process thereof, he shall be imprisoned not more than twelve months, and fined not more than three hundred dollars. Mr. Curtis charges that the offence is "a misdemeanour:" to constitute the crime, it is "not necessary to prove the accused used or even threatened active violence." "If a multitude of persons should assemble, even in a public highway, with the design to stand together, and thus prevent the officer from passing freely along the way, . . . this would of itself, and without any active violence, be such an obstruction as is contemplated by this law."

So much for what constitutes the crime. Now see who are criminals: "All who are present and actually obstruct, resist, or oppose, are of course guilty. So are all who are present, leagued in the common design, and so situated as to be able, in case of need, to afford assistance to those actually engaged, though they do not actually obstruct, resist, or oppose." That is, they are guilty of a misdemeanour, because they are in the neighbourhood of such as oppose a constable of the United States, and are "able" "to afford assistance." "If they are present for the purpose of affording assistance, though no overt act is done by them, they are still guilty under this law." They are guilty of a misdemeanour, not merely as accessory before the fact, but as principals, for "in misdemeanours all are principals."

"Not only those who are present, but those who, though absent when the offence was committed, did procure, counsel, command, or abet others to commit the offence, are indictable as principals." But what amounts to such counselling as constitutes a misdemeanour? "Evincing an express liking, approbation, or assent to another's criminal design."

" It need not appear that the precise time, or place, or means advised, were used." So all who evinced "an express liking, approbation, or assent" to the rescue of Mr. Burns are guilty of a misdemeanour; if they evinced " an express liking" that he should be rescued by a miracle wrought by Almighty God,—and some did express "approbation" of that "means,"—they are indictable, guilty of a "misdemeanour;" "it need not appear that the precise time, or place, or means advised, were used!" If any coloured woman, during the wicked week—which was ten days long—prayed [that God would deliver Anthony, as it is said his angel delivered Peter, or said "amen" to such a prayer, she was "guilty of a misdemeanour:" to be indicted as a "principal."

So every man in Boston who, on that bad Friday, stood in the streets of Boston between Court Square and T Wharf, was "guilty of a misdemeanour," liable to a fine of three hundred dollars, and to gaoling for twelve months. All who at Faneuil Hall stirred up the minds of the people in opposition to the Fugitive Slave Bill; all who shouted, who clapped their hands at the words or the countenance of their favourites, or who expressed "approbation" by a whisper of "assent," are "guilty of misdemeanour." The very women who stood for four days at the street corners, and hissed the infamous slave-hunters and their coadjutors, they, too, ought to be punished by fine of three hundred dollars and imprisonment for a year! Well, there were fifteen thousand persons "assembled" "in the highway" of the City of Boston that day opposed to kidnapping; half the newspapers in the country towns of Massachusetts "evinced an express liking" for freedom, and opposed the kidnapping; they are all "guilty of a misdemeanour;" they are "principals." Nay, the few ministers all over the State, who preached that kidnapping was a sin; those who read brave words out of the Old Testament or the New; those who prayed that the victim might escape: they, likewise, were "guilty of a misdemeanour," liable to be fined three hundred dollars and gaoled for twelve months. Excellent Fugitive Slave Bill Judge! Mr. Webster did wisely in making that appointment! He chose an appropriate tool. The charge was worthy of the worst days of Jeffreys and the second James!

We all know against whom this judicial iniquity was directed—against men who at Faneuil Hall, under the pictured and sculptured eyes of John Hancock and the three Adamses, appealed to the spirit of humanity, not yet crushed out of your heart and mine, and lifted up their voices in favour of freedom and the eternal law of God. If he had called us by our names he could not have made the thing plainer. You know the zeal of the United States Attorney, you have heard of the swearing before the Grand Jury and at the Grand Jury. Did the Judge's lightning only glow with judicial ardour and zeal for the Fugitive Slave Bill?—or was it also red with personal malignity and family spleen? Judge you!

But, alas! there was a Grand Jury, and the Salmonean thunder of the Fugitive Slave Bill Judge fell harmless— quenched, conquered, disgraced, and brutal—to the ground. Poor Fugitive Slave Bill Court! it can only gnash its teeth against freedom of speech in Faneuil Hall; only bark and yelp against the unalienable rights of man, and howl against the Higher Law of God! it cannot bite! Poor imbecile, malignant Court! What a pity that the Fugitive Slave Bill Judge was not himself the Grand Jury, to order the indictment! what a shame that the Attorney was not a petty jury to convict! Then New England, like Old, might have had her "bloody assizes," and Boston streets might have streamed with the heart's gore of noble men and women; and human heads might have decked the pinnacles all round the town; and Judge Curtis and Attorney Hallett might have had their place with Judge Jeffreys and John Boilman of old. What a pity that we have a Grand Jury and a traverse jury to stand between the malignant arm of the slave-hunter and the heart of you and me! Perhaps the Court will try again, and find a more pliant Grand Jury, easier to intimidate. Let me suggest to the Court, that the next time it should pack its jurors from the Marshal's "guard." Then there will be unity of idea; of action, too—the Court a figure of equilibrium.*

At a Fugitive Slave Bill meeting in Faneuil Hall, it is easy to ask a minister a question designed to be insulting,

---

* The experiment was made; the brother-in-law of the Fugitive Slave Bill Judge was put on the jury, and indictments were found in October and November.

and not dare listen to the proffered reply ; easy to bark at justice, and howl at the unalienable rights of man ; easy to yelp out the vengeance of a corrupt administration of slave-hunters upon all who love the Higher Law of God ; but He himself has so fashioned the hearts of men that we instinctively hate all tyranny, all oppression, all wrong ; and the hand of history brands ineffaceable disgrace on the brass foreheads of all such as enact iniquity by statute, and execute wickedness as law.   The memory of the wicked shall rot.   Scroggs and Jeffreys also got their appointment as pay for their service and their character—fitting blood-hounds for a fitting king.   For near two hundred years their names have been a stench in the face of the Anglo-Saxon tribe.   Others as unscrupulous may take warning by their fate.

Thus has Slavery debauched the Federal Courts.

VII. Alas me ! Slavery has not ended yet its long career of sin.   Its corruption is seven-fold.   It debauches the elected offices of our City, and even our State.   In the Sims time of 1851, the laws of Massachusetts were violated nine days running, and the Free Soil Governor sat in the State House as idle as a feather in his chair.   In the wicked week of 1854, the Whig Governor sat in the seat of his predecessor ; Massachusetts was one of the inferior coun-ties of Virginia, and a slave-hunter had eminent domain over the birthplace of Franklin and the burial-place of Hancock !   Nay, against our own laws the Free Soil Mayor put the neck of Boston in the hands of a " train-band captain"—the people " wondering much to see how he did ride !"   Boston was a suburb of Alexandria ; the mayor a slave-catcher for our masters at the South !   You and I were only fellow-slaves !

All this looks as if Slavery was to triumph over Freedom. But even this is not the end.   Slavery has privately emptied her seven vials of wrath upon the nation—com-mitting seven debaucheries of human safeguards of our natural rights.   That is not enough—there are other seven to come.   This Apocalyptic Dragon, grown black with long-continued deeds of shame and death, now medi-tates five further steps of crime.   Here is the programme of the next attempt—a new political tragedy in five acts.

I.—The acquisition of Dominica—and then all Hayti —as new slave territory.

II.—The acquisition of Cuba, by purchase, or else by private fillibustering and public war,—as new slave territory.

III.—The re-establishment of Slavery in all the free States, by judicial "decision" or legislative enactment. Then the master of the North may "sit down with his slaves at the foot of Bunker Hill monument!"

IV. The restoration of the African Slave-Trade, which is already seriously proposed and defended in the Southern journals. Nay, the Senate Committee on Foreign Relations recommend the first step towards it—the withdrawal of our fleet from the coast of Africa. You cannot escape the consequence of your first principle : if Slavery is right, then the Slave-Trade is right ; the traffic between Guinea and New Orleans is no worse than between Virginia and New Orleans ; it is no worse to kidnap in Timbuctoo than in Boston.

V. A yet further quarrel must be sought with Mexico, and more slave territory be stolen from her.

Who shall oppose this five-fold wickedness ? The Fugitive Slave Bill party ;—the Nebraska Enslavement party? Northern servility has hitherto bee n ready to grant 'more than Southern arrogance dared to demand !

All this looks as if the third hypothesis would be fulfilled, and Slavery triumph over Freedom ; as if the nation would expunge the Declaration of Independence from the scroll of Time, and, instead of honouring Hancock and the Adamses and Washington, do homage to Kane and Grier and Curtis and Hallett and Loring. Then the preamble to our Constitution might read—"to establish injustice, insure domestic strife, hinder the common defence, disturb the general welfare, and inflict the curse of bondage on ourselves and our posterity." Then we shall honour the Puritans no more, but their prelatical tormentors ; nor reverence the great Reformers, only the inquisitors of Rome. Yea, we may tear the name of Jesus out of the American Bible ; yes, God's name ; worship the devil at our Lord's table, Iscariot for Redeemer !

See the steady triumph of despotism ! Ten years more,

like the ten years past, and it will be all over with the
liberties of America. Everything must go down, and the
heel of the tyrant will be on our neck. It will be all over
with the Rights of Man in America, and you and I must
go to Austria, to Italy, or to Siberia for our freedom; or
perish with the liberty which our fathers fought for and
secured to themselves—not to their faithless sons! Shall
America thus miserably perish? Such is the aspect of
things to-day!

But are the people alarmed? No, they fear nothing—
only the tightness in the money-market! Next Tuesday
at sunrise every bell in Boston will ring joyously; every
cannon will belch sulphurous welcome from its brazen
throat. There will be processions,—the Mayor and the
Aldermen and the Marshal and the Naval Officer, and, I
suppose, the "Marshal's Guard," very appropriately taking
their places. There is a chain on the common to-day—it
is the same chain that was around the Court House in
1851—it is the chain that bound Sims; now it is a
festal chain. There are mottoes about the common—
"They mutually pledged to each other their lives, their
fortunes, and their sacred honour." I suppose it means
that the Mayor and the kidnappers did this. "The spirit
of '76 still lives." Lives, I suppose, in the Supreme Court
of Fugitive Slave Bill judges. "Washington, Jefferson,
and their compatriots!—their names are sacred in the
heart of every American." That, I suppose, is the opinion
of Thomas Sims and of Anthony Burns. And opposite the
great Park Street Church, where a noble man is this day,
I trust, discoursing noble words, for he has never yet been
found false to Freedom—"Liberty and independence, our
fathers' legacy!—God forbid that we their sons should
prove recreant to the trust!" It ought to read, "God
forgive us that we their sons have proved so recreant to
the trust!" So they will celebrate the 4th of July, and call
it "Independence Day!" The foolish press of France,
bought and beaten and trodden on by Napoleon the Crafty,
is full of talk about the welfare of the "Great Nation!"
Philip of Macedon was conquering the Athenian allies
town by town; he destroyed and swept off two and thirty
cities, selling their children as slaves. All the Cassandrian

eloquence of Demosthenes could not rouse degenerate Athens from her idle sleep. She also fell—the fairest of all free States; corrupted first—forgetful of God's higher law. Shall America thus perish, all immature!

So was it in the days of old : they ate, they drank, they planted, they builded, they married, they were given in marriage, until the day that Noah entered into the ark, and the flood came and devoured them all!

Well, is this to be the end? Was it for this the pilgrims came over the sea? Does Forefathers' Rock assent to it? Was it for this that the New England clergy prayed, and their prayers became the law of the land for a hundred years? Was it for this that Cotton planted in Boston a little branch of the Lord's vine, and Roger Williams and Higginson—he still lives in an undegenerate son—did the same in the city which they called of peace, Salem? Was it for this that Eliot carried the Gospel to the Indians? that Chauncey, and Edwards, and Hopkins, and Mayhew, and Channing, and Ware laboured and prayed? for this that our fathers fought—the Adamses, Washington, Hancock? for this that there was an eight years' war, and a thousand battle-fields? for this the little monument at Acton, Concord, Lexington, West Cambridge, Danvers, and the great one over there on the spot which our fathers' blood made so red? Shall America become Asia Minor? New England Italy? Boston such as Athens—dead and rotten? Yes! if we do not mend, and speedily mend. Ten years more, and the liberty of America is all gone. We shall fall, the laugh, the byword, the proverb, the scorn, the mock of the nations, who shall cry against us. Hell from beneath shall be moved to meet us at our coming, and in derision shall it welcome us :—

"The heir of all the ages, and the youngest born of time!"

We shall lie down with the unrepentant prodigals of old time, damned to everlasting infamy and shame.

Would you have it so? Shall it be?

To-day, America is a debauched young man, of good blood, fortune, and family, but the companion of gamesters and brawlers; reeking with wine; wasting his substance in riotous living; in the lap of harlots squandering the life which his mother gave him.   Shall he return?   Shall he perish?   One day may determine.

Shall America thus die?   I look to the past,—Asia, Africa, Europe, and they answer, "Yes!"   Where is the Hebrew Commonwealth; the Roman Republic; where is liberal Greece,—Athens, and many a far-famed Ionian town; where are the Commonwealths of Mediæval Italy; the Teutonic free cities—German, Dutch, or Swiss?   They have all perished.   Not one of them is left.   Parian statues of liberty, sorely mutilated, still remain; but the Parian rock whence Liberty once hewed her sculptures out—it is all gone.   Shall America thus perish?   Greece and Italy both answer, "Yes!"   I question the last fifty years of American history, and it says, "Yes."   I look to the American pulpit, I ask the five million Sunday school scholars, and they say, "Yes."   I ask the Federal court, the Democratic party, and the Whig, and the answer is still the same.

But I close my eyes on the eleven past missteps we have taken for Slavery; on that seven-fold clandestine corruption; I forget the Whig party; I forget the present administration; I forget the Judges of the Courts;—I remember the few noblest men that there are in society, Church and State; I remember the grave of my father, the lessons of my mother's life; I look to the spirit of this age— it is the nineteenth century, not the ninth;—I look to the history of the Anglo-Saxons in America, and the history of mankind; I remember the story and the song of Italian and German patriots; I recall the dear words of those great-minded Greeks—Ionian, Dorian, Ætolian; I remember the Romans who spoke, and sang, and fought for truth and right; I recollect those old Hebrew prophets, earth's nobler sons, poets and saints; I call to mind the greatest, noblest, purest soul that ever blossomed in this dusty world;—and I say, "No!"   Truth shall triumph, justice shall be law!   And, if America fail, though she is one fortieth of God's family, and it is a great loss, there are other nations behind us; our truth shall not perish, even if we go down.

But we shall not fail!   I look into your eyes—young men and women, thousands of you, and men and women far enough from young!   I look into the eyes of fifty

thousand other men and women, whom, in the last eight
months, I have spoken to, face to face, and they say, "No!
America shall not fail!"

I remember the women, who were never found faithless
when a sacrifice was to be offered to great principles; I
look up to my God, and I look into my own heart, and I
say, "We shall not fail! We shall not fail!"

This, at my side, it is the willow;* it is the symbol of
weeping :—but its leaves are deciduous; the autumn wind
will strew them on the ground; and beneath, here is a
perennial plant; it is green all the year through. When
this willow branch is leafless, the other is green with hope,
and its buds are in its bosom; its buds will blossom. So
it is with America.

Did our fathers live? are we dead? Even in our ashes
live their holy fires! Boston only sleeps; one day she
will wake! Massachusetts will stir again! New England will rise and walk! the vanished North be found
once more queenly and majestic! Then it will be seen
that Slavery is weak and powerless in itself, only a phantom
of the night.

Slavery is a "finality,"—is it? There shall be no
"agitation,"—not the least,—shall there? There is a
Hispaniola in the South, and the South knows it. She sits
on a powder magazine, and then plays with fire, while
humanity shoots rockets all round the world. To mutilate,
to torture, to burn to death revolted Africans whom outrage has stung to crime—that is only to light the torches
of San Domingo. This black bondage will be red freedom
one day : nay, lust, vengeance, redder yet. I would not
wait till that flood comes and devours all.

When the North stands up, manfully, united, we can
tear down Slavery in a single twelvemonth; and, when we
do unite, it must be not only to destroy Slavery in the
territories, but to uproot every weed of Slavery throughout
this whole wide land. Then leanness will depart from our
souls; then the blessing of God will come upon us; we
shall have a Commonwealth based on righteousness, which
is the strength of any people, and shall stand longer
than Egypt,—national fidelity to God our age-outlasting
pyramid!

* Referring to the floral ornaments that day on the desk.

How feeble seems a single nation; how powerless a solitary man! But one of a family of forty, we can do much. How much is Italy, Rome, Greece, Palestine, Egypt to the world? The solitary man—a Luther, a Paul, a Jesus—he outweighs millions of coward souls! Each one of you take heed that the Republic receive no harm!

AN ADDRESS

DELIVERED BEFORE THE NEW YORK CITY ANTI-
SLAVERY SOCIETY,

AT ITS FIRST ANNIVERSARY, HELD AT THE BROADWAY TABERNACLE,
MAY 12, 1854.

LADIES AND GENTLEMEN,—I shall ask your attention
this evening to some few thoughts on the present condition of the United States in respect to Slavery. After
all that has been said by wise, powerful, and eloquent men,
in this city, this week, perhaps I shall have scarce anything
to present that is new.

As you look on the general aspect of America to-day,
its main features are not less than sublime, while they
are likewise beautiful exceedingly. The full breadth of the
continent is ours, from sea to sea, from the great lakes to
the great gulf. There are three million square miles, with
every variety of climate, and soil, and mineral; great
rivers, a static force, inclined planes for travel reaching
from New Orleans to the Falls of St. Anthony, from the
mouth of the St. Lawrence to Chicago; smaller rivers,
a dynamic force, turning the many thousand mills of the
industrious North. There is a coast most richly indented,
to aid the spread of civilization. The United States has
more than twelve thousand miles of shore line on the continent; more than nine thousand on its islands; more than
twenty-four thousand miles of river navigation. Here is
the material groundwork for a great State—not an empire,
but a commonwealth. The world has not such another.

There are twenty-four millions of men; fifteen and
a half millions with Anglo-Saxon blood in their veins—
strong, real Anglo-Saxon blood; eight millions and a half
more of other families and races, just enough to temper

the Anglo-Saxon blood, to furnish a new composite tribe, far better, I trust, than the old. What a human basis for a State to be erected on this material ground-work!

On the Eastern slopes of the continent, where the high lands which reach from the Katahdin mountains in Maine to the end of the Apalachians in Georgia—on the Atlantic slopes, where the land pitches down to the sea from the 48th to the 28th parallel, there are fifteen States, a million square miles communicating with the ocean. In the South, rivers bear to the sea rice, cotton, tobacco, and the products of half-tropic agriculture; in the North, smaller streams toil all day, and sometimes all night, working wood, iron, cotton, and wool into forms of use and beauty, while iron roads carry to the sea the productions of temperate agriculture, mining and manufactures.

On the Western slope, where the rivers flow down to the Pacific Ocean from the 49th to the 32nd parallel, is a great country, almost eight hundred thousand square miles in extent. There, too, the Anglo-Saxon has gone; in the South, the gold-hunter gathers the precious metals, while the farmer, the miner, and the woodman gather far more precious products in the North.

In the great basin between the Cordilleras of the West and the Alleghanies, where the Mississippi drains half the continent to the Mediterranean of the New World, there also the Anglo-Saxon has occupied the ground—twelve hundred thousand square miles; in the south to rear cotton, rice, and sugar; in the north to raise cattle and cereal grasses, for beast and for man.

What a spectacle it is! A nation not eighty years old and still in its cradle, and yet grown so great. Two hundred and fifty years ago, there was not an Anglo-Saxon on all this continent. Now there is an Anglo-Saxon commonwealth twenty-four millions strong. Rich as it is in numbers, there are not yet eight men to the square mile.

All this is a Republic; it is a Democracy. There is no born priest to stand betwixt the nation and its God; no pope to entail his nephews on the Church; no bishop claiming divine right to rule over the people and stand betwixt them and the Infinite. There is no king, no born king, to ride on the nation's neck. There are noble-men, but none noble-born to usurp the land, to monopolize the government and keep the community from the bosom of the earth. The people is priest, and makes its own religion out of God's revelation in man's nature and history. The people is its own king to rule itself; its own noble to occupy the earth. The people make the laws and choose their own magistrates. Industry is free; travel is free; religion is free; speech is free; there are no shackles on the press. The nation rests on industry, not on war. It is formed of agriculturists, traders, sailors, miners—not a nation of soldiers. The army numbers ten thousand—one soldier for every twenty-four thousand men. The people are at peace; no nation invades us. The government is firmly fixed and popular. A nation loving liberty, loves likewise law; and when it gets a point of liberty, it fences it all round with law as high up as the hands reach. We annually welcome four hundred thousand immigrants who flee from the despotism of the Old World.

The country is rich—after England, the richest on earth in cultivated lands, roads, houses, mills. Four million tons of shipping sail under the American flag. This year we shall build half a million tons more, which, at forty dollars a ton, is worth twenty millions of dollars. That is the ship crop. Then, the corn crop is seven hundred millions of bushels—Indian corn. What a harvest of coal, copper, iron, lead, of wheat, cotton, sugar, rice, is produced!

Over all and above all these there rises the great American political idea, a "self-evident truth"—which cannot be proved—it needs no proof; it is anterior to demonstration; namely, that every man is endowed by his Creator with certain inalienable rights, and in these rights all men are equal; and on these the government is to rest, deriving its sole sanction from the governed's consent.

Higher yet above this material groundwork, this human foundation, this accumulation of numbers, of riches, of industry—as the cross on the top of a tall, wide dome, whose lantern is the great American political idea—as the cross that surmounts it rises the American religious idea —one God; Christianity the true religion; and the worship of God by love; inwardly it is piety, love to God; outwardly love to man—morality, benevolence, philanthropy.

What a spectacle to the eyes of the Scandinavian, the

German, the Dutchman, the Irishman, as they view America from afar! What a contrast it seems to Europe. There liberty is ideal, it is a dream; here it is organic, an institution; one of the establishments of the land.

That, ladies and gentlemen, is the aspect which America presents to the oppressed victims of European despotism in Church and in State. Far off on the other side of the Atlantic, among the Apennines, on the plains of Germany, and in the Slavonian lands, I have met men to whom America seemed as this fair-proportioned edifice that I have thus sketched out before your eyes. But when they come nearer, behold half the land is black with Slavery. In 1850, out of more than two hundred and forty hundred thousand Americans (24,000,000), thirty-two hundred thousand (3,200,000) were slaves—more than an eighth of the population counted as cattle; not as citizens at all. They are only human material, not yet wrought into citizens—nay, not counted *human*. They are cattle, property; not counted men, but animals and no more. Manhood must not be extended to them. Listen while I read to you from a Southern print. It was recommended by the Governor of Alabama that the Legislature should pass a law prohibiting the separation of families; whereupon the *Richmond Inquirer* discourses thus :—

"This recommendation strikes us as being most unwise and impolitic. If slaves are property, *then should they be at the absolute disposal of the master*, or be subject only to such legal provisions as are designed for the protection of life and limb. If the relation of master and slave be infringed for one purpose, it would be difficult to fix any limit to the encroachment."

They are property, no more, and must be treated as such, and not as men.

Slavery is on the Atlantic slopes of the continent. There are one million six hundred thousand (1,600,000) slaves between the Alleghany range and the Atlantic coast. Slavery is in the central basin. There are a million and a half of slaves on the land drained by the Mississippi. Spite of law and constitution, Slavery has gone to the Pacific slopes, travelling with the goldhunter into California. The State whose capital county "in three years committed over twelve hundred murders" has very appropriately legalized Slavery for a limited time. I suppose it is only preliminary to legalizing it for a time limited only by the Eternal God. In the very capital of the Christian democracy there are four thousand purchased men. In the Senate-house, a few years ago, a Mississippi senator belched out his imprecations against *that one New Hampshire senator* who has never yet been found false to humanity. Mr. Foote was a freeman, a citizen, and a "Democrat;" and while, in the halls of Congress, he was threatening to hang John P. Hale on the tallest pine tree in Mississippi, there toiled in a stable, whose loft he slept in by night, one of that senator's own brothers. The son of Mr. Foote's father was a slave in the capital of the United States, while his half-brother—by the father's side—threatened to hang on the tallest pine in Mississippi the only senator that New Hampshire sent to Washington who dared be true to truth and free for freedom.

But a few years ago, Mr. Hope H. Slatter had his negro market in the capital of the United States; one of the greatest slave-dealers in America. He was a member also, it is said, of a "Christian church." The slave-pen is a singular institution for a democratic metropolis, and the slave-trader a peculiar ornament for the Christian Church in the capital of a democracy. He grew rich, went to Baltimore, had a fine house, and once entertained a "President of the United States" in his mansion. The slave-trader and the democratic President met together—Slatter and Polk! fit guest and fitting host!

In all the three million square miles of American land there is no inch of free soil, from the St. John's to the Rio Gila, from Madawasca to San Diego. The star-spangled banner floats from Van Couver's island by Nootka Sound to Key West, on the south of Florida, and all the way the flag of our Union is the standard of Slavery. In all the soil that our fathers fought to make free from English tyranny, there is not an inch where the black man is free, save the five thousand miles that Daniel Webster surrendered to Lord Ashburton by the treaty of 1842. The symbol of the Union is a fetter. The President should be sworn on the auction block of a slave-trader. The New Hampshire President, in his inaugural, declared, publicly, his allegiance to the slave power—not to the power of Northern mechanics, free farmers, free manufacturers, free men; but allegiance to the slave power; he swears special protection to no property but "property" in slaves; specific allegiance to no law but the Fugitive Slave Bill; devotion to no right but the slave-holder's "right" to his property in man.

The Supreme Court of the United States is a slave court; a majority of the Senate and of the House of Representatives the same. It has been so this forty years. The majority of the House of Representatives are obedient to the lords of the lash; a majority of Northern politicians, especially of that denomination which is called "dough-faces," are only overseers for the owner of the slave. Mr. Douglas is a great overseer; Mr. Everett is a little overseer, very little.

The nation offers a homestead out of its public land; it is only to the *white* man. What would you say if the Emperor of Russia offered land only to *nobles;* the Pope only to *priests;* Queen Victoria only to *lords?* Each male settler in Utah, it seems, is to have four hundred and eighty acres of land if he is not married, and a hundred and sixty more, I believe, according to one proposition, for every wife that he has got. But if he has the complexion of the only children that Madison left behind him, he can have no land at all.

Even a Boston school-house is shut against the black man's children. The arm of the city government slams the door in every coloured boy's face. His father helps pay for the public school; the son and daughter must not come in.

In the slave States, it is a crime to teach the slave to read and write. Out of four millions of children of America at school in 1850, there were twenty six thousand that were coloured. There were more than four hundred thousand free coloured persons, and there were more than two hundred and fourteen thousand thereof under the age of twenty; of these, there were at school only twenty-six thousand— *one child in nine!* Out of three and a quarter millions of slaves, there *was not one at school.* It is *a crime by the statute in every slave State to teach a slave to spell "God."* He may be a Christian; he must not write "Christ." He must worship the Bible; he must not read it! It is a crime even in a *Sunday school* to teach a child the great letters which spell out "Holy Bible." I knew a minister, he was a Connecticut man, too, who went off from New Orleans because he did not dare to stay; and he did not dare to stay because he tried to teach the slave to read in his Sunday school. He went back to Connecticut, whence he will, perhaps, go as missionary to China or Turkey, and find none to hinder his Christian work.

At the North, the black man is shut out of the meeting house. In heaven, according to the theology of America, he may sit down with the just made perfect, his sins washed white "in the blood of the Lamb;" but when he comes to a certain Baptist church in Boston, he cannot own a pew. And there are few churches where he can sit in a pew. The rich and the poor are there; the one Lord is the Maker of them all; but the Church thinks He did not make the black as well as the white. Nay; he is turned out of the omnibus, out of the burial ground. There is a burial ground in this State, and in the deed that confers the land it is stipulated that no coloured person or convict can ever be buried there. He is turned out of the grave-yard, where the great mother of our bodies gathers our dust when the sods of the valley are sweet to the soul. Nowhere but in the gaol and on the gallows has the black man equal rights with the white in our American legislation!

The American press—it is generally the foe of the slave, the advocate of bondage.

In Virginia, it is felony to deny the master's right to own his slave. There is an old law, re-enacted in the revision of the Virginia statute, which inflicts a punishment of not more than one year's confinement on any one guilty of that offence. It was proposed in the Virginia Legislature, last winter, that if a man had conscientious objections to holding slaves, he should not be allowed to sit on any jury where the matter of a man's freedom was in question. Nor is that all. There is a law in Virginia, it is said, that when a man has three-quarters white blood in his veins, he may recover his freedom in virtue of that fact. It is well known that at least half the slaves in Virginia are half white and one-quarter of them three-quarters white. Accordingly, it was proposed in one of their newspapers that that old law should be re-pealed, and another substituted, providing that no man

should recover his freedom in consequence of his complexion, unless he had more than nine-tenths white blood
in his veins.

The slave has no rights; the ideas of the Declaration
of Independence are repudiated; he is not " endowed by
his Creator" with " certain inalienable rights" to "life,
liberty, and the pursuit of happiness." Accomplished Mr.
Agassiz comes all the way from Switzerland to teach
us the science which God has stored up in the ground
under our feet—the perennial Old Testament—or in the
frames of our bodies, this living New Testament of
Almighty God in man; and he tells us this: " *The
Mandingo and the Guinea negro*" together " *do not
differ more from the Orang Outang than the Malay
or white man differs from the negro.*" So, according
to Mr. Agassiz, the negro is a sort of *arithmetic mean
proportional* between a man and a monkey. The upright form, the power of speech, the religious faculty,
permanence of affection, self-denial, power to master the
earth, and smelt iron ore, as the African has done, and is
doing still, every year, do not distinguish the black man
from the *Orang Outang.*

> "O star-eyed science! hast *thou* wandered there,
>   To waft us home the message of despair?"

Mr. Agassiz is an able man, of large genius, industry that
never surrenders, and was a bold champion of freedom on
his own Swiss hills. He comes to America; he is subdued
to the temper of our atmosphere; and, from a great man of
science, he becomes the *Swiss of Slavery.* Southern journals rejoice at the confirmation of their opinion. Listen
to what a Southern editor says. I am quoting now from
one of the most powerful Southern journals, printed at the
capital of Virginia, the *Richmond Examiner;* and the
words which I read were written by the American *charge
d'affaires* at Turin. He says: " The foundation and right
of negro Slavery is in its utility and the fitness of things;
*it is the same right by which we hold property in domestic
animals.*" The negro is " *the connecting link between the
human and brute creation.*" " The negro is not the white man.
Not with more safety do we assert *that a horse is not a hog.*
Hay is good for horses—but not for hogs; liberty is good

for *white men,* but not for *negroes."* *"A law rendering perpetual the relation between a negro and his master is no wrong, but a right."*

Then, in reply to some writer in the *Tribune,* who had asked, "Have they no souls?" he says, "They may have souls for aught he knew to the contrary; so *may horses and hogs."* Then, when somebody quotes the Bible in behalf of the rights of men, he answers: "The Bible has been vouchsafed to mankind for the purpose of keeping us out of hell-fire and getting us into heaven *by the mysteries of faith and the inner life;* not to teach us *a government political economy,"* &c.

The American Church repudiates the Christian religion when it comes to speak about the African. It does not apply the golden rule to the slave. The *"servants"* of the New Testament, in the slave language, were "slaves," and the American Church commands them to be obedient to their masters. There must be no *marriage*—the affectional and passional union of one man and one woman for life— only transient concubinage. Marriage is inconsistent with Slavery, and the slave wedlock in the American Church is not a Sacrament. "Manifest destiny" is the cry of politicians, and that demands Slavery: "the will of God" is the cry of the priests, and it demands the same thing. I am not speaking of *ministers of Christianity;* they are very different sort of men, and preach a very different creed from that—only of the ministers in the churches of commerce. According to the popular theology of all Christendom, Jesus Christ came on earth to seek and to save that which is lost. The good physician does not go among the whole, but among the sick. If he were to come here to seek to relieve the slave, the leading men in the American denominations would tell him he came before he was called; he ran before he was sent—that it was no mission from God to break a single American fetter, nor to let the oppressed go free. Is not the "Constitution" above "Conscience," and the Fugitive Slave Bill more holy than the Bible? the Commissioner of more authority than Christ?

> "O Faith of Christians, hast thou wandered there
> To waft us home the message of despair?
> Then bind the palm *thy sage's brow to suit,*
> *Of blasted leaf and death-distilling fruit."*

Such is the aspect of America when the immigrant comes near and looks the nation in the face. What a spectacle that is to put alongside of the other! Europe repudiates bondage—Scandinavia, Holland, France, England. Since Britain emancipated her slaves, the present Emperor of Russia has set free over *seven million of slaves* that belonged to his own private domain, and established more than *four thousand schools*, free for those seven millions of emancipated slaves; and did he not fear an outbreak in a country where "revolution is endemic," he would set free the other five and thirty millions that occupy his soil to-day. And when he extends his territory, he never extends the area of bondage, only the area of what in Russia is freedom.

What a spectacle! A country reaching from sea to sea, from the gulf of tropic heat to Lake Superior's arctic cold, and not an inch of free soil all the way! Three millions of square miles, and not a foot where a fugitive from Slavery can be safe! A democracy, and every eighth man bought and sold!

It is the richest nation in the world, after England; yet, we are so poor that every eighth man is unable to say that he owns the smallest finger on his feeblest hand. So poor are we amid our riches, that every eighth woman is to such an extent a pauper that she does not own the baby she has borne into the world, nor even the baby that she bears under her bosom! Maternity is put up at public vendue, and the auctioneer says, "So much for the mother and so much for the hopes and expectations of another life that is to be born!"

America calls herself " the best educated nation in the world," and yet, in fifteen democratic States, it is a felony by statute to teach a child to know the three letters that spell " God." What a spectacle is that!

Nor is that all; but able men, well-educated and well-endowed, come forward to teach us that Slavery is not only no evil, but is right as a principle, and is divine—is a part of the divine revelation which the great God miraculously made to man. What a spectacle!

Four hundred thousand immigrants come here openly every year, and a thousand fugitives flee off by night, escaping from American despotism. They go by the underground railroad, shut up in boxes smaller than a coffin, or, as lately happened, riding through the storms of ocean in the fore-chains of a packet ship, wet by every dash of the sea, and frozen by the winter's wind. Far off in the South the spirit of freedom came in the Northern blast to the poor man, and said to him, "It is better to enter into freedom halt and maimed rather than, having two hands and two feet, to continue in bondage for ever;" and he puts himself in the fore-chains of a packet ship, and, half frozen, with the loss of two of his limbs, he gets to the North, and thanks God that he has got one hand and one foot to enter into freedom with. Alas! he is carried back, halt and maimed, to die; then he goes from bondage to that other Commonwealth, where even the American slave is free from his master, and democrats "cease from troubling."

America translates the Bible—I am glad of it, and would give my mite thereto—into a hundred and forty-seven different tongues, and sends missionaries all over the world; and here at home are three and a quarter millions of American men who have no Bible, whose only missionary is the overseer.

In the Hall of Independence, Judge Kane and Judge Grier hold their court. Two great official kidnappers of the middle States hold their slave-court in the very building where the Declaration of Independence was decreed, was signed, and thence published to the world. What a spectacle it is! We thought, a little while ago, that Judge Jeffries was an historical fiction; that Scroggs was impossible. We did not think such a thing could exist. Jeffries is repeated in Philadelphia; Scroggs is brought back to life in various Northern towns. What a spectacle is that for the Swiss, the German, and the Scandinavian who come here!

Do these immigrants love American Slavery? The German, the Swiss, the Scandinavian hate it. I am sorry to say there is one class of men that come here who love it; it is the class most of all sinned against at home. When the Irishman comes to America, he takes ground against the African. I know there are exceptions, and I would go far to honour them; but the Irish, as a body, oppose the emancipation of the blacks as a body. Every sect that comes from abroad numbers friends of freedom—except the Catholic. Those who call themselves infidels from Germany do not range on the slave-holder's side. I have known some men who take the ghastly and dreadful name of Atheists; but they said, "there is a law higher than the slave-holder's statute." But do you know a Catholic priest that is opposed to Slavery? I wish I did. There are good things in the Catholic faith—the Protestants have not wholly outgrown it—not yet. I wish I could hear of a single Catholic priest of any eminence who ever cared anything for the freedom of the most oppressed men that are here in America. I have heard of none.

Look a little closer. The great interests prized most in America are commerce and politics. The great cities are the head-quarters of these, too. Agriculture and the mechanic arts, they are spread abroad all over the country. Commerce and politics predominate in the cities. New York is the great metropolis of commerce; Washington of politics. What have been the views of American commerce in respect to freedom? It has been against it, I am sorry to say so.

In Europe commerce is the ally of freedom, and has been so far back that the memory of man runs not to the contrary. In America, the great commercial centres, ever since the Revolution, have been hostile to freedom. In Massachusetts we have a few rich men friendly to freedom—they are very few; the greater part of even Massachusetts capital goes towards bondage — not towards freedom. In general, the great men of commerce are hostile to it. They want first money, next money, and money last of all; fairly if we can get it—if not, unfairly. Hence the commercial cities are the head-quarters of Slavery; all the mercantile capitols execute the Fugitive Slave Bill — Philadelphia, New York, Boston, Buffalo, Cincinnati—only small towns repudiate man-stealing. The Northern capitalists lend money and take slaves as collateral; they are good security: you can realize on it any day. The Northern merchant takes slaves into his ships as merchandise. It pays very well. If you take them on a foreign voyage, it is "piracy;" but taken coastwise, the domestic slave trade is a legal traffic. In 1852, a ship called the "Edward Everett" made two voyages from Baltimore to

New Orleans, and each time it carried slaves, once twenty, once twelve.

A sea captain in Massachusetts told a story to a commissioner sent to look after the Indians, which I will tell you. He commanded a small brig, which plied between Carolina and the Gulf States. "One day, at Charleston," said he, "a man came and brought to me an old negro slave. He was very old, and had fought in the Revolution, and been very distinguished for bravery and other soldierly qualities. If he had not been a negro, he would have become a captain at least, perhaps a colonel. But, in his old age, his master found no use for him, and said he could not afford to keep him. He asked me to take the revolutionary soldier and carry him South and sell him. I carried him," said the man, "to Mobile, and I tried to get as good and kind a master for him as I could, for I didn't like to sell a man that had fought for his country. *I sold the old revolutionary soldier for a hundred dollars to a citizen of Mobile,* who raised poultry, and he set him to attend a hen-coop." I suppose the South Carolina master drew the pension till the soldier died. "Why did you do such a thing?" said my friend, who was an anti-Slavery man. "If I didn't do it," he replied, "I never could get a bale of cotton, nor a box of sugar, nor anything to carry from or to any Southern port."

In politics, almost all leading men have been servants of Slavery. Three "major prophets" of the American Republic have gone home to render their account, where the servant is free from his master and "the wicked cease from troubling," and the "weary are at rest." Clay, Calhoun, Webster; they were all prophets of Slavery against Freedom. No men of high political standing and influence have ever lived in this century who were sunk so deep in the mire of Slavery as they during the last twenty years. No political footprints have sunk so deep into the soil — their tracks run towards bondage. Where they marched Slavery followed.

Our Presidents must all be pro-Slavery men. John Quincy Adams even, the only American thus far who inherited a great name and left it greater, as President, did nothing against Slavery that has yet come to light; said nothing against it that has yet come to light. The brave

old man, in his latter days, stirred up the nobler nature
that was in him, and amply repaid for the sins of omission.
But the other Presidents, a long line of them—Jackson,
Van Buren, Harrison (they are growing smaller and
smaller), Tyler, Polk, Taylor (who was a brave, earnest
man, and had a great deal of good in him—and now they
begin to grow very rapidly small), Fillmore, Pierce—can
you find a single breath of freedom in these men? Not
one. The last slave President, though his cradle was
rocked in New Hampshire, is Texan in his latitude. He
swears allegiance to Slavery in his inaugural address.

Is there a breath of freedom in the great Federal officers — secretaries, judges? Ask the Cabinet; ask the
Supreme Court; the Federal officers; they are, almost
without exception, servants of Slavery. Out of forty thousand government officers to-day, I think thirty-seven
thousand are strongly pro-Slavery; and of the three thousand who I think are at heart anti-Slavery, we have yet
to listen long before we shall hear the first anti-Slavery
lisp. I have been listening ever since the 4th of March,
1853, and have not heard a word yet. In the English
Cabinet there are various opinions on important matters;
in America, they "are a unit," a unit of bondage. In Russia, a revolutionary man sometimes holds a high post and
does great service; in America, none but the servant of
Slavery is fit for the political functions of Democracy. I
believe, in the United States, there is not a single editor
holding a government office who says anything against the
Nebraska Bill. They do not dare. Did a Whig officeholder oppose the Fugitive Slave Bill or its enforcement?
I never heard of one. The day of office, like the day of
bondage, "takes off half a man's manhood," and the other
half it hides! A little while ago, an anti-Slavery man in
Massachusetts carried a remonstrance against the Nebraska
Bill, signed by almost every voter in his town, to the post-
master, and asked him, "Will you sign it?" "No, I
shan't," said he. "Why not?" Before he answered, one
of his neighbours said, "Well, I would not sign it if I was
he." "Why not?" said the man. "Because if he did,
he would be turned out of office in twenty-four hours; the
next telegraph would do the business for him." "Well,"
said my friend, "if I held an office on that condition, I

would get the biggest brass dog-collar I could find and put it around my neck, and have my owner's name on it, in great, large letters, so that everybody might see whose dog I was."

In the individual States, I think there is not a single anti-Slavery government. I believe Vermont is the only State that has an anti-Slavery Supreme Court; and that is the only State which has not much concern in commerce or manufactures. It is a State of farmers.

For a long time the American Government has been controlled by Slavery. There is an old story told by the Hebrew rabbis, that before the flood there was an enormous giant, called Gog. After the flood had got into full tide of successful experiment, and everybody was drowned except those taken into the ark, Gog came striding along after Noah, feeling his way with a cane as long as a mast of the "Great Republic." The waters had only just come up to his girdle. It was then over the hill tops, and was still rising—raining night and day. The giant hailed the Patriarch. Noah put his head out of the window and said, "Who is there?" "It is I," said Gog. "Take us in; it is wet outside!" "No," said Noah, "you're too big; no room. Besides, you're a bad character. You would be a very dangerous passenger, and would make trouble in the ark; I shall not take you;" and he clapped to the window. "Go to thunder," said Gog: "I will ride after all;" and he strode after him, wading through the waters and keeping out of the deep holes, and *mounting on the top of the ark*, with one leg over the larboard and the other over the starboard side, steered it just as he pleased, and made it rough weather inside. Now, in making the Constitution, we did not care to take in Slavery in express terms. It looked ugly. So it got on the top astride, and it steers us just where it pleases.

The slave power controls the President, and fills all the offices. Out of the twelve elected Presidents, four have been from the North, and the last of them might just as well have been taken by lot at the South anywhere. Mr. Pierce, I just now. said, was Texan in his latitude. His conscience is Texan; only his cradle was New Hampshire. Of the nine Judges of the Supreme Court, five are from the slave States—the Chief Justice from the slave States. A part of the Cabinet are from the North—I forget how many; it makes no difference; they are all of the same Southern complexion; and the man that was taken from the farthest north, Caleb Cushing, I think is most Southern in his Slavery proclivities.

The nation fluctuates in its policy. Now it is for internal improvements: then it is against them. Now it is for a bank; then a bank is unconstitutional. Now it is for free-trade; then for protection; then for free-trade again—protection is altogether unconstitutional. Mr. Calhoun turns clear round. When the North went for free-trade and grew rich by that, Calhoun did not like it, and wanted protection. He thought the South would grow rich by it. And when the North grew rich under protection, he turned round to free-trade again. Now the nation is for giving away the public lands. Sixteen millions of acres of "swamp lands" are given, within seven years, to States. Twenty-five millions of the public lands are given away gratuitously to soldiers—six millions in a single year. Forty-seven millions of the public lands to seventeen States for schools, colleges, &c. Forty-seven thousand acres for deaf and dumb asylums. And look; just now it changes its policy, and Mr. Pierce is opposed to granting any land—it is not constitutional—to Miss Dix, to make the insane sober, and bring them to their right minds. He may have a private reason for keeping the people in a state of craziness, for aught I know.

The public policy changes in these matters. It never changes in respect to Slavery. Be the Whigs in power, Slavery is Whig; be the Democrats, it is Democratic. At first, Slavery was an exceptional measure, and men tried to apologize for it and excuse it. Now it is a normal principle, and the institution must be defended and enlarged.

Commercial men must be moved, I suppose, by commercial arguments. Look, then, at this statement of facts.

Slavery is unprofitable for the people. America is poorer for Slavery. I am speaking in the great focus of American commerce—the third city for population and riches in the Christian world. Let me, therefore, talk about dollars. America, I say, is poorer for Slavery. If the three and a quarter millions of slaves were freemen, how much richer would she be? There is no State in the Union but it is poorer for Slavery. It is a bad tool to work with. The educated freemen is the best working power in the world.

Compare the North with the South, and see what a difference in riches, comfort, education. See the superiority of the North. But the South started with every advantage of nature—soil, climate, everything. To make the case plainer, let me take two great States, Virginia and New York. Compare them together.

In geographical position Virginia has every advantage over New York. Almost everything that will grow in the Union will grow somewhere in Virginia, save sugar. The largest ships can sail up the Potomac a hundred miles, as far as Alexandria. The Rappahannock, York, James, are all navigable rivers. The Ohio flanks Virginia more than three hundred miles. There is sixty miles of navigation on the Kanawha. New York has a single navigable stream with not a hundred and fifty miles of navigation from Troy to the ocean. Virginia has the best harbour on the Atlantic coast, and several smaller ones. Your State has but a single maritime port. Virginia abounds in water-power for mills. I stood once on the steps of the capitol at Washington, and within six miles of me, under my eyes, there was a water-power greater than that which turns the mills of Lawrence, Lowell, and Manchester, all put together. In 1836 it did not turn a wheel; now, I am told, it drives a grist mill. No State is so rich in water-power. The Alleghanies are a great watershed, and at the eaves the streams rush forward as if impatient to turn mills. New York has got very little water-power of this sort. Virginia is full of minerals—coal, iron, lead, copper, salt. Her agricultural resources are immense. What timber clothes her mountains! what a soil for Indian corn, wheat, tobacco, rice! even cotton grows in the southern part. Washington said the central counties of Virginia were the best land in the United States. Daniel Webster, reporting to Virginians of his European tour, said he saw no lands in Europe so good as the valley of the Shenandoah. Virginia is rich in mountain pastures favourable to sheep and horned cattle. Nature gives Virginia everything that can be asked of nature. What a position for agriculture, manufactures, mining, commerce ! Norfolk is a hundred miles nearer Chicago than New York is, but she has no intercourse with Chicago. It is three hundred miles nearer the mouth of the Ohio; but if a Norfolk man wants to go to St. Louis, I believe his quickest way lies through New York. It is not a day's sail farther from Liverpool; it is nearer to the Mediterranean and South American points. But what is Norfolk, with her 23,000 tons of shipping and her 14,000 population ? What is Richmond, with her 27,000 men— 10,000 of them slaves? Nay, what is Virginia itself, the very oldest State? Let me cipher out some numerical details.

In 1790 she had 748,000 inhabitants; now she has 1,421,000. She has not doubled in sixty years. In 1790 New York had 340,000; now she has 3,048,000. She has multiplied her population almost ten times. In Virginia, in 1850, there were only 452,000 more freemen than sixty years before; in New York, there were 2,724,000 *more freemen than there were in* 1790. There are only 165,000 dwellings in Virginia; 463,000 in New York. Then the Virginia farms were worth $216,000,000, yours $554,000,000; Virginia is wholly agricultural, while you are also manufacturing and commercial. Her farm tools were worth $7,000,000; yours $22,000,000. Her cattle $33,000,000 ; yours $73,000,000. The orchard products of Virginia were worth $177,000; of New York $1,762,000. Virginia had 478 miles of railroad; you had 1,826 miles. She had 74,000 tons of shipping; you had 942,000. The value of her cotton factories was not two millions ; the value of yours was four and a quarter millions. She produced $841,000 worth of woollen goods; you produced $7,030,000. Her furnaces produced two millions and a half ; yours produced eight millions. Her tanneries $894,000; yours $9,804,000. All of her manufactures together were not worth $9,000,000 ; those of the *city of New York* alone have an annual value of $105,000,000. Her attendance at school was 109,000 ; yours 693,000.

But there is one thing in which Virginia is far in advance of you. Of native Virginians, over twenty years old, who could not read the name of "Christ" nor the word " God"—free white people who cannot spell *democrat* —there were 87,383. That is, out of every five hundred free white persons, there were *one hundred and five* that could not spell PIERCE. In New York there are 30,670— no more; so that, out of five hundred persons, there are *six* that cannot read and write. Virginia is advancing rapidly upon you in this respect. In 1840 she had only 58,787 adults that could not read and write; now 28,596 more. So, you see, she is advancing.

Virginia has 87 newspapers; New York 428. The Virginia newspaper circulation is 89,000; New York newspaper circulation is 1,622,000. The *Tribune*—and I think it is the best paper there is in the world—has an aggregate circulation of 110,000; 20,000 more than all the newspapers of Virginia! Virginia prints every year 9,000,000 of copies of newspapers, all told. New York prints 115,000,000. The New York *Tribune* prints 15,000,000—more than the whole state of Virginia put together. Such is the state of things counted in the gross, but I think the New York *quality* is as much better as the quantity is more.

Virginia has 88,000 books in libraries not private. New York 1,760,000; a little more than twenty times as much. Virginia exports $3,500,000; New York $53,000,000. Virginia imports $426,000; New York $111,000,000. But in one article of export she is in advance of you—she sends to the man-markets of the South about $10,000,000 or $12,000,000 worth of her children every year; *exports slaves!* The value of all the property real and personal in the State of Virginia, *including* slaves, is $430,701,882; of New York $1,080,000,000, without estimating the value of the men who own it. Virginia has got 472,528 slaves. I will estimate them at less than the market value—at $400 each; they come to $189,000,000. I subtract the value of the *working people of Virginia*, and she is worth not quite $242,000,000. Now, the State of New York might buy up all the property of Virginia, *including the slaves*, and still have $649,000,000 left; might buy up all the real and personal property of Virginia, except the working-men, and have $838,000,000 left. The North appropriates the rivers, the mines, the harbours, the forests, fire and water—the South *kidnaps* men. Behold the *commercial* result.

Virginia is a great State—very great! You don't know

how great it is. I will read it to you presently. Things
are great and small by comparison. I am quoting again
from the *Richmond Examiner* (March 24th, 1854).
"Virginia in this confederacy is the impersonation of
the well-born, well-educated, well-bred aristocrat" [*well-
born*, while the children of Jefferson and the only *children
of Madison* are a "connecting link between the human
and brute creation;" *well-educated*, with 21 per cent. of
her white adults unable to read the vote they cast against
the unalienable rights of man ; *well-bred*, when her great
product for exportation is—the *children of her own loins!*
Slavery is a "patriarchal institution;" the Democratic
Abrahams of Virginia do not offer up their Isaacs to the
Lord; that would be a *sacrifice*, they only *sell them.* So];
"she looks down from her elevated pedestal upon her *par-
venu*, ignorant, mendacious Yankee vilifiers, as coldly and
calmly as a marble statue ; occasionally she condescends to
recognise the existence of her adversaries at the very
moment when she crushes them. But she does it without
anger, and with no more hatred of them than the gardener
feels towards the insects which he finds it necessary occasionally to destroy." "She feels that she is the sword
and buckler of the South—that it is her influence which
has so frequently defeated and driven back in dismay the
Abolition party when flushed by temporary victory. Brave,
calm and determined, wise in times of excitement, *always
true to the slave power*, never rash or indiscreet, the waves
of Northern fanaticism burst harmless at her feet; the
contempt for her Northern revilers is the result of her
consciousness of her influence in the political world. *She
makes and unmakes Presidents ; she dictates her terms to
the Northern Democracy, and they obey her. She selects
from among the faithful of the North a man upon whom
she can rely, and she makes him President."* [This latter
is true ! The opinion of Richmond is of more might
than the opinion of New York. Slavery, the political Gog
on the outside, steers the ark of commercial Noah, and
makes it rough or smooth weather inside, just as he likes.]
    "In the early days of the Republic, the superior saga-
city of her statesmen enabled them to rivet so firmly the
shackles of the slave, *that the Abolitionists will never be
able to unloose them.*"

"A wide and impassable gulf separates the noble, proud, glorious Old Dominion from her Northern traducers; the mastiff dare not willingly assail the skunk!" "When Virginia takes the field, she crushes the whole Abolition party; her slaughter is wholesale, and a hundred thousand Abolitionists are cut down when she issues her commands!"

Again (April 4th, 1854), "A hundred Southern gentlemen, armed with riding-whips, could chase an army of invading Abolitionists into the Atlantic."

In reference to the project at the North of sending Northern Abolitionists along with the Northern slave-breeders to Nebraska, to put freedom into the soil before Slavery gets there, the *Examiner* says:—" *Why, a hundred wild, lank, half-horse, half-alligator Missouri and Arkansas emigrants would, if so disposed, chase out of Nebraska and Kansas all the Abolitionists* who have figured for the last twenty years at anti-Slavery meetings."

I say Slavery is not profitable for the nation nor for a State, but it is profitable for *slave-owners.* You will see why. If the Northern capitalist owned the weavers and spinners at Lowell and Lawrence, New England would be poorer, and the working-men would not be so well off, or so well-educated; but Undershot and Overshot, Turbine Brothers, Spindle and Co., would be richer, and would get larger dividends. Land monopoly in England enfeebles the island, but enriches the aristocracy. How poor, ill-fed, and ill-clad were the French peasants before the Revolution; how costly was the *château* of the noble. Monopoly was bad for the people; profitable for the rich men. How poor are the people in Italy; how rich the Cardinals and the Pope. Oppression enriches the oppressor; it makes poorer the down-trodden. Piracy is very costly to the merchant and to mankind; but it enriches the pirate. Slavery impoverishes Virginia, but it enriches the master. It gives him money—commercial power—office—political power. The slave-holder is drawn in his triumphal chariot by two chattels: one, the poor black man, whom he " owns legally;" the other is the poor white man, whom he owns morally, and harnesses to his chariot. Hence these American lords of the lash cleave to this institution—they love it. To the slave-holders, Slavery is money and power!

Now the South, weak in numbers, feeble in respect to

money, has continually directed the politics of America,
just as she would.   Her ignorance and poverty were more
efficacious than the Northern riches and education.   She is in
earnest for Slavery ; the North not *in earnest for Freedom !
only earnest for money.*   So long as the Federal Government grinds the axes of the Northern merchant, he cares
little whether the stone is turned by the free man's labour
or · the slave's.   Hence, *the great centres of Northern
commerce* and manufactures are also the *great centres of
pro-Slavery politics.*   Philadelphia, New York, Boston,
Buffalo, Cincinnati, they all liked the Fugitive Slave Bill;
all took pains to seize the fugitive who fled to a Northern
altar for freedom ; nay, the most conspicuous clergymen in
those cities became apostles of kidnapping ; their churches
were of commerce, not Christianity.   The North yielded
to that last most insolent demand.   Under the influence
of that excitement she chose the present Administration,
the present Congress.   Now see the result !   Whig and
Democrat meet on the same platform at Baltimore.   It
was the platform of Slavery.   Both candidates gave in
their allegiance to the same measure—Scott and Pierce—
it was the measure which compromised the first principles
of the American Independence—they were sworn on the
Fugitive Slave Bill.   Whig and Democrat knew no
" higher law," only the statute of slave-holders.   Conscience bent down before the Constitution.   What sort of
a government can you expect from such conduct !   What
representatives !   Just what you have got.   Sow the wind,
will you ? then reap the whirlwind.   Mr. Pierce said in
his inaugural, " I believe that involuntary servitude is
recognised by the Constitution ;" " that it stands like
any other admitted right.   I hold that the compromise
measures (*i.e.*, the Fugitive Slave Bill) are strictly constitutional, and *to be unhesitatingly carried into effect.*"   The
laws to secure the master's *right* to capture a man in the
free States " should be respected and obeyed, *not with a
reluctance* encouraged by abstract opinions as to their propriety in a different state of society, *but cheerfully* and
according to the decision of the tribunal to which their
exposition belongs."   These words were *historical* — re-
miniscences of the time when "*no higher law*" was the
watchword of the American State and the American

Church ; they were *prophetic*—ominous of what we see to-day.

I. Here is the Gadsden Treaty which has been negotiated. How bad it is I cannot say ; only this. If I am rightly informed, a tract of 39,000,000 acres, larger than all Virginia, is " re-annexed" to the slave soil which the " flag of our Union" already waves over. The whole thing, when it is fairly understood by the public, I think will be seen to be a more iniquitous matter than this Nebraska wickedness.

II. Then comes the Nebraska Bill, yet to be consummated. While we are sitting here in cold debate, it may be the measure has passed. From the beginning I have never had any doubts that it would pass ; if it could not be put through this session—as I thought it would—I felt sure that before this Congress goes out of office, Nebraska would be slave soil. You see what a majority there was in the Senate ; you see what a majority there is in the House. I know there is an opposition—and most brilliantly conducted, too, by the few faithful men ; but see this: the Administration has yet three years to run. There is an annual income of sixty millions of dollars. There are forty thousand offices to be disposed of—four thousand very valuable. And do you think that a Democratic Administration, with that amount of offices, of money and time, cannot buy up Northern doughfaces enough to carry any measure it pleases ? I know better. Once I thought that Texas could not be annexed. It was done. I learned wisdom from that. I have taken my counsel of my fears. I have not seen any barrier on which the North would rally that we have come to yet. There are some things behind us. John Randolph said, years ago, " We will drive you from pillar to post, back, back, back." He has been as good as his word. We have been driven " back, back, back." But we cannot be driven much farther. There is a spot where we shall stop. I am afraid we have not come to it yet. I will say no more about it just now—because, not many weeks ago, I stood here and said a great deal. You have listened to me when I was feeble and hollow-voiced ; I will not tax your patience now, for in this, as in a celebrated feast of old, they have "kept the good wine until now!" (alluding to Garrison and Phillips, who were to follow).

. If the Nebraska Bill *is* defeated, I shall rejoice that iniquity is foiled once more. But if it become a law—there are some things which seem probable.

1. On the 4th of March, 1856, the democrats will have *leave to withdraw* from office.

2. Every Northern man who has taken a prominent stand in behalf of Slavery will be *politically ruined.* You know what befell the Northern politicians who voted for the Missouri Compromise; a similar fate hangs over the men who enslave Nebraska. Already, Mr. Everett is, theologically speaking, among the *lost;* and, of all the three thousand New England ministers whose petition he dared not present, not one will ever pray for his political *salvation.*

Pause with me and drop a tear over the ruin of Edward Everett, a man of large talents and commensurate industry, very learned, the most scholarly man, perhaps, in the country, with a persuasive beauty of speech only equalled by this American (Mr. Phillips), who surpasses him; he has had a long career of public service, public honour—Clergyman, Professor, Editor, Representative, Governor, Ambassador, President of Harvard College, alike the ornament as the auxiliary of many a learned society—he yet comes to such an end.

> "This is the state of man : to-day, he puts forth
>   The tender leaves of hope; to-morrow, blossoms,
>   And bears his blushing honours thick upon him ;
>   The third day comes a frost, *Nebraska's* frost ;
>   And, when he thinks, good easy man, full surely,
>   His greatness is a ripening, nips his root,
>   And then he falls ————."

>   "Oh, how wretched
>   Is that poor man that hangs on *public* favours !
>   There is betwixt that smile *he* would aspire to,
>   That sweet aspect of *voters*, and their ruin,
>   More pangs and fears than wars or women have ;
>   And when he falls, he falls like Lucifer,
>   Never to hope again ! "

Mr. Douglas also is finished; the success of his measure is his own defeat. Mr. Pierce has three short years to serve; then there will be one more ex-President—ranking with Tyler and Fillmore. Mr. Seward need not agitate,

——— " Let it work,
For 'tis the sport to have the engineer
Hoist with his own petard."

III. The next thing is the enslavement of Cuba. That is a very serious matter. It has been desired a long time. Lopez, a Spanish fillibuster, undertook it and was legally put to death. I am not an advocate for the *garrote*, but I think, all things taken into consideration, that he did not meet with a very inadequate mode of death : and I believe that is the general opinion, not only in Cuba, but in the United States. But Young America is not content with that. Mr. Dean, a little while ago, in the House, proposed to repeal the neutrality laws—to set fillibusterism on its legs again. You remember the President's message about the "Black Warrior"—how *black warrior* like it was; and then comes the "unanimous resolution" of the Louisiana legislature asking the United States to interfere and declare war, in case Cuba should undertake to emancipate her slaves. Senator Slidell's speech is still tingling in our ears, asking the Government to repeal the neutrality laws and allow every pirate who pleases to land in Cuba and burn and destroy. You know Mr. Soulé's conduct in Madrid. It is rumoured that he has been authorized to offer $250,000,000 for Cuba. The sum is enormous; but, when you consider the character of *this* Administration and the Inaugural of President Pierce, the unscrupulous abuse made of public money, I do not think it is a very extraordinary supposition.

But this matter of getting possession of Cuba is something dangerous as well as difficult. There are three conceivable ways of getting it: one is by *buying*, and that I take it is wholly out of the question. If I am rightly informed, there is a certain Spanish debt owing to Englishmen, and that Cuba is somehow pledged as a sort of collateral security for the Spanish bonds. I take it for granted that Cuba is not to be bought for many years without the interference of England, and depend upon it England will not allow it to be sold *for the establishment of Slavery;* for I think it is pretty well understood by politicians that there is a regular agreement entered into between Spain on one side and England on the other, that at a certain period within twenty-five years every slave in Cuba shall be set free. I believe this is known to men somewhat versed in the secret history of the two cabinets of England and of Spain. England has the same wish for land which fires our Anglo-Saxon blood. She has islands in the West Indies; the Morro in Cuba is only 100 miles from Jamaica. If we get Cuba for Slavery, we shall next want the British West Indies for the same institution. Cuba filled with fillibusters would be a dangerous neighbour.

Then there are two other ways: one is by fillibusterism; and that Mr. Slidell and Mr. Dean want to try; the other is by open war. Now, fillibusterism will lead to open war, so I will consider only this issue.

I know that Americans will fight more desperately, perhaps, on land or sea, than any other people. But fighting is an ugly business, especially with such antagonists as we shall have in this case. It is a matter well understood that the Captain-General of Cuba has a paper in his possession authorizing him discretionally to *free the slaves and put arms* in their hands whenever it is thought necessary. It is rather difficult to get at the exact statistics of Cuba. There has been no census since 1842, I think, when the population was estimated at a million. I will reckon it now at 1,300,000—700,000 blacks, and 600,000 whites. Of the 700,000 blacks, half a million are slaves and *two hundred thousand free men*. Now, a black free man in Cuba is a very different person from the black free man in the United States. He has *rights*. He is not turned out of the omnibus nor the *meeting house* nor the *graveyard*. He is respected by the law; he respects himself, and is a formidable person; let the blacks be furnished with arms, they are formidable foes. And remember there are mountain fastnesses in the centre of the island; that it is as defensible as St. Domingo; and it has a very unhealthy climate for Northern men. The Spaniard would have great allies. The vomito is there; typhoid, dysentery, yellow fever—the worst of all—is there. A Northern army even of fillibusters would fight against the most dreadful odds. "The Lord from on high," as the old Hebrew would say, would fight against the Northern men ; the pestilence that swept off Sennacherib's host would not respect the fillibuster.

That is not all. What sort of a navy has Spain? *One hundred and seventy-nine ships* of war! They are small mostly, but they carry over 1,400 cannon and 24,000 men —15,000 marines and 9,000 sailors. The United States has *seventy-five ships* of war ; 2,200 cannon, 14,000 men— large ships, heavy cannon. That is not all. Spaniards fight desperately. A Spanish armada I would not be very much afraid of ; but Spain will issue letters of marque, and a Portuguese or Spanish pirate is rather an uncomfortable being to meet. Our commerce is spread all over the seas ; there is no mercantile marine so unprotected as ours. Our ships do not carry muskets, still less cannon, since pirates have been swept off the sea. Let Spain issue letters of marque, England winking at it, and Algerine pirates from out the Barbary States of Africa and other pirates from the Brazilian, Mexican, and the West Indian ports, would prowl about the coast of the Mediterranean and over all the bosom of the Atlantic ; and then where would be our commerce? The South has nothing to fear from that. She has got no shipping. Yes, Norfolk has 23,000 tons. The South is not afraid. The North has nearly *four million tons* of shipping. But touch the commerce of a Northern man and you touch his heart.

England has conceded to us as a measure just what we asked. We have always declared " free ships make free goods." England said " enemies' goods make enemies' ships." Now she has not affirmed our principle ; she has assented to our measure. That is all you can expect her to do. But, if we repeal our neutrality laws and seek to get Cuba in order to establish Slavery there, endangering the interests of England, and the freedom of her coloured citizens, depend upon it England will not suffer this to be done without herself interfering. If she is so deeply immersed in European wars that she cannot interfere directly, she will indirectly. But I have not thought that England and France are to be much engaged in a European war. I suppose the intention of the American Cabinet is to seize Cuba as soon as the British and Russians are fairly fighting, thinking that England will not interfere. But in " this

war of older sons" which now goes on for the dismember-
ment of Turkey, it is not so clear that England will be so
deeply engaged that she cannot attend to her domestic
affairs, or the interest of her West Indies. I think these
powers are going to divide Turkey between them, but I
do not believe they are going to do much fighting there.
If we are bent on seizing Cuba, a long and ruinous fight
is a thing that ought to enter into men's calculations.
Now, let such a naval warfare take place, and how will
·your insurance stock look in New York, Philadelphia, and
Boston? How will your merchants look when reports
come one after another that your ships are carried in as
prizes by Spain, or sunk on the ocean after they have
been plundered? I speak in the great commercial metropolis of America. I wish these things to be seriously considered by Northern men. Though I would not fear a
naval war, let the Northern men look out for their own
ships. But here is a matter which the South might think
of. In case of foreign war, the North will not be the
battle-field. An invading army would attack the South.
Who would defend it—the local militia, the "chivalry" of
South Carolina, the "gentlemen" of Virginia, who are to
slaughter 100,000 Abolitionists in a day? Let an army
set foot on Southern soil, with a few *black regiments;* let
the commander offer *freedom to all the slaves and put arms
in their hands;* let him ask them to *burn houses and butcher
men;* and there would be a state of things not quite so
pleasant for gentlemen of the South to look at. "They
that laughed at the grovelling worm and trod on him may
cry and howl when they see the stoop of the flying and
fiery-mouthed dragon!" Now, there is only one opinion
about the *valour* of President Pierce. Like the sword of
Hudibras, it cut into itself,

> —— "for lack
> Of other stuff to hew and hack."

But would he like to stand with such a fire in his rear?
Set a house on fire by hot shot, and you don't *know how
much of it will burn down.*

IV. Well, if Nebraska is made a slave territory, as I
suppose it will be, the next thing is the possession of
Cuba. Then the war against Spain will come, as I think,

inevitably. But even if we don't get Cuba, Slavery must be extended to *other parts of the Union.* This may be done *judicially* by the Supreme Court—one of the powerful agents to destroy local self-government and legalize centralization ; or *legislatively* by Congress. Already Slavery is established in California. An attempt, you know, was made to establish it in Illinois. Senator Toombs, the other day, boasted to John P. Hale, that it would "not be long before the slave-holder would sit down at the foot of Bunker Hill monument with his slaves." You and I may live to see it—at least to see the attempt made. A writer in a prominent Southern journal, the *Charleston Courier* (of March 16, 1854), declares "that domestic Slavery is a constitutional institution, and cannot be prohibited in a territory by either territorial or congressional legislation. It is recognised by the Constitution as an existing and lawful institution . . and by the *recognition and establishment of Slavery eo nomine* in the district of Columbia, under the constitutional provision for the acquisition of and exclusive legislation over such a capitoline district; and by that clause also which declares that the citizens of each State shall be entitled to all the privileges and immunities of citizens in the several States." " The *citizens of any State . . cannot be constitutionally denied the equal right . . of sojourning or settling . . with their man servants and maid servants . . in any portion of the widespread Canaan* which the Lord their God hath given them, *there to dwell unmolested in* person or PROPERTY." Admirable exposition of the Constitution ! The free black man must be shut up in gaol if he goes from Boston in a ship to Charleston, but the slave-holder may bring his slaves to Massachusetts and dwell there *unmolested with his property in men.* South Carolina has a white population of 274,567 persons, considerably less than half the population of this city. But, if South Carolina says to the State of New York, with three million men in it, let us bring our slaves to New York, what will the "Hards," and the "Softs," and the "Silver Greys" answer? Gentlemen, we shall hear what we shall hear. I fear not an officeholder of any note would oppose the measure. It might be carried with the present Supreme Court, or Congress, I make no doubt.

But this is not the end. After the Gadsden Treaty, the enslavement of Nebraska, the extension of Slavery to the free States, the seizure of Cuba, with other islands— San Domingo, &c.—there is one step more—THE RE-ES-TABLISHMENT OF THE.AFRICAN SLAVE-TRADE.

A recent number of the *Southern Standard* thus develops the thought: "With firmness and judgment we can open up the African slave emigration again to people the whole region of the tropics. We can boldly defend this upon the most enlarged system of philanthropy. It is far better for the wild races of Africa themselves." " The good old Las Casas, in 1519, was the first to advise Spain to import Africans to her colonies. . . Experience has shown his scheme was founded in wise and Christian philanthropy. . . The time is coming when we will boldly defend this emi-gration [kidnapping men in Africa and selling them in the Christian Republic] before the world. The hypocritical cant and whining morality of the latter-day saints will die away before the majesty of commerce. . . We have too long been governed by psalm-singing schoolmasters from the North. . . The folly commenced in our own govern-ment uniting with Great Britain to declare slave-importing piracy." . . " A general rupture in Europe would force upon us the undisputed sway of the Gulf of Mexico and the West Indies. . . With Cuba and St. Domingo, we could control the . . power of the world. Our true policy is to look to Brazil as the next great slave power. . . A treaty of commerce and alliance with Brazil will give us the control over the Gulf of Mexico and its border coun-tries, together with the islands; and the consequence of this will place African Slavery beyond the reach of fanaticism at home or abroad. These two great slave powers . . ought to guard and strengthen their mutual interests. . . We can not only preserve domestic servitude, but we can defy the power of the world." . . " The time will come that all the islands and regions suited to African Slavery, between us and Brazil, will fall under the control of these two powers. . . In a few years there will be no investment for the $200,000,000 . . so profitable . . as the development . . of the tropical regions" [that is, as the African slave-trade]. . . "If the slaveholding race in these States are but true to themselves, they have a great destiny before them."

Now, gentlemen and ladies, who is to blame that things have come to such a pass as this? The South and the North; but the North much more than the South,—very much more. Gentlemen, we let Gog get upon the Ark; we took *pay for his passage.* Our most prominent men in Church and State have sworn allegiance to Gog. But this is not always to last; there is a day after to-day—a FOR-EVER behind each to-day.

The North ought to have fought Slavery at the adoption of the Constitution, and at every step since; after the battle was lost then, we should have resisted each successive step of the slave power. But we have yielded— yielded continually. We made no fight over the annexation of slave territory, the admission of slave States. We should have rent the Union into the primitive townships sooner than consent to the Fugitive Slave Bill. But as we failed to fight manfully then, I never thought the North would rally on the Missouri Compromise line. I rejoice at the display of indignation I witness here and elsewhere. For once New York appears more moral than Boston. I thank you for it. A meeting is called in the Park to-morrow. It is high time. But I doubt that the North will yet rally and defend the line drawn in 1820. But there are two lines of defence where the nation will pause, I think—the *occupation of Cuba,* with its war so destructive to Northern ships; and the *restoration of the African slave-trade.* The *slave-breeding* States, Maryland, Virginia, Kentucky, Tennessee, Missouri, will oppose that; for, if the Gulf States, and the future tropical territories can import Africans at $100 a head, depend upon it, that will spoil the market for the slave-breeders of America. And, gentlemen, if Virginia cannot sell her own children, how will this "well-born, well-educated, well-bred aristocrat" look down on the poor and ignorant Yankee! No, gentlemen, this iniquity is not to last for ever. A certain amount of force will compress a cubic foot of water into nine-tenths of its natural size; but the weight of the whole earth cannot make it any smaller. Even the North is not infinitely compressible. When atom touches atom, you may take off the screws.

Things cannot continue long in this condition. Every triumph of Slavery is a day's march towards its ruin.

There is no higher law, is there? "He taketh the wise in their own craftiness, the council of the wicked is carried" —ay, but *it is carried headlong.*

Only see what a change has been coming over our spirit just now.   Three years ago, Isaiah Rynders and Hiram Ketchum domineered over New York; and those gentlemen who are to follow me, and whom you are impatient to hear, were mobbed down in the city of New York, two years ago; they could not find a hall that would be leased to them for money or love, and had to adjourn to Syracuse to hold their convention.   Look at this assembly now.

A little while ago all the leading clergymen were in favour of the Fugitive Slave Bill; now three thousand of New England ministers remonstrate against Nebraska. They know there is a fire in their rear, and, in theological language, it is a fire that "is not quenched." It goeth not out by day, and there is no night *there.*   The clergymen stand between eternal torment on one side and the little giant of Slavery on the other.   They do not go back! Two thousand English clergymen once became non-conformists in a single day.   Three thousand New England ministers remonstrated against the enslavement of Nebraska.   Now is the time to push and be active, call meetings, bring out men of all parties, all forms of religion, agitate, agitate, agitate.   Make a fire in the rear of the Government and the representatives.   The South is weak —only united.   The North is strong in money, in men, in education, in the justice of our great cause—only not united for freedom.   Only be faithful to ourselves, and Slavery will come down, not slowly, as I thought once, but when the people of the North say it, it will come down with a GREAT CRASH.

Then, when we are free from this plague-spot of Slavery —the curse to our industry, our education, our politics, and our religion—we shall increase more rapidly in number and still more abundantly be rich.   The South will be as the North—active, intelligent—Virginia rich as New York, the Carolinas as active as Massachusetts.   Then, by peaceful purchase, the Anglo-Saxon may acquire the rest of this North American Continent.   The Spaniards will make nothing of it.   Nay, we may honourably go farther South, and possess the Atlantic and Pacific slopes of the Northern continent, extending the area of *Freedom* at every step. We may carry thither the Anglo-Saxon vigour and enterprise, the old love of liberty, the love also of law; the best institutions of the present age—ecclesiastical, political, social, domestic. Then what a nation we shall one day become. America, the mother of a thousand Anglo-Saxon States, tropic and temperate, on both sides the Equator, may behold the Mississippi and the Amazon uniting their waters, the drainage of two vast continents in the Mediterranean of the Western World; may count her children at last by hundreds of millions—and among them all behold no tyrant and no slave! What a spectacle—the Anglo-Saxon family occupying a whole hemisphere, with industry, freedom, religion. The fulfilment of this vision is our province; we are the involuntary instruments of God. Shall America scorn the mission God sends her on? Then let us all perish, and may Russia teach justice to mankind!

A SERMON

OF THE

CONSEQUENCES OF AN IMMORAL PRINCIPLE AND FALSE IDEA OF LIFE.

PREACHED AT THE MUSIC HALL IN BOSTON, ON SUNDAY,

NOVEMBER 26, 1854.

"Be not deceived; God is not mocked: for whatsoever a man soweth, that shall he also reap."—GALATIANS, vi. 7.

I ASK your attention to a "Sermon of the Consequences which come from an Immoral Principle and False Idea of Man's Duty and the Purpose of Human Life."

Man's moral, as his industrial progress, is by experiment. Many of the experiments fail; but by repeated trials we hit the mark. America's mercantile ability to-day—her power of agriculture, mining, manufactures, commerce—is the achievement of the human race in the long history from the creation till now. So America's spiritual ability —her power of wisdom, justice, philanthropy, and religion —is not the product of this one nation, nor of this age alone, but of all time and all men; it is a part of the net result of human activity thus far. Vice, ignorance, folly, injustice, bad institutions—they represent the imperfect development of man's faculties, and consequent experiments badly planned; and so which needs must fail. The most moral man in Boston did not attain his excellence all at once, but by repeated efforts, by continuous experiments; and a great many of his efforts turned out mistakes. As he builds up his fortune, so his character, by trial, by experiment; first failure, and then success. So out of this briar, Failure, we pluck the honeyed rose, Success.

In the best man's action, there is a per-centage of

abnormal action : that is; folly, injustice, error, sin—if you choose to call it so. Put all man's moral misdemeanours together, and call them by one name—Vice. They are most conveniently dealt with if put into a basket with a single handle.

This amount of abnormal action, other things being equal, will diminish in proportion to the correctness of the man's ideal of life; and in proportion to the strength and earnestness of his efforts to make his ideal the actual fact of his life : or it will increase in proportion to the falseness of his ideal, and the feebleness of his efforts to make it the actual fact of his life. Vice is a variable, capable of being enlarged or lessened.

In all nations, likewise, there is a variable per centage of moral error—Vice. Other things being equal, this abnormal quantity will commonly depend on five causes.

First. On the amount of activity in the nation ; a people that goes is more likely to go wrong than one that goes not ; one which goes much, more than one which goes little.

Second. On the amount of property ; for property represents power over Nature, and this may be abused, directed wrong or right.

Third. On the difference in respect to property between the rich class and the poor class. Where this difference is immense, there is a vast quantity of vice ; where the difference is small, the vice is little.

Fourth. On the ideas which men of genius, culture, and station, spread abroad amongst the people as their rule of life ; on the institutions and laws. Where these are good, vice will continually diminish ; where bad, progressively multiply. National institutions, conduct, character, resemble the popular ideas as plants grow from the seed.

Fifth. On the pains taken to remove the causes of wrong,—the circumstances which occasion it ; an attempt to remove ignorance, alleviate want, cure drunkenness, end prostitution ; on the pains taken to comfort, teach, and moralize mankind.

In France, England, part of Germany, and the free States of America, great pains are taken to diminish the amount of vice by removing some of its outward causes. Wise social philosophers look upon all this abnormal action of a nation as a disease incident to the childhood of mankind, and to exposure amongst pernicious circumstances, not natural to man's constitution, but only native to certain conditions and stages of development; and these doctors of humanity seek to help mankind remove the outward occasion, and overcome the inward and transient impulse to this wrong.

Now, in these four countries, for fifty or a hundred years past, there has been a progressive diminution of vice. The amount of abnormal action first becomes smaller in proportion to the whole action, and to the whole property, a smaller fraction of the total action of the people. The amount of *tare* is diminished.

But next, the bad quality of vice also diminishes. The old error of violence disappears; the milder vices take its place. The chief object of vicious attack is not the substance of man, his person; it is an accident of man, his estate. Vices of violent instinct—lust, revenge, diminish and shade off into vices of reflective calculation—ambition, acquisitiveness, and the like.

Then, as a third thing, vice is getting confined to a smaller class of persons. Once, it was almost universal. Such vice was instantial, virtue the exception. In the age before Homer, every Greek skipper was also a pirate. Now, vice permanently infects but a small body of persons; first, the perishing class, whom poverty and its consequent ignorance makes offenders; second, the professional villains, not ignorant, not necessarily poor,—for, in the division of labour in modern society, general villany has become a profession, whereof there are various specialities —pickpockets, burglars, thieves, forgers, and the like; the same spirit of villany having divers manifestations.

So the general abnormal action is getting corrected. First, the snow is getting thin everywhere; next, it becomes less cold in all or most places; third, it gets melted away from the open land, and only lies in a few great heaps, covered up with dust, or is stretched in long lines where the walls hide it from the summer's sun. Men are attacking also this residue of ice and snow, carting it off to sunnier spots: and so the world is getting moralized; and though fresh snow falls on the ground, yet the neck of vice's winter must be considered broke. The moralization of mankind goes on continually; the proportionate quantity of vice is lessened, and its quality bettered, in England, France, part of Germany, and in free America.

In some of the other countries of Christendom, there is one great cause which hinders man's instinct of progressive development, and prevents the advancing diminution of vice, namely; the institutional tyranny exercised by the church, by society, by the state, by priests, kings, and nobles. That cause retards the normal action of the people in Russia, Turkey, Austria, the other part of Germany, in Italy, Portugal, and Spain, where the progress of man is far less rapid than in those four other countries just named. This tyranny retards also man's advance in riches, for despotism is always costly; vice is a spendthrift, and, other things being equal, a moral people will have the most power over the material world, and consequently be the richest, and advance in riches with the greatest rapidity,—for wealth is an unavoidable accident of man's development, indispensable for future progress, and the hoarded result of the past.

But here, in America, there is one cause which tends to check the progressive diminution of abnormal action, and the advancing moralization of man, and which actually is now leading to a frightful development of vice in most hateful and dangerous forms; indeed, a cause which tends to demoralize the people here, even more rapidly than tyranny itself is doing in Russia, Austria, Turkey, Italy, Portugal, and Spain. Here is the cause: it is the prevalence of an immoral principle, a false idea of man's duty, boldly set forth by men of great prominence, and within the last few years very widely spread.

To understand this false idea the better, and see how fatally it operates against us, look a little at the circumstances of the nation, wherein we differ from the other families of men. The old civilizations of Europe had two distinctive characteristic marks.

First, they were oligarchic, having a government of all, but by a few, and for the sake of a few. Sometimes it was a theocratic oligarchy—the rule of priests over the people; sometimes a monarchic oligarchy—the rule of kings over the subjects; sometimes an aristocratic oli-

garchy—the rule of the nobility over the plebeian class;
sometimes a despotocratic oligarchy—the rule of masters
over their slaves. In all these four cases, the mass of men
were deemed of no value except as servants to the oligarch.
He was "born to eat up the corn," to wear the flowers in
the garland round his brow; the mass of men were only
born to create corn for him to eat, and rear flowers for
him to wear. But if you "drive out Nature with a pitch-
fork, still nevertheless she comes back." And so the
people tended to rebellion, casting off the yoke of priest,
king, noble, master. To check this revolutionary spirit,
the ruling power spreads abroad the idea that such rebellion is the greatest offence which man can commit; it is
high treason. So in the theocratic oligarchy it was
high treason to doubt or deny the exclusive rule of the
priest; in the monarchic, the exclusive rule of the king;
in the aristocratic, the exclusive rule of the nobilitary
class; and, in the despotocratic, the exclusive rule of the
master. It was taught there was no natural right of men
above the conventional privilege of the priest, king, noble,
and master; no law of God above the enactment of earthly
rulers. This characteristic mark of the old civilization is
somewhat effaced in France and England; but still even
there the handwriting is yet so plain that he may read
who runs.

   That is the first characteristic. Here is the next.
Therein, civilization was military, not industrial; the art
to produce was put below the art to destroy. Productive
industry was counted "an illiberal art;" it was despised:
destructive fighting was "liberal" work; it was honoured.
Working was for the mass of the people, and must be
degraded; fighting, the rulers' business, and held honourable. "It is the business of a man to fight, of a slave to
work," quoth Homer. Besides, fighting was indispensable for these unnatural rulers, not only to stave off a
foreign foe, but at home to keep the mass of the people
down. This characteristic mark of all the governments of
the old world is likewise somewhat effaced in mercantile
England and France, but still writ in letters of fire, most
savagely plain. Such oligarchies do not rest on the permanent moral nature of man, but only on the transient
selfishness incident to a low stage of development. Their

support is not in the conscience of the mass of men, but in the violence of the few who rule; not in the consent of the Hungarians and Poles, but in the cannons of the Emperor and the Czar. Military violence is the complement of oligarchy, for the special privilege of the oligarch is held of his private selfishness, and against mankind; not of his human nature, and for all the people; is a conventional, not a natural accident of humanity. Hence is it also insecure: for what will not even touch firm ground with its feet must one day with its head.

Now, the American civilization has two characteristics exactly opposite to these. First, it is not oligarchic; it is a democracy; in theory, having a government of all, for all, by all. Next, it is industrial, and not military.

I. This democracy, in theory, rests on the idea that the substance of manhood, the human nature in which all are alike, is superior to any human accident wherein all must differ. Manhood is more than priesthood, kinghood, noblehood, masterhood. The qualitative human agreement of nature is more than the quantitative difference between the genius and the clown; more than the historic and conventional distinction between noble-born and common-born, rich and poor. So democracy can exist only on condition that this human substance is equally respected in the greatest and the least; in man and woman; in the largest majority, and in the minority of one, that stands on manhood. So the people is not for the ruler, but the ruler for the people; the government is the creature of the nation, not the nation of the government. Each man's natural rights are to be sacred against the wrong-doing of any other man, or of the whole nation of men—all protected against each, each against all. That is the first point.

II. Then the American civilization is also industrial. Military power is to be exceptional, subordinate; the industrial is instantial and chief. Now, industry aims at the production and enjoyment of property; for, in a word, industry is the art of making material nature into human property. Property is a natural accident of man, inseparable from his substance. The first thing he does on

coming into the world is to acquire property; first food,
then shelter.   The first thing the baby does is this: the
earliest generation of babies—baby men—their first deed
was acquisition; food for existence, flowers for ornament.
Property is the material result and test of man's normal
activity.   It is also the indispensable condition of existence
from day to day; much and permanent property is the
indispensable condition for the advance and development
of mankind, in mind and conscience, heart and soul.   It is
an accident of more value than all other external accidents
—priestly, kingly, nobilitary, and despotocratic.   In the
industrial state, money is the symbol of power, for the
individual and for the nation; it is worth more than
descent from priestly Moses, or Luther, from royal Charle-
magne, or protectorial Cromwell, or from any nobilitary
stem.   "All the blood of all the Howards" is powerless,
compared to the almighty dollar.
    Democracy is not possible except in a nation where there
is so much property, and that so widely distributed that
the whole people can have considerable education—intellectual, moral, affectional, and religious.   So much property,
widely distributed, judiciously applied, is the indispensable
material basis of a democracy; as military power is indispensable to the existence of an unnatural oligarchy—
priestly, monarchic, nobilitary, or despotocratic; and as
those tyrannical rulers must have military power to keep
the people down, so in a democracy the people must have
property—the result of their industry—to keep themselves
up, and advance their education; else, very soon there will
be a government over all, but by a few, and for the sake of
a few; and democracy will end in despotism.   But it must
be natural property resting on a basis of natural morality,
consisting of what man may own and not violate his moral
nature.   There can be no natural property which violates
natural right, the constitution of the universe.
    Accordingly, from the nature of such a government, it
becomes necessary, in every industrial democracy, to have
one thing sacred:—the natural rights of man, the substance of humanity.   This is the prime factor of all the
national product.   If the natural rights of man be not
respected, then the democracy will perish, just as the oligarchy will come to an end if the pretended privilege

of king, priest, noble, and master be denied and set at naught. The natural rights of the individual must be secured from violation by another man, or by the State. An attack on the natural rights of man is the most fatal of all things to the industrial democracy, undermining the foundation whereon its chief corner stone is laid; for rights are anterior to all "social compacts," and the earliest statutes of the oldest realm; are inherent in our nature, and therewith derived from God. Oligarchy involves a denial of the generic rights of human nature; it depends on violence, and has no permanent roots in the constitution of man; while democracy is only possible on condition of permanent respect for those rights.

When the substance of man is thus respected, and his rights in general duly honoured, all special rights are also safe: among these is the right to property, an indispensable accident of man, quite easily secured if man's substance be respected; but if not, then property itself is as insecure in the industrial democracy as freedom in a despotism. So, in a democracy, any attack on the unalienable rights of man, or any class of men, or any individual person, is an attack also on each one of the accidents of man—on property, for example; taking from beneath it the natural basis of right, whereon it might rest secure, and substituting therefore only permanent or fleeting violence. This has not been known as science by philosophers, nor seen as fact by the mass of men, but is yet fore-felt in the instinctive consciousness of enlightened nations, and partially acted on. We are wiser than we know, and build better than we plan; for the instinct of the people has told them that the substance of man must be held sacred.

Now, an industrial democracy is not the creature of man's caprice, which might be so or otherwise. It is a reproduction of the law of human nature, and the constitution of the universe; and "other foundation can no man lay than what is laid" eternally in the nature of man. Arabesques of fancy may differ, as Raphael Urbino or as Raphael Morgen paints them; they are the creatures of voluntary caprice: but the multiplication tables, made by Pythagoras or Bowditch, must be exactly alike; for they represent, not man's caprice, but a necessity of universal law, and rest thereon. So the industrial democracy can rest

only on the law of God, writ in the constitution of matter
and mind; accordingly, the greatest of all political errors,
and the most fatal to the existence of democracy, to the
rights of man, and to the security of property, one of his
indispensable accidents, is the idea that man has no obligation to respect the constitution of the universe; and the
declaration that there is no law above the statutes which
men's hands have made.   Where that idea prevails, there
is a blow struck at every man's head, and at each dollar of
property.   Tyranny may be provisional; justice alone is
ultimate; the point common to each and all, to man and
God, whereon all rights balance.

Such is the difference between the theory of American
civilization and that of the old civilizations of Asia and
Europe;—ours is the theory of a society that is only possible nineteen centuries after Christ; nine centuries after
it could not have been; and nine centuries before it could
not have been dreamed of; and such is its foundation in
man and the nature of things.

I have just said that, in virtue of certain causes, there is
a progressive diminution of man's abnormal action, and a
progressive moralization of mankind in England, France,
part of Germany, and the free States of America; but
that in some other European countries this natural diminution of wrong is retarded by the crimes of the ruling power.
Nay, even in England and France, man's moralization is
largely retarded by the corruption and selfishness of the
controlling classes of men, who spread abroad false ideas of
man's duty to himself, to his brother, and to his God;—
sometimes doing it purposely, but most often, I have charity
enough to think, doing it through mistake.   Still this diminution goes on in the manner set forth.

Now, in America, in direct opposition to this progressive
moralization of man, during the last few years there has
been a rapid increase of certain great vices, which are also
crimes; transgressions not only of God's law, but likewise
of man's statutes,—vices of appalling magnitude.   They
are offences not committed by those two classes just mentioned as concentrating a great amount of what is commonly called vice and crime—the perishing class, whom
poverty makes thieves and robbers, and the professional
villains, who make rascality their vocation.   Nor yet are

they committed under the transient and accidental stimulus of strong drink, or temporary malice, or passion, that springs upon the man,—causes which gender so many brawls and murders. These offences are committed by persons of high standing in society, done deliberately, the man knowing very well what he is about.

For convenience in my handling and your remembering, I will put these into three classes. First, offences against the property of individuals; next, offences against the life of individuals for the sake of getting their property; and third, offences against the property and the life of other nations. The first and second are individual,—personal vices; the last is national,—a collective vice.

I. Here are some cases which I put in the first class, offences against property. I will not travel out of America, nor go back more than twelve months. Let me say at the outset, of the individuals who have done the deeds I refer to, I would speak and judge with the greatest delicacy and the most refined charity. It is the deed itself on which I wish to fasten your condemnation, not the man who did it; for I want you to look through the man at the deed; through the deed, at the cause of it, lying far behind, which I will presently bring before your eye.

Here is the first in the first class. Mr. Crane, President of the New England railroad, deprived the company of I know not how large a sum of money entrusted to him. In this particular case there was much in the man's character, and has been much in his conduct since,—which, I am told, is, in general, manly and upright,—to lead to a favourable judgment of him. It is the deed I look at, and the principle which lies behind the deed, which I condemn: for the man, I have a woman's charity; for the deed and the principle behind it, a man's justice.

Here is the next case. Mr. Schuyler, at New York, plundered the public of about two millions of dollars, committing the largest fraud of the kind ever perpetrated in America or Europe.

Here is the third. In California, Mr. Meigs robbed the public of one million six hundred thousand dollars.

As a fourth thing, in New York, the Ocean Bank has robbed the public of one or two hundred thousand dollars.

As a fifth, you know in Boston the history of the Metropolitan Insurance Company and of the Cochituate Bank, two bubbles of fraud that burst, swallowing up the property of honest men.

In Ohio, banks and bankers have just now committed frauds to the extent of, I think, not less than two millions of dollars.

Then look at the conduct of the municipal governments of New York and Boston, the manner in which they squander the money of the people, veiling the uses to which it has been appropriated, and thus wasting the people's treasure. I need only refer to the rapid increase of taxes in Boston, which every property-holder knows and laments, —and I need not say there is no honest explanation for the whole thing. You all know it. Here, too, I would speak with all becoming charity.

II. Here are some cases of the next class. Not two months ago, the steamship *Arctic*, with about three hundred and eighty passengers, was coming from England to New York. She had six boats, and, if they were crowded till the gunwale kissed the sea, they would hold at the utmost only one hundred and eighty persons; so in case of wreck there were two hundred others with no chance of escape. This was the owner's fault; and dearly has he paid for it! The ship, in a fog so thick that a man could not see twice the length of the vessel before him, drives through the darkness at the rate of thirteen miles an hour, giving no warning sound of her ferocious approach. This was the captain's fault; and dearly has he paid for it! When the disaster happened, some thirty or forty men escaped,—not a woman or child! the feeble-bodied were left to die. I will not call this the *fault* of the men; it was their *disgrace* and their *sin!* If our fathers at Lexington and Bunker Hill had thrown down their muskets and turned their backs to the British, and been shot down with a coward's wound, you and I would feel disgraced till this day; but I think it would not have been half so disgraceful to run from a red-coat as to leave a woman and a baby to perish in the waters, rather than hazard one's own life. I should be ashamed to live if I had left a woman to sink in the ocean, and escaped myself. It is rumoured that a boat full of women was purposely overturned by the crew—to save their *manly* lives!

I believe about three hundred and forty persons perished. I am speaking in a mercantile town, where, if life and justice be not valued, money is. Look then at it as the destruction of human property only. In Massachusetts, the official valuation of a man, whose life is destroyed by a railroad company, is five thousand dollars. Three hundred and forty lives at five thousand dollars each, make the sum of one million seven hundred thousand dollars. That is the pecuniary value of life dashed away through the cupidity of the ship-owner and the recklessness of the ship-master! With gentleness, judge you the men; look at the principle which lies behind!

Pardon me if I try to calculate the value of a human life, estimating it at five thousand dollars! If, an hour before the "accident," some man had said to these three hundred and forty persons, "I will place at your disposal all the riches of America, Europe, and Asia, on condition you shall sink yourselves to the bottom of the sea;" do you think there was one man who would have said, "Let us take the wealth, and leave it to our heirs, and ourselves atheistically go down?" No! all the wealth of the material universe could not have purchased the sin. Men who would lay down their life for a moral principle, or a friend, would never throw it away for all the gold in California or Australia, or in the three continents of the earth besides. Pardon me for calculating in money the value of human life.

A similar case, in its origin and in its conduct, took place in the recent destruction of the *Yankee Blade,* at California. Then, scarce a week passes but some railroad or steamboat company massacres men by the wholesale,— sometimes, most commonly, through reckless cupidity and lust of gold. I believe America commits more murders than all the rest of Protestant Christendom; taking away Russia and Spanish America, probably more than all Christendom, Protestant and Catholic. But not to speak of the harvest of murders we annually reap, there is no country in Christendom where life is so insecure, so cruelly dashed away in the manslaughter of reckless enterprise!

III. Here is the third class,—offences against the property and life of other nations. You may take the whole history of the present national administration. Look at the conduct of this government for the last two years of its unhappy and disgraceful life; at the perpetual fillibustering of the government, now against Mexico, then against Hayti, then against Cuba; at that murderous attack on Greytown, not only wicked, but mean, cowardly, and sneaking! not a Narragansett Indian but would have been ashamed of such unbarbarous conduct! But it has been commended, I know not in how many journals; and one in this city declares it had "the entire approbation of the whole community." See how steadily the administration seeks to tighten the chains on the working class of the South: no Italian pope, no king, nor priest, was ever more oppressive towards his subjects than the American industrial democracy towards the three and a quarter millions of men who do the work of the South.

These three classes of cases are exceptions to the progressive diminution of abnormal action, and to the advancing moralization of the people. They are not to be explained by the common causes of vice.

Look back a little, and you will see the root out of which all this monstrous crop of wickedness has grown so swiftly up. I will omit all reference to individuals, and speak impersonally. A few years ago three axioms were published to the world as embodying the fundamentals of the party then in power. They were laid down as a programme of principles for the nation's future politics. Let it be remembered that this political party has more literary education, and more hoarded money, than any other whatsoever in the land. But the rival party affirmed the same principles, having therewith unity of idea.

Here are the maxims—

The first, which I give in my own language, is this: There is no law of God above any statutes, however wicked, which politicians make.

The next, which is not in my words, is, "Religion has nothing to do with politics; there it makes men mad."

The third is, "The great object of government is the protection of property at home, and respect and renown abroad."

Look at these—

I. "There is no higher law!" That is the proclamation of objective atheism; it is the selfish materialism of Hobbes, Hume, of De la Mettrie, and Helvetius, gone to seed. You have nothing to rely on above the politicians and their statutes : if you suffer, nothing to appeal to—but the ballot-box. The speculative materialism of Comte resolves man into blood and bone and nerves. The speculative atheism of Feuerbach resolves deity into the blind force of a blind universe, working from no love as motive, with no plan as method, and for no purpose as ultimate end. But both of these, materialistic Comte and atheistic Feuerbach, bow them down before the eternal laws of matter and mind : "These," say they, "we must keep always, come what may." But the prominent politicians of America,—they mocked at the law of nature and the constitution of mind; they outdid the "*French* materialism*" of Comte, and the "*Germanic* atheism*" of Feuerbach. Pardon me for saying *Germanic* atheism! He violated his nation's consciousness before he called himself an atheist; and then is not so in heart, only in head; it is the blood of pious humanity which runs in his nation's veins. The sailor, the machinist, and the farmer recognise a law of God writ in the matter they deal with, whereto they seek to conform ; but the American politician has no objective restraint. No God is to check the momentum of his ambition.

II. Here is the next axiom : "Religion has nothing to do with politics." That is subjective atheism, with a political application. If there be no law inherent in mind and matter above any wicked statute of a tyrant, still the instinctive religious sense of man looks up with reverence, faith, and love, and thinks there is a God, and a higher law. Materialistic Comte and atheistic Feuerbach, and those accomplished translators who set such works over to the English soil, confess to the natural religious emotions, give them sure place in all human affairs ; but in one of the most important of human transactions, where the welfare of millions of men is at stake, the American politicians declare that "Religion has nothing to do with politics ; it makes men mad." Politic Felix trembled before Paul, reasoning of self-command, righteousness, and God's judgment to come; Festus told the magnificent apostle, "Much learning hath made thee mad;" but the heathen Roman did not venture to say, "*Religion* makes men mad!" Conscience makes cowards of men who meditate their own destruction; nay, it sometimes holds the murderer's hand. But the moral feeling, the religious feeling, has nothing to do with politics!

No higher law! Religion nothing to do with politics!

See what it leads to. Come, Puritan fathers! who, feeding on clams for three months at a time, thanked God that they "sucked of the abundance of the seas, and of the treasures hid in the sands!" You were mistaken! Religion has nothing to do with politics! Bow to the Eighth Henry, to "Bloody" Mary, and Elizabeth, scarce cleaner in the hand or heart; to James the Stupid, and to Charles, whose head the righteous axe shore off! Come, Protestant martyrs; whose bodies snapped and crackled in the Catholic fire, but, as the candle decayed, your soul still flaming more ardent up to God! Come and submit! It was all a mistake! The priestly tyrants were right! There is no higher law! Come, glorious company of the apostles! Come, goodly fellowship of the prophets! Come, noble army of martyrs! Come, Jesus of Nazareth —crowned with thorns, spit upon, scourged, mocked at, and crucified! It was all a mistake! Your cross was not your crown of triumph; it was only your shame! The scribes and Pharisees were right! There is no higher law! Religion has nothing to do with politics!

Come, all ye tyrants of earth—Herods, Pilates, Dominics, and Torquemadas! Your great enemy is slain! There is no law above you! No sentiment in the human heart which has a right to protest against your iniquities! In matter, it is objective atheism; in mind subjective atheism. Religion has nothing to do with politics! Come, Americans, tear down the monuments you built at Bunker Hill, at West Cambridge and Concord and Lexington and Danvers, commemorating the heroism of a few farmers and mechanics! It was all a mistake! Nay, split to pieces the Rock of Plymouth, and grind it to powder, and tread it under foot of men! There is no heroism! The Puritans were madmen, and the fire-tried Christians fools!

III. "The great object of government is the protection of property !" It is not to protect the rights of man, to give all men their natural rights to "life, liberty, and the pursuit of happiness !" It is not to protect labour, but only property, the result of labour. "The State—that is I," said the French King. There, at least, the I, that called itself the State, was human : here it is the dollar that speaks :—God's law is to vacate the world, religion to avoid the soil, man to be turned out of the State, and the dollar to come in—more than soul, more than man, more than God !

That is the programme of principles laid down in 1850 and '51. It struck at all religion, all morality, all sound human policy. It affirmed the worst axioms of the worst oligarchy—theocratic, monarchic, aristocratic, despotocratic. A late Attorney-General of the United States, in a speech at New York, in 1851, declared, "Law is liberty : not the means of liberty, it is liberty itself." He applied his words in special to the Fugitive Slave Bill—"it is liberty !"

See the measures which were the concrete application of these three axioms—for the atheistic word must also become flesh. According to the custom of the industrial democracy of America, one man out of every eight is considered and treated, not as human, but material, as property. Now, according to that programme of principles, there is no objective law in the universe, in the nature of things or of God, which overrides this custom, and has eminent domain over American Slavery ; there is no higher law. And there is, moreover, no subjective law in man which has a right to resist this slavery in politics, for, though the religious element be there, "religion has nothing to do with politics." So nothing must be done or said to oppose the turning of every eighth American into a piece of human money.

But this class of property has one peculiarity which distinguishes it from all other chattels, and that is, it runs away ! For, as the fire mounts up, and as the water runs down, obeying the universal gravitation, so man's mind and body hates and abhors bondage, and seeks to escape therefrom ; and God has made mankind so that every natural man seeks to aid the victim escaping from torment, to comfort and shelter him.   I say every *natural* man.   If a man is "regenerated," after the fashion of Mr. Adams, of this city—not Samuel or John, but the Reverend Nehemiah Adams, who takes a "South Side View of Slavery," —or of President Lord, of Dartmouth College, who finds Slavery a sacred institution,—if a man is "regenerated" after this sort, he will aid the slave-hunters to the fullest extent, and that with alacrity; but men with natural hearts aid him who flees.   These things being so, the property being obnoxious to flight on its own limbs, and able to excite the instinctive sympathy of whoso is most human, the Government, whose great domestic object is the protection of property at home, must eminently protect this property in its special peril.   So Government, resisting the great objective law of God, which tends to moralize mankind, must seek to extend and propagate Slavery; must oppose also the special subjective law of humanity which inclines us to help a man escaping from bondage.   And so the Government must pass the Fugitive Slave Bill, and re-kidnap the runaway, remanding him to Slavery, and put the sheltering philanthropist in gaol, and fine him a thousand dollars: thereto it must seek out the vilest men; not only the villains of the gutter, but also the congenital scoundrels of the courts and the parlour, and give them a legal commission to lay their hand on any poor woman, and, if they send her back to Slavery, pay them twice as much as if they declare her free!

That programme of principles was posted all over the land, and re-affirmed by prominent politicians, Whig and Democratic; by two Baltimore conventions of the people, unusually large and "very respectable;" by hundreds of political and commercial editors, North and South; by prominent merchants,—merchant traders and merchant manufacturers,—nine hundred and eighty-seven of "our most eminent citizens" endorsing it all.   It was affirmed by judges on the bench, one judge telling the jury that, if there was a doubt in their minds, and a conflict between the law of God and the Fugitive Slave Bill, then they must "obey *both;*" God upwards and the devil downwards. It was re-affirmed by prominent ministers of all denominations.   All these five classes said, "There is no higher law !" "Religion has nothing to do with politics !" "Property is the great object of government !" Some pulpits were silent; a few spoke right out for God and against Atheism; some ministers looked up weeping, others warning, and uttered their words mildly, cautiously, yet with the might which comes from virtue backed by the Eternal. Most of these men had to smart and suffer. Some were driven from their parishes, and the bread taken from their wives' and children's mouths.

The programme of measures met a similar acceptance. Fugitive Slave Bill meetings were held in all the great cities. Faneuil Hall rocked with the giddy genius that screamed and thundered, teaching Atheism to the people; and its walls caught the scoff and scorn and mow of the merchants of Boston and their purchased clerks, hissing at conscience, at God, and the higher law. Ministers in this city affirmed the principle and supported the measures; yea, at Philadelphia, New York, Buffalo, New Haven, Andover,—all over the land. There were exceptional men in all these five classes—I honour them !—but they were very few. Judges, mayors, lawyers, mechanics, truckmen, ministers, merchants, they went for kidnapping. Soldiers were called out in Boston, paid at our cost; volunteers, fifteen hundred strong, agreed to chattelize a man. Twice Boston has endorsed this programme of measures, and twice offered a human sacrifice on this two-horned altar of objective and subjective Atheism. Twice the city of Cotton and Mayhew, the birthplace of Franklin and Samuel Adams, offered a human sacrifice — THOMAS SIMS and ANTHONY BURNS. Is that the end? There is a to-morrow after to-day; yea, a for ever !

While the nation was in that

> "———— rank sweat of an enseamed bed,
>   Stewed in corruption,"

it chose a new Administration. Look at them !—the President, the Cabinet, the present Congress, the foreign ministers, the Soulés and the Belmonts, and their coadjutors; at the United States judges appointed within four years; the government officers; the marshal's guard, last June ! Behold the first fruits of Atheism in politics ! Is that all; is it not enough? It is the commencement of the beginning.

Now, in all the frauds which destroy the property of the honest, in the recklessness which dashes away life on railroads of iron, or on the ocean's watery floor, behold the early fruits of the doctrine that there is no higher law; that religion has nothing to do with the most prominent affairs of men; that property, and not persons, is the great object of government! When the prominent men in business, in the State, in the literature, and the Church of America, lay down this dreadful programme of principles; when the nation executes such measures, spreading Slavery over every inch of Federal territory, and arming twenty-one millions of freemen to hunt down and enslave a single poor fugitive; when it plunders Mexico and Hayti, and lusts for Cuba; when a Boston Judge of Probate betrays the wanderer, steals the outcast, and kidnaps a man in our own streets; when the Mayor illegally puts the throat of the town in the hands of a militia colonel, and fills the streets with soldiers armed with the deadliest tools of death, and turns them loose to smite and kill,—and all that to steal a man accused of no crime but the misfortune of his birth, in " Christian" America; when the soldiers of Boston volunteer to desecrate the laws of God—while Nicholas, with his knout, must scourge his Russian serfs to less ignoble tasks;—while men are appointed " Judges" for services against mankind, for diabolic skill to pervert law to utter wickedness; when a judge of the United States stabs at freedom of speech in Faneuil Hall; when such a judge, using such creatures as appropriate tools of wickedness, seeks such vengeance on men, for such a work; when the Governor of the State compliments the illegal soldiers because they violate the laws which he has hoisted into his seat to enforce and keep; when America would thus exploiter man and God, do you wonder that railroad and steamboat companies exploiter the public, and swindling goes on all round the land! "No higher law!" "Religion nothing to do with politics!" "Property the great object of government!"

The first line of plain reading my mother ever taught me ran thus :—

"NO MAN MAY PUT OFF THE LAW OF GOD."

I hope it has not faded out of the American spelling-books yet; but it is writ plainly on the sky, on the earth: plainer yet in words of fire in my heart. It will be the last line I shall ever read, as it was the first: I can never get beyond it.

"No man may put off the law of God."

At one extreme of society are politicians, ministers, lawyers, mayors, governors, taking a "South Side View" of every popular wickedness, longing for money, office, and fame,—which will be their children's loathed infamy,—teaching practical Atheism as political science, or patriotic duty, or as "our blessed religion." At the other end are ignorant Americans and Irish Catholics—houseless, homeless, heedless, famine-stricken, and ignorant, a bundle of human appetites bound together by a selfish will. These things being so, do you wonder that crime against property and person runs through society; that Irishmen make brawls in the street; that Meigs exploiters San Francisco, and Schuyler New York, and others Boston; that railroads take no heed of life, and steamboats sink three hundred and forty men to the bottom of the sea? Does not the nation exploiter three and a quarter millions of American citizens, and pulpits justify the deed? You can never escape the consequences of a first principle.

Dream not that you have seen the end of this obvious wickedness. There will be more "defalcations," great and little; more swindlings, more Schuylers and Meigses. Reap as you sow—of the wind, the whirlwind. Let the present commercial crisis continue, its vortex deepening, its whirl more swift and wide; let employment be more difficult to obtain, winter cruel cold, bread and fuel dear, and labour cheap, will the almighty dollar be safe? The property of the rich will be openly called "a robbery," and plundered from such as honestly earned, and would generously use it. The world has dreadful warnings to offer. "Protection of property the great object of government!" Bottom it on justice—it stands like the continent of Asia; but put it on injustice—what then? It has sometimes happened that an idol came to an end. "Behold, Dagon was fallen upon his face to the ground before the ark of the Lord; and the head of Dagon and both the palms of his hands were cut off upon the threshold; only the stump of Dagon was left to him."

The official census gives America about seven thousand millions of dollars. Thirteen hundred millions thereof is vested in the souls of three and a quarter million men! So one-sixth of the nation's property has no natural foundation; rests on no moral law; has no conscience on its side: all religion is against it; all that property is robbery, unnatural property, inhumanly got, also held only by violence. Now the prominent men of both political parties—merchants, manufacturers, politicians, lawyers, scholars, ministers—have declared that this property in men is just as sacred as value in corn and cattle; that I may as legally, constitutionally, morally, religiously, own a man, as the pen I write with or the bread I eat; that when Ellen Craft took her body from her master in Georgia, and fled hither therewith, and appropriated it to her own use, in the eye of the law, the constitution, morality, and religion, she committed an offence just as much as Philip Marrett, when he took the money of the New England Bank and appropriated it to his own use; and that the nation is just as much bound to restore to the Georgian slave-holder the woman who runs away from bondage as to the stockholders' money plundered by the president of the bank; nay, that all who aided in her flight are also robbers, partakers of the felony, and merit punishment. The minister who shelters is a "receiver of stolen goods!" When the million is hungry, will it not one day take such men at their word? Shall not licentious and expensive clerks, who applauded a minister for his avowal of readiness to send into bondage for ever the mother that bore him; shall not covetous agents of factories, and speculating cashiers and presidents of railroads and banks, say, "It is no worse for me to steal money than for a fugitive slave to leap into freedom! Lawyers and ministers say so. One-sixth of the nation's property is robbery, yet the loudest defended; is it worse for me to steal a few thousand dollars than for America to steal thirteen hundred millions?"

No higher law, is there! So they said in Paris some eighty years ago. "After us the deluge:" it came in their own time. "No higher law! Religion nothing to do with

politics!" said the "eminent citizens" of France. "Down
with the rich!" "Off with their heads!" "Ours be their
money!" That was the AMEN of the million to that atheistic litany of the "enlightened." Whoso falls on God's
justice shall be broken; "but on whomsoever it shall fall,
it will grind him to powder!"

Everywhere is God's law, boundless above me, boundless
beneath, every way boundless. The universe is all Bible:
matter is Old Testament, man New Testament—revelations
from the infinite God. That law—it is man's wisdom to
know it; his morality to keep it; his religion to love it
and the dear God whose motherly blessing breathes through
and in it all. You cannot segregate this Bible from the
world of space: you cannot separate a particle of it from
the laws of matter. The lesser attraction holds together
the cohesive particles of leather, paper, metal, which compose this Bible under my hand; and the greater gravitation binds its attracted mass downwards to the weighty
world. Just so is it impossible to separate man, or any
one of his faculties, from the great all-encompassing laws
of God, the eternal decalogue which He has writ. Break
His law, put property above person, the accident before the
substance of man, declare that religion has nothing to do
with man's chief affairs, and that there is no law above
the appetite of the politician and the pimp—and not a life
is secure, not a dollar is safe! Subjective Atheism is chaos
in you, objective Atheism chaos on the outside; the rich
State will end in a ruffianhood of thieves; Democracy turn
out a despotism; and its masters will be the "marshal's
guard," or the men who make and control such things.
The chain which Boston sought to put round the virtuous neck of Ellen Craft seemed short and light: but
suddenly it undid its iron coil, and twisted all round the
Court House; under it crawled the Judges of the State, and
caught its hissing at God's law. Now it seeks to twist
about Faneuil Hall and choke the eloquent speech of liberty
in her own cradle. The cannon appointed to shoot down
the manhood of poor Burns is levelled also at every pulpit
where piety dares pray. The hundred festal cannons which
Boston "gentlemen"—jubilant at the triumph of their
own wickedness—fired to herald the Fugitive Slave Bill,

poured hard shot against every honest dollar in the town!
Politicians and lower-law divines look forward a great ways
—don't they? There is One who seeth the end from the beginning, and by His higher law is it imperishably writ
on every soul, "Though hand join in hand, the wicked
shall not prosper!"

Shall we be warned by what we suffer? No, not yet.
The new political party seems likely to adopt the worst
principles of the old one. We must suffer much more, I
fear, before we learn that, to be great and permanently successful, the nation must be just to all.

"Be not deceived; God is not mocked: whatsoever a man
soweth, that shall he also reap." Four years ago the nation
sowed Atheism; see what it reaps in Boston, in New York,
and San Francisco, in commercial frauds and peculation, in
dashing away human life on the land or on the sea. This
is very far from the end,—yet here may the dollar tremble!

But keep God's law; make the great object of government the security of every right; recognise that there is a
natural and unchangeable law of God which has eminent
domain over all human affairs; re-enact that into statutes;
remember that religion is the mediator between man's
desires and the Highest,—and all is well; you have wrought
after the law of God's spirit of life; your money is safe;
life will be respected; and the industrial Democracy, rooted
in the soil of God's world, obedient to God's laws, will rise
a strong and flame-like flower, abundant beauty in its leaves
and blossoms, to bear fruit, and sow the world with never-
ending life, a blessed and abiding joy.

THE GREAT BATTLE BETWEEN SLAVERY AND FREEDOM,

CONSIDERED IN

TWO SPEECHES,

DELIVERED BEFORE THE AMERICAN ANTI-SLAVERY SOCIETY AT NEW YORK.

THE PRESENT ASPECT OF THE ANTI-SLAVERY ENTERPRISE, AND OF THE VARIOUS FORCES WHICH WORK THEREIN.

DELIVERED ON THE MORNING OF MAY 7, 1856.

MR. PRESIDENT, LADIES AND GENTLEMEN,—After that Trinitarian introduction,* in which I am presented before you as one anti-Slavery nature in three persons,—a fanatic an infidel, and a traitor,—I am sure a Unitarian minister will bring his welcome along with him. And yet I come under great disadvantages: for I follow one whose colour is more than the logic which his cause did not need (alluding to Mr. Remond); and another whose sex is more eloquent than the philosophy of noblest men (referring to Mrs. Blackwell), whose word has in it the wild witchery which takes captive your heart. I am neither an African nor a woman. I shall speak, therefore, somewhat in the way of logic, which the one rejected; something also, perhaps, of philosophy, which the other likewise passed by.

Allow me to say, however, still further, by way of intro-

---

* The President, Mr. Garrison, thus introduced Mr. Parker to the audience :—
"Ladies and Gentlemen,—The fanaticism and infidelity and treason which are hateful to the traffickers in slaves and the souls of men must be well-pleasing to God, and are indications of true loyalty to the cause of liberty. I have the pleasure of introducing to you a very excellent fanatic, a very good infidel, and a first-rate traitor, in the person of Theodore Parker, of Boston."

duction, that I should not weary your ears at all this morning, were it not that another man, your friend and mine, Mr. Phillips, lies sick at home. Remember the threefold misfortune of my position: I come after an African, after a woman, and in the place of Wendell Phillips.

I shall ask your attention to some "Thoughts on the Present Aspect of the anti-Slavery Enterprise, and the Forces which work therefor."

In all great movements of mankind, there are three special works to be done, so many periods of work, and the same number of classes of persons therein engaged.

First is the period of sentiment. The business is to produce the right feeling,—a sense of lack, and a fore-feeling of desire for the special thing required. The aim is to produce a sense of need, and also a feeling of want. That is the first thing.

The next period is that of ideas, where the work is to furnish the thought of what is wanted,—a distinct, precise, adequate idea. The sentiment must precede the thought: for the primitive element in all human conduct is a feeling; everything begins in a spontaneous emotion.

The third is the period of action, when the business is to make the thought a thing, to organize it into institutions. The idea must precede the action, else man begins to build and is not able to finish: he runs before he is sent, and knows not where he is going, or the way thither.

Now these three special works go on in the anti-Slavery movement; there are these three periods observable, and three classes of persons engaged in the various works. The first effort is to excite the anti-Slavery feeling; the next, to furnish the anti-Slavery idea; and the third is to make that thought a thing,—to organize the idea into institutions which shall be as wide as the idea, and fully adequate to express the feeling itself.

I. The primitive thing has been, and still is, to arouse a sense of humanity in the whites, which should lead us to abolish this wickedness.

Another way would be to arouse a sense of indignation in the person who has suffered the wrong,—in the slave,—

and to urge him, of himself, to put a stop to bearing the wickedness.

Two things there were which hindered this from being attempted. First, some of the anti-Slavery leaders were non-resistant; they said it is wrong for the black man to break the arm of the oppressor, and we will only pray God to break it: the slaves must go free without breaking it themselves. That was one reason why the appeal was not made to the slave. The leaders were non-resistants; some of them covered with a Quaker's hat, some of them (pointing to Mr. Garrison, who was bald) not covered by any covering at all.

The other reason was, the slaves themselves were Africans,—men not very good at the sword. If the case had been otherwise,—if it had been three and a half millions of Anglo-Saxons,—the chief anti-Slavery appeal would not have been to the oppressor to leave off oppressing, but to the victim to leave off bearing the oppression. For, while the African is not very good with the sword, the Anglo-Saxon is something of a master with that ugly weapon; at any rate, he knows how to use it. If the Anglo-Saxon had not been a better fighter than the African, slave-ships would fill this side of Sandy Hook and in Boston Bay; they would not take pains to go to the Gulf of Guinea. The only constitution which slave-hunters respect is writ on the parchment of a drum-head. If the three and a half millions of slaves had been white men, with this dreadful Anglo-Saxon blood in their bosoms, do you suppose the affair at Cincinnati would have turned out after that sort? Do you believe Governor Chase would have said, "No Slavery outside of the slave States; but, inside of the slave States, just as much enslavement of Anglo-Saxon men as you please?" Why, his head would not have been on his shoulders twenty-four hours after he had said it. In the State of Ohio, when Margaret Garner was surrendered up, there were four hundred thousand able-bodied men between the ages of eighteen and forty-five; there were half a million of firelocks in that State; and, if that woman had been the representative of three and a half millions of white persons held as slaves, every one of those muskets would have started into life, and four hundred thousand men would have come forth, each with a firelock on his shoulder; and then one hundred thousand women would have followed, bringing the rest of the muskets. That would have been the state of things if she had been a white Caucasian woman, and not a black African. We should not then have asked Quakers to lead in the greatest enterprise in the world: the leaders would have been soldiers; I mean such men as our fathers, who did not content themselves with asking Great Britain to leave off oppressing them. They asked that first; and when Great Britain said, "Please God, we never will!" what did the Saxon say? "Please God, I will make you!" And he kept his word.

> "Gods!" (we should have said,)
>   "Can a Saxon people long debate
> Which of the two to choose,—slavery, or death?
> No: let us rise at once, gird on our swords,
> . . . Attack the foe, break through the thick array
> Of his thronged legions, and charge home upon him!"

That would have been the talk. Meetings would have been "opened with prayer" by men who trusted in God, and likewise kept their powder dry.

But in this case it was otherwise. The work has not been to arouse the indignation of the enslaved, but to stir the humanity of the oppressor, to touch his conscience, his affection, his religious sentiment; or to show that his political and pecuniary interests required the freedom of all men in America.

And it has been very fortunate for us that this great enterprise fell into the hands of just such men as these,— that it was not soldiers who chiefly engaged in it, but men of peace. By and by I will show you why.

The attempt was made at first, and by that gentleman too (pointing to Mr. Garrison), with others, to arouse the anti-Slavery feeling in the actual slave-holders at the South. You know what followed. He and every one who tried it there were driven over the border. Then the attempt was made at the North; and there it has been continued. It is exceedingly important to get a right anti-Slavery feeling at the North: for two-thirds of the population are at the North; three-fourths of the property, four-fifths of the education are here, and I suppose six-sevenths of the Chris-

tianity ; and one of these days it may be found out tha:
seven-eighths of the courage are at the North also. I do
not say it is so ; but it may turn out so. So much for the
matter of sentiment.

II. Now look at the next point. If the sentiment be
right, then the mind is to furnish the idea. But a statement of the idea before the sentiment is fixed helps to excite
the feeling ; and so a great deal has been done to spread
abroad the anti-Slavery idea, even amongst persons who had
not the anti-Slavery feeling ; for, though the heart helps
the head, the head likewise pays back the debt by helping
the heart. If Mr. Garrison has a clear idea of freedom,
he will go to men who have no very strong sentiment of
freedom, and will awake the soul of liberty underneath
those ribs of death. The womanhood of Lucy Stone
Blackwell will do it ; the complexion of Mr. Remond will
do it.

In spreading this idea of freedom, a good deal has been
done, chiefly at the North, but something also at the South.
Attempts have been made to diffuse the anti-Slavery idea in
this way : Men go before merchants, and say, " Slavery is
bad economy ; it don't pay : the slave can't raise so much
tobacco and cotton as the freeman." That is an argument
which Mr. May's " mercantile friend " could have understood ; and a political economist might have shown him,
that, although there were millions of dollars invested " on
account of Slavery," there were tens of millions invested
on account of Freedom ; and that latter investment would
pay much larger dividends when it got fairly to its work.

Then, too, the attempt has been made to show that it
was bad policy : bondage would not breed a stalwart, noble
set of men ; for the slave contaminated the master, and the
master's neighbour not the less.

It has been shown, likewise, that Slavery injured education ; and while, in Massachusetts, out of four hundred
native white men, there is but one who cannot read the
Bible, in Virginia, out of nine white native adults born of
" the first families " (they having none others except " black
people "), there is always one who cannot read his own
name.

All kinds of schemes, too, have been proposed to end

this wickedness of Slavery. There has been a most multifarious discussion of the idea; for, after we have the right sentiment, it is difficult to get the intellectual work done, done well, in the best way. It takes a large-minded man, with great experience, to cipher out all this intellectual work, and show how we can get rid of Slavery, and what is to take its place, and how the thing is to be done. Accordingly, very various schemes are proposed.

Now, the idea which has been attained to, the anti-Slavery idea reached by the ablest men, is embodied in these two propositions: first, NO SLAVERY ANYWHERE IN AMERICA; second, NO SLAVERY ANYWHERE ON EARTH. That is the topmost idea.

There has been an opposite work going on. First, an attempt "to crush out" the sentiment of humanity from all mankind. That was the idea of a *very* distinguished son of Massachusetts. He said "it must be crushed out." Second, to put down the idea of Freedom. That has been attempted, not only by political officers, but also by a great many other men. It is not to be denied that, throughout the South, in the controlling classes of society, the sentiment and idea of Freedom are much less widely spread than twenty years ago. The South has grown despotic, while the North becomes more humane.

III. The third thing is to do the deed. After the sentiment is right, and the idea right, organization must be attended to. But the greatest and most difficult work is to get the heart right and the head right; for, when these are in a proper condition, the hand obeys the two, and accomplishes its work. Still it is a difficult matter to organize Freedom. It will require great talent and experience; for, as it takes a master mind to organize thought into matter, and to make a Sharp's rifle or a sewing-machine, so it requires a great deal more mind to organize an idea into political institutions, and establish a State where the anti-Slavery sentiment shall blossom into an idea, and the idea grow into a national fact, a State where law and order secure to each man his natural and unalienable rights.

In the individual Northern States a good deal has been done in five-and-twenty years to organize the idea of freedom for white men, a little also for coloured men; for the feeling and thought must lead to action. But in the Federal Government the movement has been continually the other way. Two things are plain in the conduct of Congress: (1) Acts to spread and strengthen African Slavery; (2) Subsidiary Acts to oppress the several Northern States which love Freedom, and to "crush out" individual men who love Freedom. Slavery centralizes power, and destroys local self-government.

Something has been done in the Northern States in respect to awakening the sentiment and communicating the idea; but there has nothing been done as yet in the Federal Congress towards accomplishing the work. I mean to say, for the last seventy years, Congress has not taken one single step towards abolishing Slavery, or making the anti-Slavery idea an American fact. So even now all these three operations must needs go on. Much elementary work still requires to be done, producing the sentiment and the idea, before the nation is ready for the act.

Now look at the special forces which are engaged in this enterprise. I divide them into two great parties.

The first party consists of the political reformers,—men who wish to act by political machinery, and are in government offices, legislative, judicial, and executive.

The second party is the non-political reformers, who are not, and do not wish to be, in government offices, legislative, judicial, or executive.

Look a moment at the general functions of each party, and then at the particular parties themselves,—at the business, and then at the business men.

The business of the political man, legislative, judicial, and executive, is confined to the third part of the anti-Slavery work; namely, to organizing the idea, and making the anti-Slavery thought a thing. The political reformer, as such, is not expected to kindle the sentiment or create the idea, only to take what he finds ready, and put it into form. The political legislative is to make laws and institutions which organize the idea. The political judiciary is to expound the laws, and is limited thereby. The political executive is to administer the institution, and is limited to that: he cannot go beyond it. So the judiciary and the executive are limited by the laws and institutions. The legislature is chosen by the people to represent the people; that is, it is chosen to represent and to organize the ideas, and to express the sentiments, of the people; not to organize sentiments which are in advance of the people, or which are behind the people.   The political legislator is restricted by the ideas of the people: if he wants what they do not want, then they do not want him. If senator Wilson had a million of men and women in Massachusetts who entertained the sentiments and ideas of Mr. Garrison, why he would represent the sentiments and ideas of Mr. Garrison, would express them in Congress, and would go to work to organize those ideas.

In hoisting the anchor of a ship, two sets of men are at work, two machines.   One, I think, is called the windlass. Many powerful men put their levers to that, and hoist the anchor up out from the deep.   Behind them is the capstan, whose business it is to haul in the rope.   Now, the function of the non-political reformer is to hoist the anchor up from the bottom : he is the windlass.   But the business of Chase, Hale, Sumner, and Wilson, and other political reformers, is to haul in the slack, and see that what the windlass has raised up is held on to, and that the anchor does not drop back again to the bottom.   The men at the windlass need not call out to the men at the capstan, " Haul in more slack !" when there is no more to haul in. This is the misfortune of the position of the men at the capstan,—they cannot turn any faster than the windlass gives them slack rope to wind up.   That ought to be remembered.   Every political man, before he takes his post, ought to understand that ; and the non-political men, when they criticize him never so sharply, ought to remember that the men at the capstan cannot turn any faster than the men at the windlass.

If the politician is to keep in office, he must accommodate himself to the ideas of the people ; for the people are sovereign, and reign, while the politicians only govern with delegated power, but do not reign : they are agents, trustees, holding by a special power of attorney, which authorizes them to do certain things, for doing which they are responsible to the people.   In order to carry his point, the politician must have a majority on his side : he cannot wait for it to grow, but must have it now, else he loses his post. He takes the wolf by the ears; and, if he lets go, the wolf eats him up: he must therefore lay hold where he can clinch fast and continue. If Mr. Sumner, in his place in the Senate, says what Massachusetts does not indorse, out goes Mr. Sumner. It is the same with the rest. All politicians are well aware of that fact. I have sometimes thought they forgot a great many other things; they very seldom forget that.

See the proof of what I say. If you will go into any political meeting of Whigs or Democrats, you shall find the ablest men of the party on the platform,—the great Whigs, the great Democrats; "the rest of mankind" will be on the floor. Now, watch the speeches. They do not propose an idea, or appeal to a sentiment that is in advance of the people. But, when you go into an anti-Slavery meeting, you find that the platform is a great ways higher than the pews, uniformly so. Accordingly, when an African speaks (who is commonly supposed to be lower than "the rest of mankind") and says a very generous thing, there is a storm of hisses all round this hall. What does it show? That the anti-Slavery platform which the African stands on is somewhat higher than the general level of the floor, even in the city of New York. The politician on his platform often speaks to the bottom of the floor, and not to the top of the ceiling.

So much for the political reformers: I am not speaking of political hunkers. Now a word of the non-political reformers. Their business is, first, to produce the sentiment; next, the idea; and, thirdly, to suggest the mode of action. The anti-Slavery non-political reformer is to raise the cotton, to spin it into thread, to weave it into web, to prescribe the pattern after which the dress is to be made; and then he is to pass over the cloth and the pattern to the political reformer, and say, "Now, sir, take your shears, and cut it out, and make it up." You see how very inferior the business of the political reformer is, after all. The non-political reformer is not restricted by any law, any Constitution, any man, nor by the people, because he is not to deal with institutions; he is to make the institutions better. If he do not like the Union, he is to say so; and, just as soon as he has gathered an audience inside of the

Union that is a little too large for its limits, the Union will be taken down without much noise, and piled up,—just as this partition (alluding to the partition dividing the hall) has been taken down this morning, — and there will be a larger place.   The non-political reformer can say, " Down with the Constitution ! " but the political reformer has sworn to keep the Constitution.   He is foreclosed from saying that to-day : by and by he can recant his oath, and say it when he gets ready.   The non-political reformer is not restricted by fear of losing office.   Wendell Phillips can say just what he pleases anywhere : if men will not hear him in Fancuil Hall, they will, perhaps, in the Old South Meeting-house.   If they will not here him there, he can speak on the Common ; at any rate, in some little schoolhouse.

The political reformer must have a majority with him, else he cannot do anything ; he has not carried his point or accomplished his end.   But the non-political re-former has accomplished part of his end, if he has con-vinced one man out of a million ; for that one man will work to convince another, and by and by the whole will be convinced.   A political reformer must get a majority ; a non-political reformer has done something if he has the very smallest minority, even if it is a minority of one. The politician needs bread: he goes, therefore, to the baker ; and bread must be had to-day.   He says, " I am starving : I can't wait."   The baker says, " Go and raise the corn." " Why, bless you," he replies, " it will take a year to do that; and I can't wait."   The non-political reformer does not depend on the baker. The baker says, "I have not much flour."   " Very well," he says, " I am going to procure it for you."   So he puts in the seed, and raises the harvest. Sometimes he must take the land wild, and even cut down the forest, and scare off the wild beasts. After he has done that preliminary work, he has to put in the anti-Slavery seed, raise the anti-Slavery corn, and then get the public baker to make the bread with which to feed the foremost of the political reformers,—men like Seward, Hale, Sumner, and Wilson.   They do all that is possible in their present position, with such a constituency behind them : they will do more and better soon as the people command ; nay, they will not wait for orders,—soon as the people allow them. These men are not likely to prove false to their trust. They urge the people forward.

So much for the business. Now look at the business men.

I. Look first at the political part of the anti-Slavery forces.

1. There is the Republican party. That is a direct force for anti-Slavery; but, as the anti-Slavery idea and sentiment are not very wide-spread, the ablest members of the Republican party are forced to leave their special business as politicians, and go into the elementary work of the non-political reformers. Accordingly, Mr. Wilson stumped all Massachusetts last year,—yes, all the North; not working for purpose purely political, but for a purpose purely anti-Slavery,—to excite the anti-Slavery sentiment, to produce an anti-Slavery idea. And Mr. Sumner has had to do that work, even in our city of Boston. Yet New England is further advanced in anti-Slavery than any other part of America. The superiority of the Puritan stock shows itself everywhere; I mean its moral superiority. Look at this platform: how many persons here are of New England origin? If an anti-Slavery meeting was held at San Francisco or New Orleans, it would be still the same; the platform would be Yankee. It is the foot of New England which stands on that platform. It is to tread Slavery down. But, notwithstanding New England is the most anti-Slavery portion of the whole land, these political men, whose business ought to be only to organize the anti-Slavery ideas, and give expression to anti-Slavery sentiments in the Senate, or House of Representatives, are forced to abandon that work from time to time, to go about amongst the people, and produce the anti-Slavery sentiment and idea itself. Let us not be very harsh in criticising these men, remembering that they are not so well supported behind as we could all wish they were.

This Republican party has some exceedingly able men. As a Massachusetts man, in another State, I am not expected to say anything in praise of Mr. Sumner, or Mr. Wilson, or Mr. Banks. It would be hardly decorous for a Massachusetts man, out of his own State, to speak in praise of those men. And they need no praise from my

lips. And, as a New England man, I think it is not necessary for me to praise Mr. Hale or Mr. Foote, Mr. Collamer,
Mr .Fessenden, or any other eminent political men of New
England. But, as a New Englander and a Massachusetts
man, you will allow me to say a word in praise of one
who has no drop of Puritan blood in his veins; who was
never in New England but twice,—the first time to attend
a cattle-show, and the last to stand on Plymouth Rock,
on Forefathers' Day, and, in the bosom of the sons and
daughters of the Puritans, to awaken the anti-Slavery sentiment and kindle the anti-Slavery idea. I am speaking
of your own Senator Seward. As I cannot be accused of
State pride or of sectional vanity in praising him, let me
say, that, in all the United States, there is not at this day
a politician so able, so far-sighted, so cautious, so wise, so
discriminating, and apparently so gifted with power to
organize ideas into men, and administer that organization,
as William Henry Seward. I know the other men; I de-
tract nothing from them. It is a great thiug to be second
where Seward is first.

Of course, this party, as such, will make mistakes; individual republicans will do wrong things. It has been declared here that Mr. Hale says, in his place in the Senate,
that he would not disturb Slavery nor the slave-holders.
I doubt that he ever said so in public; I am sure it is not his
private opinion. I know not what he said that has been so
misunderstood. His sentiment is as strongly anti-Slavery
as our friend Garrison's; but he is just now in what they
call a "tight place:" he wants to do one thing at a time.
The same is true of Henry Wilson and of Charles Sumner:
they want to do one thing at a time. I do not find fault
with their wishing to do that. The Constitution is the
power of attorney which tells them how to act as official
agents of the people; how to govern for the sovereign
people, whose vicegerents they are. But there are republican politicians who limit their work to one special thing,
and say, "To-day will we do this, and then strike work for
ever. We do not intend to do anything to-morrow."
They say, "Please God, we will pull up these weeds to-
day." The South says, "You shan't!" And these men
say, "Let us pull up these: we will never touch those
which grow just the other side of the path." They hate

those other weeds just as much; they mean to pull them up : but I am sorry to hear them say they do not intend to : and I am glad to hear severe censure passed upon them for promising never to do that particular thing,—not for taking one step at a time. If we only find fault with real offenders, we shall still have work enough to do.

I say this party has great names and powerful men. It will gain others from the Democrats and from the Whigs alike. See what it has gathered from the Democrats! Look at that high-toned and noble newspaper, the *Evening Post*, and its editor, not only gifted with the genius of poetry, which is a great thing, but with the genius of humanity, which is tenfold greater. See likewise such a man as Francis P. Blair coming into this movement! Governor Chase is another that it has gathered from that party. There are various other men whom I might mention from both the old political parties. Then see what service is rendered to the cause of humanity by a newspaper, which, a few years ago, seemed sworn for ever to Henry Clay. I speak of the only paper in the world which counts its readers by the million,—the *New York Tribune*. The Republican party gathers the best hearts and the noblest heads out of the Whig and the Democratic parties. If faithful, it will do more in this way for the future than in the past. The Democratic party continues to exist by these two causes: (1) its admirable organization; (2) the tradition of noble ideas and sentiments. In this respect, it is to the Americans what the Catholic Church is to Europe ; the leaders of the two about equally corrupt, the rank and file about equally deceived, hoodwinked, and abused. Which is the better,—to be politician-ridden, or priest-ridden? Good men will become weary of such service, and leave the party for a better, soon as they are sure that it is better.

2. Look next at the American party, so called: it is anti-American in some particulars. This is an indirect anti-Slavery force, as the Republican party is a direct anti-Slavery force. I suppose you know what its professed principle is,—"No foreign influence in our politics." Now, that principle comes partly from a national instinct, whose function is this : first, to prevent the excess of foreign blood

in our veins ; and, secondly, the excess of foreign ideas in the American consciousness. Well, it was necessary there should be that party. It has a very important function ; because it is possible for a people to take so much foreign blood in its veins, and so many foreign ideas to its consciousness, that its nationality perishes.

In part, this principle comes from the national instinct ; and that is always stronger in the great mass of the people than it is in any class of men with "superior education:" for the superior education consists almost wholly in development of the understanding,—the thinking part,—not in culture of the conscience, the affections, and the religious element. Therefore, for the national instinct, I never look to lawyers, ministers, doctors, literary and scientific men, or, in short, to the class of men who have what is called the "best education:" I look to the great mass of the people. It seems to me that the national instinct of the Saxon had something to do in making this principle of the American party so popular.

However, I do not think the chief devotion to this principle comes from that source, but from one very much corrupter than that,—a source a great deal lower than the uneducated mass of the Northern people. It comes from political partisans,—men who want office. There are two ways of getting into high office. One is to fly there : that is a very good way for an animal furnished with wings. The other is to crawl there : that is the only way left for such as have no wings, and no legs, and no arms. Well, there was a class of men at the North who could not fly into office ; and when the way which led up to the office was perpendicular, and went up straight, they could not crawl ; they were so slippery, that they fell off : there was not strength enough in their natural gluten to hold up their natural weight. Such men could not fly there ; they could not crawl there, so long as the road went straight up ; so they took the Know-Nothing plank, which sloped up pretty gradually ; and on it Mr. Gardner crawled into the governorship of Massachusetts. A good many men, in various other States, wormed up on that gently sloping inclined plane, who else never would have been within sight of any considerable office. Now, it is this class of men, who caught sight of that principle demanded by the national

instinct, which fears an excess of foreign blood in our veins,
and of foreign ideas in our consciousness; and they said,
"Let us make use of that as a wedge upon which we can
crawl up into office." They have got in there; but before
long they will fall out of their lofty hole, or, if they stay in,
will be shrivelled up, dried clear through, and by and by
be blown off so far that no particle of them will ever be
found again. The American party just now, throughout
all the United States, I fear, has fallen into the hands of
this class of men. It does not any longer, I think, represent the instinct of the less-educated people, or the
consciousness of the more thoughtful people, but the designs of artful, crafty, and rather low-minded persons.

But let no injustice be done. In the party are still
noble men, who entered it full of this national instinct,
with these three negations on their banner,—No Priest-
craft, No Liquor, No New Slave States. Some of them still
adhere to the worst of the leaders of their party. Loyalty
is as strong in the Saxon as in the Russian or Spaniard; as
often attaches itself to a mean man. It is now painful to
see such faithful worshippers of such false "gods." "An
idol is Nothing," says St. Paul: it may also be a Know-
Nothing.

This party, notwithstanding its origin and character,
has done two good works—one negative, one positive.

First, it helped destroy the Whig and Democratic
party. That was very essential. The anti-Slavery man,
the non-political reformer, wanted to sow his seed in the
national soil. It was dreadfully cumbered with weeds of
two kinds—Whig-weed and Democrat-weed. The Know-
Nothings lent their hands to destroy these weeds; and
they have pulled up the Whig-weed pretty thoroughly:
they have torn it up by the roots, shaken the soil from it,
and it lies there partly drying and partly rotting, but, at
any rate, pretty thoroughly dead. They laid hold of the
Democrat-weed. That was a little too rank, and strongly
rooted in the ground, for them to pull up. Nevertheless,
they loosened its roots; they gave it a twist in the trunk;
they broke of some branches, and stripped off some of its
leaves, and it does not look quite so flourishing as it did
several years ago.

Now, this negative work is very important; for, if we

could get both these kinds of weed out of the soil, it would not be a very difficult matter to sow the seed and raise a harvest of anti-Slavery.

Next for the positive work. It calls out men who hitherto have never taken the initiative in politics, but have voted just as they were bid. I will speak of Massachusetts, of Boston. We had there a large class of excellent men, who always went, a week or two before the election, to the Whigs and Democrats, and said, "Whom are we to vote for?" The great Whigs said, "We have not yet taken counsel of the Lord; we shall do so to-morrow, and then we will tell you." So these men went home, and bowed their knees, and waited in silent submission; and the next day their masters said, "You are to vote for John Smith or John Brown," or whosoever it chanced to be. And the people said, "Hurrah for the great John Smith!" "Hurrah for the great John Brown!" "Did you ever hear of him before?" asked some one. "No: but he is the greatest man alive." "Who told you so?" "Oh! our masters told us so." Now, the Know-Nothings went to that class of men, and said, "You have been fooled long enough." "So we have," said the people, "and no mistake! and we will not bear it any longer." They would not be fooled any longer by the Whigs, and some of them no longer by the Democrats; but they were fooled by the Know-Nothings. Nevertheless, it was an important thing for this class of people to take the initiative in political matters. If they stumbled as they tried to go alone, it is what all children have done. "Up and take another," is good advice. So the Know-Nothings not only pulled up the Whig-weed, and left it to rot, but they stirred the land; they ploughed it deep with a subsoil plough, turning up a whole stratum of people which had never been brought up to the surface of the political garden before. That was another very important matter; and yet, allow me to say, with all this subsoiling, they have not turned up one single man who proves powerful in politics, and at the same time new. Mr. Wilson owns his place in the Senate to the Know-Nothings: he was known to be a powerful man before. Mr. Banks owes his place to this party; he also was a powerful man before. I do not find, anywhere in the United States, that the

Americans have brought one single able man before the people, who was not known to the people just as well before. You shall determine what that fact means. I shall not say just now.

At the South, this party has done greater service than at the North; for, among the non-slaveholders at the South, there is a class of men with very little money, less education, and no social standing whatsoever. That class have been deprived of their political power by the rich, educated, and respectable slave-holders; for the slave-holders make the laws, fill the offices, and monopolize all the government of the South. Those Poor-whites are nothing but the dogs of the slave-holder. Whenever he says, "Seize him, Dirt-eater!" away goes this whole pack of pro-Slavery dogs, catching hold of whomsoever their master set them upon. This class of men, having no money and no education, and no means of getting any, deprived of political influence, felt that they were crushed down; but they were too ignorant to know what hurt them. They had no newspapers, no means of concerted action. Northern men have undertaken to help those men. Mr. Vaughan established his newspaper at Cleveland chiefly for the purpose of reaching them. Cassius M. Clay, in Kentucky, said, "Let us speak to that class of men." Once in a while, you hear of their holding a meeting somewhere in Virginia, and uttering some kind of anti-Slavery sentiment or idea. Very soon they are put down. Now, the Know-Nothings went among the Poor-whites in the South, and organized American lodges. The whole thing was done in secret; so that the organization was established, and set on its legs, before the slave-holders knew anything about it: it was strong, and had grown up to be a great boy before they knew the child was born. Of course, the Southern Know-Nothing party, at first, does not know exactly what to do; so it takes the old ideas of persons that are about it, and becomes intensely pro-Slavery. That is not quite all. The Whigs at the South have always been feeble. They saw that their party was going to pieces; and, with the instinct of that other animal which flees out of the house which is likely to fall, they sought shelter under some safer roof: they fled to the Know-Nothing organization. The leading Whigs got control of the party at the South, and made that still more pro-Slavery in the South which was already sufficiently despotic at the North.   Nevertheless, there has now risen up, at the South, a body of men who, when they come to complete consciousness of themselves, will see that they are in the same boat with the black man, and that what now curses the black man will also ruin the Poor-white at last.   At present, they are too ignorant to understand that ; for the bulk of the American party at the South consists of Know-Nothings, who were such before they ever went into a lodge—natural Know-Nothings, who need no initiation.   Nevertheless, they are human ; and the truth, driven with the slave-holder's hammer, will force itself even into such heads.

Such men are not hopeless.   One day, we shall see a great deal of good come from them.   At present, they are in the same condition with the Irish at Boston—first, ignorant ; and next, controlled by their priests ; for, as the Irish Catholic in Boston and New York is roughly ridden by that heavy ecclesiastical rider, the priest, so the Know-Nothings at the South are still more roughly ridden by this desperate political rider mounted upon their backs. One day, both the Irish and the Know-Nothing master will be unhorsed, and there will be no more such riding.

So much for these two anti-Slavery forces—one direct, and the other indirect.

This, let me say in general, is the sin of the politician— he seeks office for his own personal gain, and, when he is in it, refuses to organize the anti-Slavery ideas which he was put in office to develop and represent.   After the windlass has lifted the anchor, he refuses to haul in the slack cable. That was the case with Webster ; it caused him his death. It was the case with Everett ; it brought him to private life and political ruin.   Many are elected as anti-Slavery men, who prove false to their professions.   New England is rich in traitors.   The British Executive bought Benedict Arnold with money ; the American Executive has since bought many an Arnold.   Look at the present national Administration.   In 1852, had he published his programme of principles and measures, do you think Mr. Pierce would have had the vote of a single Northern State ?   Not an electoral vote would have been given by the North for robbing the people of a million square miles of land, and bestowing it on three hundred and fifty thousand slave-holders! He is an official swindler. He got his place by false pretences—the juggling trick of the thimble-rigger. Mr. Hale says, "For every doughfaced representative, there is a doughfaced constituency." It is true; but the constituency is not always quite so soft as the delegate; it is at least *slack-baked*, and does not pretend to be what it knows it is not.

Here, too, let me say, it is a great misfortune that the North has not sent more strong men to the political work. In time of war, you take the ablest men you can find, and put them to do the military work of the people. The North commonly sends her ablest men to science, literature, productive industry, trade, and manufactures; the South, hers to politics; and so she outwits and beats us from one fifty years to another. But, in such a terrible battle as this before us now, rest assured the North cannot afford to send her strong men to callings directly productive of pecuniary value: we must have them in politics—men of great mind, able to see far behind and before; of great experience, to organize and administer. Above all must our statesmen be men of great justice and humanity, such as reverence the higher law of God. Integrity is the first thing needed in a statesman. The time may come when the men of largest human power may go to the shop, the counting-room, the farm, the ship, to science, or preaching: just now we cannot afford to make a land-surveyor out of a Washington, or turn our Franklins into tallowchandlers. When we can afford such expenditure, I shall not object: now we are not rich enough to allow Moses to tend sheep, asses, and young camels, or to keep Paul at tent-making.

Here are the anti-Slavery forces which are not political. They are various.

At first, the anti-Slavery men looked to the American Church, and said, "That will be our great bulwark and defender." Instead of being a help, it has been a hinder-ance. If the American Church, twenty years ago, could have dropped through the continent, and disappeared alto-gether, the anti-Slavery cause would have been further on than it is at this day. If, remaining above ground, every minister in the United States had sealed his lips, and said,

" Before God, I will say no word for freedom or against it,
in behalf of the slave-holder or of his victim," the anti-
Slavery enterprise would have been further on than it is
at this day. I say, that, notwithstanding the majestic
memory of William Ellery Channing, a magnanimous
man, whose voice rung like a trumpet through the continent, following that other clearer, higher, more widely
sounding voice, still spared to us on earth (Mr. Garrison's) ;
notwithstanding the eloquent words which do honour to
the name of Beecher and the heart of humanity ; notwithstanding the presence of this dear good soul (referring to
Samuel J. May), whose presence in the anti-Slavery cause
has been like the month whose name he bears, and has
brought a whole lapful of the sweetest flowers,—the
Church has hindered more than it has helped. For the
tallest heads in the great sects were lifted up to blaspheme
the God of Righteousness, and commit the sin which Mr.
Remond says is second only to Atheism,—the denial of
humanity. While the Atheist openly denied God, many
a minister openly denied man. I think the minister committed the worst sin ; for he sinned in the name of God,
and hypocritically : he wrought his blasphemy that he
might gain his daily bread, while the Atheist perilled his
bread and his reputation when he stood up, and said, " I
think there is no God." I have no respect for Atheism ;
but, when a man in the pulpit blasphemes the Divinity of
God by treading the humanity of man under His anointed
foot, I say I would take my chance in the next world
with him who speaks out of his own heart, in his blind-
ness, and says, "There is no God," rather than share the
lot of that man who, in the name of Jesus and of the
Father, treads down humanity, and declares there is no
higher law.
     There are a great many direct anti-Slavery forces.
     1. The conduct of the slave-holders in the South, and
their allies, has awakened the indignation of the North.
The Fugitive Slave Bill was an anti-Slavery measure. We
said so six years ago ; now we know it. Kidnapping is
anti-Slavery ; it makes anti-Slavery men. The repeal of
the Missouri Compromise stirred anti-Slavery sentiment in
Northern hearts. The conduct of affairs in Kansas, Judge
Kane's wickedness, and the horrible outrage at Cincinnati,

—all these turn out anti-Slavery measures. Mr. Douglas stands in his place in the Senate, and turns his face north, and says, "We mean to subdue you." The mass at the North says, "We are not going to be subdued." It is an anti-Slavery resolution. The South repudiates Democracy: the *Charleston Mercury* and the *Richmond Examiner* say that the Declaration of Independence is a great mistake when it says all men are by nature equal in their right to life, liberty, and the pursuit of happiness,—that there is no greater lie in the world. When the North understands that, it says, "I am anti-Slavery at once." The North has not heard it yet thoroughly. One day it will.

2. Then there are the general effects of education: it enlightens men, so that they can see that Slavery is a bad speculation, bad economy.

3. Then there is the progressive moralization of the North. The North is getting better, more and more Christian and humane. It was never so temperate as to-day, never so just, never so moral, never so humane and philanthropic. To be sure, even now we greatly over-look our black brother: it is because he is not an Anglo-Saxon. But he has human blood in his veins: by and by we shall see our black brother also.

4. Then the better portion of the Northern press is on our side. Consider what quantities of books have been written within the last ten years full of anti-Slavery senti-ment, and running over with anti-Slavery ideas. Think of *Uncle Tom's Cabin* and the host of books, only in-ferior to that, which have been published. Then look at the newspapers. I just spoke of the *Evening Post*, and *Tribune*: look at the *New York Independent*, with twenty thousand subscribers, with so much anti-Slavery in it. It does not go the length that I wish it did, and sometimes it does very mean things; for it is not unitary. See what powerful anti-Slavery agents are the *Evening Post*, the *Independent*, the *New York Times*, and the *New York Tribune*, and that whole army of newspapers, some of them in every Northern city; not to forget the *National Era*, at Washington. Besides these, there are the anti-Slavery newspapers proper, the *Liberator*, the *Standard*, and divers others, only second where it is praise to be inferior.

5. Then there is the anti-Slavery party proper, with its

men, its money, and its immense force in the country. What power of religion it has! I know it has been called anti-religious, anti-Christian, Infidel. Was not Jesus of Nazareth nailed to the cross, between two thieves, on the charge that He blasphemed God? How rich is this party in its morals, how mighty in its eloquence! I am sorry its most persuasive lips are not here to-day to speak for themselves and for you, and instead of me. Here is a woman also in the anti-Slavery ranks. I need say nothing of her: her own sweet music just now awoke the tune of humanity in your hearts, and I saw the anti-Slavery sentiment spring in tears out of your eyes. One day, from such watering, it will blossom into an anti-Slavery idea, and fruiten into anti-Slavery acts.

(1.) Here is the merit of this anti-Slavery party. It appeals to the very widest and deepest humanity. It knows no restriction of State or Church. If the State is wrong, the anti-Slavery party says, "Away with the State!" if the Church is mistaken, "Down with the Church!" If the people are wrong, then it says, "Woe unto you, O ye people! you are sinning against God, and your sin will find you out." It does not appeal to the politician, the priest, the editor alone; it goes to the people, face to face, eye to eye, heart to heart, and speaks to them, and with immense power. It knows no man after the flesh. Let me suppose an impossibility—that Mr. May should become as Everett, and Mr. Garrison as Webster: would their sin be forgiven by the abolitionists? No: those who sit behind them now would stand, not on this platform, but on this table, and denounce them for their short-coming and wrong-doing. They spare no man; they forgive no sin against the idea of Freedom.

They are not selfish; for they ask nothing except an opportunity to do their duty. And they have had nothing except a "chance" to do that; always in ill report until now, when you shall judge how much there is of good report awaiting them.

They are untiring. I wish they would sink through the platform, so that I could say what would now put them to the blush before so large an audience.

They appeal to the high standard of absolute right. This is their merit. The nation owes them a great debt, which

will not be paid in this life. Their reward is in the nobleness which does such deeds and lives such life: thus they
will take with them "an inheritance incorruptible, unde-
filed, and which fadeth not away."

(2.) Here, I think, is their defect. They forget, sometimes, that there must be political workmen. This comes
from the fact, that, to so great an extent, they are non-
voters, even "non-resistants." If they were the opposite,
they would have appealed to violence: being Quakers and
non-resistants, they have not done quite justice always, it
seems to me, to those who work in the political way.

This has been charged against them: that they quarrel
among themselves; two against three, and three against
two; Douglas against Garrison, and Garrison against
Douglas; the liberty-party men against the old anti-
Slavery men; and all that. That is perfectly true. But
remember why it is so. You can bring together a Democratic body, draw your line, and they all touch the mark:
it is so with the Whigs. They have long been drilled into
it. But, whenever a body of men with new ideas comes to
organize, there are as many opinions as persons. Pilate
and Herod, bitter enemies of each other, were made friends
by a common hostility to Jesus; but, when the twelve dis-
ciples came together, they fell out: Paul resisted Peter;
James differed from John; and so on. It is always so on
every platform of new ideas, and will always be so—at
least for a long time. We must bear with one another
the best we can.

I think that the anti-Slavery party has not always done
quite justice to the political men. See why. It is easy for
Mr. Garrison and Mr. Phillips or me to say all of our
thought. I am responsible to nobody, and nobody to me.
But it is not easy for Mr. Sumner, Mr. Seward, and Mr.
Chase to say all of their thought; because they have a
position to maintain, and they must keep in that position.
The political reformer is hired to manage a mill owned
by the people, turned by the popular stream—to grind
into anti-Slavery meal such corn as the people bring him
for that purpose, and other grain also into different meal. He
is not principal and owner, only attorney and hired-man. He
must do his work so as to suit his employers, else they say,
"Thou mayest be no longer miller." The non-political

reformer owns his own mill, which is turned by the stream drawn from his private pond: he put up the dam, and may do what he will with his own—run it all night, on Sunday, and the 4th of July; may grind just as he likes, for it is his own corn. He sells his meal to such as will buy. He is in no danger of being turned out of his office; for he has no master—is not hired man to any one.

The anti-Slavery non-political reformer is to excite the sentiment, and give the idea: he may tell his whole scheme all at once, if he will. But the political reformer, who, for immediate action, is to organize the sentiment and idea he finds ready for him, cannot do or propose all things at once: he must do one thing at a time, tell one thing at a time. He is to cleave Slavery off from the Government; and so must put the thin part of his wedge in first, and that where it will go the easiest. If he takes a glut as thick as an anti-Slavery platform, and puts it in anywhere, head foremost, let him strike never so hard, he will not rend off a splinter from the tough log; nay, will only waste his strength, and split the head of his own beetle!

Still, this non-political, anti-Slavery party—averse to fighting, hostile to voters under present, if not all possible, circumstances—has been of most immense value to mankind. It has been a perpetual critic on politicians; and now it has become so powerful that every political man in the North is afraid of it; and, when he makes a speech, he asks not only, What will the Whigs or the Democrats think of it? but, what will the anti-Slavery men say; what will the *Liberator* and the *Standard* say of it? And, when a candidate is to be presented for the office of president, the men who make the nomination go to the Quakers of Pennsylvania, and say, "Whom do you want?" They go to the non-resistants of Massachusetts—men that never vote or take office—and ask if it will do to nominate this, that, or the other man. A true Church is to criticize the world by a higher standard. The non-political anti-Slavery party is the Church of America to criticize the politics of America. It has been of immense service; it is now a great force.

6. Besides that, there is the spirit of the Anglo-Saxon tribe, which hates oppression, which loves justice and liberty, and will at last have freedom for all. Look at its history for

three hundred years—from 1556, when the three millions of Old England were ruled by the bloody Mary, to 1856, when the three millions of New England govern themselves! Do you fear for the next three hundred years? That historic momentum will not be lost.

7. Then there is the spirit of the age we live in. Only see what has been done in a century! A hundred years ago, there were slaves in every corner of the land. There are men on this platform, whose fathers, within fourscore years, have not only owned black, but red and white slaves also. See what a steady march there has been of freedom in New England, and throughout the North—likewise on the continent of Europe! Christendom repudiates bondage. Think of British and French emancipation, of Dutch and Danish. Slavery is only at home in three places in Christendom,—Russia, Brazil, and the south of the United States. A hundred years ago, there was not a spot in all Europe where there was not Slavery in one form or another, —men put up at auction. It is only ninety-eight years ago since men were kidnapped in Glasgow, Scotland, and sold into bondage for ever in the City of Brotherly Love, at Philadelphia. That thing took place in 1758. See what an odds there is!

It is plain that American Slavery is to end ultimately. It cannot stand. The question before us is, "Shall it ruin America before it stops?" I think it will not. The next question is, "Shall it end peaceably, as the Quakers wish, and as all anti-Slavery men wish, or shall it end in blood?" On that point I shall not now give my opinion.

THE

PRESENT CRISIS IN AMERICAN AFFAIRS:

THE SLAVE-HOLDERS' ATTEMPT TO WRENCH THE TERRITORIES FROM THE WORKING PEOPLE, AND TO SPREAD BONDAGE OVER ALL THE LAND.

DELIVERED ON THE EVENING OF MAY 7.

———

> " Oh! ill for him, who, bettering not with time,
>   Corrupts the strength of Heaven-descended will,
> And ever weaker grows through acted crime,
> Or seeming-genial venial fault,—
>   Recurring and suggesting still!
> He seems as one whose footsteps halt,—
>   Toiling in immeasurable sand,
>   And o'er a weary, sultry land,
> Far beneath a blazing vault,
>   Sown in a wrinkle of the monstrous hill,
> The city sparkles like a grain of salt."

———

AMERICA has now come to such a pass, that a small mis-step may plunge us into lasting misery. Any other and older nation would be timidly conscious of the peril; but we, both so confident of destined triumph and so wonted to success, forecast only victory, and so heed none of all this danger. Who knows what is before us? By way of warning for the future, look at the events in the last six years.

1. In the spring of 1850, came the discussions on the Fugitive Slave Bill, and the programme of practical Athe-ism; for it was taught, as well in the Senate as the pulpits, that the American Government was amenable to no natural laws of God, but its own momentary caprice might take

the place of the eternal reason. "The Union is in danger" was the affected cry. Violent speeches filled the land, and officers of the Government uttered such threats against the people of the North as only Austrian and Russian ears were wont to hear. Even "discussion was to cease." That year, the principle was sown whence measures have since sprung forth, an evil blade from evil seed.*

2. The next spring, 1851, kidnapping went on in all the North. Kane ruled in Philadelphia, Rynders in New York. Boston opened her arms to the stealers of men, who barked in her streets, and howled about the cradle of liberty,—the hiding-place of her ancient power. All the municipal authority of the town was delivered up to the kidnappers. Faneuil Hall was crammed with citizen-soldiers, volunteers in men-stealing, eager for their—

"Glorious first essay in war."

Visible chains of iron were proudly stretched round the Court House. The Supreme Judges of Massachusetts crouched their loins beneath that yoke of bondage, and went under to their own place, wherein they broke down the several laws they were sworn and paid to keep. They gave up Thomas Sims to his tormentors. On the 19th of April, the seventy-sixth anniversary of the first battle of the Revolution, the city of Hancock and Adams thrust one of her innocent citizens into a slave-prison at Savannah ; giving his back to the scourge, and his neck to the everlasting yoke.†

3. In the spring of 1854, came the discussions on the Kansas-Nebraska Bill ; the attempt to extend bondage into the new territory just opening its arms to the industrious North ; the legislative effort to rob the Northern labourer thereof, and give the spoils to Southern slave-holders. Then came the second kidnapping at Boston : a Judge of Probate stole a defenceless man, and made him a slave. The old volunteer soldiers put on their regimentals again to steal another victim. But they were not quite strong enough alone ; so the United States troops of the line were called

---

* See Mr. Parker's Speeches, Addresses, and Occasional Sermons, Vol. II., Nos. VI.—X.
† Parker, *ubi sup.* No. XI. Additional Speeches, &c., Vol. I., Nos. I., II.

out to aid the work of protecting the orphan. It was the
first time I ever saw soldiers enforcing the decisions of a
New England Judge of Probate ; the first time I ever saw
the United States soldiers in any service. This was characteristic work for a democratic army! Hireling soldiers,
mostly Irishmen,—sober that day, at least till noon,—
in the public square loaded their cannon, charged their
muskets, fixed their bayonets, and made ready to butcher
the citizens soon as a slave-holder should bid them strike a
Northern neck. The spectacle was prophetic.*

4. Now, in 1856, New England men migrate to Kansas,
taking their wives, their babies, and their cradles. The
Old Bible goes also on that pilgrimage,—it never fails the
sons of the Puritans. But the fathers are not yet dead ;—

"E'en in our ashes live their wonted fires."

Sharp's rifle goes as missionary in that same troop ; an
indispensable missionary—an apostle to the Gentiles—whose
bodily presence is not weak, nor his speech contemptible,
in Missouri. All the parties go armed. Like the father,
the pilgrim son is also a Puritan, and both trusts in God
and keeps his powder dry.

A company went from Boston a few days ago, a few of
my own friends and parishioners among them. There
were some five and forty persons, part women and children.
Twenty Sharp's rifles answered to their names, not to speak
of other weapons. The ablest minister in the United
States stirs up the "Plymouth Church" to contribute fire-
arms to this new mission ; and a spirit, noble as Daven-
port's and Hooker's, pushes off from New England, again
to found a New Haven in the wilderness. The bones of
the regicide sleep in Connecticut ; but the revolutionary
soul of fire flames forth in new processions of the Holy
Ghost.

In 1656, when Boston sent out her colonists, they took
matchlocks and snaphances to fend off the red savage of the
wilderness ; in 1756, they needed weapons only against
the French enemy ; but, in 1856, the dreadful tools of war
are to protect their children from the white border-ruffians,
whom the President of the United States invites to burn
the new settlements, to scalp and kill.

* Parker, Additional Speeches, Vol. I., Nos. V., VI. ; Vol. II., Nos. I.—IV.

In 1850, we heard only the threat of arms; in 1851, we
saw the volunteer muskets in the kidnapper's hand; in
1854, he put the United States cannon in battery; in 1856,
he arms the savage Missourians. But now, also, there are
tools of death in the people's hand. It is high time.
When the people are sheep, the Government is always a
wolf. What will the next step be? Mr. Cushing says,
"I know what is requisite; but it is *means that I cannot
suggest!*" Who knows what *coup d'état* is getting ready?
Surely affairs cannot remain long in this condition.

To understand this present emergency, you must go a
long ways back, and look a little carefully at what lies
deep down in the foundation of States.

The welfare of a nation consists in these three things;
namely : first, possession of material comfort, things of
use and beauty; second, enjoyment of all the natural
rights of body and spirit; and, third, the development of
the natural faculties of body and spirit in their harmonious order, securing the possession of freedom, intelligence,
morality, philanthropy, and piety. It ought to be the aim
of a nation to obtain these three things in the highest
possible degree, and to extend them to all persons therein.
That nation has the most welfare which is the furthest
advanced in the possession of these three things.

Next, the progress of a nation consists in two things :
first, in the increasing development of the natural faculties of body and spirit,—intellectual, moral, affectional,
and religious,—with the consequent increasing enjoyment
thereof ; and, second, in the increasing acquisition of power
over the material world, making it yield use and beauty,
an increase of material comfort and elegance. Progress is
increase of human welfare for each and for all. That is
the most progressive nation which advances fastest in this
development of human faculties, and the consequent acquisition of material power. There is no limit to this
progress.

That is the superior nation, which, by nature, has the
greatest amount of bodily and spiritual faculties, and, by
education, has developed them to the highest degree of
human culture, and, consequently, is capacious of the
greatest amount of power over the material world, to turn

R 2

it into use and beauty, and so of the greatest amount of universal welfare for all and each. The superior nation is capable of most rapid progress; for the advance of man goes on with accelerated velocity; the further he has gone, the faster he goes.

The disposition in mankind to acquire this increase of human development and material power, I will call the instinct of progress. It exists in different degrees in various nations and races: some are easily content with a small amount thereof, and so advance but slowly; others desire the most of both, and press continually forward.

Of all races, the Caucasian has hitherto shown the most of this instinct of progress, and, though perhaps the youngest of all, has advanced furthest in the development of the human faculties, and in the acquisition of power over the material world; it has already won the most welfare, and now makes the swiftest progress.

Of the various families of the Caucasian race, the Teutonic, embracing all the Germanic people kindred to our own, is now the most remarkable for this instinct of progress. Accordingly, in the last four hundred years, all the great new steps of peaceful Caucasian development have been first taken by the Teutonic people, who now bear the same relation to the world's progress that the Greeks did a thousand years before Christ, the Romans eight hundred years later, and the Romanized Celts of France at a day yet more recent.

Of the Teutons, the Anglo-Saxons, or that portion thereof settled in the Northern States of America, have got the furthest forward in certain important forms of welfare, and now advance the most rapidly in their general progress. With no class of capitalists or scholars equal to the men of great estates and great learning in Europe, the whole mass of the people have yet attained the greatest material comfort, enjoyment of natural rights, and development of the human faculties. They feel most powerfully the general instinct of progress, and advance swiftest to future welfare and development. Here the bulk of the population is Anglo-Saxon; but this powerful blood has been enriched by additions from divers other sources, — Teutonic and Celtic.

The great forces which in the last four hundred years have most powerfully and obviously helped this welfare and progress, may be reduced to two marked tendencies, which I will sum up in the form of ideas, and name the one Christianity and the other Democracy.

By Christianity, I mean that form of religion which consists of piety—the love of God, and morality—the keeping of His laws. That is not the Christianity of the Christian Church, nor of any sect; it is the ideal religion which the human race has been groping after, if happily we might find it. It is yet only an ideal, actual in no society.

By Democracy, I mean government over all the people by all the people, and for the sake of all. Of course, it is government according to the natural law of God, by justice, the point common to each man and all men, to each nation and all mankind, to the human race and to God. In a democracy, the people reign with sovereign power; their elected servants govern with delegated trust. There is national unity of action, represented by law; this makes the nation one, a whole; it is the centripetal force of society. But there is also individual variety of action, represented by the personal freedom of the people who ultimately make the laws; this makes John John, and not James, the individual a free person, discreet from all other men ; this is the centrifugal force of society, which counteracts the excessive solidification that would else go on. Thus, by justice, the one and the many are balanced together, as the centripetal and centrifugal forces in the solar system.

This is not the democracy of the parties, but it is that ideal government, the reign of righteousness, the kingdom of justice, which all noble hearts long for, and labour to produce, the ideal whereunto mankind slowly draws near. No nation has yet come so close to it as the people of some of the Northern States, who are yet far beneath ideals of government now known, that are yet themselves vastly inferior to others which mankind shall one day voyage after, discover, and annex to human possession.

In this Democracy, and the tendency towards it, two things come to all ; namely, labour and government.

Labour for material comfort, the means of use and beauty, is the duty of all, and not less the right, and practically the lot, of all; so there is no privilege for any, where each has his whole natural right.   Accordingly, there is no permanent and vicariously idle class, born merely to enjoy and not create, who live by the unpurchased toil of others ; and, accordingly, there is no permanent and vicariously working-class, born merely to create and not enjoy, who toil only for others.   There is mutuality of earning and enjoying : none is compelled to work vicariously for another, none allowed to rob others of the natural fruit of their toil.   Of course, each works at such calling as his nature demands : on the *mare liberum*, the open sea of human industry, every personal bark sails whither it may, and with such freight and swiftness as it will or can.

Government, in social and political affairs, is the right of all, not less their duty, and practically the lot of each. So there is no privilege in politics, no lordly class born to command and not obey, no slavish class born to serve and not command : there is mutuality of command and obedience. And as there is no compulsory vicarious work, but each takes part in the labour of all, and has his share in the enjoyment thereof ; so there is no vicarious government, but each takes part in the making of laws and in obedience thereunto.

Such is the ideal Democracy, nowhere made actual.

Practically, labour and government are the two great forces in the education of mankind. These take the youth where schools and colleges leave him, and carry him further up to another seminary, where he studies for what honours he will, and graduates into such degrees as he can attain to.

This sharing of labour and government is the indispensable condition for human development; for, if any class of men permanently withdraws itself from labour, first it parts from its human sympathy ; next it becomes debauched in its several powers ; and presently it loses its masculine vigour and its feminine delicacy ; and dies, at last, a hideous ruin. Do you doubt what I say ? Look then at the Roman aristocracy from two centuries before Christ to four centuries after—at the French aristocracy from Louis XIII. to Louis XVI.

If any class of men is withheld from government—from its share in organizing the people into social, political, and ecclesiastical forms, from making and executing the laws—then that class loses its manhood and womanhood, dwindles into meanness and insignificance, and also must perish. For example, look at the populace of Rome from the second century before Christ to the fourth after; look at the miserable people of Naples and Spain, too far gone ever to be raised out of the grave where they are buried now; look at the inhabitants of Ireland, whose only salvation consists in flight to a new soil, where they may have a share in political government, as well as in economic labour.

So much for the definition of terms frequently to be used, and the statement of the great principles which lie at the foundation of human progress and welfare.

Now, in the history of a nation, there are always two operating forces,—one positive, the other negative. One I will call the progressive force. It is that instinct of progress just named, with the sum total of all the excellences of the people, their hopefulness, human sympathy, virtue, religion, piety. This is the power to advance. The other I will call the regressive force; that is, the *vis inertiæ*, the sluggishness of the people, the sum total of all the people's laziness and despair, all the selfishness of a class, all the vice and anti-religion. This is power to retard. I do not speak of the conservative force which would keep, or the destructive force which would wastefully consume, but only of those named. The destructive force in America is now small; the conservative, or preservative exceeding great.

Every nation has somewhat of the progressive force, each likewise something of the regressive. Let me illustrate this regressive force a little further. You sometimes in the country find a thriving, hardy family, industrious, temperate, saving, thrifty, up early and down late. By some unaccountable misfortune, there is born into the family, and grows up there, a lazy boy. He is weak in the knees, drooping in the neck, limber in the loins, and sluggish all over. He rises late in the morning, after he has been called many times, and, in the dog-days, comes down whilst his mother is getting breakfast, and hangs over the fire. Most of you have doubtless seen such; I have, to my sorrow. That is one form of the regressive force. He is what the Bible calls a heaviness to his mother, and a grief to his father. There is a worse retarding force than this; to wit: sometimes a bad boy is born into the family with head enough, but with a devilish heart; he is a malformation in respect to all the higher faculties,—a destructive form of the regressive force. Now, a nation may have that regressive force in these two forms,—the lazy retardative, the wicked destructive.

Sometimes this progressive force seems limited to a small class of persons,—men of genius, like the Hebrew prophets, the Socratic philosophers, the German reformers of the sixteenth century, or the French *savants* of the eighteenth. But it is not likely it is really thus limited; for these men of genius are merely trees of the common kind, rooted into the public soil, but grown to taller stature than the rest.

In the Northern States of America, and also in England and Scotland, it is plain this progressive force is widely spread among the great mass of the people, who are not only instinctively, but of set purpose, eager for progress; that is, for the increasing development of faculties, and for the consequent increasing power over the material world, transforming it to use and beauty. New England is a monument attesting this fact. But still this force arrives to its highest form in men of genius. Here, in the North, you may find men of money, men of education, literary culture, and scientific skill; men of talent, able to learn readily what can now be taught—who do not share this progressive instinct, whose will is regressive; but these are exceptional men—some maimed by accident, others impotent from their mother's womb; whom no Peter and John could make otherwise than halt and lame. But all the men of genius—aboriginal power of sight, ability to create, to know and teach what none learned before—are on the side of this progressive force. In all the Northern States, I know but one exception among the men of politics, science, art, letters, or religion. Even in his cradle, the Northern genius strangles the regressive snakes of Fogydom. Still, these men of genius are not the cause of the progressive force, only expressions of it; not its exclusive depositaries.

They are the thunder and lightning, perhaps the rain, or of the cloud, sparks from the electric charge : they are no the cloud; they did not make it. Of course, where th cloud is fullest of the fire of heaven, there is the reddes lightning, the heaviest thunder, and the most abounding rain. Still, the men of genius did not make the progres sive spirit of the North ; they but express and help t(educate that force.

In the North, those two educational factors, Labour and Government, are widely diffused : more persons partake of each than anywhere else in the world. So there is no ex-clusive, permanent servile class—none that does all the work, and enjoys none of the results : there is no exclusive and permanent ruling class ; all are masters, all servants ; all command, and all obey.

So much for the progressive force.

The regressive force may consist in the general slug-gishness of the whole mass of the people : then it will be either an ethnological misfortune, which belongs to the constitution of the race—and I am sorry to say that the Africans share that in the largest degree, and, accordingly, have advanced the least of any of the races—or else an historic accident entailed on them by oppression; and that is the case also with a large portion of the Africans in America, who have a double misfortune—that of ethno-logic nature and historic position. But among the Cauca-sians, especially among the Teutons, this regressive force is chiefly lodged in certain classes of men, who are excep-tional to the mass of the people, by an accidental position separated therefrom, and possessed of power thereover, which they use for their own selfish advantage, and against the interest of the people. They commonly aim at two things—to shun all the labour, and to possess all the government.

This exceptional position was either the accidental at-tainment of the individual, or else a trust thereto delegated from the people ; but the occupiers of the trust considered it at length as their natural, personal right, and so held to it as a finality, and asked mankind to stop the human march in order that they might rejoice in their special occupation. Thus the fletchers of the fourteenth century, who got their bread by making bows and arrows, opposed the use of gunpowder and cannon; thus the scribes of the fifteenth century opposed printing, and said Dr. Faustus was "possessed by the devil." In England, two hundred years ago, every top-sawyer resisted the use of saw-mills to cut logs into boards, and wanted to draw off the water from the ponds. Forty years ago, the hand-weaver of England opposed power-looms. In 1840, the worshipful company of ass-drivers in Italy begged the Pope of Rome not to allow a single railroad in his territory, because it would injure their property invested in packsaddles and jackasses. The Pope consented, and no steam-engine dared to scream and whistle in the Papal States. In Boston, twenty years ago, the Irishmen objected to steam pile-drivers, and broke them to pieces; just now, the stevedores of Boston insist that ships shall not be unladen by horses or steam-power, but that a man, who yet has a head, shall live only by the great muscles in his arms; that all merchandise shall be taken out of ships by an Irishman hanging at the end of a rope. All these men consider that their exceptional position and accidental business is a finality of human history, a natural right, which the top-sawyer, the scribe, and the others have to stop mankind. The stevedore and hand-loom weaver must have no competitors in the labour-market; the steam-engine must be shoved off the track, in order that the donkey may have the whole country wherein to bray and wheeze.

In Europe, at this day, the regressive force is lodged chiefly in the twofold aristocracy which exists there, ecclesiastical and political. In the sixteenth century, mankind, and especially the Teutonic family, longed to have more Christianity: the priestly class, with the Pope at their head, refused, hewed the people to pieces, burnt them to ashes at Madrid and Oxford. The priest stood between the people and the Bible, and said, "The word of God belongs to us: it is for the priests only, not for you, you infidels; down with you!" He counted his stand as the stopping-place of mankind: the human race must not go an inch further—he would kill all that tried. The result attained was a finality. So the thinker must be burned alive, that the ass-driver might have the whole world to snap his fingers in and cough to his donkey! . Even now the same class of men repeat the old experiment; and, in Italy, Spain, and Spanish America, the regressive power carries the day.

In this century, when the people of Europe wished to move on a little nearer to Democracy than before, the political class of aristocrats refused to suffer it; they put men of political genius in gaol, or hung them. Kossuth and Mazzini were lucky men to escape to a foreign land; thousands fled to America. In Europe, at present, and especially on the continent, this regressive power carries the day, and the progressive force is held down. For priests, kings, and nobles, inheriting a position which was once the highest that mankind had attained to, and then taking it as a trust, now count it a right of their own, a finality of the human race, the end of man's progress.

When a nation permanently consents to this triumph of the regressive over the progressive force, allows one class to do all the government and shun all the labour, it is presently all over with that nation. Look at Italy, with Rome and Naples; at Spain, which is too far gone even to be galvanized into life. See what already takes place in France, where the son of the nephew has just been born, and the little baby is recognised as Emperor. Look at an election-day in Massachusetts, where the people choose one of themselves to be their temporary governor, responsible to them, swearing him on their statute-book: compare that with the preparation which Napoleon the Little made to anticipate the birth of Napoleon the Least! Why, the garments got ready for this equivocal baby have already cost more than the clothes of all our Presidents since "a young buckskin taught a British general the art of fighting." Eighty thousand dollars is decreed to pay for baptizing this imperial bantling. If twice that sum could christen the father, it might not be ill spent, if thereto decreed. Look at New England, and then at Spain, to see the odds between a people that has the progressive force uppermost, and a nation where the regressive force has trod the people down, and become, as it must, destructive. The Romanic nations of Italy and Spain, and the Romanized Celts of France, consent to a despotism which puts all the labour on the people, and takes all the government from them: they easily enough accept the rule of the political and ecclesias-

tical aristocracy.   But the Teutons, especially the Saxon
Teutons, and, above all others, those in the Northern States
of America, with their immense love of individual liberty,
hate despotism, either political or ecclesiastical.   They perpetually demand more Christianity and democracy ; that
each shall do his own work, and rejoice in its result; that
each shall have his share in the government of all.   The
women, long excluded from this latter right, now claim,
and will at length, little by little, gain it.   When all thus
share the burthens and the joys of life, there is no class of
men compelled by their position to hate society : so law and
order prevail with ease; each keeps step with all, nor
wishes to stay the march ; property is secure, the government popular.   But when one class does all the ruling, and
forces all the toil on another class, nothing is certain but
trouble and violence.   Thus, in St. Domingo, red rebellion
scoured black despotism out of the land, but with blood.
If a government, like a pyramid, be wide at the bottom, it
takes little to hold it up.
     So much for the regressive force.

     In the United States we have two peoples in one nation,
similar in origin, united in their history, but for the last
two generations so diverse in their institutions, their mode
of life, their social and political aims, that now they have
become exceedingly unlike, even alien and hostile; for,
though both the stems grow out from the same ethnologic
root, one of them has caught such a mildew from the
ground it hangs over, and the other trees it mixes its
boughs among, that its fruit has become "peculiar," and
not like the native produce of the sister trunk.   One
of these I will call the Northern States, the other the
Southern States.   At present, there is a governmental bond
put round both, which holds them together ; but no moral
union makes the two one.   There is no unity of idea between
them.   A word of each.

     In the Northern States we have a population fifteen
millions strong, mainly of Anglo-Saxon origin, but early
crossed with other Teutonic blood—Dutch, German, Scandinavian—which bettered the stock.   Of late, numerous
Celts have been added to the mixture, but so recently that

no considerable influence yet appears in the collective character, ideas, or institutions of the North. A hundred years hence, the ethnologic fruits of this other seed will show themselves.

These Northern Saxons, moreover, are mainly descended from men who fled from Europe because they had ideas, at least sentiments, of Christianity and democracy which could not be carried out at home. They are born of Puritan pilgrims, who were the most progressive portion of the most progressive people, of the most progressive stock, in all Christendom. They came to America, not for ease, honour, money, or love of adventure, but for conscience' sake, for the sake of their Christianity and their democracy. Such men founded the chief Northern colonies and institutions, and have controlled the doctrines and the development thereof to a great degree.

We see the result of such parentage : more than all other nations of the earth, the North has cut loose from the evil of the past, and set its face towards the future. At one extreme, it has no lordly class, ecclesiastical or political, exclusively and permanently to shun labour and monopolize government, vicariously to enjoy the result of work, vicariously to rule ; and, at the other extreme, there is no class slavishly and unwillingly to do the work, and have none of its rewards ; to suffer all the obedience, and enjoy none of the command. No class is permanent, highest or lowest. The Northern States are progressively Christian, also progressively democratic, in the sense just given of Christianity and democracy. No people on earth has such material comfort, such enjoyment of natural rights of body and spirit already possessed, such general development of the human faculties. But the attainment does not satisfy us ; for we share this instinct of progress to such a degree, that no achievement will content us. Be the present harvest never so rich, our song is—

"To-morrow to fresh fields and pastures new."

No nation has such love of liberty, such individual variety of action, or such national unity of action ; nowhere is such respect for law ; nowhere is property so secure, life so safe, and the individual so little disturbed. And, with all this, we are not at all destructive, but eager to create, and patient to preserve. The first thing which a Northern man lays hold of is a working-tool, an axe, or a plough; the last thing he takes in hand is a fighting-tool, a bowie-knife, a rifle: he never touches that till he is driven to the last extremity. He loves to organize productive industry, not war.

So much for the nation North.

Next, there are the Southern States ten millions in population. There also the original germ was Anglo-Saxon, to which additions were made from other stocks, Teutonic and Celtic, though in a smaller degree: France and Spain added more largely to the mixture. But what has most affected the ethnological character of the South is the African element. There are three and a-half millions of men in the Southern States of African origin, whereof half a million are (acknowledged) mulattoes, African Caucasians; but those monumental half-breeds are much more numerous than the census dares confess.

This is not the only human difference between the North and the South. While the Saxons, who originally came to the North, and have since controlled its institutions and ideas, were mainly pilgrims, who, driven by persecution, fled hither for the sake of establishing democracy and Christianity—the foremost people in an age of movement, when revolution shook the whole Teutonic world, bringing the most Christian and democratic institutions and ideas of their age, and developing them to forms still more human and progressive—the settlers of the South were adventurers, who came to America to mend their fortunes, for the sake of money, ease, honour, love of change. Whilst, subsequently, emigrants came from Europe to the North of their own accord, shared the Northern labour and government, partook of its Christianity and democracy, partook of its best influences, and soon mingled their blood in the great stream of Northern population: many persons from Africa were forced to immigrate to the South, and, by legal violence, compelled to more than their share of labour, driven from all share in the government; branded as inferior, and mingled with the Caucasian population only an illicit lust—which bastardized its own sons and daughters—and were made subordinate to the owners' lash. While the North, from 1620 to 1856, has aimed to spread education over all the land, and facilitate the acquisition of property by the individual, and prevent its entailment in families, or its excessive accumulation by transient corporations, the South has always endeavoured to limit education, making it the exclusive monopoly of the few—who yet learned not much —and now makes it a State prison offence to teach the labouring class to read and write: it aims to condense money into large sums, permanently held, if not in families, at least in a class.

Thus, at one extreme, the South had formed a permanently idle and lordly class, who shun labour and monopolize government.

The South culminates in Virginia and South Carolina, which bear the same relation to the slave States that New England does to the free States; that is, they are the mother-city of population, ideas, institutions, and character. As I just said, Christendom cannot boast a population in any other country where there are fifteen millions of men so nobly developed as the fifteen millions of the North; so far advanced in Christianity and democracy; with so much material comfort, enjoyment of natural rights, and development of natural powers. Compare New England with Old England, Scotland, France, Saxony, Belgium, Prussia, any of the foremost nations of Europe, and you see that it is so. But take the ten millions of the South, and see what they are: nowhere in Europe, north of Turkey and west of Russia, can you find ten millions of contiguous men who have so low a development, intellectual, moral, affectional, and religious, as the ten millions of the slave States; nowhere can you find Caucasians or any other people in Western Europe so slightly advanced above the savage. Three and a quarter millions are actual slaves. Take the States of Virginia and South Carolina, in which the South comes to its flower: there are one million one hundred and seventy thousand whites, nine hundred and twenty thousand coloured, whereof eight hundred and sixty thousand are slaves; that is to say, out of two millions, more than one-third are only human property, not counted as human persons. In South Carolina, out of a hundred native whites over twenty years of age, there are seven who cannot read the name PIERCE, the political lord they worship; in Virginia, out of a hundred native whites over twenty years, there are nine who cannot write the word SLAVE, nor spell it after it is written all over their State; whereas, in Massachusetts, out of four hundred persons over twenty, there is only one man who cannot write, with his own hand, LIBERTY FOR ALL MEN NOW AND FOR EVER!

Take the two million population of Virginia and South Carolina: there is no people in Western Europe so little advanced as they; and, in all Christendom, there are only two nations or collections of men who stand on the same level—the Russian empire and Spanish America. Behold the reason for the phenomenon which struck many with surprise,—that South Carolina and Virginia, in their politics, have recently sympathized with Russia and Brazil. Birds of a feather flock together, like consorting with like.

Here, then, are these two nations, alike in their ethnological origin, joint in their history, now utterly diverse and antagonistic in disposition and aim. The North has organized Freedom, and seeks to extend it; the South, Bondage, and aims to spread that. The North is progressively Christian and democratic; while the South is progressively anti-Christian and undemocratic. First, only the Southern measures were anti-Christian and undemocratic; now also its principles. It lays down anti-Christianity and anti-democracy as the only theory of religion and politics. In New England, man is put before property, the human substance above the material accident; in Virginia and South Carolina, property is put before man, the material accident before the human substance itself; and, of all property that which is most valued and most carefully preserved, though most "aristocratic" and sacred, is property in the bodies of men.

That is the odds between the North and the South.

Now, the progressive power of America is lodged chiefly in the North, where it is diffused almost universally amongst the people, but most conspicuously comes to light in the men of genius. Accordingly, every man of poetic or scientific genius in the North is an anti-Slavery man; every preacher with any spark of Christian genius in him is a progressive man and hostile to Slavery.

The regressive power is lodged chiefly at the South, where it is considerably diffused among the people. That wide diffusion comes partly from the ethnologic sluggishness of the African element mixed in with the population, but still more from the degradation incident to a people who have long sat under tyrannical masters. It is this which has debased the Caucasian of Virginia, Tennessee, North and South Carolina.

But as the progressive force of the North comes clearest to light in the men of genius, so the regressive force at the South is most shown in the men of eminent ability, ecclesiastical and political, of whom not a single man is publicly progressive in Christianity or Democracy. Compare the spirit of the great newspapers of the South, the *Richmond Examiner*, the *Charleston Mercury*, with those of the North, the *New York Tribune*, the *Evening Post;* compare the Southern politicians, the Masons and Toombses, with the Sewards and Chases of the North. See the odds between the mass of the people at the North and the South; between the eminent genius, all of which at the North is progressive, but all of which at the South turns its back on human progress, and would leave humanity behind. There is the difference.

This regressive force accepts Slavery as the Dagon of its idolatry, its "peculiar institution;" and Slavery is to the South what the book of Mormon or the car of Juggernaut is to its worshippers. This institution is so iniquitous and base, that in Christian Europe, all the Teutonic nations have swept it away; and all the Celtic, all the Romanic nations, even the inhabitants of Spain, have trodden bondage under their feet. Yes, the Ugrians have driven out such slavery from Hungary, from Livonia, from Lapland itself; and, of all parts of Europe, Russia, and Turkey alone still keep the unclean thing; but even there it is progressively diminishing. As a measure, it is felt to be exceptional, and publicly denounced; as a principle, no man defends it: it is there as a fact without a theory. Only two tribes in Christendom yet hold to the theory of this unholy thing,—Spanish America and the slave part of Saxon America, the two Barbary States of the New World.

All the regressive power of Christendom gathers about

American Slavery, which is the stone of stumbling, the rock of offence in the world's progress.

Slavery is the great obstacle to the present welfare and future progress of the South itself. It prevents the mass of the Southern people from the possession of material comfort,—use and beauty; from the enjoyment of their natural rights; and also, for the future, it hinders them from the increasing development of their natural faculties, and the consequent increasing acquisition of power over the material world. It hinders Christianity and Democracy, which it would destroy, or else itself must thereby be brought to the ground. It shuts the mass of the people from their share of the government of society, forces many to unnatural and vicarious labour, and robs them of the fruit of their toil. Thus it is the great obstacle alike to present welfare and future development.

The head-quarters of this regressive force are at the South, where its avowed organization and its institutions may be found. At the North it has three classes of allies. Here they are:—

1. The first class is of *base* men, such as are somewhat inhuman by birth; men organized for cruelty, as fools for folly, idiotic in their conscience and heart and soul. If there had been no "inherited sin" up to last night, these men would have "originated" it the first thing this morning; if Adam had had no "fall," and the ground did not incline downward anywhere, they would dig a pit on their own account, and leap down headlong of their own accord. These men are aboriginal kidnappers, and grow up amid the filth of great towns, sweltering in the gutters of the metropolitan pavement at Cincinnati, Philadelphia, New York. Nay, you find them even at Boston, lurking in some office, prowling about the Court House, sneaking into alleys, barking in the newspapers, to let their masters know their whereabouts, turning up their noses in the streets, snuffing after some victim as the wind blows from Virginia or Georgia, and generally seeking whom they may devour. These are "earthly, sensual, devilish." For the honour of humanity, this class of men is exceedingly small, and, like other poisonous vermin, commonly bears its warning on its face.

2. The next class is of *mean* men, of large acquisitiveness, or else a great love of approbation, little conscience, little affection, and only just religion enough to swear by. These men you can buy with office, honour, money, or with a red coat and a fife and drum. There are a great many such persons ; you find them in many places ; and, for the disgrace of my own profession, I am sorry to say they are sometimes in the pulpit, taking a South-side view of all manner of tyranny, volunteering to send their mothers into bondage, and denying the higher law of God.

3. The third class is of *ignorant* men, who know no better, but may be instructed.

At the South, this regressive force is thus distributed :— (1.) There are three hundred and fifty thousand slave-holders, who, with their families, make up a population of a million and three-quarters; (2.) There are four and three-quarter millions of non-slave-holders ; and (3.) Three and a-half millions of slaves. A word of each.

1. First, of the slave-holders. Slavery makes them rich : they own the greater part of the land, and all the slaves, and control the greater part of the coloured or white labouring population. Slavery is a peculiar curse to the South in general, but a peculiar comfort to the slave-holders. They monopolize the education, own the wealth, have all the political power of the South—are the "aristocracy." But, since the American Revolution, I think this class has not born and bred a single man who has made any valuable contribution to the art, science, literature, morals, or religion of the American people. Marshall's *Life of Washington* is the only great literary work of the South ; its hero was born in 1732, its author in 1755; and both Washington the hero, and Marshall the writer, at their death, abjured the " peculiar institution " of the South.

The Southern " aristocracy" rears two things—Negro slaves, of which it is often the father, and regressive politicians, who make the institutions to keep the slaves in bondage for ever, shutting them out from Christianity and Democracy. Behold the " aristocracy" of the South ! By their fruits ye shall know them. Of the general morals of this class I need not speak : "the dark places of the earth are full of the habitations of cruelty." Since the 1st of

January, they have burned four negroes alive, as a joyous
spectacle and "act of faith;" a sort of profession of Christianity, like the more ceremonious *autos-da-fé* of their
Spanish prototypes.   Yet among the slave-holders are
noble men; some who, but for their surroundings, would
have stood with those eminent in talent, station, and in
service, too, the forerunners of human progress.   Blame
them for their wrong, pity them for the misfortune which
they suffer.   Yet let me do the South no injustice.   Her
three hundred and fifty thousand slave-holders have ruled
the nation for sixty years; her politicians have beat the
North in all great battles.   .

Now, we commonly judge the South by the slave-
holders.   This is wrong: it is like measuring England by
her gentry, France and Germany by their men of science
and letters, Italy by her priests.   You shall judge what the
whole mass of the people are when the "aristocracy," the
picked men, are of that stamp.

2. Next are the non-slave-holders, four and three-quarter
millions of men.   Some of these are noble men, with property in land and goods, with some intelligence; but, as a
class, they are both necessitous and illiterate, with small
political power.   They are cursed by Slavery, which they
yet defend; for it makes labour a disgrace, and, if poor,
puts them on the same level with the slave himself.
Slavery hinders their development in respect to property,
intellectual culture, and manly character; yet, as a whole,
they are too ignorant to understand the cause which keeps
them down.   The morals of this class are exceedingly low:
it abounds in murders, and is full of cruelty towards its
victims.   Nay, where else in Christendom, save Spanish
America, is the Caucasian found to take delight in burning
his brother with a slow fire, for his own sport, and to please
a licentious mob?

3. The third class consists of the slaves themselves, of
whom I need say only this—that public opinion and the
law, which is only the thunder from that cloud, keep them
at labour and from government, from Christianity and Democracy, from all the welfare and development of the age,
and seek to crush out the instinct of progress from the
very nature of the victims.   The slave has no personal
rights, ecclesiastical, political, social, economical, indivi-

dual; no right to property—a human accident; none to
his body or soul—the substance of humanity itself.

But I fear you do not yet quite understand the difference
between the regressive force of slavery at the South, and
the progressive force of freedom at the North.   Therefore,
to see in noonday light the effect of each on the present
welfare and the future progress of a people, compare an
old typical slave State with an old typical free State, and
then compare a new slave State with a new free State.
1. South Carolina contains 29,385 square miles of land;
Connecticut, 4674.   In 1850, South Carolina had 668,507
inhabitants, whereof 283,523 were free, and 384,984 slaves;
while Connecticut had 370,792 inhabitants, all free.

The government value of all the land in South Carolina
was $5.08 an acre; in Connecticut it was $30.50 the acre.
All the farms in South Carolina contained 16,217,700 acres,
and were worth $82,431,684; while the farms of Connec-
ticut were worth $72,726,422, though they contained only
2,383,879 acres.   Thus Slavery and Freedom affect the *value
of land* in the old States.

In 1850, South Carolina had 340 miles of railroad; and
Connecticut 547, on a territory not equal to one-sixth of
South Carolina.   In 1855, South Carolina had $11,500,000
in railroads; Connecticut had then $20,000,000.

The shipping of South Carolina amounts to 36,000 tons;
in Connecticut, to 125,000, though she is not advanta-
geously situated for navigation.

The value of the real and personal property in South
Carolina, in 1850, was estimated by the Federal Government at $288,257,694.   This includes the value of all the
slaves, who, at $400 apiece, amount to $153,993,600.   Sub-
tracting this sum, which is neither property in *land* nor
things, but wholly *unreal* and fictitious, there remains
$134,264,094 as the entire property of the great slave
State; while the total valuation of the land and things
in Connecticut, in 1850, was $155,707,980.   In other
words, in South Carolina, 670,000 persons, with 30,000
square miles of land, are worth $134,000,000; while in
Connecticut, 370,000 men, with only 4600 square miles of
land, are worth $156,000,000.   Thus do Slavery and Free-
dom affect the *general wealth* of the people in the old States.

In 1850, South Carolina had 365,026 persons under twenty years of age; her whole number of pupils, at schools, academies, and colleges, was 40,373. Connecticut had only 157,146 persons of that age, but 83,697 at school and college. Will you say it is of no consequence whether the *coloured child* is educated or not? Then remember that South Carolina had 149,322 white children, and only sent 40,373 of them to school at all in that year; while, out of 153,862 white children, Connecticut gave 82,433 a permanent place in her noble schools.

In South Carolina, there are but 129,350 free persons over twenty years of age; and, of these, 16,564 are unable to read the word heaven. So, in all that great and democratic State, there are only 112,786 persons over twenty who know their A B C's; while in Connecticut there are 213,662 persons over twenty; and, of all that number, only 5306 are illiterate, and of them 4013 are foreigners. But, of all the 16,564 *ignoramuses* of South Carolina, only 104 were born out of that State!

Out of 365,026 persons over twenty, South Carolina has only 112,786 who can read their primer; while, out of 213,662, Connecticut has 208,356 who can read and write. South Carolina can boast more than 250,000 native adults who cannot write or read the name of their God—a noble army of martyrs, a cloud of witnesses to its peculiar institution; while poor Connecticut has only 1293 native adults unable to read their Holy Bible.

Such is the effect of Slavery and Freedom on *education* in the old States. The Southern politician was right: "Free society is a failure!"

2. Now compare two new States of about the same age. Arkansas was admitted into the Union in 1836, Michigan in 1837.

Arkansas contains 52,198 square miles, and 209,807 inhabitants, of whom 151,746 are free, and 58,161 are slaves. Michigan contains 56,243 square miles, and was entered for settlement later than her sister, but contains 397,654 persons, all free.

In Arkansas, the land is valued at $5.88 the acre; and, in Michigan at $11.83. The slave State has 781,531 acres of improved land; and Michigan, 1,929,110. The farms of Arkansas are worth $15,265,245; and those of Michigan,

$51,872,446. Thus Slavery and Freedom affect the *value of land* in the new States.

Michigan had, in 1855, 699 miles of railroad, which had cost $19,000,000; Arkansas had paid nothing for railroads. The total valuation of Arkansas, in 1850, was $39,871,025: the value of the slaves, $23,264,400, was included. Deducting that, there remains but $16,576,625, as the entire worth of Arkansas; while Michigan has property to the amount of $59,787,255. Thus Slavery and Freedom affect the *value of property* in the new States.

In 1850, Arkansas had 115,023 children under twenty, whereof 11,050 were in schools, academies, or colleges; while Michigan had 211,969, of whom 112,382, were at school, academy, or college. Or, to omit the coloured population, Arkansas had 97,402 white persons under twenty, and only 11,050 attending school; while, of 210,831 whites of that age in Michigan, 112,175 were at school or college. Last year, Michigan had 132,234 scholars in her public common schools. In 1850, Arkansas contained 64,787 whites over twenty—but 16,935 of these were unable to read and write; while, out of 184,240 of that age in Michigan, only 8281 were thus ignorant—of these, 3009 were foreigners; while, of the 16,935 illiterate persons of Arkansas, only 37 were born out of that State. The slave State had only 47,852 persons over twenty who could read a word; while the free State had 175,959. Michigan had 107,943 volumes in "libraries other than private," and Arkansas 420 volumes. Thus Slavery and Freedom affect *the education of the people* in the new States.

Now, see the effect of Slavery and Freedom on property and education in their respective neighbourhoods. I take examples from the States of Missouri and Virginia, kindly furnished by an ingenious and noble-hearted man.

1. In the twelve counties of Missouri, which border on slave-holding Arkansas, ther eare 20,982 free white persons, occupying 75,360 acres of improved land, valued at $13 an acre, or $989,932 : while in the ten counties of Missouri bordering on Iowa, a free State, though less attractive in soil and situation, there are 26,890 free white persons, with 123,030 acres of improved land, worth $19 an acre, or $2,379,765. Thus the *neighbourhood of Slavery retards the development of property.*

In those ten Northern counties bordering on Freedom, there were 2329 scholars in the public schools; while in the twelve Southern, bordering on Arkansas, there were only 339. Thus *the neighbourhood of Slavery affects the development of education.*

2. Compare the Northern with the Southern counties of Virginia, and you find the same results. Monongahela and Preston Counties, in Virginia, bordering on free Pennsylvania, contain 122,444 acres of improved land, valued at $21 an acre, or $2,784,137 in all; are occupied by 24,095 persons, whereof 263 only are slaves; and there are 1747 children in the public schools: while the corresponding counties of Patrick and Henry, touching on North Carolina, contain but 99,731 acres of improved land, worth only $15 an acre, or $1,554,841 in all; are occupied by 18,481 inhabitants, 5664 of them slaves; and have only 961 children at school. But cross the borders, and note the change : the adjacent counties of North Carolina, Rockingham, and Stokes, contain 103,784 acres of improved land, worth $14 an acre, or $1,517,520; 23,701 persons, of whom 7122 are slaves; and have only 2050 pupils at school or college: while Fayette and Green Counties, in Pennsylvania, adjacent to the part of Virginia above spoken of, contain 297,005 acres of improved land, valued at $49 an acre, or $7,618,919; 61,248 persons, all free; and 12,998 pupils at the common schools.

The South has numerous natural advantages over the North,—a better soil, a more genial climate, the privilege of producing those tropical plants now deemed indispensable to civilization. Of $193,000,000 of exports last year, $93,000,000 were of Southern cotton and tobacco. Yet such is her foolish and wicked system, that, while the North continually increases in riches, the South becomes continually poorer and poorer in comparison. Boston alone could buy up two States like South Carolina, and still have thirteen millions of dollars to spare. Three hundred years ago, Spain monopolized this continent; she exploitered Mexico, Peru, the islands of the Gulf; all the gold of the New World came to her hand. Where is it now? Spain is poorer than Italy. Is here no lesson for South Carolina and Virginia?

In civilized society, there must be an organization of things and of persons, of labour and of government; and so slavery is to be looked at, not only in its economical relations, as affecting labour and wealth, power over matter, but also in its political relations, as affecting government, which is power over men.

There are 350,000 slave-holders in the United States, with their families, making a population of 1,750,000 persons. Now, Slavery is a political institution which puts the government of all the people of the slave States into the hands of those few men : the majority are the servants of this minority.

1. The 350,000 slave-holders control the 3,250,000 slaves ; owning their bodies, and, by direct legislation, *purposely preventing their development.*

2. They control the 4,750,000 non-slave-holders, cutting them off from their share of government, and hindering them alike in their labour and their education, and *purposely preventing their development.*

3. They control the Federal politics, and thereby affect the organization of things and persons, of labour and government, throughout the whole nation, and *purposely prevent the development of the whole people.*

In all these three forms of political action, they have selfishly sought their own immediate interest, and wrought to the lasting damage of the slaves, the non-slave-holders, and the whole people. But neither the slaves nor the non-slave-holders have made any powerful opposition to this injury : the chief hostility has been shown by the North, or rather by the few persons therein who either had mind enough to see this manifold mischief clearly, or else such moral and religious instinct as made them at once revolt from this wickedness. But, ever since the Declaration of Independence, there has been a strife, open or hidden, between the South and this portion of the Northern people ; and though the battle has been often joined, yet, since 1788, the North has been beaten in every conflict, pitched battle or skirmish, until last January ; then, after much fighting, the House of Representatives chose for Speaker a man hostile to Slavery. Always before, the South conquered the North ; that is, the minority conquered the majority. The party with the smallest numbers, the least money, the meanest intelligence, the wickedest cause, yet beat the larger, richer, more intelligent party, which had also justice on its side.   There is now no time to explain this political paradox.

Between 1787 and 1851, the regressive power, Slavery, took nine great steps towards absolute rule over the United States.   These I have spoken of before.   It now lifts its foot to take a tenth step,—to stamp bondage on all the territories of this Union, and then organize them into Slave States.   Look at the facts.

We have now one million four hundred thousand square miles of territory not organized into States (1,400,934).   Of this, Kansas, Nebraska, New Mexico, and Utah make nine hundred and twenty-six thousand (926,857).   Now, THE SOUTH AIMS TO MAKE IT ALL SLAVE TERRITORY, to deliver it over to this regressive force, and establish therein such institutions that a few men shall at first own all the land; next, own the bulk of the working people ; and, thirdly, shall control the rest of the whites ; then themselves monopolize education, and yet get very little of it ; repress freedom of speech, and enact laws for the advantage of the vulgarest of all oligarchies,—a band of men-stealers.

Let me suppose that there is no immediate danger that Slavery will go to Oregon or Washington territory,— rather a gratuitous admission : there are still NINE HUN- DRED AND TWENTY-SIX THOUSAND SQUARE MILES of land to plant it on; that is, about one-third of all the country which the United States own! the South is endeavour- ing to establish it there.   Within three years the great battle is to be fought; for, before the 4th of March, 1859, all that territory of fourteen hundred thousand square miles will be either free territory or else slave terri- tory.

The battle is first for Kansas.   Shall it be free, as the majority of its own inhabitants have voted ; or slave, as the Federal Government and the slave power—the general regressive force of America—have determined by violence to make it ? This is the question, *Shall the nine hundred and twenty-six thousand miles of territory belong to three hundred and fifty thousand slave-holders, or to the whole people of the United States?* This is a question which directly concerns the material interest of every working man in the nation, and especially every Northern working man. Before the 1st of January, 1858, perhaps before next January, Kansas, with its one hundred and fourteen thousand seven hundred and ninety square miles, will be a Free State or a Slave State. See what follows, immediately or ultimately, if we let the slave-holders have their way, and make KANSAS A SLAVE STATE.

Look, first, at the effect on the welfare and progress of individuals.

1, A privileged class, an oligarchy of slave-holders, will be founded there, such as exists in the present slave States. They will own all the land, almost all the labourers; will make laws for the advantage of the slave-holder against the interest of the slave and the non-slave-holder. That is the effect on the Southern man.

2. Next see the effect on the working men of the North who emigrate to that quarter. They must go as slave-holders or as non-slave-holders.

Some will go as slave-holders, such as take a South-side view of human wickedness in general. You know what the effect will be on them. Compare the condition, the intellectual and moral character, of New England men who have settled in Georgia, and become slave-holders, with others of the same families—their brothers and cousins—who have remained at home, and engaged in agriculture, commerce, and manufactures.

But not many Northern men will go there and become slave-holders. Some will go as non-slave-holders; and you will see under what disadvantage they must labour.

1. They must live by their work, and in a place where industry is not honoured, as in Connecticut, but is despised, as in South Carolina and Arkansas. The working white man must stand on a level with the slave. He belongs to a despised caste. He will have but little self-respect, and soon will sink down to the character and condition of the poor whites in the old slave States. A scientific friend of mine, who travels extensively in both hemispheres, says that he has not found the Caucasian people anywhere so degraded as in Tennessee and the Carolinas.

2. Next, there will be no miscellaneous mechanical industry, as in New England and all the free States. Agriculture will be the chief business, almost the only business; and that will be confined to the great staples— corn, wheat, rice, tobacco, cotton; the aim will be only to produce the raw material. Agriculture will be poor, land will be low in price, and continually getting run out by unskilful culture. The slave's foot burns the soil and spoils the land; that is the master's fault. Twenty years hence, land will not be worth $16 an acre, as in sterile New Hampshire, but $4, as in fertile Georgia. There will be no rapid development of wealth; and, as the Northern man values riches, I think he should look to this, and see that the land is not taken from under his foot, and the power of creating wealth from his head and hand.

3. Then there will be no good and abundant roads, as in New England, but only a few, as in Carolina and Virginia, and those miserably poor. In Kansas, twenty years hence, there will not be 1964 miles of railroad, as in Illinois, but 231 miles, as in Missouri.

4. There will be no abundance of beneficent free schools, as in New England, but a few, and of the worst sort. Education will be the monopoly of the rich, who will not get much thereof. Laws will forbid the education of the slave, and discourage the culture of the mass of the people.

5. There will be no Lyceums, no courses of lectures; but, in their place, there will be horse-races, occasionally the lynching of an Abolitionist, or the burning of a black man at a slow fire! Yet, now and then, a Northern man will be invited thither by the slave-holders; some unapostolical fisherman will take the majestic memory of Washington, disembowel it of all its most generous humanity, skilfully arrange it as bait; and then, with bob and sinker, hook and line, this "political Micawber," "looking for something to turn up," will go angling along the shore, praying for at least a presidential bite, and possibly obtain a conventional nibble.

6. There will be no "libraries other than private," with their one hundred and eight thousand volumes, as in Michigan; only four hundred and twenty volumes, as in

Arkansas. But a noble army of ignoramuses, twenty-five men out of each hundred adult white men, will attest the value of the "peculiar institution."

7. There will be no multiplicity of valuable newspapers, with an annual circulation of three million three hundred and twenty-four thousand copies, as in Michigan; but a few political journals, scattering three hundred and seventy-seven thousand dingy sheets, as in Arkansas.

8. There will be no abundant and convenient meeting-houses, as in the North; not one hundred and twenty thousand comfortable pew-seats in neat and decorous churches, as in Michigan; but only sixty thousand benches in barns and log-huts, as in Arkansas. No army of well-educated ministers will help, instruct, and moralize the community, but ignorant ranters or calculating hypocrites will stalk through the Christian year, perverting the Bible to a Fugitive Slave Bill, and denying the higher law which God writes in man.

9. There will be no laws favouring all men; but statutes putting the neck of labour into the claws of capital, by which the strong will crush the weak, and enslave the feeblest of all; constitutions like those of South Carolina, which provide that nobody shall sit in the popular House of the Legislature, unless, in his own right, he own "ten negro slaves."

10. There will be no universal suffrage, as in Massachusetts; but a man's political rights will be determined by the colour of his skin, and the amount of his estate. One permanent class will monopolize government, money, education, honour, and ease; the other permanent class will be forced to bondage, ignorance, poverty, and shame. This is the prospect which the Northern man will find before him if Slavery prevails in the new territory.

11. That is not all: his property and person will not be safe, as in Michigan; border-ruffians will permanently have gone over the border, and a new Arkansas be established in Kansas.

Under such circumstances, Northern men will not go there; and so KANSAS, AND THEN ALL THE OTHER TERRITORY, IS STOLEN FROM THE NORTH, AS EFFECTUALLY AS IF CEDED TO RUSSIA OR ANNEXED TO THE SPANISH DOMAIN. Yes, more completely lost; for, if it did belong to Spain, we might reclaim it by *filibustering*; and the American Government would not disturb, but help us.

Then, if a Northern man wishes to migrate, he has only the poorer land of Washington and Oregon before him, and is shut out from the most valuable territory of the United States.

If the city government of Boston were, next month, to establish a piggery on Boston Common, with fifty thousand swine, and set up an immense slaughter-house of the savagest and filthiest character in the Granary Burying-ground, on Copp's Hill, and in each of the public squares; were to give all vacant land to the gamblers, thieves, pimps, kidnappers, and murderers—they would not commit a worse injustice, and they would not do a greater proportional damage to the real estate, and more mischief to the health of the inhabitants of the city, than the American Government would do the working people of the South and North by creating this nuisance of Slavery on the free soil of Kansas.

So much for the effect of this on the individual interests of the working people of America. I have only taken the lowest possible view of the subject.

See its effects on American politics—on the welfare and progress of the nation. If Kansas is made a slave State, we shall either keep united, or else dissolve the Union and separate..

1. Suppose we keep united : what follows?

First, New Mexico will be a slave State, then Utah.

California is only half for freedom now, and will soon split into two; Lower California will be slave.

Then Texas will peel off into new States; Western Texas will soon be made a new slave State.

The Mesilla Valley, bigger than Virginia, will be a slave territory.

Then we shall dismember Mexico—make slave territory there.

We shall *re-annex* the Mosquito territory: the Government wants it, and lets all manner of filibusters go there now.

We shall seize Cuba, to make that soil red with the white man's blood, which is now black with African bondage.

St. Domingo must next fall a prey to American lust for land.

Then we shall carry out the Fugitive Slave Bill in the North as never before. In 1836, Mr. Curtis asked the Supreme Court of Massachusetts to decree that a slave-holder from Louisiana might take his bondman to Boston as a slave, hold him as a slave, sell him as a slave, or, as a slave, carry him back. In 1855, Mr. Kane decreed that a slave-holder might bring his slave into a free State, and keep him there as long as he would *in transitu*. Then we must have laws to enforce these demands : Congress will *legislate*, and the Supreme Court will *rule* to put Slavery into every Northern State. In the beginning of June, 1854, this same Mr. Curtis, then become a judge, gave a "charge," in which he made it appear that, to make a speech in Faneuil Hall against kidnapping was "a mis-demeanour." Yes, if a Massachusetts minister sees his parishioners kidnapped, and makes a speech in Faneuil Hall against that iniquity, and tells the people that they are slaves of Southern masters, Mr. Justice Curtis says that that man has committed a crime, to be punished by im-prisonment for twelve months, and a fine of three hundred dollars! By-and-by, that charge will be "good common law :" *all* lawyers will be slave-hunters ; *all* judges of the Scroggs family ; *all* court-houses girt with chains ; *all* the newspapers administration and Satanic ; *all* the Trini-tarian doctors of divinity will take a South-side view of wickedness in high places ; *all* the Nothingarian doctors of divinity will send back their mothers—for a consideration! And then what becomes of freedom of speech, freedom to worship God ? What of unalienable rights to life, liberty, and the pursuit of happiness? They all perish; and the mocking of tyrants rings round the land : "We meant to subdue you," scoffs one ; "I said, 'We will crush out humanity,'" laughs forth another. Where, then, is America? It goes where Korah, and Dathan, and Abiram are said to have gone long ago. The earth will open her mouth and swallow us up ; the justice of God will visit us —our crime greater than that of Sodom and Gomorrah— for we shall have committed high treason against the dearest rights of man! He will rain on us worse than fire and brimstone ; our name shall rot in the Dead Sea of infamy, and the curses of mankind hang over our memory for ever and ever, world without end!

II. Suppose we separate. The North may at length feel some little manhood; become angry at this continual insult, and be roused by fear of actual ruin; calculate the value of the Union, and find it not worth while any longer to be tied to this offensive partner. See what may follow in the attempt at dissolution. Look at the comparative military power—the men and money—of the North and South.

Omitting California and the territories, the North has fifteen million freemen, or three million men able to do military duty; and also thirty-two hundred million dollars ($3,200,000,000); while the South has fifteen hundred million dollars ($1,500,000,000), six million five hundred thousand freemen, and three million five hundred thousand slaves. But the latter are a negative quantity to be subtracted from the whole. So the effective population is three millions, or six hundred thousand men able to bear arms. Such is the comparative personal and material force of the two. I will not speak of the odds in the quality of Northern and Southern men, looking now only at the obvious quantitative difference.

The contest could not be doubtful or long. The North could dictate the terms of separation, and would probably take two-thirds of the naval and military property of the nation, and all of the territories. Then would come the question, where shall be the line of demarcation between Freedom and Slavery? I think the North might fix the Potomac and Ohio as the Northern, and the Mississippi as the Western limit of Slavery. Depend upon it, we shall not leave more land than these boundaries indicate to the cause of bondage. Then the ten Barbary States of America might found a new empire, with despotism for their central idea; take the name of Braggadocia, Servilia, Violentia, Thrasonia, or, in plainer Saxon title, Bullydom; and become as famous in future history as the "Five Cities of the Plain" were in the past. But would Virginia, Kentucky, Tennessee, Louisiana, consent to be border States, with no Fugitive Slave Bill to fetter their bondmen?

I do not propose disunion—at present. I would never leave the black men in bondage, or the whites subject to the slaveholding oligarchy which rules them. The Constitution itself guarantees "a republican form of government" to each State in the Union : no slave State has had it yet. Perhaps the North will one day respect the other half of "the Compromises of the constitution." Certainly there must be national unity of idea, either of Freedom or of Slavery, or else we separate before long.

This regressive force, which retards the progress and diminishes the welfare of the South, and yet controls the politics of America, is determined to conquer the progressive force, to put liberty down, to spread bondage over all the North, to organize it in all the wild land of the continent. The ablest champions of this iniquity are Northern men. The same North which bore Seward and Giddings, Sumner and Hale, not to mention others equally able, is mother also to Cushing and Douglas; and one of these would "crush out" all opposition to Slavery, all love of welfare and progress; the other is reported to have said to the North, in the Senate, "We mean to subdue you." Mark the words—"WE MEAN TO SUBDUE YOU!" That is the aim of the administration, to make progress, regress ; welfare, illfare ; to make Democracy and Christianity, Despotism and anti-Christianity; that is the purpose of the oligarchy of slaveholders, to be executed with those triple Northern tools already named—*base* men, *mean* men, *ignorant* men.

The first great measure is to put Slavery into Kansas and Nebraska, into four hundred and fifty thousand six hundred and eighty miles of wild land.

To accomplish that, five steps were necessary. Here they are :—

I. The first was to pass a pro-Slavery Act to organize the Kansas and Nebraska territory. That accomplished two things :—

1. It repealed the Missouri Compromise, and laid the territory open to the slave-holder.

2. It established squatter sovereignty, and allowed the settlers to make laws for Slavery. or Freedom, as they saw fit. The South intended that it should be a slave State.

You know how this first step was taken in 1854; what was done by Congress, by the President; you have not

forgotten the conduct of Mr. Douglas, of Illinois.   Massachusetts yet remembers the behaviour of Mr. Everett.   It
is rather difficult to find all the facts concerning this Kansas
business; lies have been woven over the whole matter, and
I know of no transaction in human history which has been
covered up with such abundant lying, from the death of
Ananias and Sapphira down to the first nomination of
Governor Gardiner.   Still the main facts appear through
this garment of lies.

II. The second step was to give the new territory a slave
government, which would take pains to organize Slavery
into the land, and Freedom out of it.   So the executive
appointed persons supposed to be competent for that work,
and, amongst others, Mr. Reeder, of Easton, in Pennsylvania, who was thought to be fit for that business.   But
it turned out otherwise: he became conscientious, and refused to execute the infamous and unlawful commands of
the executive.   Finding it was so, the President—I have
it on good authority—tried to bribe him to resign, offering
him the highest office then vacant—the ministry to China.
Governor Reeder refused the bribe, and then was discharged
from his office on the pretence of some pecuniary unfaith-
fulness.   Mr. Shannon was thrust into his place, for which
he seems to the manner born; for—I have this also on
good authority—his habitual drunkenness seems to be one
of the smallest of his public vices.

III. The third step was to establish Slavery by squatter
sovereignty.   For this, two things were indispensable:
(1.) To elect a legislature friendly to Slavery; and (2.) To
get laws made by that legislature to secure the desired end.

1. This must be done by actual settlers; and then, for
the first time in this career of wickedness, a difficulty was
found.   The people were to be consulted; and no *coup
d'état* of the government could do the work.   There was
an unexpected difficulty; for, soon as Kansas was open,
great bodies went there from the North to settle and secure
it to freedom.   It soon became plain that they were numerous enough to bring squatter sovereignty itself over to the
side of humanity, and, by their votes, exclude bondage for
ever.   That must be prevented by the regressive force.   Mr.
Atchinson, Mr. Stringfellow, and others were appointed to
take the matter in hand.   Citizens of Missouri organized

themselves into companies, and in military order, with pistols and bowie-knives, and in one instance with cannon, went óver the border into Kansas to determine the elections by excluding the legal voters, and themselves casting the ballot. In ten months, they made four general invasions of Kansas, if I am rightly informed; namely, (1.) On the 29th of July, 1854; (2.) 29th of November, 1854; (3.) 30th March, 1855, and (4.) 22nd May, 1855. The third was the *great invasion,* made to elect the legislators who were to enact the territorial laws. It appears that four thousand men marched bodily from Missouri to Kansas, some of them penetrating two hundred miles into the interior, and delivered their votes, electing men who would put Slavery into the land. The fourth was a smaller and local invasion, to fill vacancies in the legislature.

I cannot dwell on these things, nor stop to speak of the violence and murder repeatedly committed by these border ruffians, under the eyes, and with the consent, and by the encouragement, of the American Executive. You can read those things in the newspapers, at least in the *New York Tribune* and *Evening Post.* But, suffice it to say, the Legislature thus chosen was wholly illegal. If Jersey City were to order a municipal election, and New York were to go there, and choose aldermen and common councilmen, and the new officers were to act in that capacity, we should have a parallel of what took place in Kansas.

Thus the slave power which controls the Federal Government secured the first requisite,—a Slave Legislature.

2. They must next proceed to make the appropriate laws. The Legislature came together on the 2nd July, 1855, at the place legally fixed by Governor Reeder: they passed an illegal Act, fixing the seat of Government at Shawneetown, on the borders of Missouri, and adjourned thither. The Governor vetoed the Act, and repudiated the Legislature, illegally chosen at first, illegally acting afterwards. But they continued in session there from July 15th to August 31st, and made a huge statute-book of more than a thousand great pages. It contains substantially the laws of Missouri; but, in some instances, they were made worse. Take this for example :—

"No person who shall have been convicted of any violation of any of the provisions of an Act of Congress" (the Fugitive Slave Bills of 1793 and 1850), "whether such conviction was by criminal proceeding or by civil action, in any courts of the United States, or of any State or territory, shall be entitled to vote at any election, or to hold any office in this territory." "If any person offering to vote shall be challenged and required to take an oath or affirmation that he will sustain the provisions of the above-recited Acts of Congress" (the Fugitive Slave Bills), "and shall refuse to take such oath or affirmation, the vote of such person shall be rejected."—Ch. lxvi. § 11, p. 332.

There is no similar provision depriving a man of his vote if he violate any other statute : but a deed of common humanity disfranchises a man for ever; nay, performing an act of kindness to a brother perpetually deprives a man of his share in the government !

Look at this statute :—

"Every free person who shall aid . . . . in any rebellion or insurrection of slaves, ... or do any other overt act in furtherance of such rebellion, ... shall suffer death."

"If any person shall . . . . induce any slaves to rebel, ... or shall . . . . circulate . . . . any book . . . . or circular for the purpose of exciting insurrection . . . . on the part of the slaves, such person shall . . . . suffer death."

"If any person shall aid . . . . in enticing . . . . any slave . . . . to effect the freedom of such slave, ... he shall . . . . suffer death, or be imprisoned at hard labour for not less than ten years."—Ch. cli. § 2, 4, 5.

Look at this :—

SECT. 11.—"If any person print, write, introduce into, publish, or circulate, or cause to be brought into, printed, written, published, or circulated, or shall knowingly aid or assist in bringing into, printing, publishing, or circulating, within this territory, any book, paper, pamphlet, magazine, handbill, or circular, containing any statements, arguments, opinions, sentiments, doctrines, advice, or innuendo, calculated to promote a disorderly, dangerous, or rebellious disaffection among the slaves in this territory, or to induce such slaves to escape from the service of their masters, or to resist their authority, he shall be guilty of a felony, and be punished by imprisonment and hard labour for a term not less than five years."

SECT. 12.—"If any free person, by speaking or by writing, assert or maintain that persons have not the right to hold slaves in this territory, or shall introduce into this territory, print, publish, write, circulate, or cause to be introduced into this territory, written, printed, published, or circulated in this territory, any book, paper, magazine, pamphlet, or circular, containing any denial of the right of persons to hold slaves in this territory, such person shall be deemed guilty of felony, and punished by imprisonment at hard labour for a term of not less than two years."

But stealing a free child under twelve is punished with imprisonment for not more than five years, or confinement in the county gaol not less than six months, or a fine of $500 (Ch. xlviii. Sect. 43).

CHAP. XV. SECT. 13.—"No person who is conscientiously opposed to holding slaves, or who does not admit the right to hold slaves in this territory, shall sit as a juror on the trial of any prosecutions for any violation of any of the sections of this Act."

That law excludes the New Testament and the Old Testament, as well as the Declaration of Independence, and the works of Franklin, Jefferson, and Madison: it shuts humanity from the jury-box.

IV. The next step was to get a pro-Slavery delegate from Kansas into the House of Representatives at Washington. So, on the 1st of October, 1855, the day appointed by the Border-Ruffian Legislature to elect a delegate, a fifth invasion was made by outsiders from Missouri, who, as before, took possession of the polls, and chose Hon. J. W. Whitfield to that office. Mr. Shannon, the new and appropriate Governor of the territory, gave him a certificate of lawful election. He is now at Washington in that capacity. But the House of Representatives has the matter under advisement; a committee has gone to Kansas to investigate the matter; and the country waits, anxious for the results.

V. The only remaining step is to enforce their slave-law, and then Kansas becomes a slave State. But this is a difficult matter: for the people of the territory, indignant at this invasion of their rights, long since repudiated the legislature of ruffians; held a convention at Topeka; formed a constitution, which was submitted to the people, and accepted by them. They have chosen their own legislature, State officers, senators, and representatives, and applied for admission into the Union as a free State. But men, who have already five times invaded the territory, threaten to go there again, and enforce the laws which they have already made.

I need only refer to the conduct of the President, and his masters in the cabinet, and say that he has been uniformly on the side of this illegal violence. You remember his Message last winter, his Proclamation at a later day, his conduct all the time. He encourages the violence of these tools of the slave power, who have sought to tread the people down.   Hence it becomes indispensable for the Northern emigrants to take arms.   It is instructive to see the old Puritan spirit coming out in the sons of the North, even those who went on theological errands.   Excepting the Quakers, the Unitarians are the most unmilitary of sects; in Boston, their most conspicuous ministers have been—some of them still are—notorious supporters of the worst iniquities of American Slavery.   Surely you will not forget the ecclesiastical defences of the Fugitive Slave Bill, the apologies for kidnapping.   But a noble-hearted Unitarian minister, Rev. Mr. Nute, "felt drawn to Kansas."   Of course he carried his Bible: he knew it also by heart.   His friends gave him a "repeating rifle" and a "revolver."   These also "felt drawn to Kansas."   This "minister at large"—very much at large, too, his nearest denominational brother, on one side five hundred miles off, on the other fifteen hundred—trusts in God, and keeps his powder dry.   Listen to this, written December 3rd, 1855.:—

"I have just been summoned to be in the village with my repeating rifle. I shall go, and use my utmost efforts to prevent bloodshed. But, if it comes to a fight, in which we shall be forced to defend our homes and lives against the assault of these border savages (and by the way, the Indians are being enlisted on both sides), I shall do my best to keep them off."

On the 10th, he writes :—

"Our citizens have been shot at, and, in two instances, murdered; our houses invaded; hay-ricks burnt; corn and other provisions plundered; cattle driven off; all communication cut off between us and the States; wagons on the way to us with provisions stopped and plundered, and the drivers taken prisoners; and we in hourly expectation of an attack. Nearly every man has been in arms in the village. Fortifications have been thrown up by incessant labour night and day. The sound of the drum, and the tramp of armed men, resounded through our streets; families fleeing with their household goods for safety. Day before yesterday, the report of cannon was heard at our house from the direction of Lecompton. Last Thursday, one of our neighbours,—one of the most peaceable and excellent of men, from Ohio,—on his way home, was set upon by a gang of twelve men on horseback, and shot down. Several of the ruffians pursued him some distance after he was shot; and one was seen to push him from his horse, and heard to shout to his companions that he was dead. A neighbour reached him just before he breathed his last. I was present when his family came in to see the corpse, for the first time, at the Free-State Hotel,—a wife, a sister, a brother, and an aged mother. It was the most exciting and the most distressing scene that I ever witnessed. Hundreds of our men were in tears, as the shrieks and groans of the bereaved women were heard all over the building, now used for military barracks. Over eight hundred men are gathered under arms at Lawrence. As yet, no act of violence has been perpetrated by those on our side; no blood of retaliation stains our hands. We stand, and are ready to act, purely in the defence of our homes and lives. I am enrolled in the cavalry, though I have not yet appeared in the ranks; but, should there be an attack, *I shall be there.* I have had some hesitation about the propriety of this course; but some one has said, "In questions of duty, the first thought is generally the right one." On that principle, I find strong justification. I could feel no self-respect until I had offered my services.

"Day before yesterday, we received the timely re-enforcement of a twelve-pounder howitzer, with ammunition therefor, including grape and canister, with forty bomb-shells. It was sent from New York (made at Chicopee). By a deed of successful daring and cunning, it was brought through the country invested by the enemy, a distance of fifty miles, from Kansas City, by an unfrequented route, boxed up as merchandise.

"*Sunday Morning*, Dec. 9.—The governor has pledged himself to do all he can to make peace; and we are told that the invaders are beginning to retreat; but we know not what to believe. Our men are to be kept under arms for twenty-four hours longer, at least. No religious meetings for the last three weeks. No work done, of course. Some of the logs to be sawed for our church were pressed into service to build a fort, of which we have no less than five, and of no mean dimensions or strength. For a time, it seemed probable that the foundation-stones for the church would be wet by the blood of the martyrs for liberty. They were piled up on the ground, and, with the earth thrown out of the excavation, made quite a fort on the hillside just outside of the line of intrenchments."

That is the report of a Unitarian missionary. You know what the Trinitarians have done: the conduct of that valiant man, Henry Ward Beecher,—the most powerful and popular minister in the United States,—and his "Plymouth Church," and other "religious bodies" at New Haven and elsewhere, need not be spoken of.

One effect of this warlike spirit is curious; "pious" newspapers are very much troubled at the talk of rifles, pistols, and cannon. In 1847, they rated me roundly for preaching against the Mexican war,—a war for plundering a feeble nation, that we might blacken her soil with Slavery: it was "desecrating the Sabbath." They liked the Sims brigade, the Burns division; they did homage to the cannon which men-stealers loaded in Boston, therewith to shoot the friends of humanity on the graves of Hancock and Adams! Now, the *mean* men and the *base* men are brought over to "peace principles:" a rifle is "not of the Lord;" a cannon is "a carnal weapon;" a sword is "of the devil." All the South thinks gunpowder is "unchris-

tian." Such a " change of heart" has not been heard of
since the conversion of St. Ananias and Sapphira.

I have no fondness for fighting; not the average " instinct of destruction." I should suffer a great while before I
struck a blow. But there are times when I would take down
the dreadful weapon of war: this is one of them for the
men in Kansas.

It is not easy for the border ruffians alone to put down
Kansas; not possible for them to break up the popular
organization, destroy the new Constitution, and hang the
officers. Will the President send the United States soldiers
to do this? No doubt his heart is good enough for that
work. We remember what he did with United States
soldiers at Boston, in 1854: the only service they ever
rendered in that town for more than forty years was to
kidnap Anthony Burns. But the President falters: there
is a North; all last winter there was a North,—Northern
ice in the Mississippi; Banks, of the North, at Washington, in the speaker's chair.

Kansas and Nebraska are " the Children in the Wood.".
They had a fair inheritance; but the parents, dying, left
them to a guardian uncle,—the President. I heard the
Northern mother say to him,—

> "You must be father and mother both,
>   And uncle, all in one."

> "You are the man must bring our babes
>   To wealth or misery.

> And, if you keep them carefully,
>   Then God will you reward;
> But, if you otherwise should deal,
>   God will your deeds regard."

It is still the old story: the Executive uncle promises
well enough: yet—

> "He had not kept these pretty babes
>   But twelve months and a day,
> Before he did devise
>   To make them both away.

> He bargained with two ruffians strong

[That is, *Straightwhig* and *Democrat*,]

> Which were of furious mood,
> That they should take these children young,
>   And slay them in a wood."

It is still the old story. One of the ruffians kills the other; but, in this case, Democrat, the strong ruffian, killed Straightwhig,—a weak ruffian, who had no "backbone,"—and now seeks to kill the babes. He is not content to let them starve,—

> "Their pretty lips with blackberries
> So all besmeared and dyed;"

he "*would make them both away*." But that is not quite so easy. Kansas, the elder, turns out a very male child, a thrifty boy: *he will not die;* he refuses to be killed, but, with such weapons as he has, shows what blood he came of. His relations hear of the matter, and make a noise about it. The uncle becomes the town-talk. Even the ghost of Straightwhig is disquieted, and "walks" in obscure places, by graveyards, "haunting" some houses. Nay, the Northern mother rises from the grave: perhaps the Northern father is not dead, but only sleeping, like Barbarossa in that other fable, with his Sharp's rifle for a pillow. Who knows but he, too, will "rise," and execute his own will? The history may yet end after the old sort:—

> "And now the heavy wrath of God
> Upon the Uncle fell;
> Yea, fearful fiends did haunt his house;
> His conscience felt a hell.
>
> His barns were fired, his goods consumed,
> His lands were barren made;
> Conventions failed to nominate;
> No office with him staid."

Kansas applies for admission as a free State, with a constitution made in due form and by the people. The regressive force is determined that she shall be a slave State; and so all the 926,000 miles of territory become the spoil of the slave-holder. See the state of things.

The majority of the Senate is pro-Slavery, of the Satanic Democracy. For once, the House inclines the other way,—leans towards Freedom. A bill for making Kansas a slave State will pass the Senate; will be resisted in the House: then comes the tug of war. The North has a majority in the House, but it is divided. If all will unite, they make Kansas a free State before the 4th of next July.

They can force the Administration to this act of justice,
simply by refusing to vote a dollar of money until Kansas
is free. If the House will determine on that course, the
two Executives—the Presidential and the Senatorial—will
soon come to terms. This is no new expedient: it was often
enough resorted to by our fathers in old England, under
the Tudors and Stuarts; nay, even the Dutch used it
against Philip II.

But perhaps there is not virtue enough in the House to
do this; then let the State legislatures which are now in
session send instructions, the people—who are always in
session—petitions, to that effect.

But perhaps the people themselves are not quite ready
for this measure; and the House and Senate cannot agree.
Then the question goes over to the next presidential election, where it will be the most important element. There
will be three candidates, perhaps four; for the straight
Whigs may put up some invertebrate politician, hoping to
catch whatever shall turn "up." It is possible there shall
be no choice by the people; then the election goes to the
present House of Representatives, where the choice is by
States. In either case, if the matter be managed well, the
progressive force of America may get into the presidential
chair. I mean to say, we can choose an *anti-Slavery president next autumn*,—some one who loves man and God, not
merely money, loaves and fishes,—who will counsel and
work for the present welfare and future progress of America,
and so promote that Christianity and Democracy spoken of
before. I shall not pretend to say who the man is: it
must be some one who reverences JUSTICE,—the higher
law of God. He must be a strong man, a just man, a man
sure for the right. Let there be no humbug this time, no
doubtful man.

If we once put an anti-Slavery man, never so moderate,
into the presidency, then see what follows immediately or
at length:—

1. The Executive holds 40,000 offices in his right hand,
and 70,000,000 annual dollars in his left hand: both will
be dispensed so as to promote the welfare and the prosperity
of the people. All the great offices, executive, judicial, diplomatic, commercial, will be controlled by the

progressive force; the Administration will be celestial-democratic, not Satanic merely, and seek by natural justice to organize things and persons so that all may have a share in labour and government. Then, when freedom has money and office to bestow, she will become respectable in the South, where noble men, slave-holders and non-slaveholders, will come out of their hiding-places to bless their land which others have cursed so heavily and so long. There are anti-Slavery elements at the South : " One swallow makes no summer ;" but one presidential summer of freedom will bring many swallows out from their wintry sleep, fabulous or real. Nay, the *ignorant* men of the North will be instructed ; her *mean* men will be attracted by the smell of dinner ; and her *base* men, left alone in their rot, will engage in other crime, but not in kidnapping men.

2. Kansas becomes a free State before the 1st of January, 1858. Nebraska, Oregon, Washington, Utah, New Mexico, all will be free States. When Texas sends down a pendulous branch, which takes independent root, a tree of freedom will grow up therefrom. Western Texas will ere long be a free State ; she is half ready now. Freedom will be organized in the Mesilla Valley. If we acquire new territory from Mexico, it will be honestly got, and Democracy and Christianity spread thither. If Central America, Nicaragua, or other new soil, become ours, it will be all consecrated to freedom, and the unalienable rights of man. Slavery will be abolished in the district of Columbia.

3. There will be no more national attempts to destroy Freedom in the North, but continual efforts to restrict Slavery. The democratic parts of the Constitution, long left a dead letter therein, will be developed, and the despotic clauses, exceptionable there, and clearly hostile to its purpose and its spirit, will be overruled, and forced out of sight, like odious features of the British common law. There will be a pacific railroad, perhaps more than one ; and national attempts will be made to develop the national resources of the Continent by free labour. The South will share with the North in this better organization of things and persons, this development of industry and education.

4. And what will be the future of Kansas ? Her 114,000 square miles will soon fill up with educated and industrious men, each sharing the labour and the government of

society, helping forward the welfare and the progress of all, aiding the organization of Christianity and Democracy. What a development there will be of agriculture, mining, manufactures, commerce! What farms and shops! What canals and railroads! What schools, newspapers, libraries, meeting-houses! Yes, what families of rich, educated, happy, and religious men and women! In the year 1900, there will be 2,000,000 men in Kansas, with cities like Providence, Worcester, perhaps like Chicago and Cincinnati. She will have more miles of railroad than Maryland, Virginia, and both the Carolinas can now boast. Her land will be worth $20 an acre, and her total wealth will be $500,000,000 of money; 600,000 children will learn in her schools.

5. There will be a ring of Freedom all round the slave States, and in them Slavery itself will decline. The theory of bondage will be given up, like the theory of theocracy and monarchy; and attempts will be made to get rid of the fact. Then the North will help the Southern States in that noble work. There will never be another Slave State nor another Slave President; no more kidnapping in the North; no more chains round the Court House in Boston; no more preaching against the first principles of all humanity.

Three hundred years ago, our fathers in Europe were contending for liberty. Then it was freedom of conscience which the progressive force of the people demanded. Julius the Third had just been Pope, who gave the cardinalship, vacated at his election, to the keeper of his monkeys; and Paul IV. sat in his stead in St. Peter's chair, and represented in general for all Europe the regressive power; while bloody Mary and bloodier Philip sat on England's throne, and, incited thereto by the Pontiff, smote at the rights of man.

Two hundred years ago, our fathers in the two Englands —old and new—did grim battle against monarchic despotism: one Charles slept in his bloody grave, another wandered through the elegant debaucheries of the Continent; while Cromwell and Milton made liberal England abidingly famous and happy.

One hundred years ago, other great battling for the

rights of man was getting begun. Ah me ! the long-continued strife is not ended. The question laid over by our fathers is adjourned to us for settlement. It is the old question between the substance of man and his accidents, labour and capital, the people and a caste.

Shall the 350,000 slave-holders own all the 1,400,000 square miles of territory not yet made States, and drive all Northern men away from it, or shall it belong to the people ; shall this vast area be like Arkansas and South Carolina, or like Michigan and Connecticut ? That is the *immediate* question.

Shall Slavery spread over all the United States, and root out Freedom from the land ? or shall Freedom spread wide her blessed boughs till the whole continent is fed by her fruit, and lodged beneath her arms—her very leaves for the healing of the nations ? That is the *ultimate* question.

Now is the time for America to choose between these two alternatives, and choose quick. For America ? No, for the North. You and I are to decide this mighty question. I take it, the Anglo-Saxon will not forego his ethnological instinct for freedom ; will not now break the historic habit of two thousand years ; he will progressively tend to Christianity and Democracy ; will put Slavery down, peaceably if he can, forcibly if he must.

We may now end this crime against humanity by ballots ; wait a little, and only with swords and with blood can this deep and widening blot of shame be scoured out from the continent. No election, since that first and unopposed of Washington, has been so important to America as this now before us. Once the nation chose between Aaron Burr and Thomas Jefferson. When the choice is between Slavery and Freedom, will the North choose wrong ? Any railroad company may, by accident, elect a knave for President ; but, when he has been convicted of squandering their substance on himself, and blowing up their engines, nay, destroying their sons and daughters, will the stockholders choose a swindler for ever ?

I think we shall put Slavery down ; I have small doubt of that. But shall we do it now and without tumult, or by and by with a dreadful revolution, St. Domingo massacres, and the ghastly work of war ?

Shall America decide for wickedness,—extend the dark

places of the earth, filled up yet fuller with the habitations of cruelty ? Then our ruin is certain,—is also just. The power of self-rule, which we were not fit for, will pass from our hands, and the halter of vengeance will gripe our neck, and America shall lie there on the shore of the sea, one other victim who died as the fool dieth. What a ruin it would be! Come away! I cannot look, even in fancy, on so foul a sight.

If we decide for the unalienable rights of man; for present welfare, future progress; for Christianity and Democracy; and so organize things and men that all may share the labour and government of society—then what a prospect is before us! How populous, how rich, will the land become! Ere long, her borders wide will embrace the hemisphere—how full of men! If we are faithful to our duty, one day, America, youngest of nations, shall sit on the Cordilleras, the youthful mother of the continent of States. Behind her are the Northern lakes, the Northern forest bounded by Arctic ice and snow; on her left hand swells the Atlantic, the Pacific on her right—both beautiful with the white lilies of commerce, giving fragrance all round the world; while before her spreads out the Southern land, from terra firma to the isles of fire, blessed with the Saxon mind and conscience, heart and soul; and, underneath her eye, into the lap of the hemisphere, the Amazon, and the Mississippi—classic rivers of freedom—pour the riches of either continent; and behind her, before her, on either hand, all round, and underneath her eye, extends the new world of humanity, the commonwealth of the people, justice, the law thereof, and infinite perfection, God; a Church without a bishop, a State without a king, a community without a lord, a family with no holder of slaves, with welfare for the present, and progress for the future, she will show the nations how divine a thing a people can be made.

> " Oh, well for him whose will is strong!
> He suffers, but he will not suffer long;
> He suffers, but he cannot suffer wrong:
> For him nor moves the loud world's random mock,
> Nor all calamity's hugest waves confound,
> Who seems a promontory of rock,
> That, compassed round with turbulent sound,
> In middle ocean meets the surging shock,
> Tempest-buffeted, citadel-crown'd."

THE PRESENT ASPECT OF SLAVERY IN AMERICA, AND THE IMMEDIATE DUTY OF THE NORTH.

A SPEECH

DELIVERED IN THE HALL OF THE STATE HOUSE, BEFORE THE MASSACHUSETTS ANTI-SLAVERY CONVENTION, ON FRIDAY, JANUARY 29, 1858.

MR. PRESIDENT, LADIES AND GENTLEMEN :—I shall not hold you long to-night. There are others to speak after me who have better claims to your attention—the one (Mr. Remond) for his race, the other (Mr. Phillips) for the personal attributes of eloquence which, in America, have never reached a higher height, or exhibited themselves in so fair a form. The hand of the dial shall pass round once, and I leave this spot, to be filled more worthily. During these sixty minutes, I ask your attention to some thoughts on the "Present Aspect of Slavery in America, and the immediate Duty of the North."

Mr. Guizot—one of the most learned and humane of the European statesmen — prefaced one edition of his *History of Representative Government*, by stating that the conditions of national welfare were far more difficult than the too sanguine hopes of mankind had ever led them to expect. If that were so in Europe, where centuries of bitter experience have taught men to be cautious in their hopes, how much truer it is in America, where we think liberty is so natural to the soil and congenial to man, that it needs no support from the people, but will thrive of its own sweet accord !

In some respects, our experiment is simpler than the great attempts at freedom made before us in the Old World; in some others it is more complex and difficult. All the old

forms of civilization were based on unity of race.   It was
so with the Romans, Greeks, Persians, Hebrews, Egyptians,
East Indians.   The same holds good of the Moors, who
mark the transition from ancient to modern times.   All the
mediæval attempts at improvement had the same character
—in Spain, Italy, France, Germany, England itself. Civilization hitherto has belonged only to the Caucasian race.
The Africans have remained strangers to it in all times
past ; they could not achieve it for themselves at the time,
hitherto never rising above the savage or the barbarous
state; no other people brought it to them, or them to it,
save in small numbers.

It was left for America to begin a new experiment in the
history of civilization — to bring divers races into closest
contact.   The Catholic Spaniard began the experiment: he
mixed his blood with the red man, whose country he subdued; he brought hither also the black man.   Thus the
African savage, the American barbarian, and the civilized
Caucasian of Spain, became joint stockholders in this new
coparceny of races.   The Protestant Briton continued what
his Catholic predecessor had begun ; and, while the Puritan
was painfully voyaging to Plymouth, in the wilderness
seeking an asylum where the Apocalyptic woman might
bear her manchild to grow up in freedom, other Saxons
were bringing a ship-load of negroes to the wilderness, to
become slaves for ever.   Thus the African came to British
and Spanish America.   Out of the 60,000,000 inhabitants
of this continent, I take it about 9,000,000 are of this unfortunate race.

In the United States to-day, four of the five great races live
side by side.   There are some 60,000 or 80,000 Mongolian
Chinese in California, I am told ; there are 400,000 American Indians within our borders ; perhaps 4,500,000 Africans ; and 26,000,000 Caucasians.   The union of such
diverse ethnological elements makes our experiment of
democracy more complex, and perhaps more difficult than
it would otherwise be.

The Mongolians are few in numbers, and so transient in
their stay that nothing more need now be said of them.

It is plain where the red man will go.   In two hundred
years, an Indian will be as rare in the United States as
now in New England.   Like the bear and the buffalo, he ·

OF SLAVERY IN AMERICA.289

perishes with the forest, which to him and them was what cultivated fields, towns, and cities are to us. Our fathers tried to enslave the ferocious and unprogressive Indian; he would not work—for himself as a freeman, nor for others as a slave: he would fight. He would not be enslaved—he could not help being killed. He perishes before us. The sinewy Caucasian labourer lays hold on the phlegmatic Indian warrior; they struggle in deadly grasp—naked man to naked man, hand to shoulder, knee to knee, breast to breast; the white man bends the red man over, crushes him down, and chokes him dead. It is always so when the civilized meets the savage, or the barbarian—naked man to naked man: how much more fatal is the issue to the feeble when the white man shirted in iron has the small-pox for his ally, and rum for his tomahawk! In the long run of history, the race is always to the swift, and the battle to the strong. The Indian will perish—utterly and soon.

The African is the most docile and pliant of all the races of men; none has so little ferocity: vengeance, instantial with the Caucasian, is exceptional in his history. In his barbarous, savage, or even wild state, he is not much addicted to revenge; always prone to mercy. No race is so strong in the affectional instinct which attaches man to man by tender ties; none so easy, indolent, confiding, so little warlike. Hence is it that the white men have kidnapped the black, and made him their prey.

This piece of individual biography tells us the sad history of the African race. Not long since, a fugitive slave told me his adventures. I will call him John—it is not his name. He is an entire negro—his grandfather was brought direct from the Congo coast to America. A stout man, thick-set, able-bodied, with great legs and mighty arms, he could take any man from this platform, and hurl him thrice his length. He was a slave—active, intelligent, and much confided in. He had a wife and children. One day his master, in a fit of rage, struck at him with a huge club, which broke both of his arms; they were awkwardly set, and grew out deformed. The master promised to sell the man to himself for a large sum, and take the money by instalments, a little at a time. But, when more than half of it was paid, he actually sold him to a trader, to be taken further South, and there disposed of. The appeals of the wife, the tears of the children, moved not the master whom justice had also failed to touch. As the boat which contained poor John shot by the point of land where he had lived, his wife stood upon the shore, and held her babies up for him to look upon for the last time. Descending the Mississippi, the captain of the boat had the river fever, lost his sight for the time, and John took the command. One night, far down the Mississippi, he found himself on board a boat with the three kidnappers who had him in their power, and intended to sell him. They were asleep below—the captain still blind with the disease—he watchful on deck. " I crept down barefoot," said John. " There they lay in their bunks, all fast asleep. They had money, and I none. I had done them no harm, but they had torn me from my wife, from my children, from my liberty. I stole up noiselessly, and came back again, the boat's axe in my hand. I lifted it up, and grit my teeth together, and was about to strike : and it came into my mind, ' No murderer hath eternal life.' I put the axe back in its place, and was sold into slavery. What would you have done in such a case ?" I told him that I thought I should have sent the kidnappers to their own place first, and then trusted that the act would be imputed to me for righteousness by an all-righteous God ! I need not ask what Mr. Garrison would do in like case. I think his Saxon blood would move swift enough to sweep off his non-resistant creed, and the three kidnappers would have started on their final journey before he asked, " *Where shall I go ?*"

John's story is also the story of Africa. The stroke of an axe would have settled the matter long ago. But the black man would not strike. One day, perhaps, he will do what yonder monument commends.

At this moment, we have perhaps 4,500,000 men of African descent in the United States ; say 4,000,000 slaves, 500,000 free. They are with us, are of us ; America cannot be rid of them if she would. Shall they continue slaves, or be set free ? What consequences will follow either result ? This is the great question for America. It is the question of industry, of morals, of religion ; it is the immediate question of politics. It does not concern the 4,000,000 slaves alone, but also each of the 26,000,000 Caucasian freemen. On it depends the success or the failure of our experiment of Democracy. The bondage of a class may continue in a despotism; there it is no contradiction to the national idea. It is different in a Democracy which rests on the equality of all men in natural rights. So here the question of Slavery is this: "Shall we have an industrial Democracy, or a military despotism?" If you choose Slavery, then you take the issue of Slavery, which can no more be separated from it than cold from ice. No nation can escape the consequences of its own first principle of politics. ·The logic of the idea is the "manifest destiny" of the people. If Slavery continues, Democracy goes down; every form of republicanism, or of constitutional monarchy, will perish; and absolute military despotism take their place at last. From despotism, as seed reared in the national garden, comes despotism, as national crop, growing in the continental field.

This question of Slavery does not concern America alone; all Christendom likewise is party to the contest. To all men it is a question of industry, commerce, education, morals, religion; to the civilized world, it is the great question of civilization itself. Shall this great continent be delivered over to ideas which help the progress of mankind, or to those which only hinder it?

Every year brings America into closer relations with the rest of mankind. Our Slavery becomes, therefore, an element in the world's politics. See, then, for a moment, how the various Christian nations stand affected towards it.

Just now, there are but five great national powers in the civilized or Christian world. Spain, Italy, and Greece pass for nothing—they have no influence in the progressive movements of mind, are no longer a force in the world's civilization. They are not wholly dead; but so far as they affect other peoples, it is only by the thought of past generations, not the present. I pass those three decaying nations by, and look at the live peoples. There is (1) the Russian power—a great Slavic people holding Mongolians in subjection; (2) the French power—a great Celtic people variously crossed with Basque, Roman, and Teutonic tribes; (3) the German power — a great Teutonic people, in many nations or States, with Slavic and Celtic elements mixed in; (4) the English power—a great Saxon-Teutonic people, with Celtic annexations; and (5) the American power—

a great English-Saxon-Teutonic people, with diverse mixtures from the rest of mankind. All the four act on the fifth, and influence our treatment of this question of Slavery.

I. Russia is mighty by itsv ast territory, its great natural resources, its immense population, its huge army—appointed and commanded well—its strong central government, its diplomatic talent, and the people's ability to spread. The Government is despotic, but yet one of the most progressive in Christendom. With the bondage of Africans, Russia has no direct concern ; she has much to do with that of white Caucasians. She is rapidly putting an end to Slavery in her own borders. Not many years ago, the late emperor Nicholas emancipated the serfs he had inherited as his own private property. They amounted to more than 7,500,000 men ; he established over 4000 schools for the education of their children. Alexander, his son, had not been in the imperial seat three years before he published a decree for the gradual and ultimate emancipation of all the serfs in the empire. Their number must exceed the entire population of the United States. Here is the decree, dated the 20th of last November—the 2nd of December by our New Style calendar. The proprietors of two large provinces—St. Petersburg and Lithuania (containing nearly three million souls) some weeks since asked permission to emancipate their serfs at once. Yesterday's steamer brings also the welcome news that the proprietors of Nishni-Novogorod have just done the same. This province is as large as Virginia, with a population of 1,500,000, and, with the exception of the capital and its environs, is the richest and most intellectual part of the empire. It abounds with manufactories; every year, 300,000 strangers from Asia and elsewhere trade in its fairs. You would expect the most enlightened population to demand the immediate freedom of the serfs. Russia has become an ally on our side. Her example favours freedom. So you will find a change in the Southern newspapers, and in the American Government, which they direct and control. In the Crimean war, when Russia fought for injustice, they sustained her as the ally of their own despotism, and fought against England as their foe. All that will soon change ; and already Southern papers denounce the enfranchisement of the Russian serf: "The example is dangerous;" "the condition of the British West Indies, and of Hayti, might have taught Alexander a better lesson."

II. The French are powerful through the character of the people—the most military in the world—their science, letters, art, the high civilization of the land. France has had a long and sad connection with African Slavery. Once she was the most cruel of cruel masters. In her first Revolution, of 1789, the chain was broken, but its severed links united again. In the last Revolution, of 1848, at the magic word of Lamartine, expressing the revolutionary thought of the people, the fetters were not only broken off, but cast into the sea. France, for a moment, was the ally of Freedom—and of course encountered the noisy wrath of the Southern States. But the Celtic French, the most fickle people in the world, revolution their normal State, perpetually turning round and round, have elected a tyrant for their master, and now worship the Emperor. He has "crushed out" Freedom from the French press as completely as our own Mr. Cushing wished to do in America. The new tyrant attempts to revive the African slave trade, and has already made arrangements for kidnapping 5,000 savages in Africa, and sending them as missionaries to Christianize the West Indies! What will come of this scheme, I know not. But just now the political power of France is hostile to Freedom everywhere. When the Emperor has padlocked even the French *mouth*, no wonder he finds it easy to chain the negro's hands. No doubt the intellectual and moral power of France are on our side as before; but both are silent and of no avail. The French Emperor is the "little Napoleon" of the African slave trade. Great is the joy thereat in the Southern States: already their newspapers glorify the "profound policy," "the wise and humane statesmanship of the great Emperor."

"A fellow feeling makes us wondrous kind."

III. The Germans are of our blood and language—bone of our bone, and flesh of our flesh—with the same blue eyes, the same brown hair and ruddy cheek, and instinctive love of individuality. The people which began the civilization of modern times by inventing the Press, and originating

he Protestant Reformation, can it ever be false to Free-
lom ?   Germany acts on mankind by thought—by great
ideas.   What France is for war, England for commerce,
and Russia for the brute power of men, that is Germany
for thought.   The Germans have had connection with
African Slavery, but have ended it.   Sweden begun the
work some years ago ; then Denmark followed ; now,
within the last few months, Holland has finished it.   Here
are the documents.   Soon the last footsteps of German oppression will be covered up by the black man rejoicing in
his freedom.   Though their rulers are often tyrants, our
German kinsfolk are on our side—God bless them !

IV. England has great influence by her political institutions, her army and navy, her commerce and manufactures,
her power of practical thought, her large wealth, her mighty
spread.   She and her children control a sixth part of the
globe, and nearly a fourth part of its people.   No tribe of
men has done such service for Freedom as the Anglo-Saxons,
in Britain and America.   England has had connection with
African Slavery, her hand has been dyed deep in the negro's
blood.   She planted Slavery in her provinces throughout
the continent and its many islands ; the ocean reeked with
the foul steam of her slave-ships.   She was a hard master,
and men died by millions under her lash.   But nobly did the
dear old mother put this wickedness away.   She abolished
the slave trade, making it piracy ; at length, she repudiated
Slavery itself, and in one day threw into the sea the fetters
of 800,000 men.   Well did Lord Brougham say—it was
" the greatest triumph ever won over the foulest wrong man
ever did against man."   England need not boast of Agin-
court, Cressy, Poitiers, and many another victorious fight,
at Waterloo, Sebastopol, or Delhi ; the most glorious victory
her annals record was achieved on the 1st of August, in the
first year of Victoria, when justice triumphed over such
giant wrong.   Nobly has she contended against the slave
trade, rousing the tardy conscience of Brazil, and not quite
vainly galvanizing Spain into some show of humanity.   She
has shamed even the American Government—and I think
we have a sloop-of-war on the African coast, which we
yearly hear of in the annual appropriation bill !

But this nobleness is exceptional even in England ; the
world had seen no such example before.   That emancipa-

tion was not brought about by the privileged class, the royal and nobilitary, who officially reign, or the commercial class, who actually govern the nation; but by the moral class, whose conscience stirred the people, and constrained the Government to do so just a deed. Of course a reaction must follow. We see its effect to-day. There is a party which favours African Slavery. Mr. Carlyle is the heroic representative thereof. Personally amiable, in his ideas he is the Goliath of Slavery. Just now, the London *Times* appears to favour this reactionary movement, and its powerful articles are reprinted with great jubilation in the American newspapers, which hate England because they love the Slavery which she has hated so long. There is no time to inquire into the cause of this reaction. It affects the political class, and still more certain commercial classes to whom "cotton is king." Great is the delight of the South; the slave power sings *Te Deums* to *its* God. A bill was before the Senate, not long since, appropriating $3750 to pay the masters for twelve slaves who ran away and were carried off by the British in the war of 1812, whom the captors, even then, refused to deliver up to "democratic bondage." Mr. Hale opposed the bill, because it recognised the doctrine that there may be property in human beings, declaring that neither by vote nor by silence would he ever recognise so odious and false a doctrine. Mr. Seward joined in the opposition. But Mr. Fugitive Slave Bill Mason came to the rescue; and after referring to the anti-Slavery opinions of the British, declared he was *"gratified to see those opinions are rapidly undergoing a change."* What signs of such a rapid change he may have seen, I know not; nor what sympathies with the slave power the accomplished British minister, new in this field, may have expressed to him: "Diplomacy is a silent art." But I think Mr. Mason greatly mistakes the British public, if he believes they will be fickle in their love of right. The Anglo-Saxon has always been a resolute tribe. I believe John Bull is the most obstinate of all national animals. When his instinctive feelings and his reflective conscience command the same thing, depend upon it he will not lack the will.

There may have been a change in the British Government, though I doubt it much; there has been in the

5

London *Times.* In the "cotton lords," I take it, there is no alteration of doctrine, only an utterance of what they have long thought. The opinion of the British people, I think, has only changed to a yet greater hatred against Slavery. The anti-Slavery party in England has immense power—not so much by its numbers, or its wealth, as by its intelligence, and still more by that justice which, in the long run of time, is always sure of the victory. At the head of this party I must place Lord Brougham, now drawing near the end of a long and most laborious life, not without its eccentricities, but mainly devoted to the highest interests of the human race. Within the four seas of Britain, I think there lives no man who has done so much to proclaim ideas of justice and humanity, and to diffuse them among the people. If he could not oftener organize them into law, it was because he took too long a step in advance of public opinion; and he that would lead a child must always keep hold of its hand. Nearly fifty years ago (June 14, 1810) he fought against the slave trade, and drew on him the wrath of men "who live by treachery, rapine, torture, and murder, and are habitually practising the worst of crimes for the worst of purposes." Long ago he declared—"There is a law above all the enactments of human codes—the same throughout the world, the same in all times; it is the law written by the finger of God on the heart of man; and by that law, unchangeable and eternal, while men despise fraud, and loathe rapine, and abhor blood, they will reject the wild and guilty phantasy that man can hold property in man." When the little tyrant of France revives the slave trade, the great champion of human right roused him once more for battle, and the British Government has taken the affair in hand. The British love of justice will triumph in this contest. Why, the history of England is pledged as security therefore.

Such to-day is the opinion of the four great nations of Christian Europe. What if the despotic power of the French Emperor be against us; what if, for a moment, the cotton lords of England lead a few writers and politicians to attempt the restoration of bondage; the conscience of England and her history, the intelligence of France and Germany, the example of Russia are on our side. Yes,

the teachings of universal human history. All these come
with their accumulated force to help the moral feeling of
America sustain the rights of man.

The American Government has long been on the side of
Slavery. The present administration is more openly hostile
to Freedom than any of its predecessors. Mr. Buchanan is
no doubt weak and infatuated, strong only in his wrong-
headedness; his cabinet is palsied with Slavery. But he
has done one service which was thought hopelessly difficult,—he has already made President Pierce's administration respectable. We complain of the New Hampshire
general, but the little finger of Buchanan's left hand is
thicker than Pierce's whole loins.

Since we met last the Federal Government has committed two outrages more.

I. The first is the Dred Scott decision. The Supreme
Court is only the dirty mouth of the slave power, its chief
function to belch forth iniquity, and name it law. Of the
decision itself, I need not speak. It is the political opinion
of seven partisans appointed to do officially that wickedness which their personal nature also no doubt inclined
them to. That Court went a little beyond itself,—out-
Heroding Herod.

Two Northern judges, only two, McLean and Curtis,
opposed the wrong. I think nobody will accuse me of any
personal prejudice in favour of Judge Curtis, or any undue
partiality towards him. His conduct on other and trying
occasions has been justly condemned on the anti-Slavery
platform, and is not likely to be soon forgot, nor should it
ever be. But I should do great injustice to you and him,
and still more to my own feelings, if I let this occasion
pass without a word of honest and hearty praise of that
able lawyer and strong-minded man. He opposed the
"decision," with but a single Northern judge to support
him, with two Northern judges to throw technical difficulties in his way and oppose him by coward treachery,
with five Southern judges openly attacking and brow-
beating him, with both the outgoing and incoming administration to oppress and mock at him, with subtle and
treacherous advisers at home to beguile his steps and
watch for his halting, did Judge Curtis stand up at Wash-

ington, amid those corrupt and wicked judges, and in the name of history which they falsified, of law which they profaned, of justice which they mocked at, with a manliness which Story never showed on such occasions, he pronounced his sentence against the wicked Court. I remember his former conduct with indignation and with shame; but no blackness of the old record shall prevent me from turning over a new leaf, and with golden letters writing there—*In the Supreme Court* JUDGE CURTIS DEFENDED ONCE THE HIGHER LAW OF RIGHT.

I am truly sorry his manhood did not stay by him and continue his presence in that Court. The defence of his resignation is found in the inadequacy of the salary. It was $4500 when he took it, $6000 when he left it. A pitiful reason—by no means the true one. Samuel Adams was a poor man; I do not think he would have left his seat in the revolutionary Congress because more money could be made by the cod-fishery or by privateering.

II. The Dred Scott decision was the first enormity. The next is General Walker's filibustering expedition. I regard this as the act of the Government. "What you do by another, you do also by yourself," is a maxim older than the Roman law which preserves it. I am not inclined generally to place much confidence in Walker's word, but he sometimes tells the truth. In a recent speech at Mobile, he says he had an interview with the President, last summer, and declared his intention of returning to Nicaragua: his (filibustering) letter was published with the President's consent. A member of the cabinet sought a confidential interview with him, told him where he might go with safety, where only with danger; and added, "You will probably sail in an American vessel, under the American flag. After you have passed American limits, no one can touch you but by consent of this Government." A cabinet minister told one of Walker's friends, if he made an alliance with Mexico, and *attempted the conquest of Cuba,* "*means shall not be lacking to carry out the enterprise.*" Walker says the Government arrested him, not because he attacked Nicaragua, but because he did not attack Mexico! I hold the Federal Government responsible alike for the conduct of Walker and the Supreme Court.

But omitting particulars, looking only at the general

course of the Government, you find it favours Slavery with continued increase of intensity. Let not this rest on my testimony alone, or your judgment. Here is "An Address delivered before the Euphemian and Philomathean Literary Societies of Erskine College, at the Annual Commencement, Wednesday, August 12th, 1857, by Richard Yeadon, Esq., of Charleston, S. C." Mr. Yeadon is a representative man, editor of the *Charleston Courier*, and a staunch defender of the peculiar institution. He tells us he comes "rather to sow the good seed of truth, than to affect the arts or graces of oratory; to teach the lessons of history, and impress the deductions of reason, than to twine the garlands of science, or strew the roses of literature;" he would "combine the didactic in large measure with the rhetorical." He discusses the character of the Federal Government and its relation to Slavery, "on which rest the pillars of the great social fabric of the South." He attempts to show that the Constitution was so framed as to uphold Slavery and check Freedom; and that the Federal Government has carried out the plan with such admirable vigour, that now Slavery can stand by its own strength. But you must have his own words :—

"The new Constitution not only recognised, sanctioned, and guaranteed it [Slavery] as a State institution, sacred within State limits from Federal invasion or interference, but also so far as to foster and expand it, by Federal protection and agency, wherever it was legalized, within State or territorial limits; to uphold it by Federal power, and the Federal arm against domestic violence or foreign invasion; and, to make it an element of Federal organization and existence, by adopting it as a basis of Federal representation, and a source of Federal revenue."

"From that day to this, the institution of domestic Slavery, within the several States, has been regarded and held sacred as a reserved right, exclusively within State jurisdiction and beyond the constitutional power of Congress or of the general Government, except for guarantee, protection, and defence; it being one and the chief of those 'particular interests' which the Convention had in view, as enhancing the difficulty of their work."

"The general Government and the co-States are bound by constitutional duty and Federal compact to uphold and defend the institution, wherever it lawfully exists, in any of the States."

"Indeed, so unquestionable is the exclusive jurisdiction of State sovereignty, except in the way of guarantee and protection, over the institution of Slavery within State limits, that even the high-priest and archfiend of political free-soilism, William H. Seward, in his speech in Congress, on the admission of California into the Union, thus conceded it— 'No free State claims to extend its legislation into a slave State. None

claims that Congress shall usurp power to abolish Slavery in the slave
States ;' and the wildest fanatics of abolitionism, of the Parker and Garrison school, acknowledge that their atrocious crusade against the South
can only achieve its unhallowed aims by trampling as well on the Constitution of their country, as on the oracles of God."

He has admiration for one Northern man who has been
remarkably faithful to the ideas and plans of the slave
power. He says it is the duty of the General Government
to protect Slavery by suppressing insurrectionary movements, or attempts at domestic violence, and to turn out
the whole force of the Republic, regular and militia :—

"It was in contemplation of such a contingency, such a *casus fœderis*,
that the eloquent, accomplished, and gifted Everett (now dedicating his
extraordinary powers of composition and elocution, under the auspices of
the *Southern Matron*, a patriot daughter of the Palmetto State, to the
purchase and consecration of the home and the grave of Washington, as
the Mecca of America), in his maiden speech as the representative in
Congress of the city of Boston, in 1826, then fresh from the pulpit, in
honourable contrast with the dastardly Sumners and bullying Burlingames
of the present day, thus patriotically and fervently spoke—' Sir, I am no
soldier. My habits and education are very unmilitary ; but there is no
cause in which I would sooner buckle a knapsack on my back, and put a
musket on my shoulder, than that of putting down a servile insurrection
in the South.' "

The newspapers say, with exquisite truth, that Mr.
Everett is " the monarch of the platform," the " greatest
literary ornament of the entire continent of America." So
he is : but to Mr. Yeadon, he is also a great hero, the iron
man of courage, unlike the " *dastardly Sumners*," and
"*the dishonoured and perjured miscreants, Seward, Sumners,
et id omne genus,* who advocated the ' higher law doctrine.' "

He thus sums up the whole of our history :—

"The American Union . . . has been the great bulwark of . . .
Southern Slavery, and has, in fact, nursed and fostered it, from a feeble
and rickety infancy, into a giant manhood and maturity, and self sustain-
ing power, able to maintain itself either in the Union or out of the Union,
as may best comport with the future policy and welfare of the Southern
States."

"Finally, to crown all, comes, in august majesty, the decision of the
Supreme Judicatory of the United States in the case of Dred Scott, pro-
nouncing the Missouri restriction unconstitutional, null and void, and
declaring all territories of the Union, present and future, when acquired
by purchase or conquest, by common treasure or common blood, to be
held by the General Government, as a trustee for the common benefit of
all the States, and open to every occupancy and residence of the citizens

of every State, with their property of every description, including slaves reposing under the ægis of the Constitution."

"The cheering result, then, is, that the Southern States stand now on stronger and higher ground than at any previous period of our history; and this, under the progressive and constitutional action of the General Government, blotting out invidious lines, establishing the broad platform of State equality, demolishing squatter sovereignty, retrieving the errors of the past, and furnishing new securities for the future."

"The number of slave-holding States has been increased to fifteen, out of an aggregate of thirty-one States, with a fair prospect of further increase in Texas, and in other territory, acquired or to be acquired from Mexico, in the Carribean Sea, and still further south."

The slave States, he says, no longer "conceding domestic Slavery to be a ' moral, social, and political evil,' any more than any other system of menial and prædial labour, but able . . to defend it as consistent with scriptural teachings, and as an *ordinance of Jehovah for the culture and welfare of the staple States,* and the civilization and Christianization of the African." To them he says, " Cotton is king, and destined to rule the nations with imperial sway."

The slave-holders feel stronger than ever before. This privileged class, the " Nobility of Democracy," counts only 350,000 in all. Feeble in numbers, the slave power is strong in position—holding the great federal offices, judicial, executive, and military, stronger in purpose and in will. "The hope, the courage of assailants, is always greater than that of those who act merely on the defensive." At the South, it rules the non-slaveholders, as at the North it has had also the Democratic party under its thumb. There is a secret article in the creed of that party which demands unconditional submission to the infallibility of the negro-driver. Senator Toombs has no slaves in Georgia who yield to his will more submissively than to the whim of the Southern master crouches Hon. Mr. Cushing, whose large intellectual talents, great attainments, and consummate political art, in this hall, so fitly represent the town of Newburyport. It is the glory of the Northern Democratic party that it has been the most cringeing slave to the haughtiest and unworthiest master in the world. All individuality seemed " crushed out," to use Mr. Cushing's own happy phrase. Within eight months every Northern State has had a State Democratic Convention, each of which has passed resolutions endorsing the Dred Scott decision. This act implies no individuality, of thought or

of will. The Southern master gave command to each
Northern squad of Democrats—"Make ready your resolutions in support of the Dred Scott decision!" They
"make ready." "Consider resolutions!" They "consider." "Vote aye!" They "vote aye."

The slave power, thus controlling the slaves and slave-
holders at the South, and the Democratic party at the
North, easily manages the Government at Washington.
The Federal officers are marked with different stripes—
Whig, Democrat, and so on. They are all owned by the
same master, and lick the same hand. So it controls the
nation. It silences the great sects, Trinitarian, Unitarian,
Nullitarian : the chief ministers of this American Church—
threefold in denominations, one in nature—have naught to
say against Slavery; the Tract Society dares not rebuke
the "sum of all villanies," the Bible Society has no
"Word of God" for the slave, the "revealed religion" is
not revealed to him. Writers of school-books "remember
the hand that feeds them," and venture no word against
the national crime which threatens to become also the
national ruin. In no nation on earth is there such social
tyranny of opinion. In Russia, Prussia, Austria, France,
Italy, and Spain, the despotic bayonet has pinned the public
lips together. The Democratic hands of America have
sewed up her own mouth with an iron thread—that and
fetters are the only product of the Southern mine. In
Washington not a man in the meanest office dares open
his lips against the monster which threatens to devour his
babies and his wife. No doctor allows himself a word against
that tyrant—his business would forsake him if he did. In
Southern States, this despotism drives off all outspoken men.
Mr. Underwood, of Virgina, made a speech against the
extension of Slavery into Kansas,—he must take his life in
his hand, and flee from his native State. Mr. Helper, of
North Carolina, writes a brave, noble book, ciphering out
the results of freedom and of bondage,—even *North* Carolina is too hot to hold him. Mr. Strickland, at Mobile, sells
now and then an anti-Slavery book,—the great State of Alabama drives him out, scares off his wife, and will not allow
him to collect his honest debts ! At the North, you know
the disposition of men who hold office from the Federal
Government, or who seek and expect it : the Federal hand

is raised to strangle Democracy. They never give the alarm: it would be to "strike the hand that feeds them." Nay, they crouch down and "lick the hand just raised to shed *our* blood." Even at Washington, Slavery has sewed up the delegated Northern mouth, else so noisy once. It is nearly two years since a Southern bully, a representative man of South Carolina, stole upon our great senator, with coward blows felled him to the ground, and with his bludgeon beat the stunned and unconscious man. He meant to "silence agitation:" he did his work too well. Excepting the discussion which followed that outrage, do you remember an anti-Slavery speech in the Senate since Charles Sumners', in May 1856? Can you think of one in the House? If such have been spoken, I have not heard either, though I have listened all the time. Now and then some one has made an apology for the North, promising not to touch Slavery in the part most woundable. But I believe there has been no manly anti-Slavery speech in House or Senate till Mr. Hale broke the silence with a noble word. The slave power dealt the blows upon one Northern man, and nearly silenced all the rest! "The *safer* part of valour is discretion!" The South has many slaves not counted in the census. Ought they to represent the North?

The slave power is conscious of strength, and sure of victory. It never felt so strong before. Look at this: the Treasury Department has just instructed the collectors not to permit a free negro to act as master of a vessel,—he is not a citizen of the United States! See what the Southern States are doing. A bill has been reported in the Senate of Louisiana, authorizing that State to import five thousand African slaves. If it becomes a law the Government will not prevent the act; our worst enemy, the Supreme Court, is ready to declare unconstitutional the law which forbids the African slave trade. The South may import as many slaves as she likes; the Government is for her wickedness, not against that—only against justice and the unalienable rights of man. Another bill is pending before the Virginia Legislature to banish or enslave all the 75,000 free coloured persons in that State, where more than one President has been the father of a mulatto woman's child. The law to enslave them all may pass; the Federal Government cares nothing about it. African Rachel may mourn in vain for her first-born, and refuse to be comforted, because the Virginian Jacob chains the parti-coloured Joseph that she bore to him; let her mourn! What does the Federal Herod care that in all Virginia there is a voice heard of lamentation, and weeping, and great mourning from the poor Rachel of Africa?

Stronger than ever before, at least in fancy, and yet more truly impudent than fancied strong, the slave power proposes two immediate measures :—

I. To pass the Lecompton Constitution through Congress, and force Slavery into the laws of Kansas, against the oft-repeated vote of the people.

II. To add seven thousand men to the standing army of the United States. They are nominally to put down the polygamous Mormons in Utah—Satan contradicting the lies he is the father of!—but really to support the more grossly polygamous slave-holders; to force the Lecompton Constitution upon Kansas with the bayonet; in all the North, to execute the Fugitive Slave Bill, and the Dred Scott decision, already made, and the Lemmon decision, about to be made, and establish Slavery in each free State; and also to put down any insurrection of the coloured people at the South. The Mormons are the pretence no more; the army is raised against the Democracy of Massachusetts, not the Polygamy of Utah.

Ladies and gentlemen, both of these measures will pass the Senate, pass the House. If it were the end of a presidential term, I should expect they would be defeated. But men worship the rising sun, not the setting, who has no more *golden* light for them. A Boston merchant, with but $87,000, could bribe men enough to pass his tariff bill! The new Presiden, the has more than $87,000,000—offices for three years to come. The addition to the army will cost at least $5,000,000 a year, and the patronage that gives will command votes enough. I know how tender are the feelings of Congress; I know how politicians reject with scorn the idea that money or office could alter their vote; but we all know that a President, his pocket full of public money, his hands full of offices, can buy votes of honourable senators and honourable representatives just as readily as you can buy pea-nuts of the huckster down stairs. I need not go from this hall, or its eastern neighbour, I need not go back seven years to find honourable members of the " Great and General Court of Massachusetts" who were bought with a price. I shall tell no names, though I know them only too well. Peter did repent and Judas may—I will give him a chance. I expect, therefore, that both these measures will pass. Then you will find the Northern " Democracy" supporting them ; future conventions will ring with resolutions in favour of the Lecompton Convention, and A GREAT STANDING ARMY will be one of the acknowledged "principles" of the Democratic party—a toast on Independence Day.

When the two immediate measures are disposed of, there are three others a little more remote, which are likewise to be passed upon.

I. The first is to establish Slavery in all the Northern States—the Dred Scott decision has already put it in all the territories. The Supreme Court will make a decision in the Lemmon case, and authorize any one of the Southern masters of the North to bring his slaves to any Northern State, and keep them as long as he pleases. Coloured men " have no rights which white men are bound to respect"— so says the Supreme Court, which is greater than the Constitution ; and if that be true generally, everywhere, then it will be true specially in Massachusetts. I have no doubt the Supreme Court will make the decision. We have no Judge Curtis to sit in that Court, and give his verdict for law and justice ; his place is occupied by Hon. Nathan Clifford—a very different man, if I am rightly informed. When his nomination was before the Senate, Mr. Hale opposed it, and said Mr. Clifford was not reckoned a first class lawyer in his own district—which comprises the greater part of New England ; nor in his own State— the State of Maine ; nor in his own country ; nor even in his own town ! .

Then, after Mr. Hale had reduced this vulgar fraction of law to his lowest terms, the Senate added it to the sum of the Supreme Court. He is strong enough for his function—to create new law for Slavery. His appointment must needs cause a judgment against him, but let us give him a fair trial. When the Court has given the expected decision in the Lemmon case, then this new article will be voted into the apostolic creed of the Demo-

cratic party, published by authority, and appointed to be
read in caucuses and conventions. It may be "said or
sung," as follows:—"I believe in the Fugitive Bill; I
believe in the Kansas-Nebraska Bill; I believe in the Dred
Scott decision; I believe in the Lemmon decision. As it
was in the beginning, is now, and ever shall be, world
without end. Amen."

II. The next measure is to conquer Mexico, Central America, and all the Northern Continent down to the Isthmus;
to conquer Cuba, Hayti, Jamaica, all the West India Islands,
and establish Slavery there. This conquest of the Islands
might seem rather a difficult work—it might require some
fighting; but the late Hon. Senator Butler, of South Carolina,
was very confident it would be done. You remember how
he spoke of those islands in a rambling speech that he once
made, which was truth-telling, because drunken. You smile;
but if *in vino veritas* be good Latin, *à fortiori* is it good
American to say, *there is more truth in whisky, which is
stronger?* In one of his fits of "loose expectoration," that
distinguished senator, a representative man, like Bully
Brooks, instantial and typical of his State, spoke of "OUR
Southern Islands," meaning Cuba, San Domingo, Jamaica,
Trinidad, St. Thomas, and the rest. He called them *our*
islands, not that they were so then, or because he had any
personal knowledge that they ever would be; but "being in
the spirit" (of Slavery), and the spirit (of whisky) being
also in him—*imperium in imperio*—by this twofold inspiration (of Slavery from without and whisky from within), and
from this double consciousness (out of the abundance of
the stomach the mouth also speaking), he prophesied (this
medium of two spirits), not knowing what he said.

That is the second measure,—to re-annex the West
Indies and the Continent.

III. The third measure is to restore the African slave
trade. Now and then the South puts forth a *feeler*, to try
the weather; the further South you go the more boldly are
the feelers put out. South Carolina and Louisiana seem
ready for this measure; and of course the Supreme Court
is ready. You must not be surprised if yet another article
be added to the Democratic creed, and we hear Mr. Cushing
deacon off this new Litany of Despotism, with—"I believe
in the African Slave Trade."

To carry all these measures, the slave power depends on
the Federal Government. But it never pesters the Government with petitions on paper; it sends its petitions in *boots*.
They are not referred to Committees in House or Senate;
the petitions in boots are themselves the Committee of
House and Senate. Gentlemen, the slave power has got
the Federal Government, especially the Supreme Court—a
constant power.

It relies also on the Democratic party North for its aid in
this destruction of Democracy. Gentlemen, it has got that
party—will it keep it? Heretofore the two have seemed
united, not for better but for worse, " so long as they both
do live." Witness the arguments of Mr. Cushing, yesterday, in this hall, against the personal liberty law; and he
faithfully and consistently represents the Northern Democratic party as it was.

The slave power depends on the four great commercial
cities of the North—Cincinnati, Philadelphia, New York,
and Boston. Gentlemen, it has the support of these four
cities, and will continue to have it for some time to come.
If the two immediate and the three remote aggressive
measures I have just mentioned were to be passed on by
the voters of these four towns, I think they would vote as
the slave power told them. They did so for the Fugitive
Slave Bill, for the Kansas-Nebraska Bill;—they will vote
for the Lecompton Bill, the Army Bill; and when their
help is wanted for the *Americanization* of the rest of the
continent, by filibustering; for the *Southernization* of the
North, by the Lemmon decision; for the *Africanization* of
America, by restoring the African slave trade, they will
do as they are bid.

If these five measures were left to the voters of Boston
alone, the result might be doubtful,—nay, I think it would
be adverse to the South. But look at the matter a little
more nicely. Divide the Boston voters into four classes:—
the rich—men worth $100,000 or more; the educated—
men with such culture as pupils get at tolerable colleges;
the poor—the Irish, and all men worth but $400 or less;
the middling class—the rest of the male citizens. If the
question were submitted to the first three, I make no doubt
the vote would be for the South, for the destruction of
Democracy. The educated and the poor would do as the

x 2

rich commanded them—they would not "strike the hand that feeds them," for they know how

> " To crook the pregnant hinges of the knee,
>   Where thrift may follow fawning."

I speak of the general rule, and do honour to the exceptions. I hope you think me harsh in this judgment. Many of you, I see, are members of this House, and do not know exactly the city you are strangers in. I believe it the best city in the world; but it has some faults which warrant my conjectural fear. Two things have happened, Mr. President, since our last annual meeting, which show the proclivity of the controlling class in Boston to support Slavery. The first took place on the 17th of June. One or two haberdashers and the hotel-keepers of Boston were anxious to celebrate the eighty-second anniversary of the battle of Bunker Hill. The State and the City united in that good work. There was a Committee of the Massachusetts Legislature, joined with a Committee of the City Council. Here is the book, "printed by authority," giving an account of some of the proceedings. The Committee invited distinguished champions of Slavery to come and consecrate the statue of Warren. Here is the reply of Governor Wise, of Virginia. It contains an admirable hint. He hopes *the Revolutionary times will return.* So do I.

Here are letters from the Hon. Mr. Hilliard, of Alabama, from ex-President Tyler, and from similar people, too numerous to mention in an anti-Slavery speech. There is a bill to be paid by the Commonwealth by and by, and some of you, gentlemen, will have an opportunity to vote the money of Massachusetts to pay for the liquor which intoxicated some of the great champions of Slavery whom the Committee invited to do honour to Bunker Hill by their bodily presence, and to Boston by their subsequent carouse. There will be a bill amounting to $1067.04 which I would advise the legislators to look at carefully, and see what the "*items*" are, and ascertain who consumed the "*items.*" But let me return to the "great celebration,"—almost equal in glory to the battle itself.

The Committee invited the author of the Fugitive Slave Bill to partake of their festivities. Yes, ladies and gentlemen, they invited the Hon. Mr. Mason, of Virginia, the most insolent man in the American Senate, the most bitterly and vulgarly hostile to the Democratic institutions of the North, the man who had treated your own senator with such insolence and abuse; Mr. Keitt, of South Carolina, also should have been included! I shall not now speak of the men who outraged the decency of New England by asking such a man to such a spot on such a day,—they were types of a class of men whom they too faithfully serve. But on that occasion, "complimentary flunkeyism" swelled itself almost to bursting, that it might croak the praises of Mr. Mason and his coadjutors.

When the coward blows of Mr. Brooks—one of that holy alliance of bullies who rule Congress—had brought Charles Sumner to the ground, and he lay helpless between life and death, you know the people of Boston proposed to have a meeting in Faneuil Hall to express their indignation. A Committee, appointed at a previous meeting, had the matter in charge. They invited Hon. Mr. Winthrop to attend. "No," he "could not come." They asked Mr. Everett. "No," he too was "unable." It was reported at the time, and I thought on good authority, that when the Committee asked Hon. Mr. Choate, he asked "if blows on the head with a gutta-percha stick would hurt a man much?" These three were ex-senators. They all refused to attend the meeting and join in any expression of feeling against the outrage upon Mr. Sumner. Gentlemen, I respect sincerity, and I was glad that they were not hypocrites on that occasion. Twice the Committee waited on the first two gentlemen, offering the invitation, which was twice refused. But Mr. Winthrop and Mr. Everett were both at Charleston to pay that feudal homage to Mr. Fugitive Slave Bill Mason, which Northern vassals owe the slave power. With their "flunkeyism," they tainted still worse the air of that town which has a proverbial repute and name.

Then was fulfilled that celebrated threat of Senator Toombs, of Georgia. On the eighty-second anniversary of New England's first great battle, at the foot of Bunker Hill monument, the author of the Fugitive Slave Bill, the most offensive of all his tribe, called over the roll of his slaves; and men, their names unknown to fame, their personalities too indistinct for sight, at least for memory, with the City Government of Boston, the authorities of Harvard College, two ex-senators, one ex-governor, the Governor of Massachusetts (spite of the " certainty of a mathematical demonstration," now also an ex), answered to their names !

That was not all. The next day, at the public cost, in a steam-boat chartered expressly for the purpose, the City Government took Mr. Mason about the harbour, showing to him the handsome spectacle of nature, the green islands, then so fair ; and you saw, a hideous sight, the magistrates, of this town doing homage to one of the foulest of her enemies, who had purposely incited a kindred spirit to deal such blows on the honoured head of a noble senator of this State.

Nor was that all. The next night, one of the Professors of Harvard College, both a learned and most genial man, but at that time specially representing the servility of his institution, better even than his accomplishments generally represent its Greek scholarship, invited the author of the Fugitive Slave Bill to an entertainment at his house.

So the magistrates of Boston, the authorities of Harvard College, the "respectabilities of the neighbourhood," the Committee of the Legislature, the Governor of the Commonwealth, and its ex-senators said in their acts, and their words too, " Thus shall be done unto the man whom the slave power delighteth to honour."

Here is the other act. Mr. Alger, a young Unitarian minister of this town, had been invited to deliver the annual Fourth of July Address before the city authorities ; and he, good honest man, in the simplicity of his heart, like Horace Mann and Charles Sumner, long before, thought that one day in the year was consecrate to Independence, and an orator might be pardoned if, on Independence Day, he said a word in behalf of the self-evident truths of the old Declaration, and spoke of the natural and unalienable right of all men to life, liberty, and the pursuit of happiness. Mr. Alger's grandfather fought in the battle of Bunker Hill, and it was not surprising that the " spirit of '75," speaking through such a " medium," should be a little indignant at the *spirit of* '57 ! He spoke as he ought. The City Government refused to print his speech—which, however, printed itself. The act was consistent. They who had crouched to Senator Mason, and answered at the roll-call of his slaves, how could they publish a manly speech rebuking their "complimentary flunkeyism!"

These two acts may make you doubt what would be the fate of the slave power's measures if left to Boston alone; but they make me sure what it would be if left to the three classes I have just now named.

But will these measures succeed, even with such help? If I had stood in this spot on the 29th of January, 1850, and foretold as prophecy what is history to-day, would you have believed me, Mr. President? Ladies and gentlemen, *you* could not credit it: that Mason's Bill, proposed the week before, would become a law; that Boston would ever be the haunt of man-stealers, her Court-House a barracoon, Faneuil Hall crammed with soldiers hired to steal a negro boy; that her Judge of Probate would forego the benevolence of his nature, or at least of his office, and become a kidnapper, and even a pretended anti-Slavery Governor keep him in office still! No, you could not believe that Wendell Phillips would ever be brought to trial for a "misdemeanor," because, in the cradle of liberty, he declared it wrong for a Judge of Probate to turn kidnapper! No, you would not hear the prediction that the Missouri Compromise would be repealed, the Kansas-Nebraska Act be passed, and the military arm of the United States, lengthened out with Border ruffians, would be stretched forth to force Slavery into Kansas with the edge of the sword. You would have said, "The Dred Scott decision is impossible; the Supreme Court cannot declare that no coloured man is a citizen of the United States,— that the Constitution itself puts Slavery into every territory, spite of local legislation, spite of Congress itself, spite of the people's will! Should they attempt so foul a wrong, the next Convention of the Northern Democrats would rend the Court asunder! Caleb Cushing would war against it!" What have we seen abroad; what do some of you hear in this hall, day out, day in? On the 29th of January, 1858, is it more unlikely that the Federal Government will decree these three new measures,—to establish Slavery in all the North, to conquer and enslave the Southern part of the continent, to restore the slave trade? The past is explanation of the present, as the present also of the past.

There are two things you may depend on : the impudent boldness of your Southern masters ; the thorough corruption of their Northern slaves. These two are " sure as death and rates."

But opposition is made against Slavery,—some of it is quite remarkable. I begin with mentioning what comes from quarters which seemed least promising.

1. A Northern Democrat enters on the stage,—an unwonted appearance. But it is no " infant phenomenon," no stripling, "who never appeared on any stage before," making his first essay by venturing on an anti-Slavery part. It is an old stock actor—the little giant of many a tragedy. Mr. Douglas has broken with the Administration ; the author of the Kansas-Nebraska Act is now undoing his own work ; the inventor of " squatter sovereignty " (or, if Cass be the inventor, Douglas has the patent) turns round and *strikes the hand that fed him* with honours and applause. He has great personal power of work, of endurance, immense ability to talk ; all the arts of sophistry are at his command ; adroit, cunning, far-sighted, for an American politician—no man, I think, better understands the strategy of politics, and no man has been more immoral and shameless in its use. He has long been the leader of the Northern Democracy, and knows its instincts and its ideas ; his hand is familiar with the strings which move the puppets of the party. Amongst men not clerical, I have heard but one speaker lie with such exquisite adroitness, and make the worse appear the better reason. He is a senator, still holding his place on important committees ; he is rich, in the prime of life, ambitious of power : he has abandoned drunkenness, and his native strength returns to his stout frame once more. Let us not disguise it,—no mere politician in America can do the slave power such harm.

But I have no more confidence in Mr. Douglas now than in 1854. The nature of the man has not changed, nor can it change ; even his will is still the same. No man has done us such harm. You know his public measures, his public speeches—the newspapers report all that; but his frauds, his insolent demeanour, his brow-beating and violence towards the Republican senators, you do not know—only the actual spectators can understand such things. Do you remember that, after Mr. Sumner had made his last great speech, Mr. Douglas said,—"Does the senator want us to kick him?" You have not forgot that when Brooks made his attack upon Sumner, Douglas also was there, and did not interfere to prevent a continuance of the blows. He also was a part of that outrage. The man has not changed. If he were President, he would do as Buchanan does, only more so. If he were sure of his senatorial office for six years to come, I think we should hear no words from him in behalf of Kansas. But his term expires in March, next year. He knows he cannot be re-elected, unless he changes his course. So he alters his measures, and provisionally favours Freedom; not his principles, which are the loaves and fishes of power. I am sorry to hear Republicans express their confidence in him, and give him praise which leaves nothing to add to such men as Hale, Seward, and Chase. I know it is said, "Any stone is good enough to throw at a dog;" but this is a stone that will *scale* in its flight, veer off, and finally hit what you mean not to hurt, but to defend. Yet it is unexpected to find any individuality of conduct or opinion in the party. It is pleasant to see what a train of followers he has already, and to think that Democracy is not quite dead among "Democrats." He is fighting against our foes—that is an accident; he is not fighting for us, but only for Stephen A. Douglas, and if he wins that battle, he cares not who his allies are, nor who his foes.

2. The next help comes from a slave State. Here is the valuable speech of Hon. F. P. Blair, from Missouri. "The civilized world," says he, "is at war with the propagation of Slavery, whether by fraud or by the sword; and those who look to gain political ascendancy on this continent by bringing the weight of this system, like an enormous yoke, not to subject the slaves only, but their fellow-citizens and kindred of the same blood, *have made false auguries of the signs of the times.*"

Significant words—doubly important when coming from a slave State. Do not think he is alone. He has a con-

stituency behind him not of doughfaces. Here is the
speech of Mr. James B. Gardenhire, lately made in the
House of Representatives at Jefferson City, Missouri. It
is of the same tenor as Mr. Blair's, and advocates the abolition of Slavery in Missouri itself.

3. Here is something from Republican Members of Congress. Not to mention others from New England, or elsewhere, here is a speech from Hon. Eli Thayer, ironical,
sometimes, I take it, but plain and direct in substance. He
would have the free States send settlers to Northenize the
South—already he has a colony in Virginia—and New
Englandize Central America! "The Yankee," says Mr.
Thayer, "has never become a slave-holder, unless he has
been forced to it by the social relations of the slave State
where he lived ; and the Yankee who has become a slave-
holder has every day of his life thereafter felt in his very
bones the bad economy of the system." "Why, sir, he
can buy a negro power in a steam-engine for ten dollars,
and he can clothe and feed that power for one year for
five dollars ; and are we the men to give $1000 for an
African slave, and $150 a year to feed and clothe him ?"

This is an anti-Slavery argument which traders can
understand. Mr. Thayer is not so much a talker as an
organizer ; he puts his thoughts into works. You know how
much Kansas owes him for the organization he has set on
foot. One day will he not also revolutionize Virginia?
There is a to-morrow after to-day.

Here is a speech from Hon. John P. Hale. I think it is
the ablest he ever made,—the first any one has made, I
think, since the discussion caused by the assault on Mr.
Sumner. It relates to Kansas and the Dred Scot decision.
Hear what he says of the latter :—

"If the opinion of the Supreme Court be true, it makes the immortal
authors of the Declaration of Independence liars before God and hypocrites before the world ; for they lay down their sentiments broad, full,
and explicit, and then they say that they appeal to the Supreme Ruler of
the universe for the rectitude of their intentions ; but, if you believe the
Supreme Court, they were merely quibbling on words. They went into
the courts of the Most High, and pledged fidelity to their principles as
the price they would pay for success, and now it is attempted to cheat
them out of the poor boon of integrity ; and it is said that they did not
mean so ; and that when they said *all men*, they meant *all white men ;*
and when they said that the contest they waged was for the *rights of
mankind*, the Supreme Court of the United States would have you believe

that they mean it was to *establish Slavery*. Against that I protest, here, now, and everywhere; and I tell the Supreme Court that these things are so impregnably fixed in the hearts of the people, on the page of history, in the recollections and traditions of men, that it will require mightier efforts than they have made or can make to overturn or to shake these settled convictions of the popular understanding and of the popular heart.

" Sir, you are now proposing to carry out this Dred Scott decision by forcing upon the people of Kansas a Constitution against which they have remonstrated, and to which there can be no shadow of doubt a very large portion of them are opposed. Will it succeed? I do not know; it is not for me to say; but I will say this : if you force that—if you perse-vere in that attempt—I think, I hope, the men of Kansas will fight. I hope they will resist to blood and to death the attempt to force them to a submission against which their fathers contended, and to which they never would have submitted. Let me tell you, sir, I stand not here to use the language of intimidation or of menace; but you kindle the fires of civil war in that country by an attempt to force that Constitution on the necks of an unwilling people; and you will light a fire that all Demo-cracy cannot quench—ay, sir, there will come up many another Peter the Hermit, that will go through the length and the breadth of this land, telling the story of your wrongs and your outrages; and they will stir the public heart; they will raise a feeling in this country such as has never yet been raised; and the men of this country will go forth, as they did of olden time, in another crusade; but it will not be a crusade to redeem the dead sepulchre where the body of the Crucified had lain from the profanation of the infidel, but to redeem this fair land, which God has given to be the abode of freemen, from the desecration of a despotism sought to be imposed upon them in the name of ' perfect freedom' and ' popular sovereignty.'"

This is a little different from the speeches made in Congress last winter. There is nothing apologetic and depre-catory this time. Mr. Seward said, long ago, " The time for compromises has passed by."

Mr. Sumner's chair is vacant still—and yet it speaks with more power than any senator can bring to defend Slavery with. In the long line of men Massachusetts has sent to do service in the halls of Congress, there has been none nobler than Charles Sumner, none more faithful. I know how dangerous it is to praise a living man, especially a politician; to-morrow may undo the work of half a century. But here I feel safe; for, of all the men I have known in political life, he is the only one who has thereby grown stronger in the noblest qualities of a man. Already his integrity has been tried in the severest ordeal; I think hereafter it will stand any test. Massachusetts has had three great Adamses—Samuel, John, John Quincy. In their graves, they are to her what " the three Tells " are to Switzerland.   Here is a man equally noble, perhaps with a nicer culture than any of them.   He has now the same firmness, the same integrity—faithfulness to delegated trust, allegiance to the higher law of right.   His empty chair is eloquent.

4. Then there are Republicans out of Congress, in official station, who are at work.   All the New England States, New York, Michigan, Ohio, Illinois, Iowa, Wisconsin, have governors and legislatures, I think, hostile to Slavery—after the "Republican" way.   The election of Mr. Banks was a triumph in Massachusetts.   In fifty years past, no Northern State has sent a man to the House of Representatives, who in twenty-five years acquired as great influence there as Mr. Banks in four.   He has many qualities which fit him for eminence in American politics—if he only be faithful to the right.   I hear loud condemnation of him from anti-Slavery men, because, say they, " he will do wrong by and by."   Our sentence will be in season if it comes *after* the crime; and the actual offences of Republican politicians are so numerous that I will not condemn conjectural felonies before they are committed.   I hear it said he will not remove Judge Loring.   Wait and see.   This I know, that a good deal within twelve months, he said he wished him removed, by the address of the Legislature; and *if he* (Banks) *were Governor, he* (Banks) *would do it!* If he try to ride a compromise, he may depend on it he will not ride far, however long!   " The day of compromise is past."   I remember the speech he made in Wall-street, New York; also the one at Salem.   I have no defence to make for them, no excuse to offer for him.   I felt astonished and ashamed.   But to exchange his predecessor for him seemed a triumph of freedom in 1857; I hope it will prove so in years to come.

The Republican party has done considerable service, but it does not behave very well.   It is cowardly; a little deceitful; "making *I dare not* wait upon *I would.*"   Coloured waiters at public festivals say, "the Democrats treat us better than the Republicans."   Events have clearly shown that the party did not deserve to gain the Federal power in 1856; that it would have been ruinous to the party could they then have taken the great offices, and disastrous to the cause of freedom, which they would compromise.

Yet, as it is the best political party we have, I would not be over-nice in criticising it. I like not to pick holes in the thin spots of the only political coat we have in this stormy weather. I know the difficulties of the party, and have pity for its offenders—none for its mere hunters after place.

I have spoken of the services of these classes of political men. There is one trouble which disturbs all four. They are liable to a certain disease of a peculiar nature. I have a good copy of Galen, but he does not mention it; the last edition of Hippocrates, but neither he nor his commentator, though both well-lettered men, makes any reference thereto. Hence I suppose it is a new disease, which, though not exactly a doctor of medicine, perhaps I am the first to describe. So I will call it the presidential fever; or, in Latin, *Typhus infandus Americanus.** I will try to describe the specific variety which is endemic in the Northern States, the only place where I have studied the disease. I may omit some symptoms of the case, which other observers will supply. At first the patient is filled with a vague longing after things too high for him. He gazes at them with a fixed stare; the pupils expand. But he cannot see distinctly; crooked ways seem straight; the shortest curve he thinks is a *right* angle; dirty things look clean, and he lays hold of them without perceiving their condition. Some things he sees double—especially the number of his friends; others with a semi-vision, and it is always the lower half he sees. All the time he hears a confused noise, like that of men declaring votes, State after State. This noise obscures all other sounds, so that he cannot hear the still small voice which yet moves the world of men. He can bear no "agitation;" the word "Slavery" disturbs him much; he fears discussion thereof as a hydrophobiac dreads water. Yet he is fond of the "rich brogue" of the foreign population. His sense of smell is so morbid that an honest man is unbearably offensive. His tongue is foul, but he has an irresistible propensity to lick the hands of those he thinks will give him what he seeks. His organ of locality is crazed and erratic in its action; the thermometer may

* It may be the same *Herod* is said to have died of. From Sallust's description, it would seem that *Cataline* had a slight touch of it.—Bell. Cat. ch. i.

stands at 20 below zero—even lower, if long enough—the Mississippi may be frozen over clear down to Natchez, Hellgate be impassable for ice, and the wind of Labrador blow for months across the continent to the Gulf of Mexico— still he can't believe there is any North! Combativeness is irregularly active; he fights his best friends and clings to his worst enemies. Destructiveness is intense; he would abolish the negroes, enforce the Fugitive Slave Bill, and hang the abolitionists. Benevolence is wholly inert. Casuality has become idiotic; he looks into the clockwork of the State, and everywhere finds "a little nigger has got into the machinery," which he would set right by "crushing out" the intruder. Ideality fills him with the foolishest of dreams. The organ of self-esteem swells to a monstrous size—like a huge wen on the top of the head, "a sight to behold." He talks about himself excessively, *ad nauseam;* and "makes a noise town-meeting days," and is always "up" in the Legislature. Vanity is immense; he would be before the people continually; no place is too small, if only public;* he lives in the eye of the people, greedy of praise. Hope is in a state of delirious excitement; no failure disconcerts him, no fall abates desire to rise. Veracity is in a comatose state; "he will lie like Governor ———." Conscientiousness has "caved in," and in its place there is "a hole in his head." He knows no higher law above his own ambition, for which all means seem just. He often speaks of "the father of his country," but never tells his noblest deeds. His reverence is delirious in its action; he worships every graven or molten image that faces South, and lies prostrate before the great ugly idol of Slavery, rending his garments, and cries, "Baal help us! Baal help us!" Disease incurable; yields to no medicine; not hellebore enough in all Anticyra to affect the case.

I need not speak of the old anti-Slavery Society. It is not

* "Fidenarum Gabiorumque esse potestas,
  Et de mensura jus dicere, vasa minora
  Frangere, pannosus vacuis Ædilis Ulubris;
  ——— qui nimios optabat honores."

The Latin is only for doctors, who know the local applications of the geography.

necessary I should criticise their action—I have done that often enough before. If we deserve any praise, let others give it, or give it not, as suits them best.

There has been a great change in the people of the North—else, Mr. President, we were not here to-night. You remember the Legislatures of 1850, 1851, 1852— what if you had asked them for this hall! In 1851, even Faneuil Hall could not be had for a Convention of fifteen hundred as respectable and intelligent men as ever assembled in the United States, with Horace Mann at their head. We are here to-night by the will of the people of Massachusetts. For many years we have come up before the Legislature of this State; it has always heard us patiently, and I think at length has always done what we asked. Former Legislatures have done all in *their* power to remove the only Massachusetts Judge of Probate that ever kidnapped a man. I make no doubt this Legislature will as faithfully represent the conscience of the State.

I say there has been a great change in the people. Compare the old *Daily Advertiser* with the new, which I think one of the humanest as well as ablest newspapers in New England.

I recall the fate of the Northern men who voted for the Kansas-Nebraska Bill. There were thirteen Northern senators who did so. The official term has expired for ten of them. Nine of the ten lost their election—veteran old Mr. Cass at their head; the Camden and Amboy Railroad sent back Mr. Thompson to represent their rolling-stock. Stuart of Michigan, Jones of Iowa, and Douglas of Illinois, abide their time.

Forty-two Northern representatives were equally false to Democracy. Thirty-nine of them have gone to their own place, only three returned to their seats: J. Glancey Jones, and T. B. Florence of Pennsylvania, and W. H. English, of Indiana, alone remain.

If the South is more confident of victory than ever, the North is also more determined to conquer. The late elections show this: that of Mr. Banks is a very significant sign of the times. The "rebellion" of Mr. Douglas, so his old masters call it, is popular at the North. He could be elected to the Senate to-morrow by a vote of the people of Illinois. I do

not say I would vote for him; that State will. All the
West is on his side. See how many tender-footed Democrats there are who cannot walk over a majority of legal
voters in Kansas ten thousand strong, and force Slavery on
that State, even at the command of the old master. Soon
there will be *conscience Democrats,* as once *conscience
Whigs.* The Administration party may carry their measures; it will be as of old, "the counsel of the froward is
carried headlong." In 1860, the Northern Democratic
party will be where the Whig party was in 1856. There
will be a pack of men about the Federal offices in all the
great towns, united by common desire for public plunder;
but the party will be as dead as Benedict Arnold. If Mr.
Cushing will "crush out" all individualism from the
Democracy he will leave no life there!

Such is the aspect of Slavery now. It is clear what
duty the North has to do. She must choose either Freedom of the black man, with an industrial Democracy
gradually spreading over all the continent, diffusing everywhere the civilization of New England; or else the Slavery
of the black man, with a military despotism certainly
overspreading the land and crushing down the mass of
men, white and black, into Asiatic subjection. The choice
is between these two extremes.

There are 18,000,000 in the North, all free. The
power of numbers, wealth, industry, education, ideas,
institutions, all is on our side. So are the sympathies of
the civilized world, the hopes and the primal instincts of
mankind; "the stars in their courses fight against Sisera."
The Federal Government is against us—we might have
had it on our side if we would.

The last Presidential election showed who in the North
were the allies of the South. They dwell mainly in the
four great cities, and in that debatable land which borders
on the slave States, a strip of territory 200 miles wide,
reaching from New York harbour to the Mississippi. I
trust the anti-Slavery Society will send out its missionaries
to arouse and instruct the people in that border land.
There is a practical work to be done—to be attempted at
once.

Slavery is a moral wrong and an economical blunder;

but it is also a great political institution. It cannot be
put down by political economy, nor by ethical preaching;
men have not only pecuniary interests and moral feelings,
but also political passions. Slavery must be put down
politically, or else militarily. If not peacefully ended soon,
it must be ended wrathfully by the sword. The negro will
not bear Slavery for ever; if he would, the white man will
not.

If the Republican party behave wisely, there will never
be another inch of slave soil added to the national domain,
nor another slave State admitted to the Union: but Slavery
will be driven out of all the territories. Look at this fact.
There are now fifteen slave States, sixteen free. Minnesota
and Kansas will soon be admitted, Washington and Oregon
ere long—four new free States. Missouri may abolish
Slavery within four years. Then, in 1864, we shall stand
twenty-one free States to fourteen slave States. Nay,
perhaps Utah will repudiate both forms of polygamy, the
voluntary and the forcible, and be an ally in our defence.
It is easy to conquer the Southern part of the continent;
it is not easy to establish African Slavery there, in the
midst of a population made up of Africans or Indians ready
to shelter the slave, and also much more dense than that
in the Gulf States from Georgia or Florida to Texas.

If the North is wise and just, we shall choose an anti-
Slavery President in 1860, and on March 4th, 1861, incor-
porate the principles of the Declaration of Independence
and of the Constitution's preamble into the Federal
Government itself. And on the 4th of July, 1876, there
will not be a slave within all the wide borders of the
United States! For that service, we do not want a man
like Colonel Fremont, who has had no political experience;
we want no Johnny Raw for the most difficult post in the
nation. It must not be a man broken down with the Presidential fever.

But much is to be done before that result is possible. The
whole policy of the Republican party must be changed.
We must attack Slavery—Slavery in the territories, Slavery
in the district, and, above all, Slavery *in the Slave States*.
Would you remove the *shadow of a tree?* Then down
with the tree itself! There is no other way. To get rid
of the accidents of a thing, you make way with its sub-

stance. Does not the Constitution guarantee a Republican form of government to every State ? South Carolina has a Republican form of government, has she ? We must be aggressive, and kill the trunk, not maim the branches. When you attempt that, depend upon it the South will know you are in earnest. The Supreme Court is our worst enemy. I should attack it carefully by regular siege. Conquer and re-construct it.

If I were Republican Governor of Massachusetts, or a senator of the State, I should make it a part of my duty to attend every anti-Slavery Convention, and to speak there. Such men go to Cattle Shows, and Mechanics' Fairs, and meetings of Bible Societies, to show that they are at least officially interested in farming, manufacturing, and religion. So would I go to the other place, to show that I really took the deepest, heartiest interest, in the great principles of Democracy, and wished to see justice done to the humblest of human kind.

The *Daily Advertiser* gives us good counsel. In the editorial of the 26th, I find these words : " The enemies of Slavery and its extension have hitherto occupied too exclusively a defensive attitude ; its friends, by venturing on bold courses of aggression, have continually been gaining ground. If they did not carry their whole point, they always gained something by compromise. It is right to learn from one's enemy, and it will be fortunate if our friends in Congress have really learned the valuable lesson of refusing to be kept on the defensive."

I know how anxious men are for office. I take it there are 20,000 candidates for the Presidency now living. I wish they were enumerated in the census—they might come after the overseers of slaves. Certainly no man is too small for the place. The experience of Europe shows that little men may be born to high office ; America proves that they can be *chosen*—and Democratic election is as good as royal fore-ordination. But no man is likely to gain that high office by compromise. Webster tried it, and failed ; Clay also failed. If Seward, Chase, or Banks attempt the same thing, they also will come dishonoured to the ground. It is always hard to ride two horses. What if, as now, both be swift. and North runs one way, and South the other ? Anti-Slavery is a moveable stone—he that falls on it will be broken, but on whomsoever it shall fall, it will grind him to powder !

I know men say, " If you attack Slavery, the South will dissolve the Union." *She* dissolve the Union ? She does not dare. Without commerce, manufactures, schools, with no industry but Slavery, more than one-third of her population bondmen, their interest antagonistic to hers,—let her try if she will. Her threat—I will tell you what it is like. " Mamma," said a spoiled boy to a mother of ten. other and older children, " Mamma, I want a piece of pickled elephant." " No, my dear, he can't have it. Johnny must be a good boy." " No, I won't be a good boy. I don't want to be good. I want a piece of pickled elephant." " But aint he mother's *youngest* boy ? When we have some pickled elephant, he shall have the biggest piece !" " Ma'am, I don't want a *piece!* I want a *whole pickled elephant!* I want him *now!* If you don't let me have him now, I'll run right off and catch the measles. I know a boy that's got 'em first rate."

LONDON:

WILLIAM STEVENS, PRINTER, 37, BELL YARD,

TEMPLE BAR.

Printed in the United States
123840LV00003B/177/A

9 781417 946921